ON MISSIONARY ROADS

JOZEF CARDINAL TOMKO

ON MISSIONARY ROADS

Translated by
Reverend Lubomír J. Strečok
Sister Mercedes Voytko, SSCM
Sister Anna Catherine Melichar, OSF

IGNATIUS PRESS   SAN FRANCISCO

Originally published in 2003 as *Na misijných cestách II*
by Spolok Svätého Vojtecha
Trnava, Slovakia
© 2003 Spolok Svätého Vojtecha

Cover photographs © Jozef Cardinal Tomko

Cover design by John Herreid

© 2006 by Ignatius Press, San Francisco
All rights reserved
ISBN 978-1-58617-165-0
ISBN 1-58617-165-8
Library of Congress Control Number 2006921887
Printed in Canada ∞

Contents

On One of Many Journeys with John Paul II

Foreword

"The Church on earth is, by her very nature, missionary" (*Ad gentes*, no. 2). This was the striking declaration of the Second Vatican Council in its *Decree on the Church's Missionary Activity*. The decree set out in one document the foundations of the missionary theology and practice of the Catholic Church—a magna carta of mission.

Since 1622, the Church's missionary work had been organized and coordinated at the world level by the Congregation for the Propagation of the Faith in collaboration with many religious orders and congregations and with the local Churches. At the Vatican Council, the role of the Congregation was affirmed, and it was renamed the Congregation for the Evangelization of Peoples. At the same time, a strong desire was expressed for its greater effectiveness. It was acknowledged that "the Holy Spirit arouses a missionary spirit in the Church in many ways and indeed often anticipates the work of those whose task is to guide the life of the Church" (*Ad gentes*, no. 29). In a changing world, it would be important that the Congregation should be, in its members and staff, more effectively representative of the whole Church. The Council confirmed its role as "the only competent Congregation for all mission and missionary activity". Its task "is to direct and coordinate missionary work and missionary cooperation throughout the world" (ibid.).

The years that followed the Vatican Council have been a challenging time for the Congregation. The renewal proposed by the Council became more urgent as massive social and cultural changes took place with the stirring of globalization. This has affected the whole Church, not least in her mission. The debate within the Church about the nature and means of mission, though given direction by the Council decree on mission, took many turns, not all of them positive. The Holy See, under the leadership of Pope Paul VI, Pope John Paul II, and the Congregation for the Evangelization of Peoples, led from 1985 to 2001 by Cardinal Josef Tomko, have done a major work of developing the Magisterium of missionary theology for which the Council decree had laid the foundation.

The task of the Congregation is also highly practical. In new times and situations, communication between its office in Rome and the local Churches, the mission-sending religious communities, and the worldwide network of mission support organizations has taken on a new urgency.

In his years as Prefect of the Congregation for the Evangelization of Peoples, Cardinal Josef Tomko addressed himself to this task. Fully in the spirit of Pope John Paul II, he was himself present to the missionary work of the Church in all parts of the world. His concern for seminary reform, for the nomination of courageous and faithful bishops, for the development of consecrated life, and for social justice has strengthened the life of those local Churches supervised by the Congregation for Evangelization.

In his book, Cardinal Tomko describes his firsthand experience of missionary work as it takes place today all over the world. We see his reflective and sympathetic leadership in action and are given a firsthand glimpse of the Congregation for Evangelization, renewed by Vatican II and its successive prefects.

Cardinal Tomko has given us a gift in this book that can help us appreciate the Church's response today to the mission given her by Christ two thousand years ago. He deserves our gratitude too for what he has done for the missionary well-being of the Church over the years that he was Prefect of the Congregation for the Evangelization of Peoples. The book is an invitation to share in his generous missionary spirit and, like him, to do great things for the Lord.

† Francis Cardinal George, OMI
Archbishop of Chicago

Introduction

This book can be considered an invitation to become better acquainted with a world about which we speak little at all, or only under the aspect of economic globalization. It is the world of ancient religions and of young churches, which Christians call "mission territories" or simply "the missions" in its classical sense. In the Catholic Church, there has existed since 1622 a central office that has continued to coordinate missionary work and missionary cooperation throughout the world. This office is called the Congregation for the Evangelization of Peoples (formerly the *Propaganda Fide*), and it is a privileged observation post allowing one to acquire a unique and broad experience of this vast field of activity.

When the unforgettable Pope John Paul II called me to guide this Congregation in April 1985, I immediately understood it was not enough to consider the enormous questions and problems of competency and responsibility from behind a desk and only through the large number of reports and communications received every day. I saw the necessity of having direct contact with the people and the workers in the vineyard.

It was for this reason that over the course of some sixteen years I undertook a hundred or more challenging pastoral journeys to all the mission territories, fifty-two of which were in Africa alone. Moreover, during that same period of time, I was fortunate to accompany the great missionary, Pope John Paul II, on all of his missionary visits. Each of my pastoral visits involved extensive preparation and, upon my return, actions geared to ensure that these visits bore fruit. With the assistance of my generous collaborators, I also had the joy of preparing and presenting to the late Holy Father requests for establishing over 180 new dioceses or their equivalent and of ordaining sixty-two new bishops and a large number of priests. All this is not to say anything about the many new seminaries, churches, and chapels for new communities as well as the educational, healthcare, and other social services that have arisen and are maintained, thanks to the missionary cooperation efforts organized in many countries by the Pontifical Mission Societies.

If I mention these things, it is not to boast about them. I do so only to give glory to God for the missionary efforts present throughout the world. They are all part of God's gift to the Church, to the world, and to me. The experience gained from all this obliges me to offer testimony to what the Holy Spirit is accomplishing without making a big to-do over it. All these things are God's gift, a gift to be shared with others.

This book contains a little bit of everything. In addition to providing some facts about missionary geography, it offers short accounts of the history of evangelization in specific countries and regions. It is not intended to be a journal of my travels; it is essentially a testimony and an account of my personal experience in the service of the Congregation. For the statistics I have mainly used the *Statistical Yearbook of the Church 2004* (Vatican, 2006) and *Annuario Pontificio 2006* (Vatican, 2006).

This book has already been published in the Slovak language (115,000 copies) and has been distributed among families. It is now being published in English with some slight additions, thanks to Father L'ubomír Strečok's generous efforts in translation and to the help of Sister Mercedes Voytko, SSCM, and Sister Anna Catherine Melichar, OSF. Sister M. Cyrilla Kendra, RSM, and Father Albert H. Ledoux provided additional revisions. I wish also to express my thanks to His Eminence, Cardinal Francis George, OMI, who wrote the Foreword in a very obvious missionary spirit. Many other generous persons contributed to the publication of this book with their advice and interest. Among them, I would like to mention the Most Reverend Joseph V. Adamec, Bishop of Altoona-Johnston, and Reverend Monsignor John Kozar, the present National Director of the Pontifical Mission Societies in the United States.

Finally, I would like to express the hope that those who read this book will increase their admiration for the work of the Holy Spirit in the world and deepen their appreciation of the enormous efforts undertaken by so many people to bring the message of Jesus Christ to all nations.

Part One

Africa

In recent decades, Africa has become more and more of a forgotten continent. After the euphoria of liberation from the colonial powers, and after the establishment of several independent states, a period of rebuilding was to be expected. But it was then that all the imperfections left behind by colonialism were experienced, as well as those of the local people and of African society. The former rulers neither educated nor technically prepared future leaders in the art of governing a society or managing an economy. Tribal ethnocentrism remained smoldering as a flame under ashes, and at the first opportunity, in many places, it exploded into years-long civil or regional conflicts. These were sometimes driven by racial or religious considerations.

The Western powers did not surrender their economic interest in the continent's natural resources. Neither did they surrender their cultural-political influence in certain regions. Furthermore, they adopted a secret agenda of fighting for the control of larger countries. They even manipulated international aid to Africa for their own interests, while often cooperating with corrupt individuals and groups. There is still an effort to possess and to use the natural resources of Africa (minerals, diamonds, oil, and forests)—sometimes in collaboration with the local groups. International arms dealers mercilessly exploit this situation, trading their weapons for precious domestic natural resources. As a result, refugees can be counted in the millions, and very young soldiers as well as physically handicapped people are growing in numbers. In addition, there is now the new plague of the AIDS infection.

This sad picture, while containing a few bright, colorful spots, nevertheless remains dark. One of the principal reasons for the darkness is that the world forgets about Africa when important international decisions are being made. In particular, we can cite those concerning the future of our planet, about the economy, about international aid, and yet others aimed at solving the human and political problems of this continent. Africa covers over 18.5 million square miles and has a population of over 876 million people. This represents approximately 13.7 percent of the world's population. An example of "forgotten Africa" is the book *The Clash of Civilizations and the Remaking of World Order* (1996), authored by Harvard University professor Samuel P. Huntington. In this 367-page work, the author writes about world politics, but Africa is mentioned only marginally in his analytical list or index.

In spite all the negative data, the Church has faith in Africa. It can also be said that Africa trusts the Church. In 1900, there were only 2 million Catholics on this continent. One hundred years later, there were 135 million (currently, already 149 million) Catholics, which makes for 17 percent of the entire population of this part of the world. In the past few years, many countries have celebrated their centennial anniversary of evangelization. Therefore, most of the churches are young ones. The number of vocations to the priestly and religious life is growing in the Church in Africa. There are many catechists and zealous lay people as well as native bishops. With only a few exceptions, it is native bishops who lead the local communities everywhere on the continent. The African bishops have stood out during the world synods of bishops, especially during the Extraordinary Synod for Africa that met in Rome in 1994. The bishops of Africa are members of the Symposium of Episcopal Conferences of Africa and Madagascar. The first African cardinal, Rugambwa, died only a few years ago, leaving a fine number of colleagues in red.

For me personally, Africa has become part of my heart. Thanks to fifty-two trips to this continent, I can declare without exaggeration that I know it very well. I have visited practically all the countries, some of them several times. The exceptions are only those countries, such as Liberia and Algeria, where obstacles were erected against my visit. I spent long hours with the faithful African people during the celebration of the Eucharistic sacrifice. Sometimes it was on a savanna or by a lake, near a forest or in cathedrals and churches. It was always accompanied by joyful singing, liturgical dancing, and with the sound

Bernardin Cardinal Gantin, an Outstanding African

of drums and native musical instruments. As the Prefect of the Congregation for the Evangelization of Peoples, I assisted in establishing new seminaries, organizing help for the education of thousands of young students, and providing financial assistance for the construction of new church buildings, chapels, and pastoral centers. I helped to establish many new dioceses and submitted the names of many priests for episcopal nomination. I later ordained many of them personally in their respective dioceses. With the African Church, I have experienced some painful as well as some joyous moments. Among the former, I can point to the funeral of the murdered Archbishop Joachim Ruhuna in Burundi or the tragic killings of four bishops in Rwanda as well as that of Archbishop Christophe Munzihirwa Mwene Ngabo of Bukavu in Zaire—presently called the Democratic Republic of the Congo. There was the meeting with the shepherds of the countries of the Great Lakes area, as well as many other events. I have known heads of state, secretaries, ambassadors, and missionaries, as well as ordinary people. My ethnographic and photographic interests have helped me to preserve my existing memories of these people and of various occasions. To this day, I have maintained friendly relationships and contacts with them, especially with the bishops whom I ordained.

My knowledge of Africa allows me to look upon this continent with hope in my heart. With these sentiments, I would like to share my experiences from the missionary roads of Africa. My conviction that "God is calling Africa" still remains with me. I have spoken about this conviction with the late Holy Father John Paul II and with various members of the African Synod. Later I wrote about it in the first chapter of the book *Missione verso il Terzo millennio*[1] (Missions for the Third Millennium). I believe that Africa is still a continent of hope even though so much is working "against hope". I believe that the meeting of the representatives of the African and European bishops in November of 2004 in Rome, as well as the promise of the Second African Synod, have already strengthened the hope of the Church of Africa.

1. Southern Africa

I made several trips to the region of southern Africa. The territorial boundaries of the individual states have not changed. However, in the past twenty years, some have gone through important internal changes, especially in the political arena. First of all, I have in mind the Republic of South Africa. This country is well known for its former social system of racial differentiation among black and white citizens (apartheid). Other countries have gone through significant internal political changes brought about by the fall of communism in Europe, as for example, Mozambique.

The longest trip I ever made to Africa was one on which I accompanied the late Holy Father, John Paul II. This trip lasted from September 8 to September 19, 1988. We visited Zimbabwe, Botswana, Lesotho, Swaziland, and Mozambique and made an unplanned stop in Johannesburg, necessitated by an emergency landing. We had to use ground transportation through the northern part of the Republic of South Africa. At that time, the country was governed according to racist principles and had not been part of our itinerary. John Paul II

---

[1] Rome: Urbaniana University Press, 1998, also published as *Misie do tretieho tisícročia*, Bratislava: Lúč, 2000.

explained to the media on his way back to Rome, "This kind of visit can only happen under conditions that will not be misused politically."

Republic of Zimbabwe

Our first stop on this long trip was Zimbabwe. Older readers know this country as a part of the former British Federation of Rhodesia and Nyasaland. In 1964, Northern Rhodesia and Nyasaland became independent as Zambia and Malawi, respectively. The following year Southern Rhodesia (now Zimbabwe) declared its independence under white minority rule. Over a decade of guerrilla conflict ensued, with Zimbabwe ultimately achieving independence under black majority rule in 1980. The former capital of the undivided Rhodesia, Salisbury, was renamed Harare and is located in Zimbabwe. Today this country has almost 13.3 million citizens, over 1.3 million of whom are Catholics. It is five times larger than Pennsylvania and consists mostly of vast plains with farms and pastures. Zimbabwe possesses well-preserved forests and great mineral resources, as well as some basic industries. The majority of the population consists of two tribes, the Shona and the Ndebele. The two largest cities, Harare and Bulawayo, are archdiocesan sees. Besides these, there are six other dioceses. All but two of the bishops are natives.

Jesuit missionaries undertook evangelization of this region toward the end of the sixteenth century. They were able to introduce Christianity and to baptize the Monomotapa (or king). Later on, the king, influenced by Muslim merchants, turned against the Jesuits, allowing their

superior to be murdered. Only in 1879 was our Roman Congregation, then called the *Propaganda Fide*, able to establish the "Zambezi Mission" for the entire region. It was named after the local river, Zambezi. This very successful mission was headed by Jesuits. In 1927, the mission was granted the initial status of a prefecture apostolic and served as a base for establishing new dioceses over the ensuing years. In 1955, the new Church province of Southern Rhodesia was established, with its seat at Salisbury. The Jesuits were joined by other missionaries as well. Despite the presence of the Anglican church, Catholic numbers grew rapidly. During my time as Prefect, the Holy See was able to establish several other dioceses, as well as a second province with its seat at Bulawayo. Ten years after my visit with the Holy Father, I was able to return to Bulawayo to ordain the first native bishop.

The Pope is usually accompanied on his trips by the Vatican Secretary of State and the prefect of the Congregation responsible for the territory being visited. This is either the Prefect of the Congregation for Bishops, or in the missionary territories, the Prefect of the Congregation for the Evangelization of Peoples. On the 1988 trip to southern Africa, the Holy Father was accompanied by Cardinal Agostino Casaroli and me. In Harare, we were received with great joy. The local people were still trying to recover from the wounds inflicted by their long struggle for freedom and by conflicts between the two main tribes. Numerous groups from neighboring Zambia and Angola were also present. We arrived at the airport in the evening and proceeded immediately to an official visit with President Robert Mugabe (whose most recent presidential term commenced in 2002). He is a former student of the Jesuits who later became a socialist and led the battle for independence. His relationship with the Church has been reserved, since he thought the Church was not on the side of the colonists. He received us kindly. After this first official visit, John Paul II went to the newly built apostolic nunciature, where he met with bishops from the southern region of Africa. He stressed the importance of caring for migrants and refugees, who were numerous in this region. The next morning, the Holy Father was escorted to a large open space, where a crowd of several hundred thousand was awaiting him. On the way to this celebration, we were able to admire the modern, planned city of Harare. The streets of the city are wide and lined with buildings built in the British style, especially in the downtown area. The joy of the African people exploded at the arrival of the Holy Father and continued through the entire Mass.

The only European influence to be seen was the solemn clothing of the young people. The Holy Father came here as a messenger of peace and reconciliation. During the afternoon, he met with representatives of the lay apostolates at the cathedral. At the meeting, he stressed the duty of every Catholic to apply and to protect the moral standards governing family and society, "since we have to face misunderstandings and quarrels, causing changes in society and spreading ideologies that infringe upon Christian ethical principals." He added, "The family is the center of traditional African culture." The assembled listeners understood very well what the Holy Father was saying. The meeting with young people in the sports stadium was even more vibrant. Here, John Paul II stressed once again the importance of the human values of African family and culture. During this meeting, the Holy Father greeted approximately 50 million viewers from around the world who took part in "Sport Aid–88", an event that focused on the elimination of hunger.

The following day, September 12, the entire group flew to Bulawayo, the industrial center of the country. The Holy Father was greeted by Bishop Ernst Karlen, a Swiss missionary, as well as by other bishops from the southern region. Among them was an elderly Spanish missionary, Bishop Ignacio Prieto, who had some health problems. During these trips, I was able, as Prefect, to receive information from appropriate sources. At Bulawayo, Mass was celebrated in a large field where people could seat themselves on the green grass. After the celebration, they were able to eat the food that they had brought, in a way reminiscent of the practice of the early Church.

After the Mass, the Holy Father met with priests and religious in the cathedral. After that meeting, we flew back to Harare. The next morning we departed from Harare Airport for Botswana.

As I mentioned previously, I later returned to Zimbabwe for a visit that was both personal and pastoral. During this second trip, I was able to visit some other interesting sites. The main purpose of my trip was to ordain the new Archbishop of Bulawayo, Pius Alick Mvundla Ncube, a local priest, fruit of the missionary work and successor to Archbishop Ernst Heinrich Karlen, CMM. The joy of our Christians during the long ceremony in the large stadium was immense. During this stay, I also made some suggestions for the building of a new seminary. On this occasion, I was able to fulfill my desire to see the world-renowned Victoria Falls near Livingstone: first approaching the huge magnitude of the river Zambezi, and then flying over the falls in a helicopter. It

Victoria Falls on the Zimbabwe Border

surely is an impressive view. I completed this wonderful trip by navigating the Zambezi by boat, observing the hippopotamuses, crocodiles, and other animals and birds on the banks, as well as in the water. It was the best rest after a tiring pastoral visit in the tropical climate.

But I must go back to the visit of 1988 in the region of southern Africa in the company of John Paul II.

Republic of Botswana

This name will not be found in old geography books. The first time the name Botswana was used was in 1970, when the country, formerly known as Bechuanaland, became independent. Despite its political independence, Botswana depends in many respects on the neighboring Republic of South Africa.

This very young country is slightly smaller than the state of Texas. The northern part is watered by the Okavango River, which originates in neighboring Angola. As this river enters the territory of

Botswana, it spills out into marshes, creating a paradise for animals and birds. The eastern part of the country is largely covered with vegetation, while the central and western parts embrace the well-known Kalahari Desert, so often mentioned in the thrillers of Wilbur Smith. It is not surprising that the number of Botswana's citizens stands at only 1.6 million.

Missionary work in this area began quite late. Toward the end of the nineteenth century, Jesuits on their way to Rhodesia stopped in Botswana for very short periods of time. The Oblates of Mary Immaculate (OMI) initiated their mission in 1928. With greater success, Passionists undertook responsibility for the prefecture apostolic, erected by order of the Holy See in 1959. This prefecture covered the entire country. Before Botswana's independence in 1966, the Holy See elevated the prefecture to a diocese with its seat at the future capital, Gaborone. In 1981, the diocese received its first native bishop, Boniface Tshosa Setlalekgosi. In the same year, the Missionaries of the Divine Word (SVD) began to work in the northern part of the country. This young Church community, which is growing constantly, had approximately 45,000 Catholics during the Holy Father's 1988 visit. Today, there are about 84,000 Catholics. They were genuinely honored to receive a visit from the leader of the Church.

The capital of the country, Gaborone, started to develop after independence. The city has a more European than African character. The influence of Botswana's close southern neighbor is extremely high, especially in the industrial field. The diamond mines are a clear guarantee of wealth for the country, but the diamonds are processed in the

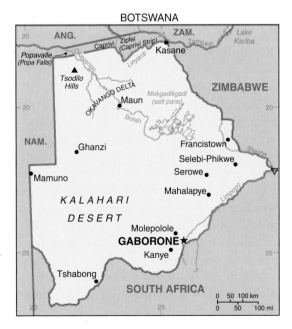

9

Republic of South Africa. This is proof of the fact that Botswana is dependent on its southern neighbor. The people of Botswana enjoy great freedom, one where racial and religious discrimination are absent. During the period of rigid apartheid in their neighbor to the south, the Holy Father called Botswana "an island of peace in a raging sea". This was a good place for him to stress basic human rights and to express his hope that the country would provide a pulse for an entire region in crisis. In the new cathedral, he spoke to the priests and religious, repeating his message with greater emphasis and inviting them to educate the laity. He asked them to condemn every kind of discrimination and to protect the poor and the oppressed. For all Christians, including those in neighboring states, it was a lesson against racial politics. In the afternoon, the Holy Father celebrated Mass in the stadium. Prior to the liturgy, young people brought in the mission cross that had traveled all over the country. In front of this cross, they promised fidelity to the gospel. During the homily, the "Roman Pilgrim" stressed once again the importance of Christian and African values and their close connection to family life.

I think that many will recall the short episode that occurred at the airport. When the Holy Father blessed the country, a few raindrops fell. Someone from the crowd mentioned that it was "pula". This word in the native language has two meanings: "blessing" and "rain". John Paul II seized upon it immediately and exclaimed, "Pula, pula." All those gathered started to applaud and repeated, "Pula, pula." The papal escort appreciated this scene very much, especially for having connected the two meanings of this word. For Africans, rain really is a blessing. Before every supper, the papal photographer would always greet us with "Pula, pula." At the airport, we later sensed a rush of activity. The Jesuit priest Roberto Tucci, presently a cardinal, who was in charge of the trip, was constantly running around and trying to arrange something. But the commotion turned out to be more than a regular delay. At our next destination, Lesotho, a severe storm had broken out. We waited, hoping that the weather would change and that we would be allowed to fly out. Finally, permission was granted to depart. It later became apparent that the concern over the weather had been warranted.

I returned to Botswana in December of 1996, on my way from Namibia, and was accompanied by the apostolic nuncio for this region, Archbishop Ambrose De Paoli. The most important reason for this visit was to attest to the conditions for the establishment of a second diocese in the country. It was to cover the northern region, which the Holy See had entrusted to the Missionaries of the Divine Word. We arrived at Francistown, the second major city, which we chose to be the diocesan seat.

Missionary work in this vast area was going very well. Among the missionaries, we could sense a very good spirit of collaboration, even though the missionaries were from Ghana, India, Poland, and from Slovakia. The Slovak missionary was glad to speak in his native language as I approached him in Slovak. He was not there long when he got infected with malaria and later had to return home. Missionary work is physically very demanding. The center for the missionaries was their religious house on the outskirts of the city. The naming of their own bishop fostered enthusiasm and hope among Christians as well as non-Christians. In the city, they built a new church, which was later to become the cathedral.

I was greeted by the mayor, who, if I am correct, was a Muslim of Asian origin. He actually begged me to establish the diocese. Later on I was told the reason for his zealous interest. Supposedly, according to old British law, the presence of either a Catholic or an Anglican bishop was a condition under which Francistown would be recognized by the government as having the status of a city. After this excursion, I let them all know that this general wish was realistic. In 1998, the vicariate apostolic was established and was confided to a religious order. From among the members of this religious order, the Holy See will name their apostolic vicar-bishop.

The Polish missionary gave me a ride from Francistown to Gaborone. The trip on a nice asphalt road took us six hours and included two short visits with our faithful. Traveling in this way, I could admire the beautiful countryside as well as the progress that had occurred during the previous eight years, especially in the capital. In Gaborone, I celebrated Mass in a beautiful cathedral. This has been a short personal update on the trip with the Holy Father. We will now continue with our next stop on the 1988 papal visit to Africa.

Kingdom of Lesotho

Our flight from Botswana to Lesotho, which, as I mentioned above, had been delayed, turned into an adventure that most of the world started to follow. As we were getting closer to the airport in Maseru, the capital of Lesotho, a severe thunderstorm erupted, accompanied by rain, strong winds, and thick fog. The airport is located in a valley in the middle of high mountains and does not have a radar system that could make landing easy. The airplane was made in the U.S. and, according to a sign that I found, it used to belong to Lufthansa. Apparently, after a general overhaul of the plane, the airline in Zimbabwe had bought it. I had a window seat and was able to observe carefully what was about to happen. The pilot tried penetrating the clouds with full-powered engines, all the while resisting the force of the wind and looking for better visibility through the thick fog. At a certain point, I was able to see the ground, but strong winds and rain forced the pilot to make a sharp turn, upon which the plane started to ascend once again. At that point, a massive rocky wall of mountains appeared alongside the plane, and one of the reporters screamed, as if the pilot were trying to kill us. Shortly, the plane reached a good altitude and direction. The pilot came to the cabin in order to explain the situation personally. He gave us three options. The first two were to fly all the way either to Mozambique or to Swaziland. The third option was to land in the nearby Republic of South Africa, which was not on the Pope's itinerary. From there, by means of ground transportation, we would be able to reach Lesotho in several hours. This last option was accepted, and after a very short flight, we landed in Johannesburg. There the airport seemed to be under a state of emergency. We had to remain seated in the plane for a long period of time, until the president, Pieter Botha, arrived from the nearby capital city of Pretoria. He expressed delight that the Republic of South Africa was able to assist the Pope in an emergency. Within moments, he had arranged accommodations, a luncheon, and ordered cars and buses for our short trip to Lesotho. During our waiting period, the reporters ran to the telephones to inform the world about the happy ending of this adventure. Some of them could not do so without adding their own speculations about the "Vatican's secret plan" for a papal stop in the country of apartheid. I thought about the fear that some of them had experienced during our unsuccessful attempt to land in Maseru. But the media like it that way. They need to fantasize.

That day, the rest of the tiring trip went fairly smoothly. The Holy Father remained exceptionally at peace during this entire time. We started the trip escorted by local police and traversed the large plain toward Bloemfontein. By evening, we crossed into Lesotho. The Holy Father then decided that we should continue on toward Roma, a city that carries the same name as the center of the Catholic Church and which was the first missionary station founded by the Oblate Joseph Gérard. The Holy Father celebrated the Eucharist at the tomb of this missionary, and we concluded the day by arriving in the capital of the country, Maseru.

Lesotho is a small country, like an island surrounded by the Republic of South Africa. Its territory is slightly smaller than that of Maryland and is home to over 2,151,000 citizens. There are 1,093,000 Catholics grouped into four diocesan churches. The arrival of the first missionaries of the Oblates of Mary Immaculate dates to 1862. Among them was Father Joseph Gérard, originally from France, who for over fifty years served the sick and orphaned throughout the entire country, which was at that time called Basutoland. He died in 1914, but his legacy still lives among the people. John Paul II came here on September 15, 1988, to beatify this missionary at an outdoor Mass. He performed this solemn act among the people whom Father Gérard had served his entire life. The seed that Father Gérard planted has yielded a bountiful harvest in the number of Catholics: 15,000 at the time of his death, 650,000 when the Holy Father visited, and today over a million. The life of Father Gérard is an example of the fulfillment of the gospel.

Many faithful, especially from the mountainous areas, were not able to come for the celebration because of the bad weather. Some pilgrims canceled because of a tragic event that had taken place on the day prior to the outdoor Mass. Four terrorists attacked a bus carrying seventy-one pilgrims from the Republic of South Africa. They kidnapped all those on board, half of whom were children escorted by religious sisters. The South African police attacked the bus, and all four kidnappers and the driver were killed. Many of the travelers were injured. In Maseru, the Holy Father and all those gathered there prayed for the victims. In the evening, he visited the injured pilgrims. This event created a very sad atmosphere for the participants in the papal visit.

The mood at the afternoon meeting with the youth was a bit happier, however. John Paul II talked to young people about the topic that interests them the most: love. He stressed that love is able to permeate emotional anger, and that love, as a social force, is able to conquer hatred. This love helps people to join in efforts for human rights, justice, and social progress. Those words, proclaimed in this poor country, made a real impact and demonstrated that the gospel is a solution for social problems. Many sons of this country have had to go to work in a neighboring state, where they often experience racial discrimination.

The Pilgrim from the Vatican was able to fulfill most of his schedule in this country, even though inclement weather and significant travel delays had caused the cancellation of the traditional welcome at the ancient royal citadel. This customary celebration was very important to the elderly king. In peace, we were then able to continue to the next destination on our trip, Swaziland.

Kingdom of Swaziland

This tiny state is only half the size of Lesotho or slightly smaller than New Jersey. The Republic of South Africa surrounds two-thirds of it. It borders Mozambique on the east. This country has over 1 million citizens, approximately 55,000 of whom are Catholics. During the visit of the Holy Father, the number of Catholics stood at about 40,000. They are under the jurisdiction of a bishop with his episcopal seat in the commercial capital, Manzini.

Because of its moderate climate, green forests and fields, good roads, hotels, and buildings, Swaziland is called the Switzerland of southern Africa. One can see there many white tourists from the neighboring Republic of South Africa. At the time of our visit, a small group of white people owned all the industry in the country. Even here we were accompanied by heavy rain, which eventually stopped. We were then able to land in Manzini without any difficulties.

Swaziland was then still a feudal kingdom, which maintained its own traditions, including polygamy. At that time, the young king himself had six wives. His seventh fiancée was from a very influential family. Through these several marriages, he was able to secure his alliances with powerful clans. His father had close to one hundred wives and was survived by seventy-six sons, not to mention the daughters.

Mass was celebrated in a beautiful stadium, where approximately 30,000 people had gathered. After we spent a good while waiting for the royal procession—which arrived fashionably late in huge cars—the celebration began. During his homily, the Holy Father gently explained Catholic teachings on marriage and family, including monogamy. From the stadium, we went to the royal palace for a courteous visit. Strangely, the royal procession arrived after us. The king introduced himself in his traditional attire, with his bare chest covered with furs. His servants approached him on their knees with deep bows. They never stood up. So, tradition is tradition, even in the twentieth century, and this in spite of the fact that the king had studied in schools with white people and rode in the finest of limousines.

We can imagine the kind of obstacles that the Catholic faithful have to face when living in this kind of society. The strengthening of their faith, following Jesus' command to Saint Peter, was one of the motives behind this visit by the Successor of Saint Peter. We have to point out that this small Church community in Swaziland is growing, thanks to the educational activities of missionaries from the Servants of the Virgin Mary. These missionaries arrived here in 1913, and in 1939, they were already able to have a vicariate apostolic erected. The vicariate became the Diocese of Bremersdorp in 1951, which was then renamed the Diocese of Manzini in 1961, seven years prior to national independence. The native Bishop Robert Ndlovu now heads the diocese.

Republic of Mozambique

From Swaziland we flew to Maputo, the capital of Mozambique, a country that presently has over 19 million citizens. Approximately 5 million are Catholics living within twelve dioceses. During the papal visit, the population stood at around 14 million.

Even this last part of the Holy Father's trip to southern Africa was not without challenges. Mozambique was then ruled by a communist government. The situation had become even more complicated because of a long civil war. After being occupied by Portugal for nearly five hundred years, this country obtained its freedom in 1975. Governmental authority was assumed by the communist party, or Frelimo. Several rebel groups, under the umbrella organization Renamo, rebelled against this government and were supported by their strong southern neighbor. The ensuing civil war cost many human lives and was accompanied by cruelty as well as uncertainty and hunger. Church buildings, missionary stations, and charitable institutions were damaged during this war. After beginning its missionary work in the territory almost five hundred years before, the Church here suffered great losses. Over a million people escaped across the borders seeking to save their lives. Many of them stopped in refugee camps. Surprise attacks by the rebels were made throughout the entire country, even in the suburbs of Maputo.

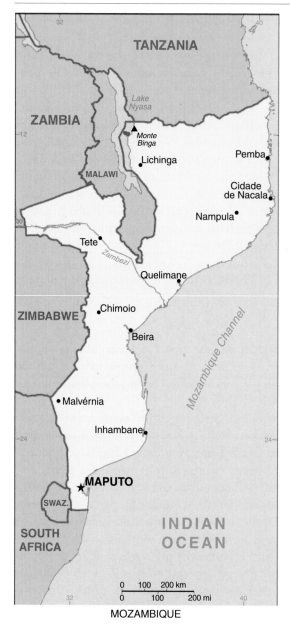

MOZAMBIQUE

The former Soviet Union supported the government (a fact made obvious to us immediately upon our arrival at the airport by the large number of Russian airplanes located there). All negotiations and attempts at reconciliation had failed.

We were greeted at the airport by the Marxist president, Joaquim Chissano. The president's speech surprised us with his appeal for gentleness, forgiveness, dialogue, and unity. However, at the president's palace, we were informed by certain foreign ambassadors that a majority of the cabinet ministers were still strong communists. I remember how the Russian ambassador responded to me, with kindness and surprise, when I greeted him in Russian.

The following day we flew to the northern part of the country for a visit to two large cities, Beira and Nampula. During his homilies and speeches, John Paul II encouraged the people amid their suffering. He emphasized, in a gentle way, that every society has to respect basic rights, as well as the moral, religious, and cultural needs of every man. Here again the Holy Father demonstrated his knowledge of Marxist propaganda and sought to build up the people's awareness of their dignity and their right to make free decisions.

On September 18, 1988, during the last day of our stay in Mozambique, the Holy Father brought up once again the pitiful situation of the people and the necessity of finally enforcing justice and peace. During his homily at the Mass, celebrated in the municipal stadium of the capital city, he used strong statements to challenge a crowd that numbered over a hundred thousand people. He called upon everyone to look for real solutions, "so that people could be more like people". These were the words of comfort and hope that had already predicted the changes that were occurring in Europe. Two years later, they helped bring about reconciliation in Mozambique as well.

In the afternoon, the Holy Father went to visit the poorest suburb of Maputo. I took advantage of this time to visit a newly built seminary in another part of the city. The army did not protect that neighborhood. To get there, I had to request one of the official governmental cars designated for the papal visit. That only created a greater risk of attack by the rebels. I was wearing a white cassock, red zucchetto, and a pectoral cross over my chest. I was hoping that the rebels would be able to recognize me and would not shoot. The official car went safely through the danger zone, all the way to the Seminary of Saint Augustine. I was greeted by the staff of the seminary and by the contractor from Portugal, who was very well paid for erecting this building. The construction of a seminary, in this land marked by the blood of so many, was a desire of my heart. This was an assurance that the formation of new priests could be developed in a better fashion after so many years of persecution and limitations. My return to the papal entourage occurred without difficulties, and with only a little tension. The car moved through streets filled with people who had lost legs, arms, eyes, or family. From my own experience, I could testify to the words of John Paul II in his farewell speech at the airport: "I saw the bleeding heart of this nation." It was September 19, 1988.

I was never again able to return to Mozambique. When I have needed to settle different problems in this country, I have met several times with the Archbishop of Maputo, Cardinal José Maria dos Santos, and with other bishops as well as with the apostolic nuncios. Luckily, the political situation later improved, and the two fighting parties came to an agreement. The Italian Catholic lay movement, "Sant' Egidio", played a very important role during the negotiations before the agreement was reached.

Republic of South Africa

In 1988, during the Holy Father's trip to the countries of southern Africa, the practice of racial discrimination was still protected by the laws of the Republic of South Africa. The Holy Father did not want to create an impression of agreeing with this sort of regime. Therefore, a visit was not planned. Black citizens did not enjoy basic human rights. They had to live in enclosed areas and travel separately from whites. They did not have access to higher education or to leading roles in industry, not to mention their lack of social and political rights.

This political situation did not impede my work, however. I was able to visit the country several times, without any significant obstacles, before and even after the abolition of the apartheid regime. In 1993, I could still experience what racial discrimination really means. Black citizens had to live on a sort of reservation, which, in some instances, was even fenced in. It gave one the impression of a ghetto or a work camp. I visited two of these reservations. One of them was located near the capital city, Pretoria. In this place, approximately 10,000 black people were living. The reservation was near an asphalt road, in the middle of arid land. In the people's eyes, one could sense their inner suffering, and even the fear and

hatred they experienced toward whites. Many of them considered white people to be their slave masters. The Church has never given her blessing to this forced situation, and so we were able, without any difficulty, to visit the religious sisters and priests who worked among these people.

The residents actually constituted a supply of workers for the nearby capital, with its architecture reminiscent of European or even British cities. I noticed a strange "hotel" in the city that was very different from the other buildings. It had too many windows located right next to each other. I found out that it had been built to house young black workers. This building had very narrow rooms, almost like prison cells, which had been designed to prevent the accommodation of families. Another similar "residential area" that grew up almost into its own city is the well-known Soweto in the suburbs of Johannesburg. I visited it with a French priest, Emmanuel Lafont (now bishop of Cayenne), who was fighting against apartheid. He was the only white person, aside from local missionaries, who could drive into Soweto without any gunshots being aimed at his car. I remember the poor apartments, the dirty streets, and the inquiring looks of the people. As soon as they recognized Father Lafont, their faces started to shine. Eventually, the priest had to leave the country because of his protests against the apartheid laws and because of his advocacy on behalf of blacks. As we were getting closer to the church on the hillside, we noticed a large number of young people involved in a protest. The police would not let us continue. We decided to detour, but we encountered armored vehicles and had to turn back.

This huge country, with an area of 762,170 square miles, has had a very troubled history. Whoever is interested in it must consult various sources. I will reduce things to a number of basic facts. It is well known that this country was initially colonized after the Reformation by the Calvinist Dutch from Europe, and then, in the nineteenth century by the British. The spread of Catholicism was forbidden, almost until the beginning of the nineteenth century. In 1870, Catholics obtained religious freedom. Missionary work was mostly conducted by the Oblates of Mary Immaculate, in cooperation with some other congregations. The Reformed Boers remained deeply anti-Catholic, so the Catholic Church needed to achieve an understanding with the Anglicans. Missionary work among black people was being done by Methodists and Anglicans. These religions practiced integration, which means solidarity among the different races. Catholic missionaries found the territory already occupied, but through their schools and charitable work, they made inroads among the native population. This serves to explain the significant delay in Catholic missionary work and in penetrating the black population. Amid a public life dominated by a Protestant leadership, the Catholic Church here was of small consequence. It could only prepare a small number of native priests and religious sisters. Even today, the Church is dependent on foreign missionaries and a white hierarchy. Compared to Protestants and Anglicans, the Catholic Church is a minority. In 1951, the territory was divided into Catholic dioceses. Racial politics have been very much in evidence over the past fifty years, especially after the year 1961, when South Africa left the British Commonwealth. Protestants started small groups, the so-called independent "churches". Later on, the larger ones grouped themselves together into the Council of South African Churches. Despite unfavorable circumstances, the increase of Catholics was quite rapid. From 1920 to 1950, the number passed from 75,000 to 375,000, and by 2004, to 3,162,000. We also need to take into consideration the increase of the entire population in the past ten years, from 30 million to 45 million. Catholics are led by twenty-seven bishops, of whom only a few are native-born. In 1965, the first cardinal was named in the person of Monsignor Owen McCann. Many years after his death, he was followed, in 2001, by Cardinal Wilfrid Napier. Both of them were natives of the country. The first, however, was white and the second of mixed European and Indian ancestry. The former constitution recognized, not only the white race, but the Asian race (Indians and Chinese), a group of interracial people, and also the black race.

However, the system of "apartheid" was applied for the black race. A long-lasting, and at times bloody, fight was led by people such as Nelson Mandela, who is known the world over. The struggle finally established equality for all races. It will take a long time until people fully attain this equality, especially in the field of industry. It is important to state that the Republic of South Africa is the most developed country, not only in this region, but also on the entire continent. It will be a challenge for skillful government representatives to preserve genuine freedom and cohesiveness among so many cultures, races, and languages. Most of the citizens speak at least English and the Boer language, "Afrikaans". The country's natural resources are substantial, and a variety of different industries exist. Both education and the health care system are very good. However, a spirit of Christian understanding and respect is necessary. Will this new capitalistic society be up to the challenge?

The Church in South Africa has an open field for its works. It needs to raise up more native black priests who could eventually become good bishops. But first of all, it must have good seminaries. As I assumed my position in the Congregation, I had to deal with two unpleasant situations in seminaries affected by racial crises. Therefore, in 1993, I visited seven dioceses and met with the bishops, priests, religious sisters, and laity from the surrounding dioceses. Another time, I went to visit three major seminaries and one experimental minor seminary. Today we cannot solve all problems from behind a desk. Sometimes it is important "to go into the field" and listen to the people. Besides my regular work in Rome, I intended through this pastoral work to get the sense of the regional situation one can gain only from being "on the ground". The knowledge and impressions that I thereby derived were extremely helpful. Through the years, they have created a precious inner wealth we often call "life experience".

John Paul II returned to the Republic of South Africa after the abolition of the racial laws. During this visit in 1995, he officially promulgated the resolutions of the Synod of Bishops for Africa. The solemn promulgation occurred in three places on the African continent: in Cameroon for western Africa, in Johannesburg for the southern region, and in Nairobi for the eastern part. During our stay in the Republic of South Africa, we were accommodated at the nunciature in Pretoria. For the public Mass, the entire group was escorted into a huge field, where a hundred thousand of the faithful awaited us in great anticipation. After the return from the colorful liturgical celebration, we met with the representatives of the new government headed by the well-known Nelson Mandela, who was at that time at the height of his glory.

My last visit to this country took place in 1998, on the occasion of the meeting of the African organization of bishops, the Symposium of Episcopal Conferences of Africa and Madagascar (SECAM), near Johannesburg. I met once again with many of my brother bishops, with whom I renewed old acquaintances and friendships. At the time that new leaders were being elected for this organization, I discreetly excused myself from the meeting. This allowed me to take a short trip to the Kruger National Park.

It turned out that all the overnight accommodations were occupied in the main areas of this huge park. Luckily, we were able to find two places in a smaller section near the airport. Our twilight "safari" through the forest was not very successful regarding our main goal, to locate a "hunting leopard". Instead, we were able to film how the intelligent elephant is able to pull up a tree along with its roots. In that way, it substitutes for a shortage of better food. The next morning we were luckier. Besides the regular antelopes, gazelles, and birds, we spotted three female lions just a few feet away from our vehicle. After their rich breakfast, they were napping next to the road and did not consider us worthy of a look. We were lucky on another occasion as well. Our ranger, after several days of searching, had finally been able to spot a leopard. The animal was right in the middle of the road, heading in the same direction as our big—and uncovered—car. It was spying on prey hiding in the nearby tall grass. I was seated on the third chair, which was elevated for a better view. This enabled me to see the leopard very well, it being only thirteen feet away from the front of our car. I could also see a baby gazelle, whose tiny head and frightened eyes were staring from the grass. The little gazelle was aware of the danger threatening her. The leopard was waiting patiently for her to jump. Meanwhile, a second car of tourists arrived. Ignoring the ranger's warning, I dared to rise a little, so that I could better capture this scene with my camera. The ranger punished me and threatened that he would leave me out there in the middle of the wilderness. Despite that, I was able to photograph this unique opportunity. After a period of waiting, the little gazelle jumped up and started to rush between the rocks and trees, where the leopard could not easily move. From the corner of my eye, I caught the leopard approximately two feet from the vehicle, right below my seat, as it dashed past quick as lightning. It was already too late for the leopard, as its prey had run too far away. The leopard pursued the gazelle for some time, as we pursued the leopard with our cameras. It was looking for the gazelle in a valley we had to bypass. We caught up with them once again, giving us another chance to experience the sensation of being frozen, as the leopard went by our car. Of course, the leopard was occupied by its thoughts of the little gazelle. We left the cat disappointed and hungry, but we were happy that the cute and defenseless gazelle had been able to get away. The story of the leopard became one of my best filmed "catches".

The trip to the national park also helped take my mind off my worries and allowed me to get a good rest.

Republic of Namibia

Many people do not even know the name of this young country, located northwest of the Republic of South Africa. Its territory is ten times larger than that of Pennsylvania, but it has less than 2.3 million citizens. During my first visit to this country in 1994, I flew from Johannesburg to the capital Windhoek with the apostolic nuncio, Archbishop Ambrose Battista De Paoli. It was then that I understood the reason for the low population density. During the flight, the native pilot poetically described the beauty of the desert and the sunsets. He did so with such enthusiasm that we began to appreciate the source of his inspiration and the richness of his descriptions. Before us extended the Kalahari Desert, which borders on the western Namib Desert that gives its name to the country. Moving northward from Windhoek, the dry desert turns into prairie and then into a more fruitful northern region adjacent to Angola.

Namibia has its own troubled history. Toward the end of nineteenth century, Namibia was a German colony. The first evangelizers were Lutheran missionaries. Catholic missionaries arrived only in 1896, but they could work more freely only in the northern territory. After the defeat of Germany in World War I, the territory passed to South African administration through a League of Nations mandate. South Africa saw Namibia as, potentially, a fifth province for their country. Finally in 1988, the United Nations was able to force the Republic of South Africa to admit an international peacekeeping force. This allowed for the move toward independence, for which the twenty-year-old South West African People's Organization (SWAPO) movement had fought. The Christian churches, with the exception of the Reformed Nederland church, respected the citizens' desire for independence. Finally, on March 21, 1990, independence was solemnly proclaimed. The newly elected president, Sam Nujoma, despite being a socialist, allowed for freedom of religion. He also was very moderate toward former enemies and let them participate in the process of rebuilding the country.

The capital, Windhoek, is very similar to the cities of South Africa, and it leaves every visitor surprised. Only the northern part of the country has preserved its typical African character. In the rest of the country, the relations and customs described by Wilbur Smith in his novel *The Fiery Coast* are now things of the past. Reminders persist in the costumes ladies from the cities wear on very special occasions. These consist of a very heavy long skirt and a large hat in the old German style. The natives of the Herero tribe are not often encountered, and itinerate "Bushmen" are very scarce. Only the northern region of Owando has preserved its typical African culture because of the better farming conditions. Our guide, the German missionary Father Bernhard Nordkamp, taught us to pronounce some words in the native tongue. This language includes sounds made by clicking the tongue against the palate.

German missionaries enjoyed great success in the northern part of the country. In 1926, Rome was already able to establish a vicariate apostolic with its seat at Windhoek. It was necessary for the southern part of the country to wait until 1949, when a vicariate was established in Keetmanshoop. In 1980, the Holy See named one of the first five native priests, Boniface Haushiku, to be bishop. In that way, evangelizing efforts could be further encouraged. Given the political realities, both of the vicariates were made part of the Bishops' Conference of South Africa. With time, missionary progress would allow for the division of this territory and the creation of another diocese. After a successful search for another good native candidate for episcopal office, Namibia later became a separate Church province. Meanwhile, the country had declared its independence from South Africa.

Plans for expanding the hierarchy came to fruition on Pentecost Sunday, May 22, 1994. I traveled to Windhoek

24

to announce the establishment of a new vicariate in Rundu and to ordain the Oblate Joseph Shikongo as its first bishop. In addition to the ordination, I announced the promotion of Windhoek to the rank of archdiocese, and its Bishop Boniface Haushiku to that of archbishop. The two other dioceses in his province would henceforth be those of Keetmanshoop and the newly established vicariate in Rundu, adjacent to Angola. The former is located in a very sparsely populated area of the south and presently has 38,000 Catholics. Rundu has 90,000 Catholics and includes the territory of the "Caprivi Strip" all the way to Victoria Falls in Zimbabwe. Windhoek has 244,000 faithful and has also received an auxiliary bishop who can prepare another diocese in the north, perhaps in Owando.

The Pentecost celebration in 1994 became almost like a national holiday. All the parishes and the missionary stations sent their faithful for this special occasion. Even the women from the remote missions living among the "Bushmen" arrived in their own dresses, or, better said, their half-dresses. In a different setting, it probably would have attracted attention. There was a bus from the "Caprivi Strip" led by a Slovak Capuchin missionary. Several bishops from South Africa were present, including my good friend Archbishop Denis Hurley, whom I had originally met during the Second Vatican Council. Many pilgrims arrived from distant Angola. They were able to use a good asphalt road that traverses Namibia all the way to South Africa. This road was used by the South African military while they were fighting in Angola. All of us were honored by the presence of representatives from the Lutheran and Anglican churches as well as those from the government. Even the elderly, former missionary bishop of Windhoek, currently living in Germany, was present for the occasion.

The entire ceremony took place in a large space in front of the beautiful cathedral. At nine o'clock, a colorful procession of altar boys and priests in flowing albs began to move from the cathedral. The priests were followed by the bishops, by the new Archbishop Haushiku, and by the young bishop-elect Shikongo. I was the last one in this procession that was greeted by the joyful singing of three very large choirs, all of whom competed with each other in their selections and performances. All in attendance accompanied the singing of the choirs with rhythmic clapping and with moderate body movements. At the start of the Mass, I could recognize the melody of a very well-known English sacred hymn. The sun was already hot, and its heat even scorched through the plastic cover above the altar. After the nuncio, Archbishop De Paoli, read the Vatican decree establishing the new province and elevating Haushiku to archbishop, a cheerful shout erupted through the entire assembly, and the loud singing of the choirs, accompanied only by the sound of drums, filled the air. The new archbishop stood up in front of the altar, and a group of religious sisters rendered him honor by dancing around him and singing in their native language. It was an expression of thanks for the honor given to their country. In this way, we spent the first hour of the celebration. We then were able to continue with the episcopal ordination. Just before the clock in the nearby modern palace announced the noon hour, the newly ordained bishop stepped down to bless the people, starting first with his elderly parents. In a spirit of ecumenical friendship, the representatives of other religions came to congratulate him. Since the president was out of the country, the representatives of his office and of the government expressed their own congratulations. Before two o'clock, our procession finally reached the shadows of the cathedral. Refreshments had been prepared in a big hall, because after five hours everyone was more thirsty than hungry.

After a short rest, Bishop Anthony Chiminello, an Italian missionary, and I started our trip by car toward the south, to the city of Keetmanshoop. During the trip, we stopped for an overnight rest and the next day continued on a deserted asphalt road. The land became more and more arid, and the prairie bushes more scarce. We stopped once to see an ostrich farm. There were hundreds of the creatures. Luckily, they were fenced in so they could not attack us with their strong beaks. Aside from that one stop, we turned twice onto dusty roads to make visits to missionary stations in this dry region. One of the stops was at old Mariental, where German religious sisters had once built a nice hospital. Because of a lack of religious vocations, the sisters had then had to leave this station. Healthcare institutions owned by the state do not exist in this difficult territory, where the residents do not like to move about. The second mission station was located in a land that resembled a moonscape. We were welcomed by an old German missionary, wearing his cassock, with a beret covering his head. He summoned his little flock to the newly built church, where I greeted and encouraged them. Life really is difficult in this area of few trees, where only goats can survive amid the hot rocks and sand. Men are working, however, in the nearby mines.

Right before sunset, we arrived at our final destination. Keetman-shoop is a small town and the administrative center for the entire southern region. It is like an oasis surrounded by two deserts: the Kalahari in the east and the Namib in the west. The Namib Desert continues along the coast to the north, where the famous Skeleton Coast is located. In front of the small cathedral, a group of faithful and religious sisters of different nationalities had gathered. Before the evening Mass began, I experienced a surprise. In the church, we heard the sounds of a waltz and saw a few couples dancing in a limited space. It seemed as though they were trying to imitate the native Africans and bring about some sort of "enculturation". The old residents did not realize that to us Europeans, the results were not harmonious.

The next day, after a short excursion and a visit of the town hall, I returned north in a small plane in order to visit the city of Rundu. There I met with the faithful and with the priests. Later, I visited the mission that gave to Namibia both of its native bishops—a fruit of excellent missionary work. I made another stop on the banks of the Okavango River, which forms part of the border with Angola. I gave my blessing to Angola, which was but a short distance away and without any border security. The entire northern part of Namibia is fruitful and cultivated. The process of evangelization also continues here very well.

I returned from Rundu to Windhoek through the Etosha National Park, which has its own interesting sights, even though it is not very well known. German tourists like to visit it, and Lufthansa has a direct flight from Frankfurt to Windhoek. In the park are a good number of wild animals, such as elephants, giraffes, zebras, gazelles, different kinds of antelopes, and a few leopards and lions. Among the antelopes, the kudu stands out because of its size and beauty. The male has long rounded legs and white stripes extending from his back to his belly. He majestically protects a herd consisting of several antler-less females and of younger males. The oryx, which is almost the size of a cow, is a very fine antelope. Its meat is very tasty, since it grazes on the savanna. Some animals live freely even outside of the national park. They can be found on the farms, which can cover several thousand acres. The asphalt roads are protected by a tall fence. Even so, antelopes can jump over the fences and run across the road. This is very dangerous for cars, especially during the night. One of our missionaries was killed in this sort of accident.

Burkina Faso: Masks from Bobo Dioulasso

I returned to this interesting country in December 1996, as a representative of the Holy Father, when Namibia celebrated its centennial of evangelization. All the tribes were present during the Eucharistic celebration on the Feast of the Immaculate Conception. Different singing and dancing groups were present, among whom the women of the Bushman tribe, dressed in their own "costumes", got most of the attention. On this occasion, I had more time for a thorough visit of the capital. The city has a European character and possesses several points of interest. Large pieces of meteoroids, which often fall in this area, were displayed in one of the squares. They look like rocks made of steel, and they are very heavy. Western funds and progress are very quickly finding their way into this country, bringing not only the good but also the bad. In its second century, evangelization needs not only to spread out horizontally, but also to sink deeper roots.

Republic of Madagascar

Once again, the following description of the lands of southern Africa comes from the trip of John Paul II of April 26 to May 6, 1989, when he and I visited Madagascar, Réunion, Zambia, and Malawi. The first two are islands, and along with the two continental countries, are almost on the same latitude.

Madagascar is the largest island of Africa, slightly less than twice the size of Arizona. As of today, it has over 18 million citizens, who are of Malaysian and Polynesian ancestry. They are so proud of their land that even the organization of the bishops' conferences of this continent includes its name: "Symposium of Episcopal Conferences of Africa and Madagascar" (SECAM). This mostly hilly country, with its narrow plains adjacent to the coasts, is occupied by approximately twenty different ethnic groups. They have a common official language with a very difficult system of pronunciation.

Catholic missionaries from Portugal were present by 1540. French Vincentians staffed the mission from the 1640s to the 1670s, after which Catholic evangelization came to a temporary end. There was no continuous presence for 130 years, and the missionaries died from illness and fatigue, not by murder. English Methodists arrived by 1830, and Catholic attempts at reestablishing the mission during that decade were frustrated. Finally, in 1861, Catholic missionaries were able to resume their work. Some Catholics even settled in the capital city. The southern part of the island, as well as some other territories, were served by the Jesuits, who did very good work among the people.

Under Jesuit supervision, Church organization slowly developed, and in 1925, the first nine native priests were ordained. The first native-born bishop of Madagascar was ordained in 1939. Rome organized a hierarchy for the territory in 1955, when several native bishops became leaders of the dioceses. The country's constitution, which dates from 1959, guarantees freedom of religion. In 1960, Madagascar achieved its independence. In 1965, Paul VI beatified the Jesuit missionary Father Jacques Berthieu, who had been martyred in 1896. In 1976, the archbishop of the capital city, Victor Razafimahatratra, SJ, became the first cardinal of Madagascar. During the sessions of the bishops' synods, we had a problem with the pronunciation of his name. I simply called him "Cardinal Victor", while others stopped at the middle of his last name and called him "Raza".

In 1975, Marxists seized power and Didier Ratsiraka became president. It was he who welcomed the Holy Father upon his arrival. In 1992, after the collapse of communism in Europe, the country approved a new constitution. But, in 1997, Ratsiraka obtained power again, and

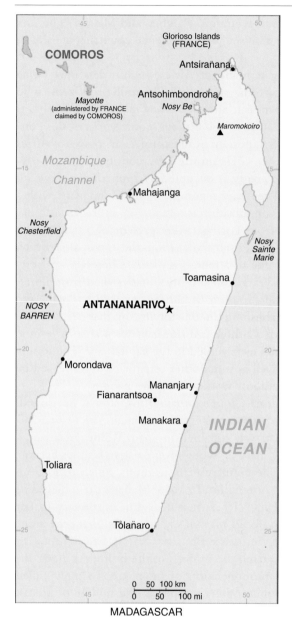

COMOROS

Glorioso Islands
(FRANCE)

Antsirañana

Mayotte
(administered by FRANCE
claimed by COMOROS)

Antsohimbondrona
Nosy Be

Maromokoiro ▲

Mozambique
Channel

Mahajanga

Nosy
Chesterfield

Nosy
Sainte
Marie

Toamasina

NOSY
BARREN

ANTANANARIVO ★

Morondava

Mananjary
Fianarantsoa

Manakara

INDIAN
OCEAN

Toliara

Tôlañaro

0 50 100 km
0   50   100 mi

MADAGASCAR

the results of the 2002 elections were ambiguous. Today 28 percent of the population is Catholic (over 9 million), while around 50 percent are animists (followers of traditional African religions) and the rest are either Protestants or members of different sects.

The visit of the Holy Father took place in three stages. After an official welcome in the capital city Antananarivo located in the center of the island, we proceeded, for our first major stop, to the Archdiocese of Antsiranana in the north, previously known as Diego Suarez and named after a Portuguese sailor. It possesses a beautiful harbor and serves as a point of departure for fishermen and tourists. Approximately half a million faithful from the surrounding mountains gathered for this occasion. I went to visit a seminary on which construction was proceeding very slowly. As usual, on this kind of trip, I had to solve some pastoral problems.

However, the centerpiece of this visit was the beatification in the capital city of the Christian mother, Victoria Rasoamanarivo, whose last name means "the beautiful, good, and rich one". She was a member of a noble family, and her mother was a lady in the royal court. At the age of thirteen, she was baptized and received a Christian name, which became a sign of her life's journey. She married an officer who was rude and unfaithful. She was very patient with him and refused the advice of many to divorce him. Finally, shortly before his sudden death, Victoria converted him to Christianity. After his death, she left the royal court and dedicated her life to the service of the poor and sick. She was really an exemplary wife and widow. This monumental celebration crowned the missionary efforts of the Catholic Church and became a strong source of encouragement for the future. After the solemn Mass, a Salesian missionary who worked in this area looked me up. He was of Slovak ancestry from the former Yugoslavia, but he had done all his studies and received his formation in the Slovak Institute of Saints Cyril and Methodius in Rome. The Holy Father met with the youth and later with the Catholic laity during special meetings. As always, the Holy Father used this opportunity to deepen catechesis.

The third stop during his visit was in the Archdiocese of Fianarantsoa, approximately 250 miles south of the capital. Mass was celebrated near the airport, in the presence of 180 lepers from a nearby institute founded by the Polish Jesuit Jan Beyzym. Father Beyzym himself later became infected with leprosy and died in 1920. These institutionalized patients brought to the altar a portrait of Our Lady of Czestochowa from their hospital. In this way, they expressed their gratitude for the Polish missionary and for their Polish Pope.

There was always a desire within me to return to Madagascar and to visit this growing Church that shows such promise in a poor country. That never happened, despite the repeated invitations from my friend Cardinal Armand, who is one year my junior. I have admired this cardinal for a long time. I was impressed when I saw photographs from his previous activities as bishop, because in a mountainous area, *per pedes apostolorum* (walking), he visited parishes that were spaced several days apart from each other. This Church has nineteen dioceses grouped into three provinces. Each has its own difficulties, but to each belongs the very important task of bringing Christ's message to the half of the population who has not yet heard it.

Department of Réunion

From Madagascar, we flew approximately 620 miles eastward over the Indian Ocean, to visit the island of Réunion. This island belongs to France, covers approximately 1,500 square miles, and has a population of 750,000. The Catholic Church in Réunion has 620,000 members. Europeans first learned of the island in the seventeenth century, and evangelization began there in the nineteenth. The bishop's seat is at the capital, Saint-Denis. Right outside the city, the high mountains are covered with lush vegetation. France maintains this island as an overseas department, or as an integral part of France, mostly because of its strategic location. The unemployment is very high, especially among young people. They live by collecting unemployment benefits because there are too few job opportunities. This creates an unhealthy situation, because the activity of working is very important for a person's psychological balance.

We were greeted by the president of the General Council from France as well as by the local bishop, Gilbert Aubry. Bishop Aubry was born on this island and became bishop when he was only thirty-three years old. John Paul II celebrated Mass on the square in front of the cathedral, and he beatified the School Brother Jean-Bernard Rousseau, locally known as Brother Scubilion. Brother Rousseau became an apostle of the island through his educational and charitable works. In his homily, the Holy Father touched upon a concrete situation. He called upon young people to maintain their hope and not get discouraged by their inability to find work.

Right after the Mass and refreshments, we went to the airport. There were two Concorde planes waiting. Those planes can fly 1,400 miles per hour. One of them was to take the president of the General Council back to France, and the other was for the Holy Father and his entourage, to take us to Zambia, which was the next destination on our trip. This plane does not carry many passengers, and it has also very strict restrictions regarding the weight of luggage. The majority of the media workers had to be satisfied with a somewhat slower airplane, which took off for Lusaka before we did, but which arrived later. Despite the clear reasons regarding the capacity of the Concorde, some of the reporters protested. The Concorde has a narrower body in comparison to other types of planes, and, so as to overcome air resistance more efficiently, has its nose tilted toward the earth during take-offs and landings. While the plane is in the air, however, its nose remains straight. The seats are relatively narrow, and the leg space too small, especially for taller people. The speed of the flight, as well as sound measurements, were displayed on a panel, but when we exceeded the speed of sound, we did not hear the famous bang. In little more than an hour, we were at the airport in the capital of Zambia, 1,925 miles from Réunion. I memorized this fact: May 2, 1989, John Paul II and I flew for the first—and probably last—time, faster than the speed of the sound.

Republic of Zambia

Zambia used to be the northern part of Rhodesia and became independent in 1964. Its counterpart to the south declared its independence the following year. Southern Rhodesia would eventually be renamed Zimbabwe in 1980, with the coming to power of the black majority. Zambia's territory is slightly larger than that of Texas. During the visit of the Holy Father, the population of the country was 7.5 million. Currently, it has surpassed 11 million. The number of Catholics stands at 3.5 million, or over a quarter of the population. Approximately the same number are animists (pagans), and 23 percent are Protestants. The visit of the Holy Father occurred during the centennial celebration of evangelization.

The first missionaries to come were the White Fathers (The Missionaries of Africa), founded by the Archbishop of Algiers, who later became a well-known cardinal, Charles Lavigerie. The Jesuits, Franciscans, and Capuchins continued their work. This territory was partially served by the Jesuit mission along the Zambezi River, in which some Polish and Slovak Jesuits used to participate. One of them, Cardinal Adam Kozlowiecki, is really exemplary and served as archbishop of Lusaka. He was born in 1911, survived imprisonment in Dachau, and then went to Zambia, where he remained as a missionary, even after being named cardinal in 1998. Missionary work was also undertaken by Slovak missionaries such as Father Jozef Švec, who is also the author of three interesting books: *Notes from Africa*, *Africa My Love*, and *Zambezi*. Also laboring in the country are Father Štefan Hirjak and religious brothers Jozef Gajdoš and Andrej Perdik. Brother Perdik built the road named after him. For their missionary works and the construction of schools, bridges, churches, and social facilities,

ZAMBIA

all of them have received prestigious state awards. Another Slovak missionary, Father Hancko, worked in Zimbabwe.

Presently Zambia is divided into ten dioceses, most of which have native bishops. Aside from this trip with the Pope, I visited the country on two other occasions, stopping at the Emmaus Minor Seminary and the Saint Dominic Major Seminary in Lusaka. I also visited the philosophical department of Saint Augustine, located far away from the capital. I had a desire to visit Livingston, the diocesan see named after the well-known explorer, which is near the famous Victoria Falls. I would later see the falls from the other side, during my second visit of Zimbabwe.

President Kenneth Kaunda welcomed us at the airport. The president had the habit of stressing the important points in his speech by waving a white handkerchief. He emphasized his stance against racism and excessive tribalism (tribal divisions), with the phrase "One people, one nation, one Africa". The proximity of the Republic of South Africa, and the presence in Zambia of probably eighty ethnic groups and of many refugees from the surrounding countries, had furnished the motivation for this sort of political platform. The Holy Father once again spoke against racism and on behalf of Christian solidarity. During the visit to the presidential palace, we were able to admire different types of gazelles and other animals that were moving freely in the nearby garden.

The following day we flew to the second largest city, Kitwe, a center of mining in the industrial region known as the "Copper Belt". It is a part of the Diocese of Ndola, which gathered around its Pope, who then celebrated the Eucharistic sacrifice. After the return to Lusaka, the Holy Father had a meeting with the diplomatic corps. To this group he delivered an interesting speech against racism, in which he declared:

> The Church considers racism and its expression in economic, social and political systems of separation, as totally opposed to Christian faith and love. Alas, the theoretical and practical expressions still exist in the world in great measure, in different forms, and in many regions, with the most dramatic and clear case embodied in the system of apartheid and separatism. To solve this moral problem, this wound of society, the Church encourages peaceful methods to effect necessary changes, and especially constructive changes. Racial separatism cannot be overcome by violence, but only by mutual reconciliation.

Who knows if these decisive words did not inspire the fall of the racist system in South Africa that happened several years later?

The principal gathering of the faithful of Zambia with the Pope was scheduled for the next morning during the celebration of the solemn Mass. During the Mass, the Pilgrim from Rome reminded those present of the centennial of evangelization and the merits of the missionaries. At the conclusion, he dedicated Zambia to the Blessed Virgin Mary. After that, we continued on our trip to the neighboring state of Malawi, where the official language is also English, since the country was once a British colony.

Republic of Malawi

Although the neighboring Zambia exceeds Malawi in size—the latter being slightly smaller than Pennsylvania—Malawi is very similar to Zambia. Its population was then almost the same as that of Zambia and today exceeds 11 million people. Many people suffer from AIDS. The mortality rate is also very high, and life expectancy is only around forty years. The number of Catholics stands at 3.3 million. The numbers of Protestants and Muslims are each a littler larger than the number of Catholics. The education and formation of priests in Malawi is proceeding very slowly because of tribal tensions. After visiting Malawi with the Holy Father in 1989, I had to return twice to this country to resolve some problems relating to seminaries and the priesthood.

The Holy Father arrived on the centennial anniversary of the arrival of the first missionaries to this country, which at that time was called Nyasaland. On May 5, 1989, he celebrated the Eucharist in Blantyre, the seat of the archbishop. During the papal visit, the political situation was pretty unpleasant. The leader of the country was a "life-long" president, a ninety-one-year-old physician, who had studied in Great Britain and who, during important visits, was able to recite long passages in Latin from *De bello gallico*. In the receiving salon of his palace, there was a small crack in the ceiling through which prying eyes and ears observed what was happening below. It was well known that instead of the president, one of the court ladies was in charge. The old president came to welcome us, escorted by women. He was dressed in a typical British tuxedo with a firm, round hat. The Holy Father kindly took his arm and escorted him to the car. During my second personal visit, I went to greet him, but shortly thereafter he was forced to resign. The country was left in a pitiful situation, from which it has still to extricate itself.

The Church in Malawi has seven dioceses. Two of the bishops are missionaries. I traveled with one of them through his diocese, which he was building up with success. He himself drove the car on an asphalt road, which was, for Africa, a very good road. We were passing through a narrow valley between two hills. From the car, he very proudly pointed to a small church built atop one of them. Then pointing to the other hill, where a tall minaret stood atop a mosque, he noted, "Those intrusive Saracens right away had to go build a mosque with a minaret that is taller than our little tower. They can afford it, because they are receiving large subsidies in petro-dollars." ("Saracens" was the name given to Muslim pirates who attacked Italian coastal cities during the Middle Ages.) While he was talking to me about the difficulties of dialogue with Islam, he often gestured with his hands, letting go of the steering wheel as he did so. I asked him delicately about his health, if he was able to drive on his own, and if he did not get sleepy while driving. He replied that he was a little worried about his diabetes, and that sometimes he would get very sleepy while traveling. He continued jokingly that he had a good method for staying awake: when his head started to droop, he would pull out a photograph of his superior in Rome, with whom he once had a very strong confrontation, and place the picture where he could see it. Recalling the troublesome event, his blood would begin to boil, after which his drowsiness would disappear. I got a good laugh out of this technique, and I concluded that even episcopal ordination does not change one's natural temper. I strongly recommended, however, that the bishop get a good driver.

The education and formation of priests in Malawi is proceeding very slowly because of tribal tensions. After visiting Malawi with the Holy Father in 1989, I had to return twice to this country to resolve some problems relating to seminaries and the priesthood. During my first trip to Malawi, with the Holy Father, I received via radio the news from Rome that my mother's health had taken a turn for the worse, after she had been lying in a coma since March 12. Upon returning to the house of the archbishop, both Cardinal Casaroli and I were able to make radio communication with Rome. I had a feeling as to what had happened, but was then told officially that my good mother had died just an hour before. I turned myself

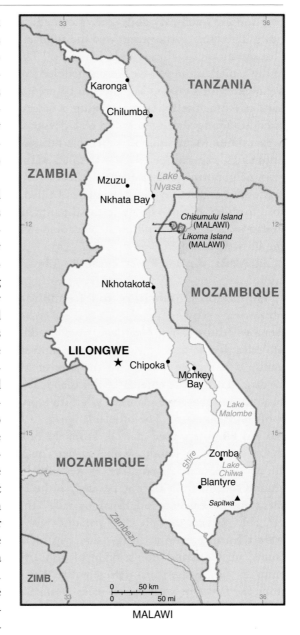

MALAWI

over to God's will. My colleague informed the Holy Father of the sad news. The Holy Father embraced me right at the door, with the words "So, the mother is already in God's glory." The next day, after the Mass in the capital Lilongwe, we were scheduled to return to Rome. I placed my request for a visa, so as to able to be present at the funeral. We were back in Rome the following evening, a Saturday, and I was still able to attend the funeral of my mother in Udavske, Slovakia (Czechoslovakia at that time). Many still remember that funeral because, in spite of many difficulties, the entire village was filled with the faithful, both those from neighboring areas as well as others from farther away. The funeral procession was led by sixty priests and filled the entire length of the road from my parents' house to the distant church. It was more a manifestation of faith than a funeral. We could sense changes in the air and the growth of hope.

In Africa, this hope was spread by John Paul II.

Republic of Mauritius and Republic of Seychelles

Another nearby island, *Mauritius*, could be added to the southern region of Africa. It measures only 1,158 square miles and has 1.2 million inhabitants. It is located not far to the east of Madagascar in the Indian Ocean. Many of the citizens of this island are a mix of the descendants of slaves and the descendants of white Europeans, but the largest group is of Indian ancestry. The official language is English, but French Creole and Hindi are used as well. From the religious aspect, one half of the population is Hindu, while 27 percent are Catholics, 16 percent are Muslims, and 5 percent are Protestants. It is a beautiful island and attracts tourists from Europe because, as the Holy Father appropriately mentioned, "balance and harmony rule" there. In October 1989, I was able to visit this piece of paradise with the Holy Father, as we were returning from a tiring Asian trip to Korea and Indonesia. We landed on the island after a flight of 3,550 miles. I returned to Mauritius in 1997 as the papal representative. I will amplify my knowledge from the first trip with experiences gleaned from the second.

The papal visit of Mauritius can be credited to two prestigious individuals: the French missionary Jacques Laval, who was one of the first to be beatified by John Paul II, and Cardinal Jean Margéot, the excellent shepherd of this country, who welcomed us very kindly. Our first stop was at the tomb of Father Laval. The next day, the Holy Father celebrated Holy Mass on a small hill, next to a statue of the Virgin Mary. A crowd of a hundred thousand people gathered on the hillside. The theme of the homily was family life. The Pope entrusted the families to the protection of the Queen of Peace, whose statue was enthroned on the mountain overlooking the capital Port Louis. The main Eucharistic celebration on the occasion of the closing of the Diocesan Synod would take place on the same spot in 1997. The entire country is actually one diocese. The Holy Father then met with the representatives of other religions and praised the spirit of reconciliation that ruled among all of them.

The following day, we flew to the island of Rodriguez, located four hundred miles to the north along with some other, smaller islands, all of which are part of the Republic of Mauritius. The population makeup is similar, and the people are poor. The inhabitants of this island feel isolated, and many of them are moving out to find jobs. The Holy Father was very attentive to them during Holy Mass. I comforted them several years later when I visited a number of locations on the island. Even at the time of the papal visit, I was looking for a way of fostering local responsibility in the Church. The sea here has a fairytale quality, but sometimes there is drought.

John Paul II concluded his visit to Mauritius by meeting with youth. They prepared a lively program for him and chose five most interesting questions for him to answer. Besides other topics, they asked him how to build unity on this multiracial island, how to discover the genuine value of love in the middle of moral decadence, and similar questions. His lifelong work with the young provided the Holy Father with beautiful words regarding human love. He called their attention to the fact that "in the life of man and woman there can be sufficient love apart from the sexual sphere. Likewise sexual life is possible without love." It is necessary to distinguish between love and sexuality and not accept a false impression of love. During the farewell ceremony in Mauritius, one of the children called John Paul II a "super-pope", and the prime minister, who was Hindu, thanked him for the message of peace, solidarity, and love.

During my personal visit as the papal representative in 1997, I broadened my knowledge of the island with a slow walk around the harbor of Port Louis and a trip to the coast, where I dedicated a new church building. I also was able to spend at least half a day and one night in the northern part of the island, where I could take a short dip in the sea. I took a ride in a boat with a transparent bottom and passed over a coral reef. I admired and filmed the different shapes and colors of coral that almost resembled stone bouquets and photographed the multi-colored fish as well.

During this trip, on the last day of October, the Catholic Indian community celebrated their own liturgical Feast of Light, called *divali*. They gave a Christian character to it when, during the Mass, with typical Indian processions, garlands, and dances, they celebrated Jesus Christ as the light, peace, and love of the world. The rite of *arati* was not missing from this celebration either. During the singing of the doxology, "Through him, with him, and in him . . .", young Indian girls in their colorful dresses, or saris, slowly circled the altar with plates filled with flowers and frankincense.

I also attended the Diocesan Synod. During a session held in a beautiful park, appropriately called "Tabor", I delivered a speech in French to approximately a thousand representatives from all the parishes and organizations. The park, which includes a castle, is the property of the diocese and was donated by a certain family to Cardinal Margéot. Now it is a center of Church activities. During the papal visit, we stayed there overnight. The day of the synod, however, the house was filled with participants chatting, singing, and eating sweets. It was truly a beautiful community. This property stands next to a steep precipice, through which a waterfall rushes. Looking through that valley, one can see all the way to the sea and to the airport. From there I set out for a short pastoral visit of the archipelago of Seychelles.

It is difficult to count *Seychelles* as part of Africa, especially as a southern part of it. It is located at the same latitude as Kenya and consists of a group of small islands, half of which are uninhabited. The black population is only 3 percent, while 90 percent are Creole, and 5 percent are Indians. The official languages are English and French. The people use French Creole. There are 81,000 inhabitants, concentrated in small towns on the main islands. One-third of the population lives in the capital Victoria, which is the episcopal seat. I stopped there for the first time with the Holy Father on our return trip from our longest visit of Asia, the Pacific, and Australia in 1986. It had been mostly a technical stop during the long flight. This time, however, I spent two full days there and performed my pastoral visit on the main island of Mahé. On November 1, I celebrated a parish Mass at the cathedral during a severe period of heat, which is even more noticeable there because of the high humidity. With Bishop Xavier-Marie Baronnet, the French Jesuit, we went around the island and visited some parishes. The bishop lived with several priests and had only a small room to himself. He prepared the breakfast and sometimes even the dinner. He showed me his pet turtles, which were of considerable size. In his garden, I filmed red birds that carry the name of "cardinals". Finally I was able to see them alive, and not merely painted as in New York, where one of my relatives jokingly gave me a sport shirt carrying the picture of that bird.

The principal industries for the local people are tourism and fishing. There is almost no land for farming, but the tropical vegetation is rich in fruits. I could pick my favorite papaya in the garden. The country became independent of Great Britain in 1976 and is a republic. Initially it was a democratic country, but the president later changed his ideological colors. Despite the shift, he was able to retain his office. The climate and tourism lead to a kind of apathy and irresponsible behavior. Pastoral work is relatively difficult, and a new evangelization is necessary also for the Catholics, who represent 90 percent of the population.

2. Central Africa

Southern Africa and especially the adjacent islands are not very typical of this continent. Their population is mixed and includes people of European and Asian descent. The further we move into the central part of Africa, the more the picture changes, and we move closer to the heart of this part of the world, to its primarily equatorial regions. West Africa and East Africa are located above it on the map. Central Africa is identified with the color green. Traveling north, passing from the tropical regions to the pre-Sahara Sahel to the actual Sahara Desert, the colors shift to yellow and brown. Deserts divide the western from the eastern part of Africa. To continue in order, let us therefore turn our attention to central Africa.

The following states comprise central Africa: Angola, Congo and Democratic Congo, Gabon, the Central African Republic, and two states that used to be united: Burundi and Rwanda. All are located near the equator. The Congo River with its many branches waters the larger part of this area. Forests and savannas cover other portions. A "rift", or area of geological depression, passes through the center of the African continent from north to south, giving rise to many lakes. In fact, the rift portion of Africa is often called the "region of the Great Lakes". Because of tragic events and conflicts that still prevail, much has been said about this area over the past decade. As concerns evangelization, this region has its own history. Nevertheless, I would like to add some general comments, because important changes have occurred there over the past twenty years.

At the end of the fifteenth century, evangelization of the central region went in two directions. One flow started from Portugal, whose sailors and merchants returned to their native land with a group of men from Angola. These later converted and returned to Africa as zealous catechists. The king of the region around the Congo River also requested missionaries from Portugal, to serve especially at the mouth of the river where it joins the Atlantic Ocean. With the help of the king, who received baptism, the Catholic faith spread quickly. The native king Alfonso I, who reigned from 1509 to 1543, sent his son Henrique along with a delegation to Rome to see Pope Leo X in 1512. In 1518, Henrique became the first native priest. In 1532, he became the bishop of his native country. Rome established a diocese under the title "Congo and Angola" in 1596. Apart from the Jesuit missionaries, Capuchins also evangelized the region. A very interesting report is to be found in the archives of *Propaganda Fide*, where a missionary describes the land, its customs, and conditions. His description of the queen is very detailed. He painted a picture of her and added it to his report. These archives house many interesting documents serving as an important source of history for mission countries that possess no other early written documentation. Another precious memento in the archive is an early map of Australia that predates the "discoverer" James Cook. In many instances, the reports of missionaries are often a country's only source of written history.

Returning to our mission history of the region, the first great successes of the Portuguese missionaries did not endure. They were affected by a decline of enthusiasm in western Europe, by the difficult climate and health conditions, and by the slave trade. Missionary activity appeared once more at the end of the nineteenth century. During the past one hundred years, missionary activity has been able to develop freely, due in part to the formation of new communities such as the Congregation of the Holy Spirit and others. Through God's grace, the Church has been able to achieve impressive results. Catholics in this region account for half and, in some places, even two-thirds of the population. Their faith and morals, however, need deeper roots.

A second flow of evangelization took place inland around the Great Lakes. Here, the process of evangelization occurred because of the beneficial activities of the Missionaries of Africa (better known as the White Fathers). They proclaimed the gospel in Burundi and Rwanda. Over the last century, the White Fathers have continued to obtain excellent results.

Republic of Angola

From June 4 to 10, 1992, while accompanying the Holy Father, I visited Angola and the adjoining islands. On the latter, São Tomé e Príncipe (Saint Thomas Island and Prince Island), the population of 140,000 is mostly Catholic. Angola is a large country, slightly less than twice the size of Texas, with over 14 million people. Approximately 60 percent of the population of less than 8 million are Catholics, and these are divided into fifteen dioceses. Angola is a former colony of Portugal that became independent in 1975. From the Church's point of view, this country was also dependent on Portuguese missionaries. Only in 1970 did Angolans get their first native bishop, not counting Prince Henrique at the beginning of the sixteenth century. Currently, the country has a majority of native African bishops, and since 1983 they also have their own cardinal, in the person of Cardinal Alexandre Do Nascimento. The northern part of the country contains rich mineral deposits and

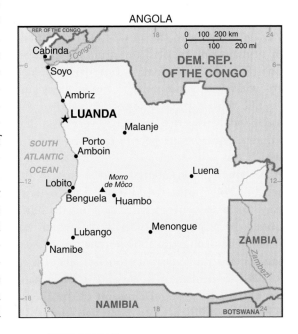

oil reserves. Until recent years, the country was wracked by civil war, one based on tribal and ideological differences. On the one side stood the governmental Popular Movement for the Liberation of Angola (MPLA), which, in looking for assistance, invited the participation of Cuban and the Soviet armies. On the other side stood UNITA (National Union for Total Independence of Angola), led by Jonas Savimbi until his death in battle. President José Eduardo dos Santos, the leader of the MPLA who underwent a shift in his ideological thinking, sent the Cubans home and recently declared an end to the twenty-five-year-long war. As usual, it was the poor people who had suffered the most. Hundreds of thousands were killed, while even more lost their homes and ran off to find whatever refuge they could.

The Supreme Shepherd of the Catholic Church arrived amid this situation to bring comfort and to encourage reconciliation. On June 4, 1992, we landed at the capital, Luanda. At the time, it had a population of 1.5 million, but by now this has doubled. After the official visit to the president, the Holy Father began his pastoral work by meeting with the clergy and laity in the cathedral. The following day we flew to Huambo, on the other side of the battle lines, where we were able to observe the consequences of the war. We then went to Lubango, where my good friend Archbishop Manuel da Costa welcomed us with a very touching speech. In it, he documented the consequences of the war by pointing to the misery of the injured people and the number of orphans. He recalled the cruel persecution and murders of one of our Roman missionary students, Leonard Sikufundo, and his co-workers—religious sisters and seminarians.

The third day we flew to the island of São Tomé. It is actually an independent island state that is very beautiful but has few job oportunities. Most of the people from the island attended the papal Mass, which was celebrated under the hot tropical sun near a gorgeous bay. A certain reporter offered a straw hat to the Pope. Though at that time, nobody in the world realized the extent to which these apostolic trips taxed the energies of the Holy Father. The Holy Father mentioned the plague of the slave trade, which was fully developed on this island. The main part of the homily was dedicated to the family, because the institution of marriage on this island is in a sorry state.

After returning to Luanda, our trip reached a high point the following day with the celebration of the Eucharist, in thanksgiving for the gift of faith received here five hundred years earlier. It was the

Feast of Pentecost, and the wide space overlooking the sea was filled with a great crowd. The view from the elevated altar was exceptional, and, from there, the Successor of Peter called upon all present to involve themselves in the work of evangelization with a new energy. He challenged them to destroy the walls of separation and, together, to start rebuilding the country. As if applying a healing balm, he said, "Dear people of Angola, I would like very much to bestow self-confidence and courage upon all of you who feel oppressed, lost, or marginalized. I really wish to erase from the hearts of children and youth the terrible images of blood and destruction!" In the afternoon, the Holy Father visited a hospital and followed this with a visit to the seminary that the Marxist government had just returned to Church control. It was undergoing extensive renovations. A visit to the capital could not end without a meeting with young people. The Holy Father met with them in a sports arena. There he engaged in a direct dialogue with a boisterous crowd of young Catholics.

On the fifth day of the trip, the Roman Pilgrim traveled to the northern city of Cabinda, where oil fields are located. During his homily, the former young worker—the Pope—expressed his views on the meaning of human labor. The singing and the colorful attire were a bit different here. By noon, we found ourselves in a different northern city, M'Banza Congo. We visited the ruins of the old cathedral built by the first missionaries in 1548—an unusual phenomenon for Africa. After a simple liturgy of the Word, the Holy Father, without his usual escort, went to the shack of a poor family. Here he spoke with its members on a friendly level. He allowed himself this kind of informal visit several times on his trips. They were a cause of great joy for the poor.

On the next-to-last day of his trip, the Pope was in the south of the country, in the city of Benguela. The local shepherd, Bishop Oscar Braga, was white, but an Angolan by birth. Keeping with the schedule, there was an outdoor Mass and then a meeting, held in the cathedral, with catechists from the entire southern region. The hot weather and the spirit of enthusiasm became a part of our memories. There used to be few priests in Angola, with some regions remaining without their spiritual shepherds for many years. The religious activity of these simple, zealous Christians during those times was of great value. They actually saved the faith during times of persecution.

The following morning, reporters conversed with the Vatican Pilgrim during the seven-hour flight back to Rome. They asked why he visited Africa so often. With sincerity, the Pope replied, "There are many reasons. Maybe you already have taken time to think about the African Mass or the African liturgy. Try to understand the deeper meaning of all parts of the liturgy. That is one of the reasons that I return to a place where values are born."

Let us hope that Angola has finally embarked on the path of reconciliation and peace, as well as the rebuilding of a single homeland and the rebuilding of one Church.

Democratic Republic of the Congo

Both the territory and population in the Democratic Republic of the Congo are the largest of central Africa. In the past, the country was called Zaire, to distinguish it from its smaller, northern neighbor, the Republic of the Congo. The population exceeds 57 million, and its territory is slightly less than one-fourth the size of the United States. Catholics comprise over half of the inhabitants, with the membership around 30 million. One-third consist of other Christians, while 10 percent are animists, followers of traditional African religions. This country received its first native priest in 1917; its first native bishop in 1956; a Catholic department of theology, which was the beginning of the Lovanium University, in 1957; and its own cardinal in 1969.

The Congo River flows west through the entire country, all the way to the Atlantic Ocean. This river has many tributaries, from the north and from the south. It is bridged in few places, therefore main roads are not numerous in the country. The northern part is heavily forested, while Shaba, covering the eastern and southern regions, contains some of the world's richest mineral deposits. These mines, from which diamonds, gold, copper, uranium, and other metals are taken, draw the attention of many businessmen and foreign countries. Shaba and the eastern region next to the Great Lakes, called Kivu, have therefore been centers of turmoil and war.

The country came into being in 1885, as the Congo Free State, a personal possession of King Leopold II of Belgium. No independence was involved. It was managed as a feudal fief. The country obtained real independence in 1960 under the leadership of the communist Patrice Lumumba. In 1965, the young Colonel Joseph Mobutu came to power and ruled as dictator until 1997. In that year, a socialist revolutionary, Laurent Kabila, invaded Congo without any difficulties and had his efforts seconded by Uganda and Rwanda. In 2001, Kabila was assassinated by his own friends, and his son Joseph was named head of state. In October 2002, the new president was successful in getting the occupying Rwandan forces to withdraw from eastern Congo. Two months later, an agreement was signed by all remaining warring parties to end the fighting and set up a government of national unity.

The people still suffer because of the war, and, with the people, the Church suffers as well. Uncertainty lies everywhere, along with self-motivated armed groups. I remember in 1999, around Christmas time, I received a phone call through the satellite system. Archbishop Laurent Monsengwo of Kisangani described to me how one of the militant groups had shot into his office using a small cannon. Luckily, the archbishop was in the neighboring room and ran immediately out the back entrance. He had called me from the nearby mission station to tell me what had happened. The role of the Prefect overseeing the missions also includes suffering with those who are suffering.

During my 1983–84 Christmas and New Year's vacation, I paid my first visit to the Democratic Republic of the Congo, which was then called Zaire. At that time, I limited my visit to three places: Kinshasa, the capital; Goma, an important small town in the heart of the eastern Kivu region; and Lubumbashi, a highly populated city in the center of the Shaba region. Lubumbashi is located on the bank of the Congo River. During the time of my visit, it already had over 3 million inhabitants. There were only a few asphalt

roads with streetlights and a telephone wire system built by the Belgian colonial government. According to African custom, public properties had not been maintained. The maintenance category is not a part of the local mentality. We saw occupied taxies run out of gas, with the passengers obliged to help push them to the closest gas station. In a certain parish in Zaire, I concelebrated Holy Mass with the auxiliary bishop in the local rite and language, Lingala. It lasted two and a half hours, with only a few differences from our liturgy. They had the penitential rite just before the Liturgy of the Eucharist, in light of the words of the gospel, "If you are offering your gift at the altar, and there remember that your brother has something against you, leave your gift there before the altar and go; first be reconciled to your brother" (Mt 5:23).

The flight to Goma was an adventure from its start. The passengers all had to spend the entire night next to the plane. In the morning, people had to run to get a place, because there were more passengers than available seats. Some of the travelers were actually piglets and chickens. On New Year's Day, I concelebrated Mass with the bishop in the new cathedral. I thanked the bishop for his warm welcome, indicating the words of a new sign written on the wall in Swahili, *Modje katiko Jesu Kristo*—"One in Jesus Christ". In the city, noticeable restoration works were under way after the eruption of a nearby volcano. The blackened lava had stopped at the first houses, but a smaller flaming stream still flowed from the side of the volcano. As we were going around a nearby lake, the bishop observed the dark clouds above the volcano and worried about another eruption. It would in fact occur, although a few years later, at which time the lava damaged a large portion of the city, including the cathedral. We flew around the volcano in a small plane, locally called *petit porteur* (small carrier), heading toward the neighboring Diocese of Butembo-Beni. We had a nice view of the active volcano, which was already signaling danger. Our two-engine Cessna plane made us feel more secure than when we had flown over Lake Kivu, where recently a small, one-engine Cessna had crashed. After our plane landed, our car got stuck on a muddy road—a very common occurrence in Africa. Bishop Emmanuel Kataliko was very kind and prepared a trip by jeep for us to a remote mission, from which we continued into the forest. To reach our final destination, we later had to walk on footpaths toward the settlements of pygmies. I met here for the first time with this interesting, partially nomadic tribe.

We were already well informed about them by a missionary from Belgium.

Our adventure continued with a visit to the Virunda National Park. Due to lack of time we were not able to go to the Bukavu Forest, where the orangutans live. However, the Virunda National Park provided adventure enough. We arrived there very late. The bishop was carefully driving the jeep along a forest road, using only the lowest beams on the headlights. Suddenly he stopped. In front of the car, a snake resembling a boa constrictor hung from a branch. If that kind of snake falls on a car or wraps itself around the wheels, it can cause an accident. As we continued on our way, the bishop, with his African eyes, spotted two hippopotamuses crossing the road. At night, they can be especially dangerous because, with their weight and strong jaws, they can tip over or destroy a car. Luckily, we arrived early at the park center's lodging area. From there, in the morning, an experienced ranger led us into the savanna. Allegedly, our ranger had at one point served as a guide for a king of Belgium, and his hand bore the marks of a lion's claws. He showed us some snakes and lions during their morning hunt. An old lion and four lionesses were resting after their breakfast near a swamp. One was finishing up a young hippopotamus, which this prowling group had still been able to conquer. We had difficulties, right there, in getting out of the muddy soil. The bishop shifted to four-wheel drive, and with small maneuvers we were able to get out. With a few minor motions, he was also able to force the old lion to get out of our way. They say that the smarter ones (or those that are well fed) give in. Our driver showed off his African knowledge of animal "psychology".

After our return to Goma, we asked why they have a transmitter at the mission station. They explained to us that that is the only means of rapid communication in a country without sufficient roads, which are often cut by the many rivers, and where there are but few bridges. People and cars are transported from one riverbank to the other by ferry. Missionaries and bishops communicate via radio at appointed times. The missionaries are then asked about their needs. Better conditions prevail in areas situated near airports, but there are not many of these. We also had to fly almost 750 miles from Goma, near Shaba, to Kinshasa, and then almost the same distance to Lubumbashi. The entire region of Shaba, or Katanga, is very rich in gold, diamonds, and minerals. We visited copper mines, of both the strip and underground varieties. Along the road we saw chips of green malachite. This natural wealth is of interest to foreign markets and gives rise to wars. Meanwhile the local citizens remain poor.

After our return flight to Brussels on Air Zaire (which is often called *Air Peut-être* or the "Maybe Airline": it might fly—or then again it might not), I derived one more experience from this very educational trip. On the plane, an eighty-year-old Benedictine missionary sister approached me. She had worked for many years in the savanna and was returning home for the first time. She had only one concern: that her mother superior might not allow her to go back to the missions because of her advanced age. Her desire was to die in Africa. She was wearing only a light coat and sandals on her bare feet. We saw her in Brussels, where she was shivering from the cold. It was snowing and windy outside. She was the embodiment of a true missionary!

A year and a half later, this heroic missionary world became a part of my life and ministry. In August 1985, accompanying John Paul II, I returned to Zaire—the Democratic Republic of the Congo, now as the Prefect for the Congregation for the Evangelization of Peoples. From my new experiences, I would like to mention the fine cooperation of Bishops Laurent Monsengwo and Faustin Ngabu, and of Cardinal Frédéric Etsou, who were the leaders of the conference of bishops. I ordained the first African Jesuit provincial, Christophe Munzihirwa, to the order of bishop. He later became the Archbishop of Bukavu and died a martyr. After his death, I helped name his successor, the excellent shepherd Bishop Emmanuel Kataliko, who was chased out of his diocese by invaders. After many protests from the Vatican, he was allowed to return. Later he attended the Symposium of Episcopal Conferences of Africa and Madagascar (SECAM) in Rome. A few hours after our concelebrated Mass, he died from a stroke, caused by all the suffering he had undergone.

During a very difficult situation, when the Democratic Republic of the Congo was divided politically and militarily, the bishops were not even able to assemble. During that time, in early November 1999, I called a meeting of the three bishops' conferences: those of the Democratic Republic of Congo, Rwanda, and Burundi. We met in Nairobi, Kenya, where all were able to arrive, despite all sorts of detours. Some of them arrived from Kinshasa, some through Uganda, and some even through Zambia, after traveling for several days. I personally arrived from India, where I had accompanied the Holy Father. I brought his greetings to the bishops, and I actively attended their meetings, which lasted several days. The bishops asked me to be the celebrant and homilist at their opening and closing liturgies.

In the beginning, I spoke about serving as their point of unity amid their suffering and told them that I had sympathy for their situation. I also had words of encouragement for the shepherds of the suffering Church in those three countries, where two of the nations were at war against the third. In the French language, I spoke to the hearts of the bishops asking them to remain under the cross. At the same time, however, I challenged them: "What are we doing, and what are we going to do in the service of peace?" They responded to this emphatic call with a common proclamation on behalf of reconciliation and an appeal for peace on the part of the assembled bishops. Here were demonstrated the power of the gospel and the light of the Holy Spirit over tribal hatred and vengeance. In the spirit of Jesus Christ, those sixty shepherds were able to come unanimously to this appeal. This was a demonstration that the African Church is able to react rightfully and prudently, even in the most difficult situations.

The bishops of the Democratic Republic of the Congo used this opportunity to stay a few more days for their own meeting. Because of the conflict occasioned by the war, they had not been able to assemble for several years. I left Nairobi with a feeling of satisfaction from our common work with the bishops. It was a heartfelt joy for the Prefect for Evangelization, and one for which I am thankful to God.

Republic of the Congo and Republic of Central Africa

On the northern side of the Congo River is located another country that carries the same name as the river. To distinguish it better from its southern neighbor, the name of the capital city has been appended to that of the country. The result is Congo-Brazzaville, or in abbreviated form, Congo-Brazza. In 1987, I spent an African Christmas in this country. In the capital, I celebrated a solemn Mass in a modern church building. The sun was mercilessly generating heat, while moist tropical air penetrated through the unglazed windows. The church was packed, with the exception of the center aisle, which was used for the ritual dance and liturgical procession—as well as by restless children. The choir of university students provided beautiful French and African songs. For the first time, I came to like local jazz, accompanied by singing, and similar to African-American spirituals. Everything was so different from Christmas in Slovakia or Italy. There were no Christmas trees and no snow, but the same Nativity set and the same joy that "Christ the Lord was born unto us."

During the Christmas season, I visited several parishes in Brazzaville. Polish priests from the dioceses of Kraków and Tarnow, Poland, administered one of them. On the Feast of Saint Stephen, this parish served as the gathering place for Polish missionaries and religious sisters from the entire Congo. They invited me as well. We sang Christmas carols and ate *opłatky* and other Slovak Christmas food. One of those present from the Gora region of Poland (close to the Tatry mountains) added a few Goral songs and jokes to the festivities. African boys peeked through the windows and rejoiced with us. It was a gathering of family and an encouragement amid difficult missionary work.

The following day we went to Kinkala, where I installed the first bishop into office in the newly established diocese. Under the merciless sun, I presided at the solemn Mass that was celebrated in an open space. Later, as I proclaimed the papal decree, the joy of the faithful overcame all fatigue and exertion. My own joy came from the growth of this young Church. My subsequent schedule included a visit to the Diocese of Nkayi and to another place that we designated as a possible seat for a future diocese. Bishop Ernest Kombo chartered an old two-engine plane for fourteen people. We had to wait a little until the pilots were able to move the plane. An hour into the flight, because of the clouds and the fact that the airport lacked a radar system for connections in bad weather, the pilots

realized that they were not able to locate the town of Nkayi. As we descended below the clouds so the pilots could better orient themselves, our plane appeared above the mountains and very close to earth, but not close to the so-called airport. Luckily, after a longer period of circling among the clouds, we were able to land at an airport at which we were scheduled to land the same day, except later in the afternoon. After we landed, despite the change of time, we were very kindly welcomed. After the celebration, they served us a meal of roasted chicken, fish, and rice in the yard of the missionary station.

African food could fill a chapter of its own, but I could fully rely on the meal served at that station. The meat prepared by Africans cannot be digested by all stomachs. We can say the same about the very spicy sauces, and it is better not to try to learn their ingredients. Besides rice, I was saved by the African potatoes, called *manioc*. They are very similar to our potatoes, but with a somewhat different taste. I also trusted the porridge made out of millet, called *fu-fu*. With *fu-fu*, I usually ate cooked *manioc* leaves, which, as I knew, could not cause me any harm. The leaves of *manioc* have a taste similar to that of spinach, but you have to be careful that those in charge of preparation do not add too many hot spices to it. Also, the cakes made of corn or some other flour are rather safe.

In the afternoon, after the sky had cleared, we could fly out and successfully land in Nkayi, the seat of the diocese. The people had been awaiting our arrival since seven o'clock in the morning. After the celebration at the cathedral, we had to rush back to the airport. That way we were able to complete our flight in daylight, a necessary requirement because the airport did not have any lighting. On the following days, I had several meetings with bishops, priests, lay workers, missionaries, religious sisters, and seminarians.

At this point I would like to add some information to complete the picture of this country, which has partially changed over the last few years. Unlike its southern neighbor, Congo-Brazza used to be a French colony. The French influence is still very strong, especially in the economy where the Elf Company dominates oil production, as well as in the area of culture. The country became formally independent in 1960. Three years later, Marxists took over the government. From 1979 until 1992, the country was under the dictatorship of General Denis Sassou-Nguesso. After a five-year hiatus, and with the help of Angola, Sassou-Nguesso regained his powers in 1997 and had these confirmed in the elections of 2002. Congo-Brazza is slightly smaller than Montana and has over 3.8 million citizens. Over fifty percent of the population are Catholics, divided into six dioceses and one prefecture.

The light of faith arrived in this country from the coast in the early sixteenth century, during the reign of the Congolese King Alfonso I. Later on, it encountered significant obstacles, especially because of the slave trade. In the late nineteenth century, missionaries began a consistent evangelization. In 1973, Pope Paul VI named the first Congolese cardinal, Emile Biayenda, who was killed four years later. John Paul II visited this country in 1983. Some tribal problems also exist in this country, especially among the members of the Lari and Vili tribes. The Church here is slowly recovering from its wounds, caused by political and tribal conflicts that are still not settled.

I left Congo-Brazza, as it is frequently called, flying to Bangui, the capital of the Republic of Central Africa. During some well organized days, I was able to visit all six existing dioceses, to ordain an Auxiliary bishop for Bossangoa, to prepare the plans for two new (now existing) dioceses, to pay a visit to some mission stations and to the pygmies in the forest. A French missionary who piloted the one-engine Cessna was very helpful on this extremely hectic and adventurous trip. We landed on open fields and flew about five thousand miles through this poor country of fewer than four million people and 792,000 Catholics. As the end of my stay, I visited the head of the state, General Kolingba, successor of the famous Bokassa, known by his "imperial" coronation imitating the glorious Napoleon Bonaparte.

Gabonese Republic

The tropical forests of the northwestern Congo continue into Gabon, covering a significant part of this country, which is slightly smaller than Colorado. Its population is only 1.35 million, of whom approximately 60 percent are Catholics. Gabon has a similar civil and ecclesiastical history to Congo. It gained its independence in 1960. Because of its low population and rich oil fields, this country should be one of the richest of the African states. Instead, it is hard to find wealth among ordinary citizens. Huge companies such as Shell and Elf own the oil production.

Evangelization began centuries ago, but the results only became more noticeable at the end of the nineteenth century. The number of native priests is growing slowly, and three of the four bishops are native to the country. In 1982, John Paul II stopped in the capital, Libreville. I ordained a native bishop in Franceville in 1997 and another missionary bishop in Mouila. I took advantage of this trip to visit the Archdiocese of Libreville as well as the Diocese of Oyem. In the capital, I had a liturgical meeting with the laity, and I also met with the country's president. I paid a visit to the newly established sem-

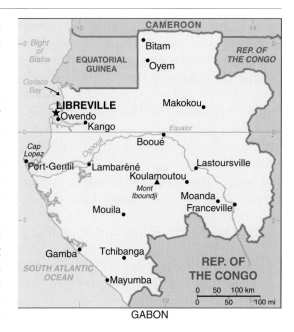

inary, which was directed by alumni of our Urbanium College in Rome. The accommodations were very humble and quite cramped, with insufficient room for all the seminarians. We therefore decided that a new facility needed to be built. The rector at that time later became an auxiliary bishop and three years later was named diocesan bishop of the newly established Diocese of Port-Gentil.

Near Libreville, we visited a contemplative religious order of sisters, where all but one of the members were native Africans. I was able to see the humble residence of the apostolic nuncio, who commutes to this area from Brazzaville. I saw a very interesting church, where African art was incorporated into the carved wooden altar, pillars, baptismal font, and statuary. There is a factory in Gabon where the so-called "soap stone" is processed into sculpted works. African religious art is very beautiful and stands out in wood and stone carvings, as well as in paintings. I saw exceptional art products with an African influence as well in Cameroon, Malawi, Zambia, Ghana, Togo, and several other countries.

The flight to Oyem was an adventure as well. The president offered a plane to us, along with its French pilot. First, we had to wait for the thick haze hanging over the runway in Oyem to dissipate. Because of limited visibility, we did not risk colliding with the tall surrounding forest. When they were ready to start the plane, one of the engines would not turn over, and we had to disembark. They had to warm up the engines on a second plane, and finally we were able to take off because the haze had started to lift. I was watching our landing in Oyem, which was not very simple. Despite low visibility in a milky fog, we landed successfully, thanks to the experience of the pilot and his knowledge of the terrain. The entire crowd was waiting patiently and cheered as they heard the engines of the arriving plane. The Eucharistic celebration began with a small delay, but the sun began to shine and melted the haze, which further increased the enthusiasm of the people. That is how life goes in this part of the world.

Republic of Burundi and Republic of Rwanda

Two countries located east of the Great Lakes have many things in common. Both are slightly smaller than Maryland and have the same structure of population, which consists of people from two tribes. The Hutu tribe, who originally were herders, are shorter in appearance and more peaceful by nature. They form 80 to 85 percent of the entire population. The members of the Tutsi tribe are taller, with a more explosive character and an inclination to govern. They constitute 14 to 19 percent of the population. Aside from these two tribes, approximately 1 percent of the inhabitants are pygmies. After the First World War, both countries, then known as Rwanda-Urundi, were governed by Belgium. This lasted until independence in 1962. The Hutu tribe in both countries felt oppressed and rebelled against the governing minority. That caused a state of perpetual turmoil, even to the point of producing bloody fights and massacres. While on his way to attend a conference in Canada, the Burundian dictator Jean-Baptiste Bagaza (who for a long time was anti-religious) was overthrown in September of 1987 by a young member of the Tutsi tribe, Pierre Buyoya. In 1993, the first democratic elections brought more justice into the government, but after the assassination of the Hutu presidents of both Rwanda and Burundi, the turmoil started again. In Rwanda, General Juvénal Habyarimana of the Hutu tribe seized power in 1973. His dictatorship lasted until 1994, when he was murdered.

From the missionary standpoint, it suffices to say that in less than a century over half of the Rwandan and two-thirds of the Burundian population received the Catholic faith, from out of their respective populations of 8.9 million and 7 million. The fostering of native vocations played an important role and also resulted in the foundation of local religious orders. Before the turmoil, those religious orders were sending missionary groups into the surrounding countries. It is noteworthy that Rwanda obtained its first black bishop, Thaddée Nsengiyumva, in 1952. Four

BARUNDI

years later, he ordained André Perraudin to the episcopate, the first time in history that a black bishop ordained a white one. This was a fine demonstration of the universal and colorblind attitude of the Catholic Church.

John Paul II visited both countries in 1990. I accompanied him on that trip. I also visited Burundi in 1987, and Rwanda in 1992, and then in September 1996 I visited both countries. I first went to Burundi in December 1987, right after the fall of the dictator Bagaza. I was invited by the bishops' conference. This visit lasted a week and culminated with a pilgrimage on the Feast of the Immaculate Conception. The pilgrimage was to the hilltop of Mugera. A jeep took me all the way to the altar, where I acted as the special representative of the Holy Father. There was no shrine, but two hills created a kind of spacious, natural amphitheater. Over a hundred thousand people gathered on this hillside, having come to thank God for freeing them from their oppressors. The altar stood on a lower part of the hill and had a small roof over it. Under the open sky, one could hear Easter songs of redemption from slavery. I preached about the necessity for true reconciliation among the tribes: "While our spirit remains closed in egoism, and our hearts are filled with hatred; while our minds are blinded by the desire for vengeance and cruel retribution, we remain far away from God and cannot obtain his peace in our hearts." During the homily, a strong wind suddenly arose and brought with it dark clouds. The tropical downpour became so strong that it seemed as if someone were emptying buckets of water over us. Everyone got completely drenched, but shortly thereafter the tropical sun came out and dried all our clothes. I could then finish my homily.

Another interesting event I can recall was the bishops' meeting, where representatives from both tribes spoke openly for the first time about methods for achieving reconciliation and ethnic equality. My meeting and dialogue with the new head of the country, Major Buyoya, were also very interesting.

The Holy Father stopped in both countries upon his return from Tanzania in early September 1990. After arriving and being welcomed by the Burundian president at the airport in the capital city, Bujumbura, the Holy Father gave an important speech to the bishops in the chapel of the nunciature. He spoke about a modern plague that affects Africa in a special way: "AIDS is threatening not only some nations and society, but the entire population. It knows no geographical, racial, or age distinctions, nor social circumstances. This epidemic is not only a medical problem, but an ethical and human one as well. It is not enough just to inform. It is not enough just to practice prevention. Mankind can escape from this scourge if everyone is emotionally mature and has his sexuality in order." During the solemn celebration of the Eucharist, in the nearby outdoor square, the Holy Father ordained twenty-five deacons to the order of priesthood.

After lunch, we went by car through the picturesque mountains to Gitega, the seat of Archbishop Joachim Ruhuna of the Tutsi tribe. Archbishop Ruhuna was very objective and consistently worked for reconciliation, a fact that caused radical leaders from both tribes to count him as their enemy. In Gitega, the Vatican Pilgrim touched upon another great issue: responsible parenthood. A Polish missionary and medical doctor Henryk Hozer, from the Pallottine order, had already developed a nationwide apostolate reflecting the spirit of good parenthood. The Holy Father stressed in his homily that married couples should "receive children that they wish for and can raise. That calls for mutual respect and a mastery over their life of intimacy." The theme of reconciliation marked every speech of the Successor of Peter. Reconciliation was also the message given to the people of Burundi as we were departing for Kigali, the capital of Rwanda.

Rwanda: *Joy at the Ordination of the Bishop*

On Saturday, September 8, 1990, we started our motor coach trip to nearby Kabgayi, which is the cradle of the Catholic Church in Rwanda. At that time, we had no idea that the old cathedral would become, five years later, a staging point for the mass murders of three bishops and great numbers of faithful. The Eucharist was celebrated outdoors near the cathedral. A similar celebration took place in Kigali.

I returned to Rwanda in June 1992. The main reason for my trip was the ordination of two new bishops. Meanwhile, I visited some dioceses and Church communities. In a small town in the southern part of the country, Gikongoro, I ordained to episcopacy Augustin Misago from the Hutu tribe. He was a very peaceful man who would never harm anyone. As usual, it was a very fine celebration of the faithful, which took place in a spacious stadium. Ritual dancing, African music, and singing enhanced the celebration. A small roof offered us some protection against the tropical sun. In the nearby second diocesan seat, the elderly Bishop Jean-Baptiste Gahamanyi welcomed us. We then visited the first missionary station, located in Sava, and the following day the church and aforementioned cathedral in Kabgayi.

Later on, I started my trip to the northern areas, to the city of Ruhengeri, where the elderly Bishop Phocas Nikwigize welcomed me. Next, I made a trip to Kibunga, which is located in the southeastern part of the country. There, I ordained Frédéric Rubwejanga to the episcopacy, a priest from the Tutsi tribe. After this joyous and heartwarming celebration, I had a short and not very pleasant dialogue with General Habyarimana, who had come to the ordination by helicopter.

All these names appeared again in the world media in the ensuing years and in connection with tragic events. The first chapter in the tragedy occurred with the invasion of Tutsi refugees who had been living in neighboring Uganda. After they invaded the northern part of Rwanda and fought against the government, the local people of that region had to flee to various camps, leaving behind their possessions. I visited one of the camps, which was located on a hillside. We had to go by helicopter, because at that time automobile travel in the valleys was too dangerous. More than ten thousand people lived in the camp amid dust and trash, and in shacks made out of branches and straw. Whatever they received through international aid, they cooked on open fires in front of their shacks. The danger posed by fire, disease, and hunger was very great, and the number of new refugees was growing rapidly. I remember the sad and questioning eyes of the women and children. I left a small sum of money there to assist them in their need. We then flew to the next camp, which was located on yet another hill closer to the area of fighting. This camp consisted only of people who had been recently displaced from the nearby villages, where cannon fire could be heard. In a panic, the people already covered the entire hill. We were not even able to find a place for landing. That was only the beginning of the great drama that engulfed the entire country two years later.

In April of 1994, President Habyarimana was returning from peace talks in Arusha (Tanzania), in the company of the Burundian president. At the Kigali airport, Rwandan rebels shot at and downed the airplane, killing both presidents. In Rwanda, the death of the president called for a bloody revenge against the members of the Tutsi tribe, and even against the more moderate members of the Hutu tribe. Thus began the massacres that took the lives of almost a million people. Then, under the leadership of Paul Kagame, an organized group of Tutsi exiles from Uganda took over the entire country as well as the government, while many hundreds of thousands sought refuge in neighboring countries. In 1997, this new government also aided the coup d'etat of socialist Laurent Kabila, sending its army to the eastern region of the Democratic Republic of Congo (Zaire) with the excuse of pursuing its Hutu enemies. They then refused to give up control of the occupied territory, preying on the natural resources of the Kivu region.

Meanwhile, the Church was also under attack. The elderly Bishop Phocas disappeared without a trace, while returning as a refugee to his own diocese, Ruhengeri. In the cathedral in Kabgayi, a Tutsi soldier shot three bishops along with a number of the faithful. Kagame's government accused the Catholic Church of genocide, trying to lay the "responsibility" of the murders on the Church. Bishop Misago was forcefully imprisoned while he was traveling, and his faithful were not able to protect him. The Rwandan government tried him in court, but fortunately without success. Thanks to world and public opinion, and the honesty of the judge, the bishop was set free. The government also planned to transform the historic church in Sava into a genocide memorial, by piling up human bones there. I was strictly against it and brought up the issue later in Rome, when I met with two representatives from Rwanda. The Church needs to protect herself from wickedness and to defend truth and freedom, no matter the cost. There have been many occasions when my position has required me to defend the freedom of the Church and religious beliefs in meetings with dictators, ambassadors, and other officers. These efforts also strengthen the faith and courage of our brothers and sisters.

My return to Burundi also took place against a tragic background. The situation in this country was very pitiful. The murder of the two Hutu presidents was followed in Burundi by a brief democratic interlude. But Pierre Buyoya, the former Tutsi president of Burundi, regained power in 1996 in a military coup. He is still in charge. The more radical Hutus organized themselves into a partisan movement and launched guerilla warfare against the military government, which consisted only of members of the Tutsi tribe.

The Church always proclaims reconciliation and offers the opportunity for dialogue, which the extreme wings of both tribes refused for different reasons. It was in this context that Archbishop Joachim Ruhuna, a member of the Tutsi tribe from Gitega, was murdered. He always proclaimed the gospel as a solution, with its values of reconciliation and justice. While traveling along the road from northern

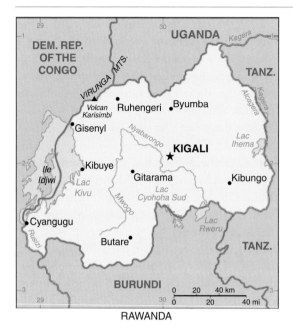

UGANDA

DEM. REP.
OF THE
CONGO

VIRUNGA MTS.

Kagera

TANZ.

Volcan
Karisimbi

Ruhengeri

•Byumba

Alcagera

Kagera

Gisenyl

Nyabarongo

Lac
Ihema

KIGALI
★

Kibuye

Ile
Idjwi

Lac
Kivu

Gitarama

Lac
Cyohoha Sud

Mwogo

Kibungo

Cyangugu

Rusizi

Butare•

Lac
Rweru

TANZ.

BURUNDI

0   20   40 km

0   20   40 mi

RAWANDA

Rwanda to Gitega, the archbishop's car was attacked, and he was shot. His body was carried off, and nobody knew where it had been taken. The Holy Father sent me to Burundi to celebrate the funeral in his own name in the archdiocesan seat. It was just before September 15, 1996, and close to the anniversary of my episcopal ordination, which the Pope himself had administered to me. I therefore asked the Holy Father for a special blessing, not only for the dangerous trip, but also on the occasion of my anniversary. The Holy Father looked at me, closed his eyes, and said, "Yes, it was September 15, 1979, on the Feast of Our Mother of Sorrows, the patroness of Slovakia, in the Sistine Chapel." Again, I had proof of his exceptional memory. I started my trip through Brussels to Kigali in Rwanda. No airlines were flying to Burundi, because after the start of the military uprising, all international airlines had declared an embargo on the country. The trip by car from Kigali to Gitega was well known for attacks, as had been the case with Archbishop Ruhuna. Luckily, there was a small special plane on its way from Kigali to the capital of Burundi, Bujumbura. The plane was carrying food from the United Nations World Food Programme and was operated by the U.S. Embassy out of Burundi. With my diplomatic passport, I got on the plane as the eighth passenger, joining several ambassadors already on board. We encountered another problem in the trip from Bujumbura to Gitega, because that road was also the scene of ambushes. Originally, we had booked a small four-seater plane that was only allowed to travel within the country. However, the evening before my arrival, the plane had been damaged before taking off on a flight. The situation was solved by the

United Nations' plane, which flew all the way to Gitega. All of the bishops were gathered there, and the following day, Pierre Buyoya, the head of state, whom I knew from our previous meetings, flew in.

One could sense the concern over a possible guerrilla attack. As we began the procession of bishops and priests from the house of the archbishop, I walked as celebrant, but escorted by two armed soldiers. In the distance, I spotted a military patrol. Buyoya was already inside the cathedral, which was packed. Soldiers stood outside the door, and tension was in the air. I broke the mournful silence by conveying the sympathies of the Holy Father, and by stressing an appeal for this fratricidal warfare to stop and for a pathway to be opened toward reconciliation and justice. It was there that I saw how Africans, especially those of this country, grieve. They did it with reverence, very quietly, and without tears in their eyes, but with tears in the depths of their hearts. As we were leaving the cathedral, we noticed a commotion around President Buyoya. We learned that he just received news regarding the body of Archbishop Ruhuna, discovered after nine days, hidden and buried in a field. I decided to stay and to celebrate the funeral Mass the following day with the remains of the archbishop. The body was brought in late that night. The body had been embalmed in a hospital, and the following morning, in company with the bishops, we officially identified it. Meanwhile, a grave was excavated in the cathedral floor, where we buried the archbishop amid a very moving ceremony. I used my stay among the bishops and priests for a meeting that resolved several problems. The meetings with the people, and the messages of the Holy Father as well as my own, strengthened the faith and hope of this local Church. Also, the meeting with government representatives would contribute to attaining the longed-for peace and reconciliation, based on justice.

The Church in Rwanda and Burundi has learned a great deal from this tragedy, which culminated in a massacre in 1994, and actually continues to this moment in a manner that is not yet being solved. The presence in the neighboring Democratic Republic of Congo of the Rwandan military, who claim to be protecting themselves against Hutu refugees, and the existence of Hutu guerilla groups inside Burundi, testifies to the persistence of intertribal tensions. The world awaits a democratic solution, while the minority retains its grip on power through military force. Fostering reconciliation, justice, and mutual respect remains the task for society and Church. Acknowledging the mistakes of the past, doing away with mutual hatred, and creating conditions for fraternal living—these are the tasks facing the Catholic Church in renewing her evangelization efforts in these countries.

3. Western Africa

Most of the countries of western Africa border on the Atlantic Ocean, while a few others touch the Sahara. In fact, the hot and dry sub-Saharan Sahel reaches at least partially into each of these countries. With the exception of Liberia, Guinea-Bissau, and Equatorial Guinea, all are former colonies of Great Britain or France, and all have retained either English or French as their official language. The two former colonial powers continue to exercise an economic and cultural influence in their now-independent former colonies. The economic, trading, and political interests of the European Union and the United States are also represented. Because tribal identity constitutes a stronger force for unity than does the concept of nation or state, the independence of these African countries is not at all stable. Those in power often seek to enhance the material prosperity of their own family or clan. Under such circumstances, even humanitarian assistance can sometimes be frustrated, going no further than the hands of those who should be distributing it to the poor. In addition, international borders were established with no consideration for such concrete data as common language and sensitivities, roads, or rivers. Instead, colonial or local governments created borders to maintain their own power—sometimes delineating artificial lines on a map after a table discussion. As a result, some tribes who possess their own language are divided between two countries that use two different official languages. In spite of all this, it would be dangerous at this time to revise the borders and reconstitute countries on a different basis. A feeling of unity, albeit a partial one, does exist in certain countries. In addition, different tribes are learning gradually to coexist peacefully within the various national borders.

This summary, which can also be applied to other African countries, illustrates the direction and circumstances under which evangelization has had to proceed. While it is true that the presence of colonists allowed for the arrival of missionaries, it is also true that this same presence was often an obstacle to spreading the Catholic faith. It is therefore a historical error to identify missionary work with the colonization of Africa or of any other continent.

Republic of Cameroon

Cameroon is a country slightly larger than California. Its present population stands at over 16.5 million, of whom 4.3 million, or 28 percent, are Catholics. Protestants account for 15 percent, Muslims for 22 percent, and animists for 30 percent of the population. Missionary efforts are chiefly directed toward this last group.

The country has a very interesting history, even if we restrict our study to the last century and a half. At the end of the nineteenth century, Cameroon became a German protectorate. This created a situation under which German Pallottine missionaries could enter the country. They founded a mission at Marienberg and in 1890 obtained the establishment of a prefecture apostolic. After the First World War, the administration of the country was divided between Great Britain and France. This explains the fact that the official language in one part of the country is French, while it is English in the other. Most educated people are fluent in both languages. Cameroon obtained its independence in 1961. The president of the country for more than twenty years has been Paul Biya, a Catholic. According to recent statistics, the country has extremely high number of people infected with HIV, and many are infected with tuberculosis.

After World War I, mission work continued to develop through the efforts of the Congregation of the Holy Spirit and later the Oblates of Mary Immaculate. The Catholic Church grew rapidly, and in 1955 an ecclesiastical province was established. Archbishop Jean Zoa, of the capital city Yaoundé, whom I knew very well, was the youngest archbishop to attend the Second Vatican Council. At the time of his episcopal ordination in 1961, he was only thirty-seven years old. In 1988, Cameroon received its first cardinal in the person of Archbishop Christian Wiyghan Tumi of Douala. Currently there are twenty-three dioceses in the country.

After my initial visit to Cameroon in 1981, I revisited the country in 1985 while accompanying John Paul II. In 1991, I represented the Pope at the centennial anniversary of evangelization. In 1995, I once more accompanied the Holy Father for the publication of the decisions of the African Synod. Those four trips, especially that of 1991, when I was able to travel for several days throughout the country, left me with vivid impressions that I would now share.

December of 1991 saw the conclusion of the centennial celebration of the evangelization of Cameroon, which I attended as the papal representative. I flew to Douala by way of Paris. Beforehand, using the diplomatic pouch, I mailed commemorative medals of John Paul II, rosaries, and other religious items that I planned to distribute. Among these were special artistic medals for the president and other individuals whom I was to meet. The papal envoy represents his superior and has diplomatic immunity. According to general customs, the local national government is responsible for his security, and the papal representative usually meets with the head of state and other public officials.

My trip did not start very well. My luggage containing my ceremonial clothing did not arrive from Paris. Thankfully, after my protest to the airlines, they were able to deliver it by the next flight and, under my supervision, to load it onto the airplane bound for Douala. After my arrival, I found that the package I had mailed to Douala had gotten lost somewhere in customs. It was found only after I complained to the minister of foreign affairs that I would not be able to offer the Holy Father's gift to the president.

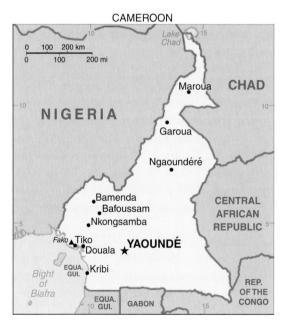

The high point of the schedule was the celebration of a Pontifical Mass on the Feast of the Immaculate Conception. It was to take place in a hilltop setting where the construction of the Jubilee Basilica had already begun. This was a typical African celebration, rich in joy and enthusiasm, and it occurred in the presence of the entire national episcopate and of bishops from abroad. The newspapers published the entire homily, even though it had not been a short one. (If I had not preached at some length, the faithful would have wondered why I had made such a long trip to deliver such a short homily.)

After the celebration, the president of the republic hosted a reception in his modern "state house" for invited guests. I was seated at the head table, and my meal was brought to me. The rest of the guests obtained their food buffet-style. The person sitting next to me described the food, quietly mentioning that they were offering crocodile meat. It was light in color and seemed to be soft, so I took some. I found that it tasted like cooked fish, and that it was very mild. The whisperer then prepared me for another "delicacy" offered at solemn meals: smoked snake. After hearing this, I began pondering how I might avoid it. Luckily, none was brought to me. In Africa, it is a very delicate matter to refuse a dish once it is offered. This is especially serious in the countryside, where doing so is considered to be an insult.

The second important event of the jubilee celebration was the opening of the newly built Catholic Institute in Yaoundé. This is actually a Catholic university for central Africa. John Paul II had requested its establishment in 1985. Six years later, I was able to bless the entire complex of new buildings, which included a fine church. The construction was made possible through the efforts of a zealous Jesuit, Father Denis Maugenest. My speech touched upon the role of the Catholic university at the service of education, science, and culture. The current minister of education immediately requested a copy of the talk. I visited the local seminary, as is my custom, because that is where new shepherds of the Church are formed.

I then attended various pastoral meetings, the first of which assembled the entire Episcopal Conference of Cameroon. I spoke to them about the placement of priests and the education of seminarians as the main agents for a second century of evangelization. A serious discussion followed. The official reports that bishops send to Rome every five years enabled me to participate fully in the dialogue.

I had an opportunity to fly to the northern part of the country, to the Archdiocese of Garoua, where priests from the surrounding dioceses had gathered. I noted the progress of construction of a new cathedral, sitting on a hillside and taller than the minaret of the nearby mosque, itself built by Muslims with the assistance of Arabic countries. At the airport in Garoua, I remembered the solemn Mass celebrated by John Paul II during his short visit in 1985 and concelebrated by the Vatican Secretary of State, Cardinal Agostino Casaroli, and by me. It had featured the celebration of the sacraments of baptism and confirmation and had taken place in an the open area near the airport where people where gathered in their traditional attire. Among those present were Muslim sheiks on their horses. The altar was elevated on metal scaffolding. Suddenly, dark clouds appeared on the horizon, and a strong wind pushed them toward us. As the wind made the pipes of the scaffolding rattle, the Holy Father poured baptismal water generously onto the heads of catechumens, both young and old. The sun was bright and very hot. Despite the threat of a tropical rain, the people stayed until the end. That picture has remained impressed in my memory as a symbol of evangelization in Cameroon, even as I was now returning from Garoua to Douala.

The latter is an important seaport and center for trade. Here I met the priests of this coastal Church province and visited the regional seminary, whose construction we had helped to finish with funds collected the world over from the annual World Mission Sunday in October. I had lunch with the priests and seminarians, as had been my custom during the many years of my assignment at the Roman College of Saint John Nepomucene.

A pilgrimage to Marienberg, the first mission and cradle of the Catholic Church in Cameroon, occupied an entire day. It consists of a complex of old buildings and a church on the Atlantic coast, several hours away by car from Douala. The mission was built by German Pallottines, who spread the gospel in the surrounding region. Many of them are buried there, as the crosses on their graves indicate. A number died from malaria and other tropical illnesses. In the old days, missionaries did not expect to return home. They remained in their new homeland until death.

During this jubilee visit, I could not omit visiting the youngest (most recently established) diocese of Yokadouma, which is located in the midst of a tropical forest. I officially installed the new missionary bishop, the Polish Oblate Eugeniusz Juretzko. The trip was a complicated and dangerous one. We initially flew from Douala into the heart of the jungle on board a small plane belonging to a lumber company. We landed in a small clearing adjacent to a storage area for cut tree trunks and then struck out through the forest over a narrow road. Tree trunks were transported over this narrow road to a wider one,

Cameroon: *Among the Pygmies*

over which they then traveled to port. We were able to visit a sizable mission for pygmies. The people were very glad that I had stopped, and together we prayed the Our Father, each, of course, doing so in his own language. The pygmies live only from hunting and from farming on small tracts cleared in the forest. After this very agreeable visit, we continued in SUVs along a muddy road that was so narrow that other vehicles could not pass. On that particular day, the government halted the heavy trucks that transport the enormously long and thick logs of precious wood. In one place, we saw a truck flipped onto its side.

After several hours, we arrived at the main missionary station in Yokadouma. It consists of older buildings built of dark bricks, and a small church, all in the middle of a meadow. Only a few houses could be seen, and these belonged to the officials of this civil administration center. The place did not at all resemble a bishop's seat, but that is how things commence, and there is no other way to go about it. In these mission territories, the Church exhibits a great deal of courage. She therefore also assists with civil development. The following morning the whole region was immersed in a dense fog, with a humidity that could be felt even in one's bones. Later, it became even warmer. The sun came out, and the faithful started to emerge from the forest, accompanied by a few curious onlookers. The Eucharistic celebration was followed by lunch and departure to a small new "airport".

A small airplane awaited us there, at the end of a four-hour drive that very much taxed our spines. After we arrived, I looked about for my suitcase, but without any success. My guide had forgotten it at the mission, along with my airplane tickets and passport. The following afternoon I was supposed to depart for Paris and Rome. What to do? Our small plane had to be in Douala before dark, and no car was capable of bringing me my luggage and documents before the departure of the plane. So we took off and tried to resolve the situation by telephone from Douala. We were lucky, because the following morning a small plane flew even closer to the mission center. My luggage was brought to that plane and, from there, was transported to Douala. Otherwise, I would have been obliged to wait several days—while all my obligations in Rome would have gone unmet. I learned the lesson that, while I must trust my travel guides, I should also double-check out of the corner of my eye. Some of my co-workers labeled it "distrust", but I preferred to call it "verified trust". Who was right?

My extensive pastoral visit as papal representative helped to give added impetus to evangelization. Numerous speeches, homilies, and presentations from the visit were later published in a sixty-six-page book. Both the local people and I have memories of this special occasion, as well as of the encouragement that it gave to the subsequent evangelization.

Federal Republic of Nigeria

Nigeria lies northwest of Cameroon. Its long coastline and the adjacent areas are humid and muddy, especially in the broad delta created by the Niger River as it enters the Atlantic Ocean. Moving northward and inland, the climate becomes dryer. The land also rises in elevation, sometimes yielding a dried-out tableland that is the precursor of the Sahara Desert.

Nigeria is one of the largest African states in terms of area and population, but also with respect to the number of its Catholics. It is slightly more than twice the size of California, and its population stands at 130 million. Half the people are Muslim. About 40 percent are Christian, of whom 19.3 million are Catholic. Lastly, approximately 9 percent are animists. The population consists of four main ethnic groups. In the south are the Ibo (or Igbo) and Yoruba tribes, and in the north the Hausa and Fulani, all of whom have their own languages. Christianity is present mostly in the south, while the northern part is more likely to be Muslim territory. In reality,

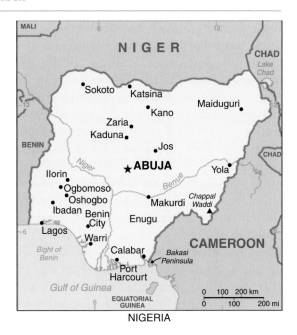

NIGERIA

Christians and Muslims live side by side everywhere, but not always in peace. Several inland states with a Muslim majority are now enforcing Islamic law (Shariah) on all the citizens and acting aggressively against Christians. I experienced this on my trip in 1986, when I visited the northern region. At that time, a fanatic Muslim group destroyed 152 Christian churches and attacked our small seminary in Zaria, which I had visited just a few days prior to the attack.

Nigeria was a British colony for a very long time and became independent only in 1960. Between 1967 and 1970, the country experienced civil war in Biafra, the name taken by the southeastern region that was seeking its independence. It is home to the largest number of members of the Ibo tribe and also to the greatest number of Catholics. After the civil war was put down, military rule with strict controls was imposed on the region. Neglected roads and public services persist as reminders of this time. The military dictatorship surrendered power only a few years ago. Nigeria possesses very rich oil fields, but these are owned by international companies.

The evangelization of Nigeria began as early as the 1400s, but in the following centuries was not very successful. At the end of the nineteenth century, the Holy Spirit Fathers arrived in the area and began their mission work in the region of Onitsha, among the people of the Ibo tribe. They persevered here, in spite of obstacles erected by the British administration and the military, who favored Anglican missionaries and who also did not wish to anger the Muslim emirs. Bishop Joseph Ignatius Shanahan established a Catholic school system and, in this way, was able to penetrate into families and educate future local leaders. The second secret for success was the education of a native clergy. Of note is the ordination of several native priests by 1929. By 1950, Rome was able to divide the country into ecclesiastical provinces. Monsignor Dominic Ignatius Ekandem became the first native bishop in 1953; he was later named a cardinal, in 1976. At the conclusion of the Biafran War, when ninety-seven missionaries were expelled, the young Church did not lose courage. At that time, the Church in Nigeria had over one hundred native priests. The seminaries and religious houses filled up. God blessed the country with many vocations, while lay merchants, teachers, and refugees began spreading the faith throughout the nation. Cardinal Ekandem even had the courage to establish the Society of Saint Paul for local and foreign missions, a group that now consists of over 150 priests.

Presently, Nigeria has forty-nine dioceses. For the most part, these are led by native bishops, nine of whom have the title of archbishop. In addition, the former Archbishop of Onitsha, Cardinal Francis Arinze, represents Nigeria with dignity as the Prefect of the Congregation for the Sacraments at the Holy See in Rome. Nigeria is also home to the Catholic Institute of West Africa (CIWA), a university that serves the entire western portion of the continent. The Church in Nigeria welcomed Pope John Paul II in 1998. During his visit, the Holy Father blessed the nunciature building in Abuja, and in Onitsha he beatified the native priest Cyprian Michael Tansi, whom Cardinal Arinze still remembered. I took part in this papal trip as well.

Apart from the trip with the Holy Father, I visited Nigeria on two other occasions. The first was in 1986 when I attended a five-day meeting of all English-speaking bishops from West Africa, united under the name Association of Episcopal Conferences of Anglophone West Africa (AECAWA). After the meeting, the following week, I used public and private planes to visit the principal regions of the country. The second time I visited, in 1997, I went to Warri, in the heart of the Niger Delta. There I ordained two bishops. One of them was a missionary and the other a native of the country. Another role for me on this trip was to foster peace amid the tensions then afflicting the region. The memories of these three trips, taken over a span of twelve years, are of great importance to me as I write these pages.

At the time of my first visit, Lagos was in most respects still the capital of the country, despite the government's insistence on transferring governmental offices and embassies to Abuja, a new and more centrally located city with a better climate. Lagos is situated on the coast and sits partially on a peninsula. It is connected with the mainland by a strip of land and by a rather extensive system of roads. The area is muddy—or such is the impression as one travels from the airport through chaotic traffic toward the old city, where the cathedral and former nunciature are located. The hot, humid air and packed cathedral made the joyful celebration of the Eucharist somewhat difficult. I therefore gratefully accepted an offer to fly to the southeastern part of the country in a small plane belonging to the AGIP oil company. My destination, Port Harcourt, was the seat of a bishop who at that time was an Irish missionary. I was to resolve some difficulties regarding the Catholic Institute of West Africa. It was subsequently transferred to a nearby city, where it was enlarged.

From Port Harcourt, my trip continued to the former Biafra, or Igboland, passing through flourishing dioceses that were home to a large number of faithful. I visited Owerri with its two seminaries filled to capacity. The minor and major seminaries were built with the assistance of Cardinal Friedrich Wetter of Munich, as a statement of gratitude to the Holy Father for his visit to Munich. I cannot forget to mention the presence in Owerri of a monastery of contemplative nuns and of a native religious order of women with a fine number of vocations. This diocese really deserved to be elevated to archdiocesan rank, and it was, in 1994.

I continued my time in the former Biafra with a visit to Enugu, where I was surprised by the number of students at the Bigard Memorial Seminary, which supports the education of native clergy. The seminary was named in honor of two zealous women, Jeanne and Stéphanie Bigard, who founded the Society of Saint Peter the Apostle in 1889 to help train indigenous clergy. The seminary has two departments, one for students of philosophy and another for theologians. At the time of my visit, there were more than four hundred students in the philosophy department, and a number almost as great studying theology. In addition to the students, there was a fine number of teachers and instructors. The complex consists of two groups of buildings. These house the seminary offices, but also contain the facilities where a great number of young people live, exercise, and take their classes.

If we include the major seminaries in the two towns of Onitsha and Ikot Ekpene, we can appreciate the resourcefulness of this young Church. It did not throw up its hands after its missionaries were brutally expelled at the end of the civil war. Rather, from its own initiative, the Church grew up and was able to survive. It produces fruit to the present day. It is also a good example of how not to despair, and how resurrection can occur, even on the heels of the severest of blows.

I returned from Enugu to Lagos by plane, and the following day I took the local airline to the northeastern part of the country, to the city of Jos. The weather in this part of Nigeria is very dry, and the population chiefly a mix of Muslims and animists. Catholics account for a quarter of the population. The local seminary is dedicated to Saint Augustine and serves the surrounding dioceses. Native priests are fewer in number, and the seminary had more missionaries on staff. The young Bishop Gabriel Ganaka, who in 1994 became the first archbishop of this diocese, was a Nigerian native and very well known as the president of the African bishops' conference (Symposium of Episcopal Conferences of Africa and Madagascar, or SECAM). He died in 1999 from heart disease. While visiting the Archdiocese of Kaduna and especially the city of Zaria, I observed the situation in the north of the country and the difficulties our faithful were already experiencing at the hands of Muslim groups. In Zaria, I met with the rector of the local university, with whom I had a very respectful, but somewhat cold, meeting. Later, I visited the minor seminary, which looked very poor, was located in old buildings, and lacked any sort of chapel facilities. The staff and the students were quite delighted when I promised them financial assistance. As I mentioned earlier, shortly after my departure, a group of fanatical Muslim students organized an attack on churches and stores belonging to Christians. The seminary was also damaged. Pressure from aggressive Islam became stronger in the north in the ensuing years, especially in the areas of Kaduna and Kano. Despite this fact, we were able to establish a new diocese in Kano, the capital of the north and the center of the Islamic movement. This diocese has now 124,000 Catholic residents.

My next stop took me to the city of Abuja. From far away, we were welcomed by the radiant glitter of the tall golden mosque that was just then in the last stages of construction. It was being built by an Italian construction company. Cardinal Ekandem, who at that time administered Church affairs in this new city, was building for himself a small house and pastoral center. He was commuting there from Ikot Ekpene, because no diocese existed as of yet. Construction had just begun on the new capital city at the time of my 1986 visit, but the Muslims were already on the scene. The elderly cardinal wanted to imitate the Muslims and requested designs for a large and expensive future cathedral—one that the local Church, however, was not able to cover financially. In addition, not everyone believed that a future government would press ahead with the idea of transferring the capital. We did not even hurry with moving the nunciature. At the time, there was a small number of faithful in Abuja, with only one parish church that was still in the final stages of construction. I was able to visit the headquarters of the Missionary Society of Saint Paul, which is truly a fruit of the Church of Nigeria.

Events later confirmed the plans of the elderly shepherd, Cardinal Ekandem, who despite his poor eyesight was able to see into the future. The city grew and even today features many construction sites. On his last visit in 1988, John Paul II blessed the new nunciature. I asked the Holy Father to approve the establishment of the diocese after my trip in 1989. By 1994, Abuja became an archdiocese. This was in spite of the fact that it contained only 72,000 Catholics, or only one-tenth of the local population. Nevertheless, the Church needs to have a vision for the future.

As I think of Nigeria, I cannot omit mentioning my visit to another centrally located city, Ibadan. There is a large and very important seminary there, named for Saints Peter and Paul, which was being enlarged at the time of my visit. After the solemn welcome, I went to inspect each building. To the great surprise of my guides, I suddenly turned toward the restrooms. In this way, I demonstrated to the staff that formation should include the human as well as the spiritual, as an expression of the dignity of the whole person. Several years later, when the bishops would come to visit me as former Prefect, they would recall the event with gratitude and laughter.

I visited Nigeria again in 1997 during a more extensive trip that took me to the country of Burkina Faso. My immediate goal was to

In Western Africa, One of Many Masses

put an end to a long-lasting conflict among our faithful in the southern part of Nigeria. Tribal pride lay at the root of the problem. The matter concerned the Diocese of Warri and had been instigated by a priest from a certain tribe who was causing difficulties for his excellent missionary bishop. The conflict had even given rise to physical attacks and brawls. To bring an end to this sad situation, I ordained an excellent native priest to be Auxiliary Bishop of Warri, and another priest to be the ordinary of the newly established Vicariate of Bomadi, which I separated from the Diocese of Warri. The ordination of both bishops made for a very joyous celebration for all concerned. To satisfy the faithful in Bomadi, I flew by helicopter to install their new shepherd personally into office. Thus, I was able to see from a distance the flames of the oil fields in the broad surrounding forests and experience the humid climate of the Niger Delta region.

From this condensed description, we can state that the Church in Nigeria is developing well and for the most part is self-sustaining. Missionaries are still needed, especially in the northern area of the country, where significant numbers of animists and Muslims live. The only method of evangelization, where these two groups are concerned, is interreligious dialogue. The danger posed by Islam lies in its effort to replace civil law with Shariah, or Muslim law.

Republic of Ghana

Ghana is one of the larger states of West Africa. It is slightly smaller than Oregon with 22 million people. Well over 2.6 million Catholics reside in eighteen dioceses. Catholic missionaries arrived here in the company of Portuguese sailors at the end of the fifteenth century. In 1503, the great chief Efutu received the faith along with 1,300 of his subjects. One hundred thirty years later, Calvinists from Holland seized the coast and destroyed the flourishing mission. Subsequent attempts at evangelization were unsuccessful. Finally, toward the end of the nineteenth century, mission initiatives multiplied. This occurred in spite of the diseases that led to the deaths of many missionaries. I saw a cemetery for missionaries under a great baobab tree by Cape Coast, and I noticed that they were people whose ages ranged from twenty-five to forty. I also saw similar cemeteries near Bangui (in the Central African Republic) and Cotonou in the country of Benin.

These sacrifices were not in vain, however. Over the past century, the Church has developed on the coast as well as inland toward the north, where the White Fathers (officially known as the Missionaries of Africa) had their mission. In 1950, the Holy See was able to divide the country into ecclesiastical provinces. Ghana became independent in 1957 and the following day received its first native bishop in the person of Monsignor John Kodwo Amissah, who shortly thereafter became Archbishop of Cape Coast. He was a very good man and also my friend, who explained the local symbols and culture to me. In 1969, the African bishops founded SECAM, which was to serve the entire continent and have its main office in the capital of Ghana, Accra. In addition to the southern ecclesiastical province with its seat at Cape Coast, Rome established another province for the northern territory in Tamale, on the border of the arid Sahel. Its first archbishop was Peter Derry, the son of a former sorcerer who had wanted his son to follow in his footsteps. The archbishop himself shared this story with me. During the time of my service as Prefect, new dioceses were established as well as a new Church province in the capital city of Accra. Yet another Church province was founded among the members of the Ashanti tribe in the city of Kumasi and headed by another excellent

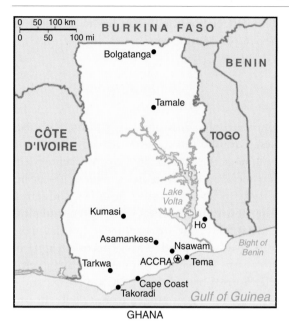

0 50 100 km
0 50 100 mi

BURKINA FASO

Bolgatanga

BENIN

Tamale

CÔTE
D'IVOIRE

TOGO

Lake
Volta

Kumasi

Ho

Asamankese
Nsawam

Bight of
Benin

Tarkwa
ACCRA
Tema

Cape Coast
Takoradi

Gulf of Guinea

GHANA

bishop, now Archbishop Peter Kwasi Sarpong. John Paul II visited Ghana in 1980.

I made several trips to this country. The purpose of the first visit was to meet the head of the state, Jerry Rawlings. A military officer, he had seized control of the government, because—as he explained to me—he had wished to protect the country and its people. During this visit, I was accompanied by the nuncio and his secretary. We went to an old fort on the coast, and, after we had waited there a fair amount of time, Rawlings arrived accompanied by several government ministers. He seated the ministers facing us, with himself in the center as if he were going to broker decisions between the two sides. A tall officer wearing dark glasses started speaking about all manner of things. I had very important topics on my agenda, especially the obtaining of entrance visas for missionaries and the relaxation of years-long tensions between the rulers and the bishops.

I began our exchange with a greeting. I also praised the asphalt road system that we had used upon the arrival—in spite of what we had been led to expect by information received in Rome. Rawlings smiled, and, in perfect English (his father was Scottish), he asked me if, after my compliments, I had any other issues to raise. I responded immediately that I did, and that they would be as sincere as my compliments. I brought up the question of missionaries. There was a problem of visas for a group of Salesians who wanted to establish a school of technology and also visas for religious sisters with nursing skills. I did not ask him for any special favors. I just needed to know if Ghana would like to have those services offered by the Church. Rawlings turned to the responsible ministers. I then commented that those responsible for such matters are actually found in subordinate offices and not in the cabinet. A decision was reached immediately to issue visas for the religious missionaries. Thus, after two years of waiting, one of the Slovak women missionaries was able to come immediately to Ghana. My other goal was more delicate because it concerned an emotional issue affecting various tribes. In my briefcase, I carried a preliminary agreement for certain conciliatory measures that had already been approved by the bishops. These were in turn accepted by Rawlings. It is interesting that during this special meeting I obtained more assistance from a Muslim minister, than from another minister who was considered to be a great Catholic. I could take my leave, not only after achieving success, but also with a smile from the ruler who would prove to be very helpful to me on the occasion of my next visit.

One of the principal reasons for the first trip was the dedication of a new cathedral in Sunyani, in the heart of the country. From the nunciature, we traveled on a newly paved road through very lovely forests. On the border of the diocese, we encountered our first welcoming ceremony, which was carried out according to local custom. The diocesan bishop and the local chiefs, who still have many special rights in Ghana, were waiting for me. The chiefs were sitting at the side of the road under colorful umbrellas. After a short welcoming speech, they placed garlands of flowers on our shoulders and poured water on the ground in front of our feet. Then, after they bowed to me and I to them, we continued our procession to the city. On the edge of town, the entire population joined in the procession. They installed me behind the driver's cab of the truck, alongside the bishop. While the crowd cheered, the principal chief, who was carried in a sedan chair and was dressed in his solemn attire, joined us on the way to the smaller town square. At the square, a solemn welcoming ceremony took place on the part of their "king". The following day I dedicated the new cathedral. The ceremony itself was rather long, and the church was packed. The roof was covered with metal, and the ventilation very poor. The procession started at nine in the morning, and we returned to the sacristy at three in the afternoon. This was, I think, the longest ceremony I ever experienced in Africa. But no one got tired, even at the end, when I presented a tall, gold monstrance as a gift from the Holy Father. At that point, it seemed as if all those in attendance held their breath, and then suddenly joined in joyful song.

From Sunyani, I traveled northward by car, passing the Benedictine monastery at Techiman. The forest vegetation became progressively thinner and eventually turned into an arid savanna, where herders tended their animals all the way to Tamale. We arrived there on a dirt road, one that the authorities had not yet had the time to pave. First I visited the flourishing Saint Vincent Seminary and, in the evening, concelebrated Mass with the elderly Archbishop Derry in his small cathedral. The folk customs and singing were particular to that region. At the end of the Mass, to my great surprise, the archbishop placed a gift upon my head. It was a miter—if we can call it that—decorated with shells, and with two horns sticking out of it. I looked like a Viking and observed that I would not be able to show up in Saint Peter's Basilica in Rome while thus attired. There were two more dioceses in the north, which I was not able to visit. I had to hurry to Kumasi, the capital of the Ashanti tribe. We arrived there in the evening, and during the Mass I delivered a homily lasting about thirty minutes. After I finished, a translator stood up. Without using any notes, and using the exact amount of time as I had, he translated my homily into the native language word for word. He had to have an excellent memory (while our memories in the Western part of the world might be by now overused). The other parts of the Mass were spoken by Bishop Sarpong in the local language and were accompanied by congregational singing. I followed the English translation. During the words of consecration, which the bishop sang in a mysterious melody, the people responded to the elevation of the Host and chalice by singing what sounded as an approval and making a deep bow. I was very impressed with the ritual, and I treasure it as a fine example of enculturation.

I then had scheduled meetings with priests, religious sisters, laity, and missionaries in the dioceses of Cape Coast, Accra, Keta-Ho, and Sekondi-Takoradi. I also visited a major seminary near Accra. I was most impressed with my visit to the fort at Elmina, constructed by wealth-seeking adventurers from Catholic Portugal who were later replaced by Calvinists from Holland. The walled castle, where native people were once imprisoned, sits right on the coast. Prisoners were taken from their cells through a very narrow passageway in the wall—an opening wide enough for only one person. The walkway ended outside the fort, where it continued as a narrow bridge leading directly onto a docked ship. Escape was therefore impossible for these slaves who had been sold by local rulers. The most painful experience, for

A Royal Welcome

me, was seeing a chapel in the middle of the complex. How could those "Christians" have been so insensitive? How far will people stoop for money, and how easily can they calm their consciences, especially if they are soldiers!

My second pastoral visit to Ghana occurred in 1995,

Enculturation, An Ecclesiastical Welcome

Ghana*: Informal Reception by the President*

Ghana*: A Smiling Christian and Bishop Sarpong*

Ghana: *A Serious Christian*

where, in the capital city, I was to ordain five new bishops from several dioceses, some of them just recently established. Among the bishops was Anthony Kwami Adanuty, a longtime co-worker from Ghana. This visit lasted nine days. I was accompanied by a group of workers from the television station in Košice, Slovakia, which is my native archdiocese. Therefore, all the main events were recorded.

The episcopal ordination ceremony took place outdoors. The venue featured two large seating areas facing each other. In the intervening space, an altar had been built on an elevated platform, so that everyone might be able to see the celebration. It was one of the best-attended ordinations I have ever witnessed, given the number of bishops present and also the number of laity, among whom sat President Rawlings. This colorful celebration, which was accompanied by beautiful singing, lasted about five hours. From the altar, one could see the ocean, where, earlier, our television team had experienced their first salt-water bath. During the celebration, the cameramen were then bathed in sunlight. This could have turned into a dangerous situation for these bold technicians, who thought that they would be able to withstand the African sun in the same way the natives do.

A subsequent meeting with the leper patients was very moving. I remember their withered hands, which I put into my own while greeting them. I could see gratitude in their eyes for having been included in my schedule. After that meeting, I could better understand the gospel passages that describe lepers as forced exiles from the human community.

We then flew by a smaller airplane to the northernmost diocese, Wa, where my schedule was quite busy. Besides visiting the cathedral, I met with the "chief" of the Muslim community and his advisors. The "chief" was pleased to receive from my hands a medal of John Paul II. He was a very calm and prudent man, who was concerned about peaceful coexistence among the different religious groups in the community. While in this area, I also received gifts from many different groups. I received two cows as well as ten sheep and goats. The pilgrims who had traveled the farthest derived the greatest joy from these gifts, which I shared with them. I kept only one sheep, which was donated to our military pilots. The soldiers loaded the sheep onto the airplane with its feet tied. Since our association with these pilots would end that evening, they were looking forward to an outdoor meal of roasted mutton with homemade beer. That same day they flew us to Kumasi, the center of the Ashanti region, after which they returned to their military base in Accra.

In the square, in front of the Cathedral of Kumasi, I was welcomed as their well-known friend. I spoke to them very briefly. The faithful became quite excited when I recalled the events and impressions of my previous visit. My translator, the one with the remarkable memory, made sure that he reintroduced himself. All those present shared their beautiful, mystical-sounding religious songs with me.

The local king, who had studied law in Great Britain, welcomed us with the traditional ceremony that is reserved for important guests. I had the same problem as the Holy Father had had during his previous visit, because this special rite lasts three hours. (A possible compromise would have been the shorter form of the celebration, or "smaller durbar", which takes only half the time.) The whole ceremony took place on a spacious meadow in front of the king's residence. The members of my "delegation" and I were seated on a small, elevated gazebo at the entrance to the field. There then commenced a parade of important civic figures and royal servants, as well as of the queen and her escort of royal ladies—all of them attired in their colorful traditional costumes. The next to pass by was the military commander, wearing an eagle headdress and other decorations. Lastly came the king accompanied by the royal advisors. All of them carried solid gold scepters representing their role and office. (British colonizers had never been able to conquer this tribe. The Ashantis had successfully protected their gold mines and freedom. Through these and other celebrations, they maintain an awareness and pride in their traditions.) The royal procession continued to the other side of the meadow, where the officers gathered under colorful umbrellas around their king. A royal representative opened the meeting and, accompanied by members of my own party, went to greet the king and his escort. The king sent his officers to greet me. After our greetings and opening addresses, we exchanged gifts. I gave the king a silver medal of John Paul II, and he gave me a chair that had been artfully fashioned from a single piece of precious white wood.

After a festive return to the king's residence, I had the honor of greeting him again in private talks. The king was an elderly man with some health problems, but he was very kind, loved by his people, and respected by the government. In Ghana, certain mutual understandings have been maintained between the central government and the traditional system of "chiefs", which elects the principal chief. The kingly office has been preserved in central Ghana, where the monarch holds only limited political power but enjoys high moral standing.

After the ceremony, I returned to Accra and met twice with President Rawlings. By then, he was the officially elected president and received me with honor. After the formal portion of the visit, he wanted to meet with me privately in his garden and offer some light refreshments. Even individuals in high positions of authority are human, and in Africa a personal relationship makes for the best diplomacy. This concluded a memorable visit.

Slovak missionaries, both male and female, labor in Ghana. During my trips, I encountered them at mission stations. I was not able to meet the devoted Father Krajčík, who, at the time, was home in Slovakia undergoing medical treatment. The local people spoke of him with respect. He had fixed the roof of the church when he was eighty years old. Most of the Slovak men are Missionaries of the Divine Word, while the sisters belong to the Servants of the Holy Spirit.

The Church in Ghana is self-sustaining and maturing. They have native bishops, full seminaries, and houses of religious. The Catholic laity is educated in religion, and there is also an organization of women devoted to good works. Archbishop Derry was raised to the cardinalate in 2006. Finally, the Church in Ghana has begun sending its own people as missionaries to other countries in Africa.

Republic of Côte d'Ivoire (Ivory Coast)

The Ivory Coast is Ghana's neighbor to the west, but their common border divides certain tribes into two parts. Colonialism caused Ghana to have English as its official language, while French was adopted in Côte d'Ivoire. Until independence, this country formed part of the overseas territories of France and had representatives in the French parliament. One of these was Félix Houphouët-Boigny, who later in his career became Ivory Coast's first president and a well-known African statesman. This country is one-fifth larger than Ghana, but poorer. Its population stands at about 18.6 million, of whom over 3.1 million are Catholics. Ivory Coast is still very much dependent on France and imitates with ease the French way of doing things.

Missionary work began in this area toward the end of the nineteenth century with the arrival of the Society of African Missions. A prefecture apostolic was established for the country at that time. Evangelization progressed rapidly, and in 1955 the country became an ecclesiastical province, headed by the Archbishop of Abidjan. Bernard Yago, a friend of mine, later became metropolitan archbishop and was named cardinal in 1983 by Pope John Paul II. Currently the country has fourteen dioceses, some of which were established during my time as Prefect for Evangelization.

I once had a humorous meeting with Cardinal Yago, when we were attempting to determine the age for his retirement. It is a known fact that every bishop has to submit his resignation to the Holy Father when he turns seventy-five. When I brought up the matter to Cardinal Yago, he only smiled at me. It seems that he had two birthdates. As he explained, when he had entered minor seminary, his pastor wrote on the application that he was two years younger than he actually was. There were no official records at that time, so he did not have any to prove his age. Apparently, the cardinal did not want to retire, and he could choose between his official and unofficial ages, pretending to be two years younger than he really was. Some people claimed that he was actually even older. This humorous episode concerning his age had no practical consequences, because John Paul II would allow bishops to serve after they reached retirement age, as long they were still in good health. After the illness and death of Cardinal Yago, a new Archbishop of Abidjan was named, in the person of the current Cardinal Bernard Agré, who is another of my close co-workers and friends.

I visited this country four times, including two visits with the Holy Father. The first time we stopped in Abidjan in August 1985. President Houphouët-Boigny welcomed us at the airport with an enthusiastic speech. He delivered his entire discourse without using notes because he was already having difficulties with his eyesight. John Paul II then dedicated the new cathedral, which had been financed by the president. Not far from the cathedral stood a Muslim mosque, which had also been a gift from the president.

This event was followed by a short visit to the president's birthplace, Yamoussoukro, where he lived. The president was already transforming this town into the future administrative capital of the country. He changed this small village, located 150 miles north of Abidjan, into a modern town with an admirable university, a convention center, and hotels. He also decided to build a basilica with a copula similar to the one atop Saint Peter's in Rome. He hurried with its construction despite a lack of enthusiasm on the part of the bishops. Several years later, when construction on the basilica was finished, the president donated an extensive adjacent property for use in building a radio station, a hospital, and a Catholic university. He finished building the church, but was not able to continue with his other projects because illness and death eventually intervened. His family was

very rich, and he himself owned a number of plantations that provided him with a substantial income. Yet a lack of financial resources kept the remainder of the president's plans from ever being completed.

The basilica was dedicated to his memory, and the bishops took it under their jurisdiction. Based on a suggestion of mine, they made it into a pilgrimage destination for the country and for all of West Africa. The Basilica of Our Lady of Peace was dedicated in 1990 by John Paul on his return trip from Tanzania. In 1998, it became the site for a world gathering of priests, where I was honored to be one of the speakers. The nearby airport allowed for a direct flight from Rome. (Some of the participants in the gathering became infected with malaria while touring the region, and, in one case, matters took a deadly turn.) On the same occasion, I ordained several new priests in the basilica. This basilica is not an example of "kitsch", as some of the German reporters wished to characterize it. With the help of Polish Pallottine missionaries, it became a beautiful pilgrimage site and a center for evangelization that continues to flourish. The neighboring clinic became a hospital under the direction of the Sisters of Saint Camille.

A longer pastoral visit in 1993 took me from Abidjan to the Diocese of Man, located in a rocky and arid region. From there, I flew north to inspect territory for a new diocese, where Islam and animism are the principal religions practiced. Today, the region is home to a new diocese, centered on the town of Odienné. On our way back to Abidjan, we went through the dioceses of Daloa, Gagnoa, and Yamoussoukro. After our arrival in Abidjan, I was greeted by all the bishops of Côte d'Ivoire. For a number of years now, all the country's bishops have been native Africans with a French cultural background. It is apparent that they also enjoy lively meetings— a fact I was able to experience during our gathering and also later in Rome during their *ad limina apostolorum* visits (to the tombs of the Apostles Peter and Paul), which all bishops perform every five years.

The Church in this country also has to face different difficult situations, but it is going forward and growing. The cultural influence of the Catholic Church is greater than the number of Catholics would suggest. A certain restrictive attitude toward foreign missionaries does not help the process of evangelization. The Insititut Catholique pour l'Afrique Occidentale (ICAO) or university center in Abidjan, which at one point the Congregation for Evangelization wanted to expand for French-speaking West Africa, remains an important center for Catholic growth in this area, despite various obstacles.

Republic of Benin

Between the eastern border of Ghana and the western border of Nigeria lie the two narrow countries of Benin and Togo. Their territory stretches northward from the Atlantic Ocean in the form of two strips of land. The mutual border was artificially drawn by colonizers, but both countries have many things in common. Tribes whose lands straddle the border, for example, maintain their own languages. The climate of the southern seacoast region is warm and humid, but the land gradually becomes dryer as one moves northward. Tropical vegetation eventually gives way to a savanna, and then to the arid territory of the Sahel.

Benin is twice the size of Togo, but its population is only one-third larger. Of its 7.2 million inhabitants, Catholics number 1.8 million, or about a quarter of the whole. The beginning of its Christian history is symbolized by a large chapel situated on the coast near Ouidah, and not very far from the former capital of Cotonou. The chapel marks the site of the first Catholic mission, founded by the Portuguese in 1680. French missionaries undertook a broader evangelization two hundred years later and opened several mission stations. In 1883, a prefecture apostolic was established for the region with its seat in Dahomey (the present Benin). A seminary opened in 1913 at Ouidah, and in 1928 its first native student was ordained. Twenty years later, other prefectures and vicariates were established because the number of Catholics had rapidly increased. Thirty-five-year-old Bernardin Gantin became a bishop in 1957, and three years later succeeded to the Archdiocese of Cotonou. In 1971, Archbishop Gantin was invited to work in the Roman Curia and in 1977 was elevated to cardinal. In 2002, this good friend of mine resigned his position as Dean of the College of Cardinals and returned to Benin. Mission work continues in the north of the country, where I prepared the establishment of several new dioceses. Evangelization goes forward, and, at this point, all the bishops of Benin are native-born.

John Paul II visited Benin twice. He spent some time in the capital but also in the northern part of the country and the important town of Parakou. After our arrival, we were greeted by local sheiks on small

Arabian horses. I recall the meeting with Muslim leaders where the Holy Father stressed the need for peaceful coexistence and interfaith dialogue. Moving out from this large archdiocese, we scheduled papal visits to three new dioceses that were already being administered by zealous young bishops. Those prelates have had to resist attempts at introducing Islamic religious law, or Shariah—a movement having its roots in neighboring Nigeria.

I visited Benin on several other occasions. In 1989, I arrived in Cotonou at four in the morning, after a delay of several hours. After arriving at the archbishop's residence and refreshing myself from the tiresome flight, I received an official message that President Mathieu Kérékou would be ready to receive me at nine o'clock in the morning. The president of Benin was known around the world as one of Africa's "socialist" dictators. When I walked into the reception hall, the president set aside his staff of office and sat down on a wooden chair in the middle of the room. After offering my greetings in a spirit of dialogue, I began to explain very carefully that the Church requests no privileges, but only the freedom to serve her people and to proclaim the gospel. To my surprise, the president, who was in fact baptized but was not a Roman Catholic, delivered a long speech on the importance of Jesus Christ and His message. It was at that point that I realized that the Marxist ideology of some African dictators did not have strong foundations and in fact was only a political cover. In this way, they cultivated possibilities for economic assistance and were able to satisfy certain younger leaders who had been educated in Moscow.

During this visit, a celebration was held in a stadium where I ordained an impressive group of priests and deacons. They still, on occasion, proudly remind me that they were ordained by me, a Vatican Prefect. Such meetings are always enjoyable, especially if it is with one of the sixty-two bishops whom I have ordained. I also visited the cathedral where the first missionary archbishop of Benin is buried. Next to the cathedral, however, is located a "church of snakes", where people pay homage to those creatures. It is an indication for us that missionary work is still necessary. During my visit to the seminary in Ouidah, I was pleasantly surprised by the students at the celebration of a liturgy that was sprinkled with a number of African songs. In a nearby minor seminary that stood near a lake, younger students welcomed me with expressions of deep joy. When I asked them if I could take their young rector away for more important ministry, they began to protest. Their attachment to their rector pointed favorably toward an episcopal nomination, which in fact came to pass a few years later. As we continued on our journey, we arrived at an interesting pilgrimage place in the Diocese of Abomey. The site is not a church building, but rather an altar situated among some granite boulders, with a statue of the Immaculate Conception standing behind them. A path passes among the trees, which widens as it approaches the altar, creating a natural shrine where people like to go to say their prayers. They need not worry about cold weather, and the rain is always considered a blessing. My trip then continued through the Diocese of Lokossa, where construction on a

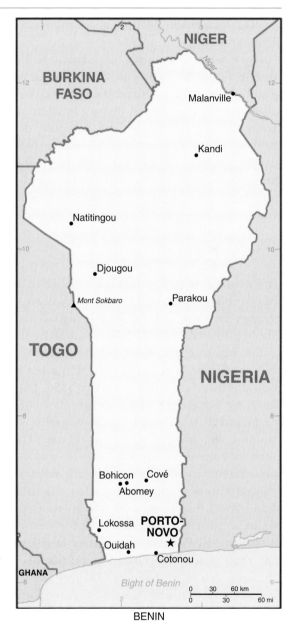

BENIN

sizable cathedral had just begun. The facility was to be affiliated with the seminary in Ouidah, where the original structure could no longer accommodate all the seminarians. In the next diocese, Porto Novo,

I celebrated solemn Mass in an overflowing cathedral and met with clergy and laity.

If we were to evaluate the Church in Benin, we would have to stress its future promise. This Church has already produced its share of great bishops, such as Cardinal Gantin and Archbishop Izidor de Souza, who died early from heart disease. In addition, the local native priests have a missionary spirit, which is especially demonstrated in the movement founded by the Bishop of Parakou, Nestor Assogba. The young native episcopate conducts an effective seminary in Ouidah that has given hundreds of alumni priests to Benin and to neighboring countries. Various religious orders, with their own programs of formation, constitute a promising guarantee for the future.

Togolese Republic

The country of Togo is slightly smaller than West Virginia and has over 5 million inhabitants. Approximately 1.5 million of these, or 30 percent, are Catholics. Lomé, the capital city, is located on the coast. The missionary history of the country has its beginnings at the end of the nineteenth century, with the arrival of the founder of the mission, Father Jeremiah Moran. He came to Togo from neighboring Dahomey (presently Benin) in 1886, but after one year was poisoned by sorcerers. Evangelization continued through the work of the Missionaries of the Divine Word, who were instrumental in constructing the historic Cathedral Lomé. This country was once a German colony. Perhaps because of that connection, the cathedral was restored many years later with financial help from Germany. Evangelization in Togo proceeded smoothly, and by the start of World War I there were 15,000 Togolese Catholics—a sufficient number to warrant the establishment of a vicariate apostolic. At the end of the war, all German missionaries were expelled from the country, and their place was taken by priests of the Society of African Missions, based at Lyon in France. By 1930, Togo received its first native priest, and mission work continued to penetrate inland. When the country became independent in 1960, there were only two dioceses. There were four dioceses in existence at the beginning of my term as Prefect, and, during my tenure, three additional ones were established. Presently the 1.3 million Catholics are spread among seven dioceses, all under the jurisdiction of native bishops. I ordained three of them in the archdiocesan city of Lomé. I was also the celebrant at the dedication ceremony of the new cathedral in Atakpamé.

On my first visit to Togo in 1985, I accompanied John Paul II. After our arrival in Lomé, we stayed at the archbishop's residence, which was round in shape and built in the African style. In the immediate neighborhood, construction had already begun on a new seminary building. Later, the Congregation for Evangelization sent financial assistance so that construction could be completed. The Pope celebrated a solemn Mass outdoors near the city of Lomé. Subsequently, the faithful from the central and northern parts of the country had their celebration with the Holy Father near the airport in Kara, where he also ordained several priests.

Kara is the birthplace of General Gnassingbé Eyadéma,

93

who constructed a multistory home there for himself, complete with marble siding, in the midst of the hovels of the poor. Next to the house stood a mausoleum where his mother was buried in a marble-decorated tomb. When we visited his family, the general asked us to say a prayer at the tomb of his mother. The mausoleum was directly accessible from the second floor of the house. Cardinal Casaroli and I gladly joined the Holy Father in prayer.

Out in the fields near Kara, we witnessed the unexpected visit of John Paul II to a shack of a poor family. We were traveling along, and the Pope suddenly requested that the driver stop the vehicle. The Holy Father entered the shack and proceeded to talk with the members of a small family about daily problems and concerns. By the time our guides recovered from their surprise, the Vatican Pilgrim was already returning to the car from his visit. For the local people, this stop assumed historic proportions. It is described on a commemorative plaque by the side of the road, where tourists and travelers stop, and which I saw on the occasion of my next visit.

The next point of the Vatican Pilgrim's itinerary was a shrine dedicated to the Blessed Mother near Togoville, which we reached by ferryboat across the lake from Lomé. It was an interesting trip especially for the media, because next to the shrine stood a forest that was sacred to the pagan practitioners of voodoo. Voodoo leaders were present at our prayer service and greeted the Pope, who began a dialogue with them. It was something of a foretaste of the gathering of religious leaders at Assisi the following year. I remember rather well a more private meeting with the voodoo leaders because of the interesting discussion that ensued. The members of this small group were dressed in bright colors and were led by some sort of intellectual leader. The Holy Father received a gift from them consisting of a wooden statue of a woman, more than two feet tall, holding in her hand some kind of "mystery box" whose contents would be revealed at some point in the future. They were still awaiting the revelation of God's mystery, while for us the mystery has already been revealed in the person of the Messiah, Jesus Christ. Where did they get this kind of faith? I asked myself this question several times. Another surprise came from one of the leaders, when he proudly announced that his son was studying at the seminary and would shortly be ordained a Catholic priest. I recalled my friend Archbishop Derry, the son of a sorcerer from Ghana.

My own personal trips to Togo were interesting as well. The longest started with a celebration of a Pontifical Mass in a parish church in Lomé, which took place there because the cathedral was under renovation at the time. It was also at that time that an agreement was finalized for the construction of a seminary. Traveling by car, I was able to view the endless African plains and knolls, as well as experience genuine African life in the countryside and observe working people with their small market stalls under the baobab trees. I passed through Sokodé and Kara, where I stopped at the house where John Paul II made his memorable unexpected visit. In the morning, we continued through the high mountains. After we crossed the ridge, a plain spread out that reached toward the town of Dapaong and the Sahel (or pre-Saharan region). The entire valley and plain in front of us was covered with something resembling fog, while a cold wind stirred up the fine sand. This was the well-known *harmatan* wind of the Sahara, which lowers visibility and causes a scratchy feeling in the throat and eyes. The dark dust swirled about, staining my shirt and settling in our throats as an oily substance. After the evening Mass in Dapaong, which was attended by many missionaries and religious sisters, we

Togo: In Front of Home Visited by John Paul II

partook of refreshments. These included a light homemade beer that helped to clear the dust from our throats.

Another trip to Togo brought me to Atakpamé, where I dedicated a new cathedral. The bishop of the diocese was a former co-worker of mine from the Congregation of Evangelization in Rome. The dedication ceremony lasted five hours, with the sun radiating its extreme heat through the glass gate. At the end of the ceremony, when I met with four or five European ambassadors who had been in attendance, they wished to let me know how they had watched the ceremony with great interest. They had especially appreciated the symbolism of anointing the altar with holy chrism, as well as the thick incense smoke that had risen toward heaven from a bowl placed on the altar. They had not suspected the richness of our liturgy. On another occasion, I ordained three bishops during a Mass in the Lomé stadium. That ceremony was attended by General Eyadéma and other members of the government. The political situation at that time was very tense, and several African dictators were worried about maintaining power. The general did not have the best of reputations because he himself had deposed his predecessor. Even the archbishop had to worry because of the unsettled circumstances and would spend his nights in various locations. Against this background, I began my meeting with the general by reminding him of the visit of the Holy Father to his home in Kara and the prayers that had been said at the tomb of his mother. As he recalled the event and felt moved, he added, "We can get older, but a mother is still a mother." The rest of our talks then proceeded peacefully. Finally, he asked me what my next scheduled trip was. I was supposed to fly to Senegal and join the official mission of John Paul II to that country, but my flight had been canceled. The general immediately offered me his airplane. I went to the airport, where a French "Mirage" fighter, remodeled into a private airplane, was waiting. French pilots flew me to Dakar within two hours.

Republic of Senegal

Senegal, on the west coast of Africa, was once a French colony. It is slightly smaller than South Dakota, and has nearly 10.5 million inhabitants. Catholics account for 544,000 of these, with the majority of the population being Muslim and animist. Evangelization was begun by priests from Portugal and later carried on by French missionaries who were more successful. By the middle of the nineteenth century, a vicariate apostolic was founded in Senegambia, and one hundred years later a hierarchy was established. The first native bishop was Hyacinthe Thiandoum, who in 1976 was named cardinal by Paul VI. During my time as Prefect, the Diocese of Ziguinchor was divided in the region of Casamance, and a new diocese was established there. Efforts have been made in this region toward acquiring independence from Senegal. The country uses the French language and is influenced by French culture. Its first president, Léopold Senghor, was a Catholic and also a well-known poet. He wrote in French, and in his poems he described the beauty of Africans, or *négritude*.

I made several trips to Senegal, one of them, in 1992, with John Paul II. After the solemn Eucharist, in the packed Cathedral of Dakar, we visited the nearby island of Gorée, where African slaves were once exported over the oceans. The Pope was moved when he stepped through a door where chained slaves in single file had once boarded the ships. There he made an intense and pained speech, in which he condemned the transgressions of unworthy Christians and asked Africans for forgiveness for those crimes. As we returned by ship to Dakar, the Holy Father expressed pain once again. The observation made by Cardinal Thiandoum—that native tribal leaders had also collaborated with European slave traders—was of no avail. There is not much discussion about this topic in America and in Europe, because of a fear that Africans will seek compensation and reparation. Also, native Africans are now more cautious with their own comments because of the collaboration of their ancestors in the

97

transatlantic slave trade—a fact that engenders in them a certain amount of guilt. Slaves were also traded to Arabic rulers and merchants. Even today, many years after the abolition of slavery in the world, situations amounting to slavery still persist, such as child labor and prostitution. Indeed, human malevolence did not die out with the end of the slave trade.

After this stop, which reminded me of Fort Elmina in Ghana, we continued to Ziguinchor, which is located on the southern border with Guinea-Bissau. A tribal question agitated the region, where the border divided a tribe and its lands into two parts. The possibility was being discussed of establishing a new tiny country or that the contested area might become a part of Guinea. The Pope's visit did not deal with those problems, and the entire trip maintained a religious character.

One of my very eventful, personal trips to Senegal occurred when, as papal legate, I attended a celebration at the Marian shrine at Pogonguine. The sanctuary is a small one, and any large celebrations must take place in an outdoor amphitheater. This town is the birthplace of

*Poponguine (**Senegal**): Pilgrims*

Cardinal Thiandoum. The former president Abdou Diouf also had his summer residence there, where I was able to have an audience with him. Another of my destinations on this trip was the seat of the Diocese of Tambacounda, which had recently been elevated to diocesan rank from that of a prefecture apostolic. It is a small town in a dusty region, where the sand-covered streets and the heat of the Sahel made us realize how close we were to the desert. However, the town has an airport with several daily flights. Young Bishop Jean-Noël Diouf is spreading the gospel in this sandy country and is still looking for missionaries for some villages. Those remote outposts are seeking Catholic missionaries and refusing Islam, because they remember the attacks of certain Muslim groups who took not only their possessions, but also their women and children. During this visit I stopped at the seminary in Dakar, which serves the entire country. At the time of my visit, it could not accommodate all the country's seminarians, so the bishops had to build a new facility, located to the south.

Missionary efforts in Senegal are moving slowly. While the neighboring countries are already over 25 percent Catholic, the figure stands at only 5 percent for Senegal. Islam is more aggressive here. To cite but one example, a local caliph once threatened to demolish a newly built Catholic church in Thiavouane. In spite of these obstacles, the priests and laity of the Catholic Church are very respected in public life. This is especially due to the personality of the now-deceased Cardinal Thiandoum and the labors of various other bishops, priests, and laity.

Republic of Mali

As we landed at the airport in Bamako, the capital of Mali, the view of the surrounding area revealed that we had entered the Sahel. In fact, the Sahara Desert covers the whole northern portion of the country. A population of 13.4 million people, including the dark-clothed Tuaregs and members of other racial groups, inhabits an area of about 479,000 square miles. The number of Catholics stands at 232,000, which is not even 2 percent of the population. It is a young Church. On the occasion of the centennial anniversary of their evangelization, in 1988, I ordained two native bishops. At the same time, the last of the missionary bishops submitted his letter of resignation. Today, there are six dioceses in Mali, all of which are headed by native bishops.

The start of evangelization here was sprinkled with the blood of missionaries. Cardinal Lavigerie, the well-known founder of the White Fathers, sent two groups of missionaries to Timbuktu in northern Mali, but the members of both groups were murdered. Later the Missionaries of the Holy Spirit and the White Fathers began to proclaim the gospel with better success from the south, from their base in Senegal. In 1921, Bamako became the seat of a vicariate apostolic that covered much of the Sahara. It became an archdiocese in 1955. When, in 1960, Mali became independent of France, the Church already had a native candidate for the post of archbishop, in the person of Monsignor Luc Auguste Sangaré. I stayed at his residence while representing John Paul II as legate during the celebrations marking the centennial of evangelization.

During that visit, I discovered the advantages and disadvantages of being a papal legate. He has international diplomatic protection, which is provided by the government of the country being visited. He has a right to a guard, and in Mali this consisted of a squad of men in beautiful uniforms. They took their turns in the courtyard of the archbishop's house. Apart from them, I was always escorted by police. When I wanted to visit one of the dioceses, the nuncio pointed out that it was against protocol and quite impossible. The farthest I could go was to the nearby Niger River. A celebration took place in the city stadium that was attended by about fifteen thousand people, including visitors from neighboring dioceses. On the elevated altar in the middle of the stadium, I ordained two bishops—a most beautiful gift to this young Church and a promising step into the next century of

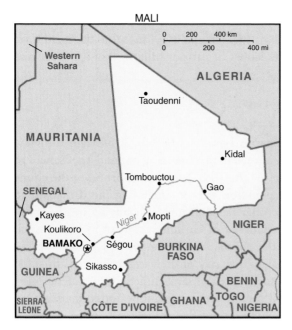

evangelization. At the exit of the stadium, a man dressed in a turban threw up his arms saying, "Monseigneur, I am Muslim, but I thank you, because this is a celebration for all of us." In Mali, as in other neighboring states, Islam is more tolerant toward the Christian religion. It is an Islam with very old roots. But even here, Muslims are becoming less tolerant and more prone to attack, because their young leaders are studying in Arab countries and are supported financially by those countries in exchange for propounding new reforms. After the celebration in the stadium, I had a meeting with the laity in the cathedral. On the way back to the archbishop's residence, once again being escorted by police, we drove past a flea market. After I saw this interesting and colorful manifestation of daily life, as well as the different faces and the clothing and goods for sale, I asked my driver to stop. I stepped out of the car with my camera and walked among the people. The police finally realized what had happened, turned around, and came back after me. I was walking in my white cassock and red sash among the merchants and customers, who were glad to pose for my camera. After this non-protocol "escape", I went to visit the new Seminary of Saint Augustine near Bamako. Then, after an official visit with the president, I was to catch a flight for Abidjan. From there, I was to proceed to other destinations on my itinerary. On the way to the Bamako airport, many people, cows, and goats thronged the road, and a policeman tried to make room for my car with his motorcycle. He was actually standing on his motorcycle, steering with his knees and hands, and yelling to clear the road for the car. The airplane did not arrive, and we had to return to the city. I then flew out late in the evening. It is not without reason that they call this airline *Air Peut-être*, since it "might fly" or it "might not". At least one does not need worry about a precise schedule!

John Paul II took me on another trip to Mali as his guide, when he stopped during his visit to West Africa in 1989. It was but a short stay, featuring only the celebration of the Eucharist and a visit with the president at his residence on a hill overlooking Bamako.

The small and young Church in Mali is growing. The number of Catholics has doubled since their centennial. The entire north of the country is predominantly Muslim, with a few followers of traditional African religions. This mission, which began to grow on land sprinkled with the blood of the first missionaries, is in my prayers and my memories. I am sorry that I was not able to visit the northern parts of

Mali: *River Niger near Bamako*

the country, especially Timbuktu, which is a tourist attraction and therefore remains open to the world.

Burkina Faso

The large, land-locked country of Burkina Faso is bordered by Côte d'Ivoire, Ghana, Togo, and Benin in the south, Mali in the west, and on the east by the Saharan republic of Niger. In the past it was called Upper Volta because of its river. It is slightly larger than Colorado and has 13.4 million people. There are nearly 1.6 million Catholics, which represents 11 percent of the population. Catholic numbers have grown in the past hundred years thanks to the work of the White Fathers, who started their mission in this area in 1900. They desired to educate a native clergy, but these efforts had to begin with the basics of reading and writing. In 1926, they founded a minor seminary, and in 1933 a major seminary, which produced the first native priests in 1942. The missionaries were also mindful of the need for women religious, and so native sisters were able to found their own order in 1930. After the establishment of an ecclesiastical province in 1955, and the achieving of independence from France in 1960, Paul Zoungrana, a native priest and former student of the White Fathers, was named archbishop of the capital city, Ouagadougou. He was

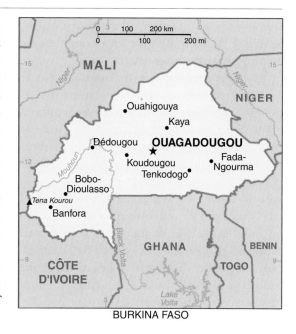

BURKINA FASO

later named cardinal in 1965, by Paul VI. Given the growing number of faithful, the number of dioceses has also grown, even during my term as Prefect. Presently there are thirteen dioceses, including three archdioceses.

John Paul II first visited this country in 1980. He did so again in 1990, while I accompanied him as the one having responsibility for missions in this territory. I still remember the pilgrimage site of Yagma near the capital, where the church sat on a large sandy plain, with young trees planted around it. The entire space was full of people who had come from a great distance to greet the head of the Church. They were unable to find shade to protect them from the hot sun, and the unpleasant conditions were made worse by the hot wind and sand of the Sahel. Many parts of the Mass were celebrated in the native language and included melodies that were pleasant to all our ears. Our visit to Bobo-Dioulasso was also memorable, since we witnessed there an easy method for memorizing the gospel. A deacon sang the gospel, and the people responded by repeating each sentence. In that way, even people who could not read or write could remember entire passages of the gospel and meditate on them. The fact is that Africans have remarkable memories. During his second trip, the Holy Father announced the creation of a foundation to assist the people of the Sahel. In this way, he gave an example of the more fortunate nations helping those who are less fortunate.

My first personal trip to Burkina Faso led me once again to the sanctuary of Yagma, where I ordained two bishops. I later represented the Holy Father at the funeral of our common friend, Cardinal Zoungrana, who toward the end of his life lost his eyesight but still assisted the Church by his prayers, his peaceful example, and his valuable insights. I flew into Ouagadougou late in the afternoon and went that same evening to say my prayers alongside the body of this servant of God, who was being viewed at the cathedral. The church was full of people who came and went in turn throughout the night. The following morning, the casket was brought into a large stadium, where about thirty thousand people had gathered. These ranged from governmental officials to simple shepherds. I began my homily by saying, "The old baobab [a large African tree] has fallen." The whole congregation loudly gave voice to their grief, since they could relate to the comparison. After the long funeral Mass, the procession continued for several hours through the streets of the city. This great African really deserved to be honored in this way.

The Church in Burkina Faso is growing also in missionary spirit. It shared one of its diocesan priests with Niger, who later became Auxiliary Bishop of Niamey and was recently entrusted with building up a new diocese in the eastern part of that Saharan state. In addition, the bishops of Burkina Faso also sponsored a mission in the neighboring state of Niger. This is a sign of the high quality of Church life and could serve as an example of missionary spirit among the priests of other countries.

Republic of Niger

The Saharan republic of Niger is located in central Africa, east of Burkina Faso. This country covers 459,000 square miles and is home to about 12.3 million people. These are all settled in the southern part of the country, since the rest of the territory is covered by the unoccupied Sahara desert. Only about 16,000 Catholics live here, most of whom reside in the western region around the capital city, Niamey. Evangelization in Niger started in 1935. In addition to the first diocese at Niamey, another one was established in the southeast in recent years. The people are mostly Muslim. The clergy consists for the most part of Redemptorist Fathers and of diocesan priests from Burkina Faso.

Republic of Chad

Niger shares its long eastern border with Chad, which is very similar in size and climate. Both have a small population. In the north, Chad borders on Libya and in the east on Sudan. Out of nearly 9.1 million citizens, about 881,000 are Catholic. The majority are Muslims in the north or pagan animists in the south. Attempts at evangelization, before the arrival of French missionaries, were carried out by a unique group of Capuchins and Jesuits. At the end of the nineteenth century, the country found itself part of a vicariate apostolic for central Africa. More effective evangelization was undertaken by the Fathers of the Holy Spirit, who arrived from the south, and in 1929 founded a mission station in the southern part of Chad. These were followed by French and Italian Jesuits, and in 1938 by two Capuchins who had been expelled from Ethiopia. In 1947, a prefecture apostolic was established under Jesuit leadership in the capital, which was at that time called Fort-Lamy. In 1955, the Holy See had the courage to establish a hierarchy for this young Church, with the archbishop's seat in the capital. The first native priest was ordained only in 1957. Evangelization continued rapidly, and after the establishment of the first dioceses in Moundou, Sarh, and Pala, others were added. The eighth and newest one is located in the east near the border with Sudan, while the rest of the dioceses are in the south. This young Church already has two native bishops in Moundou and in Sarh. I personally ordained the latter one in his diocesan seat.

My first visit to Chad, which became independent in 1960, took place in the company of John Paul II in 1990. We experienced some difficulties landing in the capital, because of the sand storms, which can be very dangerous even for larger airplanes. I can still remember the tension of the pilots and guides as we were landing with fully powered jet engines amid the strong winds. Through the window of the plane, I could see a nearby lake that was almost dry. Flying quite often, one must expect to encounter difficult situations of which one does not ordinarily hear. During this visit, the Holy Father celebrated solemn Masses in N'Djamena and Moundou. The only native bishop at

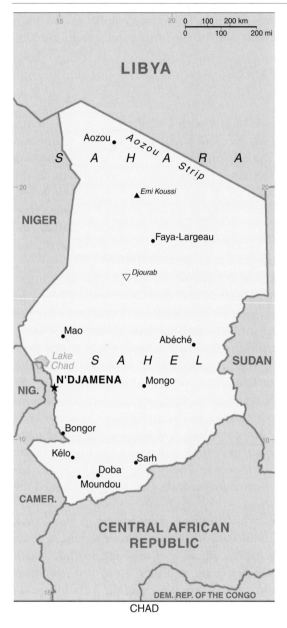

that time, Monsignor Matthias N'Garteri, was able to have the Holy Father celebrate an unplanned Mass in his native Diocese of Sarh, which was then awaiting the nomination of a shepherd.

I returned to Chad when the second native bishop, the young Edmund Jigantar, was named. The trip was planned in such fashion as to permit me to ordain him bishop. Sarh is not a very large town and is located in the transitional zone between the green south and the dry northeast. The four-hour-long ordination ceremony, which took place in the open air, went quickly. This was in spite of the sun's heat, which in fact was lessened by the small roof over the altar and by the surrounding trees. African songs and dances formed part of the ceremony. Muslim missionaries had been entering this area from Sudan to spread Islam. But the young bishop and his own missionaries immediately got to work, zealously proclaiming the faith

106

Chad: *Diocese of Pala, Before the Mass*

throughout the region. The bishop founded a new seminary in Sarh, so that he could ease the overcrowding at the Saint Luke Seminary near the capital. I would visit the latter institution after my return from Sarh on a small plane.

Part of my visit included a stop in the Diocese of Pala, located on the border with Cameroon. While there, I saw a number of piles of cotton in the local fields, all produced in this area. The merchants were transporting the cotton from the fields to a factory where cotton fabrics were woven. This was one of the rare cases of local industry in Africa. Then, by small plane, we flew along the border of northern Cameroon. This elicited memories of my previous visit to that country. I was even able to recognize some familiar features as we flew along. Finally, we landed in Moundou, which is located in the southern part of Chad. From there, we used ground transportation to take us to the seat of the new Diocese of Doba. Along the way, we stopped at some missions, observing the work of our missionaries and the life of our Christians in this part of central Africa. Most of the missionaries in the diocese were Italians, members of the group founded by Bishop Daniele Comboni that bears his name (the Comboni Missionaries of the Heart of Jesus). The local bishop was also a member of that group. All the missionaries from the area gathered in Doba, and I was able to speak to them. After my address, we celebrated the Eucharist in the neighboring cathedral where a large crowd was in attendance. At that time, I was convinced that this large country needed new dioceses. As I mentioned earlier, there are currently eight of them in Chad.

From this, we can conclude that the Church in Chad is growing. As of now, it has only two native bishops, but there are already a significant number of native priests who have all been educated in the two seminaries. This allows us to hope that the gospel will take root in the native soil.

Republic of Guinea-Bissau

As we travel together in the pages of this book, we have gone deep into the heart of Africa, which nonetheless has certain affinities with the western part of the continent. We have omitted, however, some smaller countries along the Atlantic coast that deserve our attention because we sometimes read about them in the pages of daily press. In contrast to the greater part of West Africa, where the official language is French, these lands were colonized by countries other than France and therefore have different official languages. Gambia, Sierra Leone, and Liberia have English for their official tongue, while Portuguese is spoken officially in Guinea-Bissau. We must also note the existence of a second "Guinea" to which the name of the capital city Conakry is appended, as a way of distinguishing it from its neighbor to the north. Its official language is French. And to be thorough, we must also mention Equatorial Guinea, which is located further south along the African coastline. Of its 507,000 citizens, 460,000 are baptized, and its official language is Spanish.

Guinea-Bissau was a Portuguese colony until 1975, when it became independent. It is not a large country, having an area slightly less than three times the size of Connecticut. Of its population of over 1.3 million people, 122,000, or 9 percent of the total, are Catholics. The Portuguese did not place a high priority on evangelization in this country, and so it was only in 1955 that a prefecture apostolic was established under the name of Portuguese Guinea. After independence was achieved, the capital Bissau became the seat of the diocese, which was

made directly respon-
sible to the Holy See.
An energetic Francis-
can, Settimio Fer-
razzetta from Verona,
was named bishop of
the diocese. With the
help of benefactors
and priests from his
native diocese in Italy,
he was able to give
strong encouragement
to evangelization. In
the civil war of 1998–
1999, he was quite
instrumental in the
process of reconcilia-
tion, but because of
exhaustion he became

GUINEA-BISSAU

seriously ill. A second diocese has been established only recently.

I visited Guinea-Bissau in 1990, serving as guide for the Holy Father.
We spent some time at the seminary, which still gave off the odor of
fresh paint. We marveled at how faithful workers and builders from Europe
can help advance the missions. The visit featured two main scheduled
events: a solemn Papal Mass, which was attended by people from across
the country, and a short visit to an institution for patients with leprosy.
As we walked out of the institution, where no one could remain unmoved
at the sight of the residents, John Paul II chose not to get into the waiting
car. Instead, he walked over to the nearest house, which was occupied
by a single family. He looked around their home and spoke kindly with
the members of the household. This new "escape" signaled the Pope's
interest in the real-life experience of the country's poor.

Sad to say, the fight for power in this country injured the people as
well as damaged some of the projects built up by Bishop Ferrazzetta. One
thing that has not been destroyed is the missionary work itself, which
continues to be carried out by impassioned workers from different congregations of men and women. The successor to the exceptional Bishop
Ferrazzetta, whom I have met on several occasions, is native-born. This
also is a sign of vigorous growth for the Church in Guinea-Bissau.

Republic of Guinea (Conakry)

Guinea borders upon several countries because of its large size, which is slightly smaller than the area of Oregon. Only 233,000 of its citizens are Catholic, out of a population of over 8.6 million, and these are spread out among three dioceses.

Missionary work in this country began at the end of the nineteenth century. In 1920, the Prefecture Apostolic of French Guinea was raised to the level of a vicariate apostolic. Later, this territory was subdivided into three dioceses and, in 1962, the first native bishop, Monsignor Raymond-Maria Tchidimbo, was named. After the country gained its independence in 1958, Marxists took control of the government. In 1967, the dictator Sékou Touré expelled all European missionaries, who up until then had been partially subsidized by the Holy See. Archbishop Tchidimbo was imprisoned by the dictator for nine years, from 1970 until 1979. He was then permitted to leave the country for exile. The Holy See tended to his needs, and he lived in Rome for several years in an apartment next to my own. Sékou Touré died in 1984, after which the country resumed diplomatic relations with the Vatican. These events serve to explain why evangelizing efforts slowed and why the numbers of faithful have remained low. The issue of Church development presented a difficult task to the young Archbishop Robert Sarah, who succeeded Archbishop Tchidimbo, and whom John Paul II recently asked to serve as Secretary of the Congregation for Evangelization in Rome.

John Paul II visited this country in 1992. In addition to the Papal Mass, I was able to witness an interesting conversation with Muslim leaders. Islam in Guinea has its roots in ancient history and has been marked by tolerance and peacefulness. But even here, some Muslims have been influenced by pressure from rich Arabic countries and from Libya.

Republic of the Gambia

This is a small country, almost twice the size of Delaware, and extends as a narrow strip into Senegal. There are only 1.4 million inhabitants. Its missionary history is connected to that of Senegal, and in the past the entire territory was known as Senegambia. Only in 1931 was an independent mission established for Gambia. It was administered by the

Irish Missionaries of the Holy Spirit and became a diocese in 1957. It was centered on the capital city of Banjul, then called Bathurst. I would eventually visit there, in the company of the Holy Father. The entire diocese currently has around 42,000 faithful. There are also a sizable number of Episcopalians present, but the traditional religion is Islam.

Republic of Liberia and Republic of Sierra Leone

During my time as Prefect of the Congregation for the Evangelization of Peoples, I was not able to visit Liberia or Sierra Leone. When I was ready for a visit, civil war, or rather intertribal war, was still going on. The conflict is based on control of the diamond mines. Certain countries have an interest in the diamonds and minerals, and in exchange for the gems, they give weapons to the local rivals.

Liberia is slightly larger than Tennessee and has nearly 3.5 million people. Sierra Leone is slightly smaller, but its population stands at nearly 5.2 million. In Liberia, there are 172,000 Catholics, and in Sierra Leone 196,000. Each country is divided into three dioceses.

Evangelization began here in the sixteenth century and was conducted by Portuguese missionaries based out of Cape Verde. At the end of the eighteenth century, the Sierra Leone capital of Freetown was founded as a settlement for liberated slaves. In 1821, former slaves from the United States began settling in Liberia. These achieved their independence in 1847. Five years earlier, Father Edward Barron had arrived from Philadelphia. He became vicar apostolic of a territory that encompassed both Liberia and Sierra Leone in

1843. Few missionaries could deal with the difficult climate, which constituted a significant obstacle to evangelization. Actual dioceses were established only after 1950. Efforts at evangelization have suffered substantial setbacks during the turmoil of the past ten years. Responsibility for this situation is traceable to the greed of both local people and foreigners. Because of them, the entire population suffers, along with the small Church community.

In 2004, I was finally able to visit Sierra Leone. The missionary bishop from Makeni invited me to celebrate the tenth anniversary of the African Synod and to bless two small church buildings whose construction I had assisted. I also blessed a new church near the capital and laid the cornerstone for yet another house of God. In the capital, I visited the archbishop, as well as various parishes and some Salesian schools. My trip continued to Bo and Kenema and finally to Makeni, where, in the context of a single solemn Mass, I celebrated all the sacraments, with the exception of confession. I baptized several adult women as well as little children, administered the sacrament of confirmation and the anointing of the sick to an elderly man, ordained two deacons and four priests, and witnessed the marriage of seven couples.

The consequences of the senseless civil war were visible in the wounded and handicapped children, the destroyed mission stations, the refugees whom I visited in the camps, and the uncertainty that hangs thick over the heads of the people. The Church is doing important work here that will foster the spiritual and physical healing of the population.

Republic of Cape Verde

John Paul II visited this country in the beginning of his trip to Africa in January 1990. This country consists of ten larger and several smaller islands in the north Atlantic Ocean, located west of the African continent. The uninhabited islands were discovered and colonized by the Portuguese in the fifteenth century. The people of Cape Verde gained their independence in 1975; however, they remained united with Guinea-Bissau until 1980, when both of the former colonies, which used to share common Portuguese colonizers and their language, split into two independent countries.

The area of Cape Verde is only 1,557 square miles and has more greenery in its name than in reality. It is a very dry land of volcanic origin, with a population of 473,000 citizens on the islands and approximately 700,000 spread throughout foreign countries. The population growth rate is pretty high, but the fishing industry is not able support them all. The people are mostly of mixed races (mulatto), who communicate in Crioulo (a blend of Portuguese and West African words) and Portuguese languages. Ninety-three percent of the inhabitants are Roman Catholics.

When we landed in Espargos for the papal visit, at the only international airport on the narrow Isla de Sal (Island of Salt), we were welcomed by a rocky and sandy hostile land. A smaller airplane transported us to the main island, where the seat of the Diocese of Santiago de Cabo Verde is located as well as the seat of the civil government. The people are of good spirit, but without any vision for the future of their homeland. We continued our trip by visiting one more island but, because of a major windstorm, we had to use a strong military airplane known as Hercules. During that visit, I was also studying the possibility of establishing another diocese. Only toward the end of 2003 was this plan executed, and the Holy See erected the Diocese of Mindelo with its center on the Island of São Vicente. Both of the dioceses are immediately subjected to the Holy See and are members of the Bishops' Conference of Senegal, Mauritania, Cape Verde, and Guinea-Bissau (Conférence des Evêques du Sénégal, de la Mauritanie, du Cap-Vert, et de Guinée-Bissau).

As our airplane from Cape Verde landed in Guinea-Bissau, we were welcomed by an African green landscape with its typical flora. But the Church lives where the people live and in the way that they live.

4. Eastern Africa

Eastern Africa possesses a different character than the central and western parts of the continent. This is not only due to differences among the people, but also to the influence of British colonialism, which left impressions on the local culture and on society. Colonialism in this region had a specific method for regulating missionary work. On the one hand, priority was given to the Anglican church, and, on the other hand, specific territories were attributed to certain religions. Another important aspect of this region's character is the Kiswahili, or Swahili, language, which in this part of Africa can be understood by about a hundred million people. That is a huge number, compared to the users of other African languages. Also, the racial differences are more clearly in evidence. In addition to the Bantu anthropological type, we find a more slender people living here. From the racial point of view, Ethiopia and Eritrea deserve their own special attention, because it is doubtful if their people are truly of the African type.

For the most part, these are large countries, with respect to both territory and population. Here we can include the following, beginning in the south: Tanzania, Kenya, Uganda, Sudan, Ethiopia, and Eritrea. With the exception of the last, I was able to visit all of them. In some countries, I traveled extensively. I will attempt to summarize missionary efforts in the individual countries as well as relating my personal experiences.

United Republic of Tanzania

This country is twice the size of California and is located between the Indian Ocean and the Great Lakes. It lies adjacent to the Great Rift Valley, which extends through all of East Africa and basically creates its western border. Evangelization hereabouts proceeded inland from the coast, specifically from the Island of Zanzibar. As of 1499, Augustinians erected a monastery on the island to serve the needs of European Christians. In 1698, the Augustinians were expelled by Arabs. In the second half of the nineteenth century, the Missionaries of the Holy Spirit arrived on Zanzibar, and a prefecture apostolic was founded. These same missionaries later undertook the mission in the territory of the Great Lakes, which rapidly spread toward the south. In the beginning of the the twentieth century, an order of native religious sisters was founded—a sign of productive evangelization. The education of native priests is also an important vehicle for evangelization. A vicariate apostolic was established in the current capital of Dar es Salaam early in the twentieth century, after which the number of dioceses began to grow. In 1953, it was possible to establish a hierarchy for the entire country with two archdioceses, one at Dar es Salaam and the other at Tabora. Lauréan Rugambwa, who was ordained bishop in 1952 and became archbishop of Dar es Salaam in 1968, was created Africa's first cardinal by Blessed Pope John XXIII in 1960. He was a very good friend of mine until the end of his life. Currently, Tanzania has 37.6 million people, of which over 10.8 million are Catholics, spread among thirty dioceses and four provinces. The present archbishop in Dar es Salaam is the young Cardinal Polycarp Pengo.

I visited Tanzania for the first time in 1986, on the occasion of the twenty-fifth anniversary of the foundation of the Association of Member Episcopal Conferences in Eastern Africa (AMECEA), held at Moshi near Mount Kilimanjaro. At the same time I ordained a new bishop, Amedeus Msarikie. The first jubilee celebration took place in a not very large, but filled to capacity, stadium, where approximately eighty

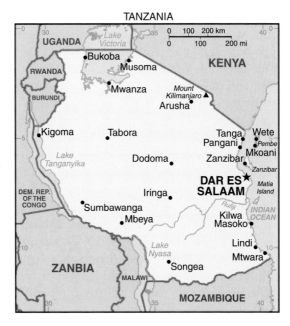

East African bishops and a good number of the faithful had gathered. Mass was followed by a banquet for five hundred people. As an honorary guest, I was seated with the dignitaries on an elevated stage. Toward the end of the meal, they announced that the last course would be "cake", which I thought would be something sweet, and so therefore I was expecting torte. Some men entered carrying a table, and on the top of the table was something large and covered. When they solemnly took the cover off, we could see a large goat that had been roasted on a spit over a fire. You could still smell the burning fat, which began to cause particular sensations in my stomach. The situation became worse, when I was chosen to do the "rite of tasting". I was expected to cut the first piece of meat from the goat and, after tasting it, was supposed to pronounce the meat well prepared. I was worried about the consequences of eating it, and I quickly excused myself over my lack of knowledge of the local culture. Then I delegated Cardinal Maurice Otunga from Nairobi to take my place. But I was not free for very long, because after my colleague tasted the first piece, he offered the second one to me, as the guest of honor. I could feel that piece of meat in my stomach for the next two or three days.

I had to experience a more difficult situation a few days later when, after the beautiful ordination celebration of the bishop in Moshi, we had a banquet in this same hall amid pleasant company. On my left at the table sat the very important Julius Nyerere, a Catholic and former president of the country, and on my right was Cardinal Rugambwa. At the end, I was asked to pronounce the toast with my "solemn message". They placed into my hands a hollowed-out oblong watermelon with a small stick inserted into the side that was supposed to serve as a handle for this unusual "glass". Inside I spotted a not very appealing liquid covered with dirty foam. I thought, "Oh my, it's homemade beer!" As I tried to put my thoughts in order before speaking to these special guests, the nuncio, who was seated behind me, tugged at my sleeve and stared at me. He repeated in Italian, "Don't drink it! Don't drink it!" At that point, several images ran through my mind, as, for example, in the South American Andes where old toothless Indian women chew corn and spit the results into a container where it acts like a necessary yeast for beer production. I knew that I had to avoid drinking that beer, even more so because the following day I had scheduled a safari tour in the national park. As I finished my speech, I put my teeth on the edge of the watermelon and closed my lips tightly. I raised the "cup" until I felt the gray foam touch my nose. Subsequently I said, "Your African beer is very good." At the same time my neighbor indulged himself with a generous sip of the beer. Suddenly everyone in the hall stood up and applauded me, because I had honored their product. I just thought to myself that I had neither drunk it nor lied about it. Later I asked the nuncio why he was so insistent that I not drink the beer. He did not want to comment, but referred to the fermentation process, the fact that the local beer-makers use different methods, and that we were in the land of the cattle herders—the Maasai. He then added, "*Sapienti sat!*"—he who is wise understands. I therefore always repeat that the most difficult part of enculturation is the enculturation of the stomach, because there, even good will is of no avail.

The following two days we traveled through the lands occupied by the Maasai tribe. Near the Ngorongoro Crater, on the edge of a paradise for wild animals, I concelebrated Mass. Among the other concelebrants, there were two Maasai priests. We then hastened along on a government road that led through the Serengeti National Park. We arrived late, however, and the park was closed for the night. Despite having permission from the government, we had to beg the rangers to let us enter. We later understood their objections, when our driver, a bishop from Musoma, passed alongside the shining eyes of wild animals. Once the bishop informed us, "That one was a lion, which does not like car headlights and can sometimes even attack a vehicle." After a longer period of traveling, we spotted the missionaries, who came to welcome us with their flashlights. They escorted us to a central facility called Serenella Lodge. I fell asleep right away in a room located on the second floor, where the British queen had once stayed. In the morning, I was able to watch the animals right out the window, and during the breakfast, a baboon crawled up right next to our table.

The following day was very tiring and included a meeting with the employees of the park and then the brave crossing of a small stream, which overnight rains had made very dangerous. In addition, our car with its waterproof windows was attacked by a swarm of tsetse flies as we traveled through the marshes on the edge of the park territory. We arrived at Musoma in the evening. The schedule for my two-day pastoral visit of this diocese was very packed. At the end of my visit, we crossed the border into Kenya, and from Nairobi, I took a flight back to Rome. This trip was very impressive, because of the events that I have shared with you and also because of other events I did not describe.

My trip in the company of John Paul II in September of 1990 brought me to the capital city, then to the southern Church province of Songea, and later to Tabora, Moshi, and Mwanza. In Dar es Salaam, the Vatican Pilgrim met with clergy in the cathedral and with diplomats in the presidential palace. He spoke to government officials about the AIDS problem, which is very acute in Tanzania and in other African countries. During his speech, he pointed to the necessity of looking for a solution, stating, "The epidemic illness of AIDS demands a tremendous effort of international collaboration from governments, medical doctors, scientists, and all people who can, with their influence, develop the sense of moral responsibility in society." The Church is convinced that without moral renewal and responsibility, as well as without a stress on "basic moral values, any kind of program based only on information, will be ineffective and will lead toward the opposite results." John Paul II had a private visit with the president, who is Muslim. He also had a friendly meeting with the former president Julius Nyerere, a Christian politician, whom I had met previously in Moshi in 1986. The very demanding schedule of the Holy Father commenced with a Sunday meeting with numerous groups of bishops. In his address to them, the Holy Father spoke about the formation of priests. After the meeting, he went to the suburbs of the city, where he celebrated an outdoor Mass. During the liturgy, he ordained forty-three priests. In the afternoon, he met with representatives of different religions. Muslims in Tanzania represent 25 percent of the population. During the meeting, he pronounced the memorable statement, "The world expects rightfully that religions will be messengers of harmony and peace. It is scandalous if, in the name of religion, divisive efforts and hostilities are spread." The meeting with clergy and religious was done in African style, as the church was filled to capacity. It was already evening when the Holy Father arrived at the residence of the first African cardinal, Lauréan Rugambwa. The visit of the Pope was the highest possible honor for the old cardinal.

The southern metropolitan city of Songea had the honor of hosting the Pope for six hours, where he celebrated the Eucharistic Liturgy and administered the sacrament of confirmation to several children. After lunch, he traveled north, visiting the city of Mwanza, which is located on the southern shore of Lake Victoria. There, the Holy Father celebrated an outdoor Mass and visited a hospital where a young American missionary and medical doctor labored, whom I had previously met. He had dedicated himself to the care of AIDS patients. This young doctor escorted us through crowds of people with pained expressions in their eyes, who were awaiting the end of their physical life. I was present during the short interview of the Pope with this young

Kilimanjaro (19,340 feet), from the North

specialist, who had unusual experiences in the medical as well as in the pastoral field.

Another seat of a Church province, Tabora, is located in the central region of the country. We were greeted by droughtlike conditions. Here the Vatican Pilgrim celebrated the Liturgy of the Word. Afterward, we flew northeast to the city of Moshi. As we got closer to Mount Kilimanjaro, the pilot circled the 19,340-foot-high peak, which was partially covered with snow. As he saw this majestic peak, John Paul II reminisced about his days of hiking in the mountains. The members of the Chagga and Maasai tribes, who live in this region, demonstrated their abilities and artistic talents during the celebration of the Eucharist, which marked the centennial of their evangelization. The gifts presented during the offertory procession were truly exquisite.

Tanzania is a promising land for the gospel because of the high numbers of clergy, religious brothers, and sisters, and the number of lay catechists. It has a solid native episcopal hierarchy, which has replaced the missionary bishops. It still requires much effort for the evangelization of non-Christians, as well as a deeper evangelization of the Catholics.

Republic of Kenya

Kenya is a large country, slightly more than twice the size of Nevada with a population of nearly 33.6 million. There are almost 8.4 million Catholics spread throughout twenty-six dioceses. I myself presented several possibilities for new dioceses to the Holy Father for his approval. During my sixteen years as Prefect, I ordained fourteen bishops for the Church of Kenya with the rites of ordination taking place in their particular dioceses. I therefore know this country very well, and I have a close, personal relationship with it, especially with our faithful people and their shepherds.

This Church, as well, was born from the blood of martyrs. The first Portuguese missionaries were already present in the sixteenth century in the port of Mombasa on the Indian Ocean. The sultan at Mombasa initially received the sacrament of baptism, but later left the Catholic faith. This led to the murders of two priests and 270 faithful, who are now honored by the Church as the Martyrs of Mombasa. Effective evangelization was begun at the end of the nineteenth century by the Missionaries of the Holy Spirit from Zanzibar, and in the early twentieth century by Italian Consolata Missionaries and English missionaries from the Society of Mill Hill. Pope Pius XI established an apostolic delegation in Mombasa, which was responsible for the English colonies of East Africa, extending all the way to Arabia. From this delegation, the Holy See was thereby able to assist all the missionary works of the region. Evangelization was successful, and in 1953 a Church hierarchy was established, with an archdiocese in Nairobi and dioceses in Kisumu, Meru, and Nyeri. At the same time, there was a growing movement for independence in Kenya, led by Jomo Kenyatta, who later became the first president of the country. I remember him from my first visit to Kenya in 1976. Efforts on behalf of the education of native priests brought their first fruits when Maurice Otunga became Auxiliary Bishop of Kisumu (1956). In 1971, he was named Archbishop of Nairobi and two years later was created a cardinal. The organizational structure of the Church in Kenya was further expanded when, after the ordination of a new bishop in Eldoret in 1990, I announced the promotion of Mombasa, Kisumu, and Nyeri to archdiocesan rank. They were to be headed by archbishops, whose names I then made public. The resulting shouts of joy were augmented with enthusiastic congratulations, and with songs and dancing. At that point, I thought of the Church province in Slovakia and the difficulties that accompanied its establishment.

I could write an entire book about my trips to Kenya. My first visit during the Christmas holidays in 1976 featured so many episodes that I can only mention them in a summary fashion. Our arrival at Nairobi started with an adventure. When it was time to land, we instead continued to circle the airport for a long period of time. As the passengers found out, the brake mechanisms on the wings were defective and were not extending. There was a danger that we would have to land at a high speed, and maybe even hurtle beyond the runway. As we touched the ground, we saw emergency vehicles and fire trucks along the illuminated runway. Luckily, nothing happened, because the brakes started to function properly. The entire city was on alert, however, because of this emergency situation. Even the Italian ambassador came to the airport.

From Nairobi we traveled east to Mombasa and then along the coast to Malindi, while going into the forest. On the way we visited missionaries. One of them had just returned from a hermitage and just needed to converse with someone. Another missionary offered us some Italian wine, which he had received as a gift from technicians working on the nearby satellite base. We saw a young Irish missionary who had been attacked by malaria. The second phase of our trip took us north, toward the equator and around the tall Mount Kenya. We went through Isiolo and continued through the savanna toward Marsabit. The main road was quite bumpy, and it shook us up rather well in our jeep. Around noon, we got to the

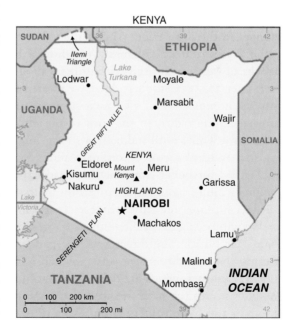

KENYA

121

midpoint of our trip, when we came to a fallen bridge, which had been destroyed during the rainy season. We had to push our jeeps across the dry sandy riverbed.

We stopped at the mission in Laisamis, where students from Rome had built several houses for the Samburu. Most of these herders still preferred sitting in front of small shacks made of dry branches. I had a very unpleasant experience there, when one of the men threatened me with a lance for having taken a picture of his son without his permission. We watched with interest a public judicial inquest regarding a lost goat, where an old herder acted as the judge. Most interesting was an old man with a worn-out hat and a very old piece of cloth wrapped around his naked body. He smiled as one of our guides nervously pointed to his wristwatch, trying to indicate that we had to leave soon, because we still had far to go and did not know what we might experience along the road. When we asked him why he was smiling, the old herder smiled once more, responding, "I am laughing, because you have such a beautiful watch, but you do not have time." It was a lesson for our civilization!

In Marsabit and its surrounding area, we were guided by the now-deceased Bishop Carlo Maria Cavallera, who founded the missionary diocese in Nyeri. Later he handed over the leadership of the diocese to a native bishop, and he went to the northern part of the country to evangelize the local tribes, this despite the prohibition of the British colonial government. Currently, the diocese has 22,000 faithful, but it has already allowed for the establishment of another diocese in Maralal with over 30,000 Catholics. After we returned to Nairobi, we stopped to see Thompson Falls. The next stop was at the station of the missionaries from Padua. In the yard of the mission, we honked the car horn for a while, until suddenly a strong nun ran out the door, holding in her hand a pair of ordinary pliers gripping a big tooth. She apologized for being late, since she had experienced some problems pulling a rather large tooth from one of the African patients. As we can see, missionaries assist wherever they can.

We witnessed another interesting experience in the Aberdare National Park near Nyeri. The director of the park gave us a two-hour tour. During this expedition, we were able to see many animals, including five rhinoceroses, which are difficult to find. On our return trip toward the entrance of the park, we took a narrow road between tall trees. I stood in the middle of the roof opening of our Landover taking a video. Rounding a curve, we came face to face with a huge elephant. The animal got scared, began trumpeting, and waved its big ears. Our British guide stopped the engine immediately and let the car slowly come to a stop. All of us turned white, and I slowly moved back into the car. We waited to see if the elephant would attack us. Our driver then started to make popping sounds, which calmed the elephant down. It moved to the side of the road and, after awhile, disappeared into the forest. We let the car go downhill without turning on the engine. All of us were pale, and, after going a certain distance, we started to question our experienced guide, asking why he had not immediately stepped on the brakes and to explain the sounds that he had made. He said that in "elephant psychology" an immediate stop would have appeared to him as our preparation to attack him, which would then have prompted the elephant to attack us. The popping sounds were an imitation of the greeting of two elephants who, though not able to see each other in the forest, would nonetheless announce their friendly presence in the area.

I could not anticipate the extent that the experiences from the first visit would be helpful ten years later, during my future trips to Kenya as Prefect of the Congregation for Evangelization. During the night flight from Rome to Nairobi, I was seated behind Mother Teresa of Calcutta. Before the arrival, we had to fill out customs declaration forms. Mother Teresa asked me, what amount she should declare, since she was not even carrying a penny. I explained to her that nobody was going to believe that she came to Africa without any money. I myself wrote a certain amount on her declaration and gave her that exact amount in dollars. As we claimed our luggage at the airport, suddenly a number of boxes and cartons started to arrive in our claim area, totaling 950 pounds of crackers, dry milk, clothing, and other goods for the poor. Everything was transferred free as the personal belongings of Mother Teresa. Her sisters then had enough to carry. That was Mother Teresa's way of living out poverty and love. We said farewell at the airport, and I began fulfilling the busy schedule of my pastoral visit.

First, I dedicated a new cathedral in Eldoret. Later, I had an interesting talk with President Daniel arap Moi, and for the first time used the Swahili language for much of the conversation. Then I visited mission stations in the foothills of Mount Elgon. We continued our trip, driving through the savanna all the way to northern Lodwar, accompanied by the first bishop of this completely missionary diocese. We visited the surroundings areas of Lodwar, and I met missionaries and religious sisters, visited schools, laid the cornerstone of a new small church building on the savanna, and celebrated the Eucharist with members of the Turkana tribe.

I flew by a small airplane to the farthest missionary station, Kakuma, located almost on the border with Uganda. There I met with a nurse and two volunteers from London. The native catechist served as my translator, and a certain elderly man with a gray beard and crippled leg, who supported himself with a strong cane, in turn supported me with his prayers. He had the look of a prophet. I was surprised by his public prayers. First he praised God for life, good weather, rain, green grass, and for cows and goats. At the end, he pleaded with God not to allow thieves from the other side of the border to steal the cows and goats. During the celebration of the Eucharist, I noticed that many children were coughing because they were infected with tuberculosis. The "hospital" did not have enough medication.

From Lodwar, I continued my trip by plane. We flew over Lake Turkana on our way to Loyangalani, where the Italian missionary had not even built the church yet, but had taught the people how to farm and fish, so their food could have greater variety than cow and goat milk. Our ensuing flight above the savanna to Maralal was an adventure. We could not locate our landing strip, and it was getting dark. We landed on the meadow while almost touching the horns of the cows pasturing on the field. As we landed, travelers passing by informed us that our small runway was not too far away. At that time, it was already dark, and, thankfully, the Bishop of Marsabit had found us at this emergency "airport".

He took us in his car to a missionary station that was well known in the area. In the early 1950s, a religious brother used to sleep in its tower, from which he was able to warn of the attacks of Mau Mau rebels. Next to the station, a minor seminary had been constructed, where I greeted students from the different tribes of the area. Currently, it is the seat of a new diocese headed by an Italian missionary bishop whom I ordained in 2001. Then we visited a hospital in the small town of Wamba. The hospital was built and is run by a praiseworthy doctor. For the structure of the building, he used his own resources and the donations of several of his colleagues from northern Italy. The meeting with the youth was very pleasant, and even nicer was the performance of the small children from the Samburu tribe, who danced and sang for me "Kalidinali Tomko".

From Wamba, I flew north over the mountains on a single-engine Cessna-type plane. Mr. Fosco, the experienced pilot, let me operate the four-passenger plane for fifteen minutes as we crossed the mountain range. I had my hands full, keeping this toy in the air as we were buffeted by the winds. We made a short stop in the Kor Desert, where only the wandering herders live. The remaining part of that day's flight led us above small craters to Marsabit, where I was welcomed by members of different tribes from the area, such as the Samburu, Turkana, Borana, Gabra, and others. All of the tribes have their own languages, habits, and specific clothing. Following the great celebration at the cathedral and on the field in front of it, we started a long flight to the town of Bungoma, where I ordained their first bishop. After the ordination, my trip continued through the clouds to Nairobi. This description of one of my pastoral visits is but a frame around a pale picture. In reality, each missionary trip for the head of the Catholic missions is a rich experience. Can anyone still call the Prefect a bureaucrat? For me, personally, it was an opportunity for spiritual growth and for gaining the experiences that God granted to me. This was only the beginning of my trips to Kenya. I will mention other instances where I participated in the visits of John Paul II, and also my own personal visits when I went to ordain new bishops.

When, in 1985, John Paul II and I landed in Nairobi for the conclusion of the International Eucharistic Congress, it was the second visit to Kenya for both of us. The newly elected Pope made his first visit in 1980. The Eucharistic Congress, attended by masses of people, took place in a large stadium where the Holy Father celebrated the Eucharist, and where several young couples from different tribes celebrated the sacrament of matrimony. The greatest amount of attention was given to the couple from the Maasai tribe, who were dressed in their own folk costumes. Right before the ceremony, their siblings arrived in an open truck with a recently killed lion. In the house of President arap Moi, whom we stopped to visit, we also saw two stuffed lions. As the president noticed our interest, he offered a live lion for the Vatican. Our representatives very politely thanked him but declined the offer, the acceptance of which would have engendered too many problems. This side episode has nothing in common with the African joy and the dignified religiosity that the faithful of Kenya and of the surrounding countries, including guests from other continents, displayed in honoring the Eucharistic Lord.

There was another celebration in Nairobi during the Holy Father's visit. He came to promulgate the resolutions of the Bishops' Synod for Africa. That ceremony took place in the broad Uhuru Park, located in the center of the capital, between the parliament building and the modern, concrete-and-steel cathedral. The latter serves its purpose but does not resemble a typical African building. During this visit, I felt as though at home in Nairobi, since I knew the city from previous stays. The plaques on the nunciature stand as reminders of the several visits of John Paul II to the city.

After my first visit to Kenya in 1976–1977, the apostolic nunciature (or the Vatican Embassy as many refer to it) became an important base of operations for a number of my trips to other countries. All of the nuncios, including my university classmate, now-Cardinal Agostino Cacciavillan, and Archbishops Clemente Faccani and Giovanni Tonucci were excellent co-workers and kind hosts during the times I stayed at the prefecture. They always stressed that the nunciature is the Pope's house, as well as the house of the prefect responsible for the territory—which therefore included me. Here I could rely on eating safe food, prepared by the religious sisters in charge of the kitchen. Initially, these were the Italian Dimesse Sisters, who were later replaced by the Polish Felician Sisters. Whenever I would arrive, my accommodations were ready. In the final years of my prefecture, a Polish sister who was also an art teacher, painted my coat of arms and placed it above the door of one of the rooms with my name and title: "Room of Cardinal J. Tomko". The nunciature is located in a pleasant part of the city. At the entrance, there are beautiful tropical trees and flowers as well as a statue of Saint Francis of Assisi with African animals lying at his feet. A short walkway takes the visitor to the main entrance of the building, which has a Vatican flag hanging above it. Off to the side is the entrance to a beautiful chapel, where a few years ago I blessed the new altar. On the other side of the building is a large garden with a walled-in fence, where the nuncio Tonucci gradually erected the Stations of the Cross. A large, artistically designed cross stands in the middle of the garden, along with a statue of Saint Clare. I sometimes went to the local market with a sister who was good at bargaining with the local merchants. Members of the Maasai tribe, in their customary attire, sell their own art at the market. Suffice it to say that I was at home at the nunciature. From there, I would walk through a small gate to a Carmelite monastery with sisters from different continents. Nearby was the private home of my friend, Cardinal Maurice Otunga. He lived in poverty, without any security, until the night when thieves broke into his house. He was a man of saintly life who did a great deal for the Church in Kenya.

The reason for many of my visits to Kenya was the ordination of new bishops for either new, or already existing, dioceses. Other times my visits had a pastoral motive. As I mentioned previously, I ordained fourteen bishops in this country, some of whom were native-born, and others who were missionaries. In this way, I became a spiritual father to the majority of the bishops of Kenya, and I could jokingly say to the president of their conference that, during their sessions, we could overturn his decisions. I ordained the bishops in the places where they were assigned, and in the company of their joyous faithful. Of particular note are the following dioceses: Embu, Bungoma (where, after the death of the first bishop, I even ordained his successor), Eldoret, Homa Bay, Kitui, Kisii, Isiolo, Kitale, Nairobi (two auxiliary bishops), Lodwar, Malindi, and Maralal. I would like to share experiences from some of the ordinations that were remarkable in their own way.

I think that the newly named bishops liked to invite me to do the ordinations, because I could employ Kiswahili, which was the language understood by most of the native faithful. Apart from the issue of language, I also had my own method for delivering homilies, which enabled everybody to follow the main ideas. Usually I began with a greeting: "*Tumsifu Jesu Kristu*" (Praised be Jesus Christ!) to which everybody present responded with joy. As I continued in their language, the applause and astonishment grew. When I delivered a part of my homily in their language, people eventually stopped clapping and began to listen attentively. After a long introduction, I explained in English the theme of the first part. I switched into English for those who did not understand Kiswahili. Then again, at the end of the part that I delivered in Kiswahili, I introduced some thoughts from the following part in English. By the end, everybody had heard the entire homily, which they remembered very well, because the memory of native Africans is exceptional.

Posing a certain challenge were the three ordinations I celebrated over the space of three days in 1996, in different cities separated by considerable distance. We began in Kitui, where I traveled with the nuncio and Cardinal Otunga. We began our journey by taking an asphalt government road toward Mombasa. We then turned onto a side road that was not in very good condition. In Kitui, I ordained an African successor to the Irish missionary Bishop William Dunne, who had developed some breathing problems and other illnesses, but who would not give up his smoking pipe. After a long celebration, we returned in the early evening to Nairobi, all bathed in perspiration.

For the following day, we had hired a small plane to take us to Kericho, because the drive would have been too long. When we arrived at the airport, the pilot was not yet there. It seemed as though he had overslept, but he later argued that he had not understood the details of our reservation. We took off after a one-hour delay, but in Africa this is no great surprise. After landing on a green meadow, we were picked by cars and eventually joined up with a singing crowd of people, at which point we could begin the ritual. After a short lunch, we had to hurry so that we might later be able to land at a regular airstrip at Isiolo and do so before dusk. Isiolo is located north of Mount Kenya, which is over 17,000 feet high, and we had to fly around this mountain range. When we were ready to land at the airfield near Isiolo, and the pilot had brought the plane close to the ground, we spotted, in the middle of the field, a donkey who had just decided not to budge at this very inconvenient time. Our pilot called it names, such us "jackass", which was correct without being insulting. We had to circle once more over the crowds of people who awaited us and were then able to land without problems.

After the welcome, we were escorted through the dusty streets to the cathedral with its high tower that exceeds the height of the nearby mosque. We were in the northern part of Kenya, where Muslim territory begins. The bishop's ordination took place the following day and was celebrated outdoors in a field. In attendance were many members of the Samburu tribe, dressed in their colorful folk costumes and with the women wearing rich decorations. To our surprise and despite his medical problems, Cardinal Otunga arrived after a long trip by car. People welcomed the cardinal very kindly and afterward listened carefully to his message. The zealous shepherd and metropolitan archbishop of all Kenya had not spared himself this tiring trip. In Isiolo, I ordained an Italian priest, Luigi Locati, from the Archdiocese of Vercelli, who, over a space of thirty years, established a community of several thousand faithful and who has now received his reward. This vicariate apostolic was never under the jurisdiction of a religious order, as is the common practice. Rather the missionaries were priests of the archdiocese mentioned above and were supervised by the Archdiocese of Cagliari in Sardinia, Italy. This is a beautiful example of how larger dioceses can sponsor the evangelization of a particular territory, bringing in the necessary missionary energy and retaining the right to submit candidates for the office of bishop.

After this beautiful ordination ceremony, I visited some mission stations and also celebrated the Eucharist under a large tree, the future site of a church building. We also crossed the Samburu National Park and visited the location where elephants had destroyed the vegetable garden of a local mission station and threatened the station itself. On our return trip through the savanna, we met up with groups of children at two locations, while tall missionaries from Somalia, in their typical white turbans, were explaining the Koran to them. We have to admire how zealously the Muslim missionaries proclaim their teaching. In this territory of mixed Christian and Muslim cultures, we need to redouble our missionary efforts, because the people are open and will be glad to receive the gospel. We also need to remember colonial history, when the British divided Kenya into three regions for missionary purposes: one for Anglicans, a second for other Christian denominations, and a third for Muslims, which actually included the area of Isiolo.

My 1998 trip was also interesting. I was escorted on this trip by the Divine Word Missionary Father Charles Bošmanský and the very experienced cameraman Mr. Paul Minárik. Father Bošmanský, as a member of a missionary society, wished to visit the missions at least once before the end of his life. Since he had been ordained in secret (underground), the former communist regime had not let him practice his charism. He later studied medicine and became an expert in the field of rheumatology. After the velvet revolution in the former Czechoslovakia, he was able to teach a course of pastoral medicine in Bratislava. The main purpose of our visit was the ordination of two bishops, one of whom was a native son, and the other a missionary. We can summarize the reactions of my travel companions with words taken from the conclusion of Mr. Minárik's twenty-two-page description of the trip: "I did not know if all the things that I experienced over those ten days were reality or a beautiful dream." Truthfully, if I were to refer to all his descriptions of the trip, I would then need at least ten books for my own notes.

*Isiolo (**Kenya**): With the Orphans before the Celebration*

Also interesting was the ordination of a bishop for the northern-most diocese, Lodwar. When the founding bishop, John Mahon, felt he could no longer govern the diocese, having expended all his energies in this difficult area ministering among the members of the Turkana tribe, a new bishop was then named. The new episcopal candidate was a member of the same missionary society as the previous bishop. Actually Father Patrick Harrington, an Irishman, had been minister-general of his society and had later served as university professor in Nairobi. I knew him well from the time he had spent in Rome. The joy I experienced at his invitation was increased by the prospect of witnessing the success of evangelization in an area much affected by drought.

We flew from Nairobi to the ordination ceremony with several other bishops aboard who had never previously seen the Diocese of Lodwar. We flew north over Lake Nakuru and the well-known Great Rift Valley. On our right, we could admire the tallest peak in the country, Mount Kenya, and, on the left side, the over-13,000-foot-high Mount

Elgon. The green colors beneath the aircraft changed to brown and then to yellow. The vegetation disappeared, or else was limited solely to the flora of steppes. All the rivers dried out, and one could barely even see their beds. As we penetrated into the desert, we spotted the small town of Lodwar, located on the side of a dark mountain. We landed on a rather rugged runway that could tolerate landings of even mid-sized planes. When we touched the ground, our airplane created a cloud of sandy dust.

As I first glimpsed the hillside, where our missionary center is located, I spotted several modest buildings. Right next to them were shacks built of wooden branches, where the native people lived, or rather where they tried to survive. As I took a walk among these poor dwellings and tried to capture the life of the people on film, I really had a difficult time. At one point, a drunken woman almost attacked me, and only one person was willing to show me the inside of his shack, of circular shape and about ten feet in diameter. As he showed me all his possessions, an odor spread from one of the containers—it held fermenting beer. The entire family slept in this small space. The center of the town, or, rather, the center of this large village, consisted of small brick houses lining three asphalt streets. The only new building was a very nice mosque, built by a Muslim merchant who had received money for it from Arabia.

The ordination of the bishop took place in a large schoolyard near the town. In attendance were local settlers, but also many nomadic people with their leaders, who had traveled a long distance. Most of them were baptized faithful, but some had come out of curiosity. All were dressed in their tribes' particular traditional costumes. Members of the Turkana tribe usually dress in dark colors. The hair of the women is cut short, with the exception of a narrow strip that extends from the forehead all the way to the neck. The men dress in robes, which are mostly red. In attendance, there were also solemnly dressed leaders of tribal groups. Members of one of the groups colored their hair red, and they dressed in dark red fabrics. As usual, joyful singing accompanied the ceremony. I had to preach in English, which then had to be translated, because not many people in this area speak Kiswahili. This also meant that I could not use my usual method for delivering my homily. The altar and the bishops were sheltered by a military tent, while most of the faithful stood under the hot sun. Right before the imposition of hands, a strong wind came up, kicking up the sand

*Lodwar (**Kenya**): Turkana Women with a Missionary*

and creating a tear in the tent directly above where the bishops were seated. Somebody commented that the Holy Spirit had cut a hole through the strong tent fabric and descended on the bishop-candidate.

I had a desire to visit the savanna, and so we went to see the chapel whose cornerstone I had blessed on my previous visit. It is a nice church that, for now, can accommodate the families of the nomadic people who live in the surrounding area. When I asked the missionary who served as my guide how much it had cost to build this church, I was surprised. The price of the materials, which all had to be carted in, was only five thousand dollars. The land, the manual labor, and other necessities were donated by the faithful. My next question was, How many of this kind of church needed to be built in the diocese? As I returned to Rome, I began to raise money to help with the construction of those small churches. In other places, the expenditures are slightly higher. It only confirmed my old plan to build these small, simple churches among the poor people of the savanna. As I retired from the Congregation for the Evangelization of Peoples, I expanded my plan for the entire continent of Africa. Each country was given money for two new churches. Right now I am receiving photographs of eighty new buildings, each of which was constructed with a ten thousand dollar donation. During this trip through the savanna, I saw children digging holes in sandy riverbeds. This allowed them to collect water into their small containers, which then had to last for the entire day. This is their daily work. As we were passing camels, some of which live in the wilderness, we met a herder and his mother from the Turkana tribe. In one hand, he had a staff, and in the other he held a small seat, which also served as his pillow at night. On his wrist, he wore a metal bracelet whose sharp endings were covered with leather that prevented him from hurting himself. This instrument was the weapon that helped protect him in case of attack by an enemy—whether man or animal. On our return trip to Lodwar, which took several hours, we stopped to visit a larger church near the town, where the people were more settled. The church was spacious enough, but the roof was covered with metal sheets. In the sun, the church became a real furnace, which only the local people were able to tolerate.

I returned to Kenya shortly thereafter in order to establish a new diocese at Malindi and to ordain their first bishop, a Capuchin from Malta named Francis Baldacchino. We joked that he would make the perfect bishop, given that he always carries his baldachin with him. I remembered Malindi from my first visit in 1976 for two reasons. There is the old chapel there, apparently built where the great missionary Saint Francis Xavier stopped on his way to India. Here also an Irish missionary shared a good Chianti with us as we concluded our Christmas celebration. It had been given to him by Italian scientists who were helping to construct an offshore satellite launching pad in the Indian Ocean. At that time, the town of Malindi had a mixed population of Christians and Muslims while the surrounding area was inhabited by our Catholics and members of traditional African religions (or animists) who were open to evangelization. The territory is located between the two Church centers of Mombasa, the province to which Malindi belongs, and Garissa, the diocese situated to the north by the Somali border. The territory around Malindi gave us the impression of being ripe for the establishment of a new diocese and the naming of a missionary bishop. I arrived on the local airline, in the company

*Nairobi (**Kenya**): The Health Center of University of Trnava, Slovakia*

of several bishops, for the ceremony where the diocese would be established and their bishop ordained. They did not have a large pastoral center at that time, so we had to stay in a hotel. The next day, we processed from the church and continued our long walk under the hot sun to the ample yard of the Catholic school, where the ceremony took place. With this procession, Archbishop John Njenga of Mombasa wanted to emphasize to the people the presence of the Catholic Church in the area. After the celebration, I withdrew to the coast. There I watched the birds diving for their food, and the rhythmic motion of the ocean waves that alternately advanced and retreated from shore. In this way, I was able to spend a relaxing evening. We also visited the Chapel of Saint Francis Xavier. Thanks be to God, his spirit is still alive in the Church.

Thus far, the last of my ordination ceremonies is that which took place in October 2001, in the newly established Diocese of Maralal, which used to be a part of the Diocese of Marsabit, whose territory had been deemed too large. I had already been retired for six months, but the division of this diocese had been planned for quite a while. It was most pleasant to be invited by the Italian missionary from Belluno, Monsignor Virgilio Pante, to impose my hands on him and to ordain him a bishop. Monsignor Pante, a young zealous priest, had worked in this area for several years, where the greatest obstacles to evangelization are the constant rivalries, and occasional outright conflicts, that exist between the two main tribes, the Samburu and the Turkana. He therefore chose the theme of reconciliation for his episcopacy and incorporated into his coat of arms that symbol of peaceful coexistence, the lion and the lamb. Leaders from both tribes delivered very moving greetings and traditional blessings during the ordination ceremony. Meanwhile the whole assembly of the faithful looked on with joy. The open area where the ordination ceremony took place sparkled with decorations and with bright colorful cloth, most especially as worn by the women of the Turkana and Samburu tribes. Local customs were incorporated very tastefully throughout the ceremony. For example, the candidate for ordination prostrated himself on sheepskins during the Litany of Saints. These served as a reminder of the shepherd culture of the region, even though the skins acted like a hot blanket over the burning ground. Here I preached once again in English and in Kiswahili.

During my visits to Kenya, I would always reserve some time for a friendly visit with my good old friend Cardinal Otunga. I once accepted the invitation of the Slovak ambassador and visited a small medical center in a suburb of Nairobi, which had been established by the University of Trnava in Slovakia. On another occasion, I blessed the new aula of the Catholic university and distributed diplomas to the graduating doctors. I was able to visit poor a neighborhood, where the Comboni Missionaries of the Heart of Jesus were assisting the people. Once, I went to see the new headquarters of the Focolare Movement, located north of Nairobi, where I received beautiful Christmas cards depicting African art. A very deep impression was left on me by a visit to a center for children infected with AIDS. They are cared for by religious sisters and volunteer nurses and by medical doctors doing research work at this institution. The center is sponsored by a certain missionary from the United States.

There are two events that I will not easily forget. The first was the terrorist attack on the United States Embassy, located in the center of the city, where many people lost their lives. The nuncio, Archbishop Raphael Ndingi, and I saw the ruins of the building, which had been several stories high. We were solemnly dressed in our white cassocks, because we were on our way to the ministry of foreign affairs to express our sympathy and solidarity. A reporter from the American television network CNN spotted us as we walked through and asked us for a short interview, which was then broadcast around the world.

The second memorable event was the gathering of all the bishops from the Democratic Republic of the Congo, and the Republics of Rwanda and Burundi after the turmoil in the area of the Great Lakes, when the two smaller countries had attacked the larger one. We had to call this meeting in Nairobi, because there was no other safe place for this kind of gathering. Would the bishops be able to find a solution for this military conflict, which had caused such suffering, mostly among the innocent? Could they be silent in the face of such injustice? The bishops assembled under difficult circumstances. They came from different directions: some through Lusaka in Zambia, others through Entebbe in Uganda, and some by way of Cameroon. Much pain was experienced at that meeting, but it was also a deeply spiritual gathering with an important message. Twice the bishops asked me to be the principal celebrant at the Eucharist, and apart from my long initial speech, I delivered two homilies. Our brotherly solidarity only increased during the meeting.

Finally, it is time to mention my visits to the national parks. After tiring trips and activities, these visits to the parks were, for me, a time of relaxation and rest. Half a day, or just several hours, sufficed for a safari, where we sought out and admired the wild animals. During my visits to Kenya, which extended over twenty-five years, I stopped at almost all the parks: Meru, Marsabit, Aberdare, Tsavo, Samburu, and a small park near Nairobi. In the last park, my Italian driver and I were in danger of sleeping overnight in the old car. Thankfully, the officer at the gate heard us arriving, and after giving us important instructions, he let us into the park. During my initial visit to this park, I was chided by the ranger. As I had been videotaping a young buffalo, which had just been killed near the road, I jumped for a minute from the covered jeep. The ranger warned me that the lion might still be hiding in the nearby bushes. I had my most enriching experiences in the Maasai Mara Park, which is a continuation of the well-known Serengeti Park in neighboring Tanzania. I was traveling with Mr. Minárik and Father Bošmanský, and we were looking for a leopard. We had an interesting encounter with a lioness hiding in a trench amid tall grass and protecting her cubs. She frightened us and the other tourists, as she jumped out from her hiding place, growled menacingly, and showed her long teeth. I promptly recorded the scene with my camera. The film became the envy of Mr. Minárik. I experienced a truly great safari during my October visit in 2001, when I was able to record several exceptional scenes. We saw three prides of lions, the first with seven members, a second one with twelve, and the last one with two. There were herds of elephants, a rhinoceros, hippos in a river, crocodiles, and many other animals such as antelopes, gazelles, giraffes, zebras, and different sorts of birds. As one watches wild animals in their natural surroundings, worries disappear and fresh thoughts occupy the mind.

In October of 2002, I had an unexpected new opportunity to visit Kenya. The Catholic University of Eastern Africa was celebrating its tenth anniversary, and honorary doctorates were to be awarded to the four founding cardinals. They included my brothers in service, Cardinals Paul Tzadua from Addis Ababa, Maurice Otunga from Nairobi, and Adam Kozlowiecki, the ninety-one-year-old, former Archbishop of Lusaka in Zambia. They added my name to the list as the former Prefect of the Congregation for Evangelization, and as an old friend of Kenya and of Africa in general. Even at my advanced age, I was the youngest among the four, and, according to African culture, it was I who was designated to celebrate the Eucharist and preach the homily. I also had to speak in the evening at the solemn dinner for the "high society" of Nairobi, and finally I had to deliver a graduation speech in the presence of about eight thousand guests of the academic senate, who were all dressed in robes fashioned in the style of European universities. They had allotted forty-five minutes for my graduation speech, but they informed me of their plan only the day before the graduation ceremony. Such are the "forgetful moments" of my African friends, who of course were expecting a solemn speech of high scientific acumen, executed in perfect English. Somehow I was able to carry out the assignment.

On this occasion, I had the opportunity of spending a day and a half among the Maasai people living at a mission station in the midst of a dry savanna near the Tanzanian border. When we arrived at our destination, we were welcomed by several missionaries who work among this partly nomadic tribe. Two of the missionaries were from Mexico, and one was from Italy, while the oldest came from Holland and had been ministering there for over forty-one years. As the last rays of the evening sun shone, the summit of Mount Kilimanjaro appeared in the distance covered with snow. With its height of 19,340 feet, it resembled a throne reaching beyond the clouds. That evening, I was able to listen to Father Frans Mol, the most knowledgeable expert on the culture, spirituality, customs, and language of the Maasai. It was he who compiled their large dictionary and who is the owner of the most extensive library on the Maasai tribe. These people are mostly herders, with their own independent system of governance. Outsiders generally photograph them because of their colorful clothing, rather than out of a desire to know them more deeply. Father Mol is an example of a missionary who dedicates himself not only to the proclamation of the gospel with the help of translators, as I had to do the following day during the celebration of Holy Mass, but who tries to learn the life of the people and their language so precisely that one of the tribal leaders called Father Mol their teacher. The four-hundred-page dictionary Father Mol had compiled, and of which he shared with me a copy, gives witness to this fact.

Part of the Mass that morning consisted of the wedding of a young couple. They and the entire wedding procession were welcomed by the one of the elders at the entrance to the church. He sprinkled us not with water, which is precious here, but with milk. After the Mass, they gave me some of the insignia of an elder, as well as other gifts. Among these was a metal-tipped lance, approximately thirty inches long. With that weapon, the younger members of the tribe are able to kill even lions, which for them is the highest of all honors. Later, we visited a *manyata* where the wedding reception and dance took place. The *manyata* is a compound for a larger family, or, more precisely, for a clan. It is surrounded by a simple fence made of wooden branches and thorns. In the middle of the area are several shacks constructed of the same branches and sealed with cow dung. Walls and roofs such as these provide protection from the heat, and from rain and wild animals. The shacks are not as tall as the height of an average adult; they have no windows, and their entrances are very narrow. These houses are also very easy to build. When the clan moves on, seeking better pastureland, they leave their shacks standing at the old location, just in case they should return. During the wedding reception, the young men danced, especially those of the warrior class. Meanwhile the women, in their colorful clothing, prepared their food and tea under the trees.

During the Stay in Maasailand: Blessing with the Milk in Front of the Church

The dancing of the men consisted of high jumping while remaining in place. It was a paradise for my video camera. To this footage, I later added some pictures of animals in their natural habitat, which I took while we stopped at the nearby Amboseli National Park.

The Church works among the Maasai people, who wander throughout the so-called "Maasailand" in Kenya and Tanzania. The missionaries try to evangelize consistently, but at a slower pace. In that way they do not destroy what is beautiful in the Maasai culture, and simultaneously they are able to correct with sensitivity whatever contradicts the gospel. The Diocese of Ndong in Kenya was established principally to care for their pastoral needs. In Tanzania, the Masai tribe form part of the dioceses of Arusha and Moshi. As of the present time, several priests have been ordained from among the people of the Maasai tribe.

If I had to evaluate briefly the Church in Kenya, I would need to stress its rapid growth, but also the necessity of deepening the faith

The Bride (at the end)
Entering the Church

With the Newlyweds in Front of Their Home

Maasai Bridesmaids

Dressed-up Maasai

of its Catholic members. I witnessed an excellent collaboration throughout the country among the native and missionary bishops, priests, and
religious sisters. There is a need for good native candidates for both
the episcopacy and the priesthood. Nairobi has become an African
Vatican City. There are many educational and religious institutions concentrated there. The Church in Kenya is a beautiful one and holds
great promise.

Republic of Uganda

This beautiful country is located north of Lake Victoria. On the east,
it borders Kenya, on the west Democratic Congo, and it extends in
the north to its border with Sudan. In area, it is slightly smaller than
Oregon, and its population is 26.7 million. There are 11.6 million
Catholics and a rather large number of Anglicans. It can be stated that
the people of Uganda are mostly Christians. The first Catholic missionaries were the White Fathers. This religious order came to Entebbe
from southern Tanganyika, currently Tanzania, in 1879. In 1885, the
local king began a persecution of the Christians. Twenty-two Catholics were tortured. These were beatified in 1920 and in 1964 declared
to be saints. In the early years of the twentieth century, other missionaries arrived in the area, especially members of the Comboni Missionaries, who evangelized the people in the northern part of the
country. The blood of the earlier martyrs enriched the vocational soil
for the local religious orders of sisters and brothers, as well as for those
called to the priesthood. In 1939, Uganda received the first African
bishop of modern times in the person of Joseph Kiwanuka. In 1953, a
Church hierarchy was established. In 1969, for the first time in history,
the Symposium of Episcopal Conferences of Africa and Madagascar
(SECAM) gathered in Uganda. The Holy Father, Pope Paul VI, attended
this meeting and delivered a memorable speech wherein he proclaimed that it was time for Africans to take a role in evangelizing
Africa. In 1976, the archbishop of the capital city Kampala was named
a cardinal.

In 1986, John Paul II sent me as papal legate to the centennial
celebration of the Martyrs of Uganda. The celebration was awe-
inspiring and took place as peace was being restored after a horrific
civil war. After the solemn welcome of the papal legate at Entebbe
airport, where, several years earlier, Israeli commandos had rescued

Jewish hostages, we continued in a long motorcar procession to the capital, Kampala. The following day, with some difficulty, we were able to pass through the crowds of faithful who had used all sorts of transportation to get to the celebration near Kampala. The place where the martyrs had been tortured resembled a natural crater with a small lake in its center. A small island

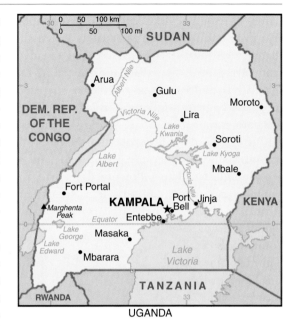

stood in the middle of the lake, on which a roofed-over altar had been erected. Because of the request of the local hierarchy, I had to wear, for the first time in my life, the long red train or *cappa magna*. The local cardinal, Emmanuel Nsubuga, was wearing one as well, and they caused us only problems as we were trying to make our way through the crowds toward the altar on the island. President Yoweri Muzeveni, whose army had already taken over nearly the entire country, arrived shortly before the celebration. In my homily, I asked everyone for reconciliation and peace.

I later traveled on a small plane in order to visit the northern cities of Gulu and Lira, which required some courage as this was still a dangerous region. As we landed on a small field, young soldiers jumped out from the bushes to protect our plane in case of attack. After the concelebrated Mass, I met with a former restaurant owner from Italy who had later become a priest. He organized humanitarian aid for the entire area, by building artesian wells and by delivering food, especially to the Karamodja region. His name was Don Vittorione (Big Victor), and he weighed about three hundred pounds. After several meetings with priests, religious sisters, and seminarians, I visited the hospital in Lacora, which had been built by a married couple named

Corti. Doctor Lucille Corti, who was originally from Canada, was at that time performing an operation. When she finished her work, she shared with me the fact that she had already performed twelve thousand surgeries. A few years after my visit, Doctor Corti injured herself. While performing an operation, she acquired AIDS, which, even then, had become widespread in Uganda. These heroic physicians, who are both now deceased, are shining examples of lay missionaries.

We returned to Kampala shortly before dusk. The African pilot was very nervous, because we had to land at an airport that lacked regular lighting. The following day I had a very long dialogue with the new president. On this trip, I learned something new about African culture. At one of the places I visited, I was greeted with a sign that read, "Welcome Holy Father". They explained to me that, according to their reasoning, a representative is honored and treated exactly as the one whom he represents. So I, as papal legate, was identified with the Holy Father. When I shared this story with the bishops, missionary Bishop Joseph Willigers from the Netherlands calmed me down with his own

Uganda:
Welcome in Gulu

story. It seems that during a confirmation in one of the small villages, the bishop was stressing to the faithful that he had come in the name of the Holy Spirit, whom he would bestow on the candidates for the sacrament. During the lunch, the leader of the village said to him, "Welcome Holy Spirit". Needless to say, my own title was not as prestigious.

I visited Uganda a second time while accompanying the Holy Father in 1993. This was during a short visit that was a part of a longer papal trip to Africa. At the airport in Entebbe, we were welcomed by President Muzeveni. By then, after the passing of several years, he knew me personally and cordially greeted me. John Paul II then visited the graves of the Martyrs of Uganda, and during a visit to the Anglican shrine he said, "I would like to express the feelings I am now experiencing at the place of martyrdom of your predecessors, both Catholic and Anglican, who burned in the same fire. It was the fire of the Holy Spirit. It is my desire that this fire might gather us together in one Church, in unity with Christ, through the Holy Spirit." Huge numbers of pilgrims had arrived at the shrine of the Catholic Martyrs from all over Uganda. The crowd even included some pilgrims from neighboring countries, such as Sudan. The visit of the Holy Father to the largest Catholic hospital in Kampala was very moving. Here, one-third of the patients were infected with the AIDS virus. The Pilgrim from the Vatican honored two other dioceses with the celebration of the Eucharist: that of Kasebe in the west, and Soroti in the east of the country.

This country of many riches, especially in those areas adjacent to the Nile, but which also has its poorer regions inhabited by herders, involved itself in military actions in Rwanda and in the Democratic Republic of the Congo, in the Kivu region as well as near Kisangani. Many are convinced that Uganda is extracting great wealth from that area, such as diamonds and gold. Uganda has no desire, therefore, to leave the occupied territories. Does it not, by these actions, make for itself new enemies?

The Church has become strong here and should exercise more leadership in religious matters in Africa. It should not slacken its efforts at evangelization and needs to continue to exercise a moral influence on Ugandan society. The local Church also needs to continue to build on the solid foundations prepared by the missionaries. Military power does not suffice to guarantee the greatness of a country and its people.

Federal Democratic Republic of Ethiopia and State of Eritrea

These two countries in northeastern Africa formed a single nation until not very long ago when Eritrea declared its independence. There have since been disagreements over the precise location of their border. This region is typical of Africa more by reason of its poverty than by the physical appearance of the inhabitants. We can, however, encounter the African physical type in the southernmost regions.

Eritrea is a small country on the Red Sea with 4.3 million people, 150,000 of whom are Catholics, in two dioceses, of the Eastern Coptic Rite. Therefore, they are not under the jurisdiction of the Congregation for the Evangelization of Peoples.

The territory of Ethiopia makes it one of the largest of African countries, apart from its 71.3 million inhabitants. Catholic numbers stand at 551,000, divided among ten dioceses. Seven of these dioceses depend on the Congregation for Evangelization, while the rest are of the Eastern Rite. All of them, however, are united in a single bishops' conference.

Christianity has its own special history here and dates from apostolic times. The eighth chapter of the Acts of the Apostles describes the trip of the Apostle Philip toward Gaza, which was located in the southern part of the Holy Land. There occurred the conversion of one of the high officers of the Ethiopian queen, who was returning from pilgrimage to Jerusalem. In the fourth century, Saint Athanasius of Alexandria ordained Saint Frumentius as bishop for Ethiopia. The Church in Ethiopia maintained its dependence on Alexandria in Egypt, which was the home of Saint Mark,

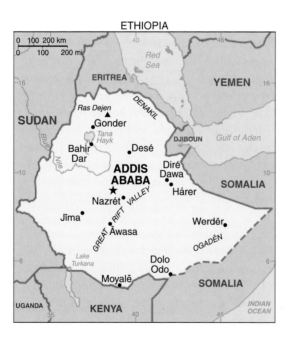

an evangelist and disciple of Peter. After the Edict of Milan of 313, whereby Emperor Constantine granted complete freedom to the Church, Christianity almost became the state religion in the empire. In the fifth century there arrived in Ethiopia monks who had had to leave Syria because of their adherence to the Monophysite heresy, which denied the divinity of Jesus Christ. They spread their false teachings in their new country.

We do not possess very much religious data from the Middle Ages in Ethiopia. However, the Catholic Church of the Coptic Rite grew stronger. Groups of Coptic Catholics were later established who use these rites until the present day. These Catholics mostly reside in the center and northern part of Ethiopia. In 1555, Jesuits tried to unite Orthodox Copts with Rome, and in 1622, Catholicism actually became the state religion. Six years later, however, bloody persecutions broke out against the Catholics. Finally, after two centuries, Saint Justin de Jacobis secretly entered Ethiopia and renewed the Catholic faith. It slowly spread, and its organization became stronger, at which point vicariates apostolic could be established. Eritrea became one of those vicariates. New missions grew to the south of Addis Ababa, where the presence of a different racial group is more significant. In that area, the Roman or Latin Rite is used. There are Catholics of both Rites, the Eastern Coptic and Western Roman, in Ethiopia today.

A short period of Italian occupation prior to World War II ended with the defeat of Italy in 1941 and the expulsion of all missionaries from the country. Later, the missionaries were replaced by members of the Capuchin and Vincentian orders, and most recently also by Salesian priests. Presently in Ethiopia, the majority of the people are members of the Orthodox Coptic church, which has its own local patriarch. Many Orthodox priests are not very well educated, and their principal role is the celebration of liturgical rites. Monks exercise a more dominant role in church life. Relations are cold between the Orthodox hierarchy and Catholics, and ecumenism is not a well-attested fact. Islam is very strong in the southeastern part of the country. Catholic missionaries use proven methods in their evangelization work. Adjacent to the western borders with Sudan and Kenya, African tribes and refugees are to be found, each with their traditional religions.

From out of the recent political past, we must mention the government of Emperor Haile Selassie, who is remembered for his role in the history of the last century. After the invasion of the Italian army in

1935, the emperor escaped to the West and stayed there until his armies defeated the colonialists and he was able to return. In 1974, political power was seized by communists who were led by the army officer Mengistu. In 1991, Mengistu's power was taken from him by members of his own political party. They forced him to leave the country, and he now lives in another African state, where he has acquired wealth and property for himself. The communist party, without any major ideological change, is still in power, concentrated in the area of Tigrai. Poverty is very much in evidence in this country, which does not enjoy an international status commensurate with the size of its population.

I spent many years preparing to visit Ethiopia. A great opportunity arose in 1994 with the ordination of two bishops, but both requested that I ordain them in Italy. Nevertheless, on my trip to Kenya in October 2001, I used the Ethiopian airlines, so I could stop for a few days in this country. Addis Ababa is a city with several million inhabitants situated from 8,200 to 9,850 feet above sea level—a height that is immediately noticeable when one gets off the airplane. It is the headquarters for the Organization of African Unity. During my visit in 2001, I stayed at the apostolic nunciature, which is referred to locally as the Vatican Embassy. The nuncio, Silvano Tomasi, was very hospitable, as were his young secretary from the United States and the sisters, who are Servants of the Holy Spirit. I was not able to visit my colleague Cardinal Paul Tzadua, who, because of age and health problems, had resigned the leadership of the diocese.

However, I was able to visit the cathedral, where some older priests sang some psalms for me and shared a liturgical ceremony in the Coptic Catholic Rite. At the seminary, located at the foot of the hill, I was able greet the seminarians and their professors, the latter being members of several religious orders. At the time of my departure from the seminary, the rector gave me a typical Coptic cross, measuring about eight inches in length. The priests of the Eastern Rites use them during their liturgies and carry them on their persons when they go out walking, in the event that people in the streets request a blessing. Apart from their liturgical use in churches, these decorated crosses of different sizes are used during pilgrimages and processions. They are richly ornamented and can be made of metal—sometimes even of gold. They can also be made of wood. Western tourists used to buy them and export them. On one occasion, a European tourist carried away a solid gold cross that weighed fifteen pounds and was of very great artistic value. Since that time, even for a simple cross, it is necessary to procure a certificate from the national museum attesting to the fact that the souvenir to be exported does not have historic or artistic value. I very much esteemed the gift of the seminary and brought it home.

One afternoon, the nuncio's secretary and I drove north of the city. We gradually ascended to an elevation of over ten thousand feet. Eucalyptus trees grew on either side of the bumpy road, and some parts of the forest looked freshly cut. We met up with what looked like a procession of women carrying heavy loads of wood on their backs, which would be used either in their own stoves or be sold in the city. On the mountain plain above the city stood two Coptic churches. The older of the two was closed, while the more recently built functioned as a place of pilgrimage. The pilgrims came to pray, never actually entering the round building, but instead offering their prayers in front of two paintings located on the outer walls of the church. They knelt while in prayer and with great piety made deep bows, as we can sometimes see Muslims do during prayer.

Descending toward the city, we stopped to visit an institute conducted by the Missionaries of Charity of Mother Teresa of Calcutta. It was not difficult to spot the large buildings surrounded by a great many poor and hungry people. The sisters care for unwanted children who are brought to the institute every morning by the police, because their poor mothers and the state are not caring for them. Another department of the institute houses patients infected with AIDS. The men are housed separately from the women. Nobody wants these patients, neither the hospitals nor their families. Apart from these residents, the sisters feed a huge number of hungry people at each meal. They never ask them about their religion or nationality. For all the work they do, the number of sisters is quite small. They are from different continents and are members of different races. I was glad to meet among them a very tall and happy sister from Romania. The sisters prepared a surprise for me in another house, where I was greeted by one of the Slovak sisters. The Missionaries of Charity also maintains a novitiate in the Republic of Slovakia.

I am not going to describe my experiences from the market, which extends over several streets and in which you can find everything imaginable. For the most part, of course, the merchants sell food, vegetables, fabric, clothing, household goods, and other necessities. It made a fine, colorful setting for the video camera, but first one has to be able to deal with the stench of some of the goods being sold, as well as the sewer, if we can even call it that. The people are all trying to survive as best as they can and purchase whatever they need and can afford in this noisy market.

I wanted to acquire a souvenir for myself. Finally, I found a small, four-sided stand topped with a small cross. Each side of the stand could be opened and was decorated with icons depicting mysteries from the life of Christ and the Virgin Mary. All together there were eight of these icons. Ethiopian icons are different from those of Russia or Greece. The most noticeable difference is in the eyes of the saints, which are generally larger and black in color. In addition, I bought a few hand-painted pictures on goatskin, as well as a set of Stations of the Cross done in the Ethiopian style. I placed the Stations in my chapel as they foster piety and are deeply expressive.

My trip to northern Ethiopia, near Lake Tana, was quite interesting. There we have a mission station in the midst of Orthodox territory. It is operated by an elderly and very pious priest, who is aided by a younger assistant from the south. The black African origins of the younger man could be easily deduced because of his racial features. Lake Tana is about twelve and a half miles long and contains dirty, yellowish water. This lake is actually the source of the Blue Nile, which generates beautiful waterfalls several miles downstream. There are a number of islands in the middle of the lake, where Orthodox Coptic monks live amid ancient monasteries and churches. We visited four of those monasteries. On one of the islands, a sign at the entrance to the monastery forbids women to enter. I did not have enough time to visit the Island of Tana Cherkos, where the monks in the Chapel of Our Lady of Zion preserve with care the legendary Ark of the Covenant from the Old Testament. Many local traditions are told concerning the Ark. Life in the monastery resembles that of the Egyptian Desert Fathers of ancient times. They eat only food they grow themselves or that others offer to them. The churches in these monasteries are real treasures because of their frescoed walls. They are circular in shape, measure thirty feet in diameter, and are surrounded by a spacious hallway. The most beautiful paintings are those on the walls of the encircling hallways. In their beauty and spiritual quality, they are equal to Byzantine icons. The monks who care for them are glad to show them to tourists. The admission fee becomes a part of their income and is used in part to buy food. These treasures deserve to be classified as international cultural artifacts. Of course, they are also of great value from a religious point of view. On Sunday morning at six o'clock, I attended the Orthodox liturgy at the nearby church. They used the *iconostas*, as do our Eastern brothers, and during the procession, they carried small, colorful baldachins over the head of the celebrant. The liturgy lasted three hours. After that, we celebrated Mass for a small group of our own faithful. Time did not allow me to visit the well-known churches in Lalibela, which are carved into the live rock of the mountainsides. Nor did I have time to visit the ruins at Axum. (At that time, its great obelisk was still in Rome, taken there by Italians in 1937. After promising its return for many years, the Italians finally brought it back in April 2005.)

The following days of my stay in Ethiopia were spent traveling by car south of Addis Ababa. Early in the morning, we took the only asphalt road in the country. We headed toward Meki, where we visited the local bishop, Yohannes Woldegiorghis. He met us with a kind smile and wore the typical black beret worn by all the other priests in the area. He reminded me again of my ordaining him bishop in Rome at the Urban College for evangelization. He recalled my quoting in the homily Jesus' words to Peter, "Do you love me more

Ethiopia:
A Coptic Monk
Showing the Gifts

Monk on the Island
in Tana Lake

than these?" (Jn 21: 15). The bishop took these words personally to heart, and at each meeting he reminded me of them. He was a bishop of a very large territory, with a small number of faithful. He died just a year after my visit.

Our final destination was the Vicariate Apostolic of Awasa, where we arrived only in the evening. This area is evangelized by the Comboni Missionaries from Italy. So successful were their evangelizing efforts in augmenting the numbers of the faithful that a prefecture apostolic was established in 1969. This was raised to a vicariate apostolic ten years later, with Monsignor Armido Gasparini as the first bishop. After he eventually submitted his letter of resignation because of age, Rome named Monsignor Lorenzo Ceresoli from northern Italy as his successor. I ordained him in his home parish on the Feast of Saint Joseph in 1994. He welcomed us at the missionary station at Awasa near the lake, where he lives with his religious brothers of the Comboni society. This has certain advantages, but the diocesan priests wish that their bishop would not be so dependent on the missionaries. It is a common problem in the mission territories.

From Awasa, we continued southward to the town of Dila. Salesians of Saint John Bosco have built large schools there and were erecting a very large church on a hill across from one where a Muslim mosque with a tall minaret already stands. The road passed through a green landscape, but soon enough the roadbed turned to dirt. We descended from the mountains to a savanna, where the territory and the people assumed a different appearance, the latter looking more African. A new mission station was going to be founded in the area. I was asked to bless a house located near the school where, not far away, a well was being dug. The Mass was celebrated in a tent. The young government prefect of the region, who was not even a Christian, translated my homily into the local dialect because nobody else could do it. We took our leave after partaking of a modest lunch for all the guests in attendance, for the missionaries of both sexes, as well as the nonbelievers because we are talking here about the early stages of evangelization.

We spent all afternoon visiting mission stations located on the side roads. We once more took our overnight accommodations with the Salesians, where the following morning I met a young man named Michael, who had been adopted at a distance by a friend of mine from Rome. (Such efforts are of great help to the missionaries.) I was also

Gorgeous Frescos in a Monastery

Missions in the South: A Health Center for Mothers

Missions (Awasa): Preschool

able to talk and joke with the assembled schoolchildren. After that, we continued on our journey in the heat of the African day, sometimes sharing the main road with people on foot, and even with animals, until we arrived in Addis Ababa in the evening.

During this short visit to Ethiopia, I realized more deeply that effective evangelization is necessary in this country, especially in its southeastern region. Cooperation and mutual understanding with the Orthodox Coptic church are also of great importance. Ecumenical contacts should be established and expanded upon. In recent years, Catholic missionary work has become more effective, but, even so, Islam continues to spread rapidly. It will also be important for the Orthodox church to revitalize its own evangelization, not only through the liturgy, but through other methods as well, so that, as Saint Paul said, "only Christ will be proclaimed".

Somalia and the Republic of Djibouti

Two neighboring countries of Ethiopia are Somalia and the Republic of Djibouti. By virtue of its territory, Somalia is considered large. It is a mostly Muslim country, where the missionary experiments of the last 120 years have all been terminated with violence. For over a hundred years, a prefecture apostolic was supervised by Franciscans. In 1927, the prefecture was elevated to a vicariate, and in 1975, to a diocese with its seat in the capital city, Mogadishu. The last bishop, Monsignor Pietro Salvatore Colombo of the Franciscan order, was murdered in 1989. I celebrated his funeral Mass in Italy, in his native village near Milan, my first contact with Somalia. After the bishop's death, Muslims destroyed the cathedral and desecrated the cross as well as a statue of Christ the Lord. They once more began persecuting the small group of Christians. Until recently, they were still a few religious sisters who staffed a small hospital. The civil war only worsened the situation. At the outbreak of the war, there were around 2,000 Catholics in the country, who were visited secretly by the apostolic administrator, Father Giorgio Bertin. He became Bishop of Djibouti in 2001, and Somalia, which is still awaiting its evangelization, then became part of his jurisdiction.

Djibouti is a small republic surrounding the city of the same name. Its area is slightly smaller than that of Massachusetts. It occupies a very strategic geographic location at the juncture of the Red Sea and the

Indian Ocean. This area was once under French jurisdiction. Even after Djibouti gained its independence in 1977, the French government has maintained a military base there. There are 7,000 Catholics, including the abovementioned soldiers. The rest of the 700,000 inhabitants are Muslims. Djibouti is a diocese, where Capuchins have been serving for over a hundred years, and where the current diocesan bishop is the abovementioned Italian Franciscan, Bertin.

5. Northern Africa

The territory of northern Africa includes those countries of the continent that border the Mediterranean, as well as Sudan, which borders the Red Sea. The Church expanded very quickly across the Mediterranean lands in Africa during the first Christian centuries. The invasion of Islamic armies between the seventh and eleventh centuries, however, destroyed many prosperous dioceses such as those that had given to the world Augustine, Cyprian, the Martyrs of the Plague in Alexandria, and many other great saints. The dioceses survive nowadays only in the form of ruins, and in the names of the titular sees given to auxiliary bishops. The history of those Christian communities serves as a reminder to us that though the gates of hell will not prevail against the universal Church throughout the world, this does not exclude the possibility that Christianity might disappear from some parts of the earth. Faith is a gift that needs to be cared for and even prayed for. An entire region can lose it. As neo-paganism spreads during our own times, the history of North Africa can serve as a warning.

Despite all that transpired in the past, we do have Catholic dioceses in this region, and this means particular churches. Not all of them are under the jurisdiction of the Congregation for the Evangelization of Peoples, and even for those under this jurisdiction, there are limitations placed on visits from its Prefect. My most memorable visit was a short trip to Morocco taken in the company of John Paul II, while he returned from the International Eucharistic Congress in Nairobi in August 1985. In the present work, our description of North Africa will commence with Sudan, which is situated west of Ethiopia. We will continue with Egypt and then move along in a westerly direction to the other countries lining the Mediterranean coast.

Republic of the Sudan

Sudan is the largest African country, covering 967,000 square miles of the continent. Most of its territory is desert. The population exceeds 34.5 million, of whom over 4 million are Catholics, spread throughout ten dioceses. The earliest evangelization began in the sixth century in the northern region, with Byzantine priests founding the first communities of the faithful. Along with their bishops, these communities later became a part of the Coptic Patriarchate of Alexandria. At the end of the thirteenth century, Muslims destroyed the Christian Kingdom of Nubia. More significant experiments in evangelization began in the nineteenth century in the southern part of the country, but the so-called Central African Mission experienced failure. Between 1872 and 1881, Blessed Daniel Comboni was assigned to this area as the vicar apostolic, but toward the end of the nineteenth century, Islam destroyed all the missions. When in 1898 the Anglo-Egyptian army took over the government in Sudan, the Comboni Missionaries of the Heart of Jesus returned, renewing their missions in the south as well as their schools in the predominantly Muslim north. From that point, evangelization continued rather quickly. The ordination of three native priests in 1944 was followed, in 1955, by that of the first native bishop. When the country declared its independence in 1956, more difficulties emerged for the missions. The Muslim government expropriated the schools of the Christian missionaries, and in 1964 all missionaries were expelled from the country. The differences

and conflicts between the predominantly Muslim north and the ani-
mistic and Christian south culminated in 1957 with the start of civil
war. This conflict was temporarily suspended in 1972, when an agreement was reached in Addis Ababa. In 1983, after the government
declared that Muslim law (Shariah) would henceforth apply to all
citizens, warfare broke out again. In 1974, a Church hierarchy was
established with seven dioceses, and evangelization continued against
many obstacles. Sudan has remained divided into two parts, which
are accustomed to fighting against each other. It is noteworthy that
Western political interests have been stirred by the discovery of oil
fields.

There are several causes for the civil war that has raged for twenty
years between north and south. The north is populated by Muslims,
while the southerners are more typically black Africans. Overall, they
are 70 percent Muslim, 17 percent Christian, and 12 percent animist,
or followers of traditional African religions. The domineering north,
with its dry climate, would like to take over the oil fields in the more
fertile south. In addition, the Arabs who control the government show
no mercy in applying their religious law to all Sudanese citizens. According to a 2001 report of the independent international organization
Amnesty International, the civil war had already cost approximately 2
million lives. Excluding half a million internal refugees, 4.5 million
people had been forced to leave the country. According to credible
sources, government airplanes bomb civilians; children in refugee camps
are forced to study the Koran; and mortality is very high. There are
also documented incidents of the kidnapping of women and children,
who are pressed into slavery. The conditions of war prevailing in the
south impede both normal living and evangelization. During the Jubilee Year 2000, Josephine Bakhita, a native of southern Sudan, was canonized. After being kidnapped and spending a harrowing time serving
cruel masters, she was acquired by the Italian consul and taken to Italy.
It was in that country that she received Christian baptism in 1890.
Italian law did not recognize her status as a slave, however, and with
her new freedom, she was able to embrace religious life. Her example
is not only proof of the heartbreaking reality of slavery in Sudan, but
also an example and an encouragement for the local people.

I visited Sudan only once, while accompanying John Paul II on his
return trip from Africa in 1993. We stopped in the capital of the country, Khartoum, and after visiting the cathedral, the Holy Father

celebrated a solemn Mass in a suburban area. Surprisingly, a large crowd gathered for this celebration, which took place next to a huge cross. Following the liturgy, we met with a governmental delegation in a palace constructed by the Chinese. The delegations sat down face to face in a great hall, which was so cold that we were chilly in our light cassocks. The leading general delivered a long speech, which was supposed to prove the existence of religious freedom in the country. The presence of an Episcopalian bishop in the governmental delegation was also supposed to confirm this fact. The Holy Father very calmly expressed the need for peace and tolerance, as well as for respecting human rights.

Despite all these difficulties, which at times should be declared an outright persecution of Catholics and black Africans, the faithful remain true, and the Church continues to grow. From the northern territory of the Archdiocese of Khartoum, Rome was able to establish a new diocese especially for refugees and those who were transferred there from the areas of conflict. This Diocese of El Obeid is practically divided in two because of the war zone. In the southern part of the country, which has its metropolitan center in the Archdiocesan See of Juba, individual dioceses continue with the evangelization process. Physical communication between the towns is difficult and dangerous. The bishops of the south sometimes hold their meetings in Nairobi across the border. The entire Conference of Bishops of Sudan have held their assemblies in Italy. The Church needs to offer social assistance to so many suffering and oppressed people. The greatest cause of pain is the inattention of the so-called "Free World", which closes its eyes to abuses of the most basic of human rights in order to safeguard its economic and political interests. It is about time that a peaceful solution to this conflict be found and for genuine respect to be accorded to human rights and religious freedom.

Arab Republic of Egypt

This country with its ancient history covers 386,000 square miles of territory, much of which is desert. The population of Egypt stands at 74.4 million, of whom only 311,000 are Catholics, of the Eastern Rites. Since these are under the jurisdiction of the Congregation for Eastern Churches, my trips to this country had more of a tourist-pilgrim character. The principal religion of Egypt is Islam. Among the Christians, the most numerous are the Orthodox Copts. The Catholic Copts are under the leadership of Cardinal-Archbishop Stephanos II Ghattas. There are also small groups representing other Catholic Rites. Egypt is divided into fifteen dioceses.

I made my first trip to Egypt over thirty years ago as part of a group of tourists. At that time, we visited Cairo with its exceptional museum, and the surrounding areas that contain the well-known pyramids and Sphinx. We also stopped at Thebes and at the Step Pyramid of Saqqara. We observed the ancient watering system in the countryside and visited the dam at Aswan. As I examined a sign written in Russian at the entrance to the dam site, I was informed why the Egyptians had expelled the Soviets who had built the dam. I was surprised by the answer. Apparently it was because the local farmers started to rebel against the Soviets, who were trying to push their atheistic, "scientific" ideology. The farmers declared that only a crazy person could deny the existence of God, whom they felt almost intuitively through their own interaction with nature.

The purpose of my second visit to Egypt around twenty years ago was to attend the ordination of my co-worker from the Secretariat for the Synod of Bishops in Rome. His name was Youssef Ibrahim Sarraf, and he became the Chaldean bishop for northern Egypt. At that time, we first flew to Aswan and visited the famous ancient Egyptian temples of Abu Simbel that had been disassembled and moved to save them from the rising lake water. Then we cruised on the Nile for two days all the way to Luxor, where we stopped to

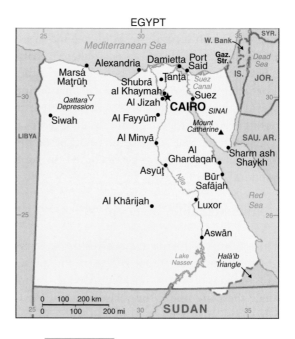

Waterfalls on the Blue Nile

see the temples and tombs in the Valley of the Kings. Finally, we returned by plane to Cairo. Because of an error on the part of our travel agent, we almost missed our flight from Luxor. When we complained to him, he just stretched out his arms and said, *"Inshallah"*— that fatalistic and miraculous expression ("God's will") that Egyptians and other Muslims use for solving all their problems. The Chaldean Rite ordination took place in Cairo in the Church of Our Lady of Fatima. That church is also very often visited by Muslim women, because they think that it is dedicated to Fatima, the daughter of Mohammed.

Egypt is the country where the Holy Family made their home for a time. After the apostles left the Holy Land, tradition holds that Saint Mark went to live in Egypt. In the first centuries after Christ, Alexandria became the center of Christian life in this area and also the seat of a patriarchate. The forceful invasion of Islam obstructed fuller evangelization of this country, where Christians of the Eastern Rites still reside. The future is in God's hands.

Libya (Great Socialist People's Libyan Arab Jamahiriya)

Libya is located west of Egypt along the Mediterranean and spreads inland all the way to the Sahara. Only about 5.7 million people live in this country measuring 679,000 square miles. Of these, 104,000 are Catholic, living in two vicariates. Two other prefectures apostolic are not able to exist separately because of local government prohibition. The population is concentrated especially along the shoreline, which is also covered by olive groves and other sorts of trees. The two largest cities, Tripoli and Benghazi, are located along the coast, as are ancient Roman ruins. The southern and central parts of the country are mostly desert, but they also contain oil wells.

The missionary history of this country is rather moving. In ancient times, the western part of the country, or Tripolitania, was more connected with the history of Carthage, while the eastern district of Cyrenaica depended more on the destiny of Egypt. Flourishing Christian communities once existed here, which tried to evangelize the south in the sixth century. However, in the middle of the seventh century, after the invasion of Muslim and Arabic armies, Christianity slipped into a slow decline. By the eleventh century, Islam became the dominant religion. Only in 1643 were Capuchins able to attempt missionary work. A prefecture apostolic for Libya was then established. Later, Italian Franciscans arrived and developed an effective evangelization, which still very often had to struggle against many obstacles. Two hundred years later, in the nineteenth century, evangelization expanded once again, and two new vicariates apostolic were

established along with two prefectures. Between World Wars I and II, Libya was under Italian influence. Two memorable battles took place between enemy armies in the vicinity of Tobruk, which eventually resulted in the complete defeat of the Germans and Italians. In 1950, Libya became independent. In 1969, the Libyan army launched a coup and seized power, expelling Italians from the country and taking over all Church property. The following year, the government gave permission for a single bishop, nine priests, and two churches to exist in all of Libya. The young Franciscan bishop, Giovanni Martinelli, who was born to Italian parents living in Libya, became vicar apostolic, with his seat in the capital city. He also oversees the two prefectures apostolic. Another Franciscan, Bishop Sylvester Magro, serves as vicar apostolic in Benghazi.

I visited Libya in April of 2000, flying from Rome to Malta, and then from Malta to Tripoli in the company of the apostolic nuncio to Malta and Libya. We flew into the capital city, which is located near the western border with Tunisia. I had my diplomatic passport and visa, and upon our arrival, one of the government officers extended courtesies to us and protected us for the entire trip. Tripoli is a beautiful city, but its location has its disadvantages. Perhaps that is why the chief of state, Muammar al-Qadhafi, began to build an administrative capital closer to the center of the country and further inland from the coast. According to his plans, it is supposed to function as headquarters for a United Nations of Africa, which he himself aspires to lead. My heart was saddened as we passed the former cathedral, built in a classic style but changed into a mosque after the revolution. Portraits of the leader hung from many tall buildings. The medium-sized Franciscan church now serves as the cathedral, and it is the only Catholic church for half the country. This is an example of how the revolution undermined the activities of the Catholic Church. Now the government carefully studies each step taken by the Church's hierarchy.

In Tripoli, I had to celebrate Masses in different languages due to the international makeup of the Catholic community in this area. The largest group, consisting mostly of African students and workers, attended the French Mass. I celebrated Mass in Slovak for a group of my countrymen and people from Poland. Many of them had come from afar, some all the way from central Libya, where they worked. Many were women who worked there as nurses. It was a nice gathering. I visited a state institute for handicapped children, where about six Catholic religious sisters were ministering. The ministry of foreign affairs had requested their presence. I remember that the sisters had some difficulties in accepting this offer, since they were not to be allowed to proclaim Jesus Christ or even to pronounce his name in public. I encouraged them at that time and told them that they would have the Lord's name inscribed on their foreheads if not in their mouths. Their subsequent work bore this out. The director of the institute, who is Muslim, mentioned that with four additional religious sisters, he could dismiss twenty local women. It was a realization that could then lead one to wonder about the source of the sisters' devotion—something that the local women lacked, even though they were better paid. The life witness of these sisters in a totally foreign country is the only way to evangelize. The Lord sends us to plant seeds, or perhaps only to prepare the ground, but not to harvest.

I made a one-day trip to Leptis Magna, where I admired the ruins of the ancient Roman city. The streets, amphitheater, victory arch, and even the Byzantine church with its baptistery are preserved.

I also visited eastern Libya with its center at Benghazi. In the middle of the city stands the Catholic cathedral, closed and empty. I celebrated Mass in a small church in Polish, because a good number of

Libya: Leptis Magna, an Ancient Roman Amphitheater

people from Poland worked there at the time. The following day we went by car even further east to the home of another group of religious sisters, where some priests had gathered who had permission from the state to work as professors in various schools. Our meeting with the priests and sisters was friendly, and I tried to encourage them. It is a fact that our missionaries need encouragement, since they cannot even use the name of Jesus. The life is a difficult one, but God is in charge of the harvest.

As we left Benghazi, we had to turn on the headlights, because a sandstorm had begun, brought in by the *gibli* wind from the Sahara. The driver had to be extremely attentive and watch for camels, because the visibility was really bad. On our return trip, we stopped in Cyrenaica, where large and well-preserved ancient Roman ruins are located. The Roman emperors used to reward their legionaries for their service by giving them territories such as these. The sandstorm soon abated, and before evening the plane could land in Benghazi to pick us up. We took off the same evening for Tripoli, and the following day I flew back to Rome by way of Malta.

From Libya I carry with me a single thought: that the Church can live and bear witness to Jesus Christ even in this way, while awaiting better times.

Tunisian Republic, People's Democratic Republic of Algeria, and Kingdom of Morocco

The three African states located to the west of Libya not only share the Sahara Desert; they also share some common history. Tunisia, with its 63,000 square miles, is the smallest of them. It is slightly larger than the state of Georgia and has a population of almost 10 million people. Algeria covers 919,000 square miles of the African continent and has a population of 32 million. Morocco covers 177,000 square miles and is home to 30.5 million people.

These three countries have a common heritage, insofar as their Catholic history is concerned. The "glory days" stretched across the first six centuries after Christ. Christianity reached this area at the end of the first century and spread rapidly throughout the second. Roman traders and soldiers were among the first to announce the Christian religion, but communities of believers and dioceses established along the coast were also very active in mission work. The faith radiated from Carthage, which used to be a lively spiritual center but now lies in ruins near Tunis. It spread to Numidia, Mauritania, and throughout all of proconsular Africa. In 256, fifteen bishops from what is now Algeria gathered at Carthage for a memorable synod, after which a Church hierarchy was established. In 354, Saint Augustine, one of the greatest Doctors of the universal Church, was born in Tagaste. Many dioceses were established in the region, and lively theological debates developed, some of which even gave birth to heresies. In 402, a universal African Council took place at Milevi, in Morocco, but several years later that area was invaded by a barbarian army from Spain. In 707, waves of Muslim invaders moved in from the east, and by fire and sword, gradually devastated the entire North African coast. By the year 1150, all the Christian communities and dioceses were gone. The Muslim armies even occupied a large part of Spain, where they remained for several centuries.

After the defeat and expulsion of the Muslims from Spain, the larger missionary attempts began in the northern coastal area of Africa. Franciscans tried to evangelize Morocco in the first half of the thirteenth century, where a diocese was even established at Marrakech. Later, the missionaries had to pay for their daring with their blood. Attempts by Trinitarians to ransom slaves in Algeria two hundred years later also remain a singular and isolated effort. Jesuits and Lazarists arrived in the seventeenth century, but more effective evangelization becomes noticeable only in the nineteenth century. France invaded Algeria in 1830, and eight years later it became possible to establish a diocese at Algiers. In 1866, it was elevated to the rank of archdiocese under the leadership of Charles Lavigerie, who later became a cardinal and founded the Society of the Missionaries of Africa (White Fathers). Spain signed an agreement with Morocco allowing for religious freedom, and in 1908, a vicariate apostolic was established at Tangier, opposite the Spanish coast. Tunisia had become a French protectorate in 1881, and the same fate befell Morocco in 1912. They would regain their independence only gradually. On the one hand, French settlement in the three countries increased the number of the faithful, but on the other hand, the missionaries were mostly French, and they exercised a very weak influence on the local population, especially with regard to forming native clergy.

When the French presence eventually ended, the number of faithful diminished as well. This explains why there is but one diocese in

Tunisia with only 22,000 Catholics. In Algeria, there are 4,000 Catholics spread out through four dioceses. Only one of these, Laghouat in the Sahara, is under the jurisdiction of the Congregation for Evangelization. The 24,000 Catholics of Morocco are divided into two archdioceses, Rabat and Tangier. An organizational peculiarity persists from the colonial era. Despite their completely missionary character, the three Algerian dioceses and the one in Tunisia are directly under the jurisdiction of the Congregation for Bishops, not the Congregation for the Evangelization of Peoples. This is a relic of the old concordat between the Holy See and France.

Currently these three countries are Muslim. One can even sense it in the general atmosphere. There is comparatively more religious freedom in Tunisia. Not too long ago in Algeria, Muslim fanatics murdered a bishop in Oran as well as seven Trappist monks in the desert. King Hassan II of Morocco kept aggressive Muslims well tethered. The pressure against the Catholic missions is rather strong, while the missionaries and their work are constantly being watched.

This general description will allow us to devote less space to each country. Besides, I have never been to Algeria, and the local Church in that country has always been more connected with the Church of France. I have, however, visited Tunisia and Morocco on two occasions.

Along with my sister, I went to Tunisia for Christmas vacation at the end of the Jubilee Year 2000. This was possible because of my acquaintance with Archbishop Fouad Twal, of the capital city, Tunis. He was originally from the Patriarchate of Jerusalem. A Palestinian by birth, he speaks several languages besides his native Arabic. He was transferred to Tunisia from the diplomatic services of the Holy See because of these attributes—which are very helpful, especially when dealing with government officials and Muslims. The entire country is a single diocese and is not under the Congregation for the Evangelization of Peoples. With the help of the archbishop, we were able to acquaint ourselves with the situation in this country, especially concerning religious issues.

The capital city, Tunis, is located on the coast and has a very European character. It is very easy to get around by speaking French. The very beautiful façade of the cathedral, which was recently renovated, borders the main square. On the opposite side of the square, which is always full of people, stand buildings once occupied by the colonial government.

TUNISIA

Not too far from the square is the entrance to the shopping quarter of the city, called the "medina". It is composed of a maze of narrow streets, lined with many small shops. Goods are displayed halfway into the street, while various artists and workers labor by the doors. One can find assorted brass containers covered with engraved images, leather purses made of camel skin, other souvenirs, colorful fabrics, clothing, food, etc., as is the case in any oriental market. Shopping is time-consuming, because of the need to haggle over prices. Shopkeepers always set their prices too high. The counter-offer needs to begin with at least one-third of the shopkeeper's price, and the final price should not be more than half of what was originally quoted.

Meanwhile there ensues a very interesting dialogue, where the shopkeeper inquires about the tourist's origins or about the health of his family. The shopkeeper might offer the tourist some Arabic tea. He will then lament the amount of money he will be losing on his merchandise by selling at such a low price to such a nice person as the tourist. This will continue until the shopkeeper realizes how strongly convinced the tourist is about the amount he has offered to pay. It seems as though they all derive a sort of national pride from robbing tourists of as much as they can. In this way, one can spend several hours in the market, looking for items and trying to get them at the best prices.

I celebrated Mass in the cathedral twice, mostly for the international community, because the local people consider Islam to be their religion. To be a Christian can cause a person difficulties in Tunisian society, in spite of the fact that Tunisians like to be considered as very tolerant. We wanted to visit a beautiful basilica located on a nearby hill next to the ruins of ancient Carthage, but it was closed because the government had taken it over and was using it as a concert hall. The museum of ancient mosaics caught my attention, because it had the largest collection from early Christian times that I have ever seen. These mosaics carry religious motifs that are known to date from the Christian era. They are preserved in their entirety, which is only possible in a hot climate and in dry sandy soil. When I discussed these unique collections with the director of the museum, who himself gave me a tour, he took me to a storage room for items that were not on display. There, he pointed out a baptistery dating from early Christian times, when people, after descending a few steps, would be baptized by immersion in a small pool. The entire baptistery was decorated with mosaics. It was a unique piece of art, and I suggested to the director that he display it publicly, instead of keeping it hidden in storage. I have no idea if he ever followed through on my suggestion.

Our three-day trip through the countryside was quite interesting. An Italian tour guide drove the car. The itinerary was unusual because it led inland and had been titled "Along the Footsteps of Saint Augustine" by the tour guide. This was the same area that been visited by the great Augustine, as he traveled outward from his episcopal seat at Hippo, which now is located in Algeria next to the Tunisian border. Over the course of his life, this saint visited numerous dioceses in the fertile center of Tunisia. These dioceses were once very numerous, but now they are only to be found in the pages of history books because they no longer exist. While I was undersecretary of the Congregation for Bishops, I used to assign their names as titular sees to newly named

Tunisia: A Walk in the Desert

auxiliary bishops. Some old church foundations have been preserved, after being exhumed by foreign archeologists who used their own funds because local historians were not interested in the ruins. As someone shared with me, for Muslims, local history and culture begins with the Islamic invasion. In one place, we saw the ruins of an old cathedral, part of which had been occupied by the orthodox faithful along with their bishop, and the other part by Novatian heretics, against whom Saint Augustine preached and wrote. That was the way disputes were settled in divided congregations.

The ancient Roman city of El Djem is located approximately in the center of the country and features ruins with preserved streets, an amphitheater, decorated arches, public baths, and a pagan temple. The entire site is located atop a hill and, at this time, is not completely excavated. It bears witness to the vibrant living conditions of ancient times. Other Roman and Christian archeological excavations and ruins were visible as we traveled across a wide, flat plain. Some were only waiting for an archeologist to excavate them. For example, from a distance, we saw a battlefield next to the town of Zama, where Romans fought Carthaginians in 202 B.C. The Nepomucene College in Rome, where I used to live for many years, is located adjacent to the Piazza Zama. It was only on this trip that I learned where the real town is located.

It was afternoon when we arrived at the town of Gafsa. We visited three religious sisters there, who give witness to Christ with great sacrifice and amid admirable poverty. They apparently enjoyed our visit. Afterward we sped on south. The cars on the road became scarcer, and the landscape drier, as could be expected of a desert. By evening we arrived in Tozeur, which is the last town before the Sahara begins. It is equipped with an airport, as well as several hotels for tourists who come here to admire the desert. We stayed overnight in this town, and the following morning we crossed the bed of a dry lake—one that fills with salty water during the rainy season. On the other side of the lake, we arrived at the Kebili Oasis. With the help of the Italian government, a certain Roman parish had opened a prep school there for workers who were interested in working in Italy. Not too far from Kebili, at the Douz Oasis, the same parish had built a recreational facility and spiritual center for small groups. We celebrated Mass there on a small altar in the company of visitors from Rome.

Next we sent our passenger car ahead of us on an asphalt road, so as to be able to pick up us in the evening after our day trip through the desert. Our entire expedition then took off into the ocean of sand in three small powerful buses. Our local drivers were experienced, and they knew the road, even in places where the stranger saw no road at all. The surface of the desert is in constant motion. It resembles the waves of the sea—as our bus driver poetically described it to us in his own language. In two places, as we were crossing over some huge dunes, our buses got stuck in the sand. Here the experience of the local people was necessary, as was the assistance of other vehicles. Later, in the middle of the road, we saw empty tents that testified to the ability of men to live here, even if only for a time. Our guides prepared hot tea for us, which is the only liquid effective here against thirst. In the afternoon, we passed an elevated spot that was topped by the ruins of a French foreign legion fort. Later we took a rock-strewn road and eventually arrived at an oasis with hot springs and tourists bathing in the waters. Other tourists were enjoying a camel ride nearby, but we opted for something to fill our stomachs.

On our return trip, we traveled along a portion of the route of the Paris-to-Dakar Rally, which traverses the Sahara and leads to the

Senegalese capital. The road was rather bumpy and poorly marked, but for our bus driver it was a highway where he could allow himself to speed up, sing local songs in his booming voice, and tap with both hands on the steering wheel. The vehicle bounced up and down wildly, and our heads almost collided with the roof of the bus. Women in the back seats began to scream, and only then did our cheerful driver slow down. We all sighed with relief when we arrived at the asphalt road where our car awaited us. We said good-bye to the tourists from Rome, and my sister and I headed for the coast. It was dusk as we reached the small village of Matmata, which is built underground. The houses here are actually cut into the hard soil, which protects the people from the heat. Even the small hotel in the village is built underground. It was almost midnight when we checked into our hotel in the city of Sfax, which is located on the coast. After an exciting day, it was wonderful to be in an air-conditioned room and to get a good night's sleep.

In December 2002, I returned to Tunisia to make a presentation on the work of volunteers in the Catholic Church, as well to celebrate the Eucharist for the diocese on the Feast of the Holy Family. Then old desires brought me back to the desert. This time I took a historical train from Tozeur, which transported us into the wild mountain country. Phosphate is mined in this area and then exported to the whole world. After that, we continued our trip for two days through a rocky and sandy desert. We visited two families in a local clan of herders and rode on their camels.

On the third day, we toured the well-known mosque of Kairouana, where the builders employed materials from earlier Christian buildings. Our tour guide pointed out to us a carved cross on one of the columns, which had escaped the attention of the Muslims and to this day is preserved as a reminder of the ancient Christian history of this country.

As I flew back to Rome, I thought about God's patience. His plans are unhurried. From us, He asks only missionary effort. He, Himself, remains the Lord of time and history, and in the last analysis, the Lord of the harvest.

As I mentioned, I have never been in Algeria, and I have no personal experiences of the country. I can only share and confirm my deep impressions from Casablanca, in Morroco, that date from the return trip of John Paul II to Kenya in 1985. I cannot forget the address of the Holy Father to Muslim youth gathered in a huge stadium that could accommodate seven thousand people. The Pope surprised the entire world as he openly and calmly spoke to this group of youth about God and Jesus Christ and encouraged their religious fervor. It was a preview of his dialogue with large religious groups, which the Pope expanded the following year later during the first meeting of religious leaders at Assisi.

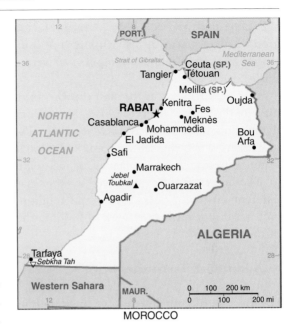

Before my trip with the Holy Father, I traveled to Morocco in 1967, with the now-deceased Monsignor Jozef Vavrovič. We went there as tourists but with religious interests. It was during our vacation after Christmas. We landed at Casablanca and visited four royal cities: Rabat, Fez, Meknès, and Marrakech. We could witness the limited freedoms enjoyed by the Catholic Church, especially with regard to schools. These were mostly conducted by French missionaries and religious sisters, but always headed by the obligatory Muslim principal. After visiting the northern cities, we crossed over the Atlas Mountains—where we could feel the colder climate—and continued to the southern part of the country and to the edge of the Sahara. We stayed overnight in a small hotel in the last oasis, which was the starting point for one-day tours of the desert vistas.

The next day, we took a ride in an old bus, which ferried us out forty miles into the desert on a road of packed sand. I took my winter jacket with me, which was useless during the day because of the heat of the sun. On the return trip, however, the bus broke down. Thankfully we were about fifteen miles away from an oasis where Bedouins had pitched their tents. While we waited for the arrival of the part needed to repair the bus, which was probably on its last legs anyway, it became dark and cold. My jacket protected me, but the rest of our group had to warm up by drinking the hot tea offered us by kindly Bedouins. Later, before midnight, we were able to start the bus and finally reach the hotel.

Our next trip led us through canyons in the Atlas Mountains, then through the Sahara Desert to Ouarzazat. After that, we continued through the mountainous Tika Pass to Marrakech. The city is made famous by its market, where you can see a mix of Bedouins and Arabs selling spring water, expertly charming snakes, or just selling ordinary goods.

The interest that I experienced in ethnography and in learning about different customs, races, tribes, and religions was even then a great preparation for my future work of heading the Congregation in charge of the missions.

Additional Territories

For the sake of completeness we must mention two territories located south of Morocco. The first is Western (previously called "Spanish") Sahara, where we have a few hundred faithful and a prefecture apostolic administered by the Oblates of Mary Immaculate. The Diocese of Nouakchott, containing several thousand Catholics, is located further to the south and is led by a missionary bishop who is a member of the White Fathers. These two territories, located on the Atlantic coast, are considered part of North Africa by virtue of their desert location and sparse population.

A Dangerous Individual **(Congo)**

An Elephant Searching for Roots **(South Africa**, *Kroeger National Park)*

Leopard, an Unusual Shot (**South Africa**, *Kroeger National Park*)

A Family of Cheetahs (**Kenya**, *Masai Mara National Park*)

*A Rhinoceros
(South Africa, Kroeger
National Park)*

*An African Boar
(Facocer)*

Thompson's Gazelles

177

An Antelope (Topi)

An Antelope (Gnu)

Zebras and Antelopes

Part Two

Asia

Asia is a continent of superlatives. It is the largest continent, larger than Africa and Europe combined. With its 3.89 billion inhabitants, it is home to almost two-thirds of the entire population of the planet. Asia is the cradle of the world's great religions: Judaism, Christianity, Hinduism, and Islam. It also gave birth to important spiritual traditions such as Buddhism, Shintoism, Taoism, Confucianism, and to other tribal religions as well. Eighty percent of the world's non-Christians live in Asia. Its nearly 113.5 million Catholics account for only 2.9 percent of its population. Most of these Catholics live in the Philippines, which is home to 67 million of them, or else in India where 17.7 million Catholics live among the 1 billion people of other faiths. In the majority of Asian lands, the Catholics are only 0.5 percent of the entire population.

Asia is genuinely a missionary continent. John Paul II wrote of it in his Encyclical Letter *Redemptoris missio* (*The Mission of the Redeemer*), where he stressed a very urgent message: "Particularly in Asia, toward which the Church's mission *ad gentes* ought to be chiefly directed, Christians are a small minority, even though sometimes there are significant numbers of converts and outstanding examples of Christian presence" (no. 37). In Manila, in 1995, before the assembled Asian bishops, the Pope expressed his hope that "as in the first millennium, the cross was planted in the soil of Europe, and in the second millennium in the soil of the Americas and Africa, it is with hope that in the third millennium we will be collecting a great harvest of faith on such a great and lively continent." The Catholic Church in Asia reaffirmed its missionary

The Synods of Bishops
for Each Continent
Were Very Helpful

endeavors during the special assembly, at the Vatican, of the Synod of Bishops for Asia, which was held from April 18 to May 14, 1998. The theme of the synod was "Jesus Christ the Savior and His Mission of Love and Service in Asia: 'That they may have life, and have it abundantly (John 10:10)'". The fruit of this gathering is the Post-synodal Apostolic Exhortation *Ecclesia in Asia* (*The Church in Asia*). It was issued on November 6, 1999, by the Holy Father in New Delhi, India, in the presence of representative bishops from all of Asia and from Rome, including me. This rich document remains to be analyzed in depth, along with its vision for the Catholic Church's evangelizing effort in Asia.

The old religions of Asia have almost become synonymous with local cultures, and it is sometimes very difficult to distinguish religious practices from cultural ones. Asia can be divided into three zones according to the largest religious groups or cultures. The zone of Islam, commencing in the west, encompasses the Middle East, Arabia, Iraq, Iran, Afghanistan, and Pakistan. It also includes parts of five former Soviet republics, northern India, Bangladesh, Malaysia, Indonesia, and the southern Philippines. This zone is characterized by a very close connection between religion and politics. The second zone, according to the countries influenced, which includes India, Sri Lanka, Myanmar, and Thailand, could be termed "Hinduist", for here the largest religions are Hinduism and Buddhism. The third zone, which encompasses China, Vietnam, Laos, Cambodia, Japan, and Korea can be labeled "Confucian", for here Confucian culture mixes with Buddhism and other religions.

The political tendencies in Asia are also very diverse. Some governments in Asia could be considered as almost democratic, such as those of Japan, South Korea, and Taiwan. Many are democratic, as is the case with India, Sri Lanka, and the Philippines. Others feature a form of dictatorship, either a communist type, as with North Korea, China, Vietnam, or Laos, or a military dictatorship, as with Myanmar and the former regime in Iraq. Lastly, there are governments with almost theocratic tendencies, as in the Islamic countries of Iran and Saudi Arabia. According to the government's ideology, some countries profess a particular state religion, some of them combat all other religions, and some consider Christians as second-rate citizens who are then denied basic human rights. In some countries, political ideology misuses religion, while some religions misuse the power of the state to combat Christianity, which they consider to be a "foreign" religion. Only a few countries in Asia allow for complete freedom in proclaiming the gospel. In most cases, the possibility for evangelization exists in a broad sense, but it must nevertheless proceed under various restrictions. There is also great diversity on the economic and social scene, to the point of encompassing extreme opposites. There are countries that are very developed, others that have embarked on industrial development, and still others that are caught in economic depression. Economic development within a free-market economy, accompanied by aggressive globalization, does not eliminate sharp economic and societal differences, especially in the region of India, where these differences are further aggravated by the caste system. Enormous cities are growing without healthy human conditions. The populations of Bombay-Mumbai and Seoul have already reached 10 million. Jakarta and Karachi each claim 9 million inhabitants. Tokyo and Istanbul have over 8 million, and Shanghai and Peking over 7 million people. Also immigration within Asia, and emigration from Asia to other continents, is on the rise. These movements are heavily influenced by poverty, wars, ethnic conflicts, and by the denial of human rights and freedom. In many areas, the people are economically, politically, or socially exploited and oppressed. During their synod, the Asian bishops protested against disgracing the dignity of women, as well as against immoral tourism. On the other hand, in many countries, we can witness enormous economic progress and the appearance of a new generation of specialized workers, scientists, and technicians. The situation on this continent is very different from that of Africa.

Most Asian nations possess important religious and human values that furnish very good soil for the gospel and sometimes even contain the "seeds of the Word". I experienced some of these values on my trips, and the bishops during their 1998 synod mentioned a number of them, as, for example, love of silence and contemplation, simplicity, harmony and conformity, nonviolence, a respect for life and compassion for every living being, a spirit of tolerance for other religions, a plurality of religions and cultures, a spiritual intuition and a form of moral knowledge, a great thirst for spiritual values and modest material aims, the honor of parents and ancestors, and a deep sense of family.

Jesus Christ has a right of domicile in Asia, as does His Church alongside Him. On this continent He became flesh and was born an Asian. He founded His Church in Asia, and from Asia He sent His apostles to proclaim the Good News to the entire world and gather the faithful into local Church communities. The Church spread from Jerusalem to Antioch, to Rome and Europe, to Ethiopia and Africa, and, according to tradition, to India with Saint Thomas. Armenia received Christianity in the third century, and toward the end of the fifth century, the kingdoms of Arabia and China were introduced to the gospel. In the early years of the seventh century, the first church building in China was erected, but after two centuries, the Church declined in that country. Even the new wave of evangelization in China, Mongolia, and Turkey that commenced during the thirteenth century did not last very long. At that time, Islam started to employ its military power in Asia. More conspicuous missionary efforts were made possible by the Portuguese sailing ships that missionaries such as Saint Francis Xavier used for their transportation. The Roman Congregation then known as *Propaganda Fide* began to organize mission work as of the seventeenth century. Through the efforts of this Congregation, Catholic groups were established in India, Sri Lanka, Bangladesh, Vietnam, and Japan. In China, the mission was greatly influenced and enhanced by the Jesuit Matteo Ricci. But the internal Church controversy regarding the Chinese rites, and a poor application of Roman directives regarding enculturation, caused grave damage in missionary development there. The Philippines were evangelized by Spain. The progress of Catholic missions in several countries, especially in India, Sri Lanka, Indonesia, and in Japan, was later disrupted by rivalry among European colonial powers that sought riches and control of the seas. The blood of martyrs in Japan, the Philippines, China, Korea, Vietnam, and Thailand fertilized the spiritual soil of Asia at various times in history and helped local Church communities to take root despite the small numbers of faithful. Since the fall of communism in central Asia, namely, in Mongolia, Siberia, and in five of the former Soviet republics, new possibilities for evangelization have emerged. Asia is still waiting for the harvest of Christ the Savior, whom the bishops of the continent have declared to be "a gift to Asia".

The entire Church needs to remember the commission and command of the risen Lord: to go out into the world and to teach all nations, including those with ancient religions. The Lord supports, and is present in, missionary work, as we read in the gospel according to Saint Matthew (28:18–20) and in other parts of Scripture. Evangelization can have different forms, but it will not be complete without open proclamation that Jesus is Lord: "'Every one who calls upon the name of the Lord will be saved.' But how are men to call upon him in whom they have not believed? And how are they to believe in him of whom they have never heard? And how are they to hear without a preacher?" (Rom 10: 13–14). The gospel is the greatest service that the Church can offer to the nations. Of course, the gospel needs to find its witness in the life of the missionary. When Jesus Christ is announced, a Christian only *announces* the gospel. He does not impose it because we cannot force the faith, which must be received freely. However, respect for freedom of conscience does not exclude proclaiming the gospel in its entirety. In the presence of the ancient and rich cultures and religions of Asia, we have to stress the words of Pope Paul VI: "Neither respect nor esteem for these religions, nor the complexity of the questions raised is an invitation to the Church to withhold from these non-Christians the proclamation of Jesus Christ" (*Evangelii nuntiandi*, no. 53). While Jesus Christ is announced as our Lord and Savior, especially in Asia, we have to progress through dialogue and enculturation, which means to implant the gospel in the local culture.

Asia was one of the destinations of my numerous visits, especially after the Holy Father gave me responsibility for evangelization. During my missionary service, I accompanied Pope John Paul II on all his

trips to the continent of Asia. My personal pastoral trips allowed me
to penetrate deeper into the different regions and to interest myself
more closely in the different cultures, religions, and ways of thinking.
I was able to know countries, governments, and the people. Because
of the political situation, however, I was not able to get into China.
Vietnam refused to grant me the required visa. Cambodia and Laos
also remained as unfulfilled points of my program, as did the former
Soviet republics, with the sole exception of Kazakhstan. My trip to
remote Siberia helped me to understand the manner in which people
live in the former parts of the Soviet Union. I still desire to visit Mongolia, where I established a mission, which after ten years was elevated
to a prefecture apostolic.

As I continue this part of my memoirs, I am convinced, along with
John Paul II and the bishops of Asia, that "the nations of Asia are in need
of Jesus Christ and his gospel, because this continent is thirsting for living water, which can be given only by Christ" (*The Church in Asia*, no. 50).

To make matters easier, it seems most appropriate to divide Asia
into cultural-religious regions, which are almost homogeneous and inte-
grated, but not always without their ambiguities. We will begin with
the part closest to Europe, where the culture produced by Islam pre-
vails. In contrast, geographical terms do not express the same meaning
in all languages. For example, the meaning of the common term "Middle East" for a particular part of Asia, varies according to the location
of the one making the observation. Similarly, for the Japanese, the
"Far East" is near and the "Near East" far away, contrary to the European view. Our chiefly religious interest therefore suggests the above
division. Each division, however, will require a brief description of its
ancient religion and culture.

1. Western Asia and Islamic Territory

Islam currently acts as a unifying force in the religious and cultural life
of the lands of western and southeastern Asia. Islam originated as a
religious movement in Arabia at the beginning of the seventh century.
It was founded by a peddler, Mohammed (570–632), who was familiar
with the Jewish and Christian sacred books and who desired that the
Arabs have one as well. According to Mohammed's testimony, God
Himself sent His word of revelation, or "Koran", wherein the earlier

teachings of prophets such as Moses, Abraham, and even Jesus, were readjusted. Mohammed proclaimed his teachings to the members of his own pagan tribe in Mecca, but after being expelled by them, he moved to nearby Medina, where he organized a religious-political society. The foundation of Islam is held to date from the time Mohamed left Mecca in 622. Several years afterward he took over Mecca, where he reigned as "caliph", or God's representative, until his death in 632.

The Koran is absolutely monotheistic, and its main profession of faith is "There is no god but Allah (God), and Mohammed is his prophet." Muslims believe in angels, consider Mohammed as the last and greatest prophet, and believe in the Koran as God's direct word. Muslims also believe in man's predestination, which nevertheless does not eliminate personal freedom. They believe in a final judgment and in everlasting life, in paradise, and even in hell. Believers, besides professing the faith, must also say their ritual prayers five times a day, give alms, and fast during the month of Ramadan. Shiite Muslims have added the concept of "jihad", namely, an effort or battle for the protection of Islam. This is interpreted by some as a spiritual fight, and by others as a real "holy war", where death is the equivalent of martyrdom and guarantees one immediate entrance into paradise. The word *Islam* means submission to the will of an almighty and merciful God. Muslims honor God with their prayer beads, whereon they repeat ninety-nine times his name and attributes. I found it a source of encouragement when I read these litanies on an old pulpit in Isfahan, in Iran, inscribed there for the honor and praise of God. It was the same emotion that I have experienced in public places, such as the train stations in Paris or Rome, when at their prayer times Muslims spread their carpets in front of everyone. Islam considers obedience to God and to his law, Shariah, as obligatory, as is the extension of this law to all of society. Islam makes no distinction between civil and religious rules, or even between secular and religious "powers". A certain Muslim ambassador tried to persuade me that religion must enforce its laws and rules through police power, as well as assume the political leadership of society. Islam actually fosters *umma*, or community, which imparts a feeling of bondedness with believers in different countries and regions. Its program is not solely religious and spiritual, but also social and political. It is rendered visible by service to one's neighbor, but can sometimes be very aggressive. Only in some territories has Islam preserved its tolerance and acceptance toward believers of other religions.

After the death of Mohammed, Islam spread rapidly, mostly by the sword and political power, but also with spiritual weapons. Before the year 700, the caliphs took over Syria, Palestine, Egypt, Iran, Afghanistan, and even some parts of North Africa. In the following centuries, they took over Iraq and the greater part of Spain. From the eleventh to the fifteenth centuries, Islam gradually displaced the Byzantine Empire, with the Ottomans settling in Turkey and extending their control through the Balkans as far as the Danube. After their defeat at Vienna in 1683, Muslim armies withdrew from the area, but their followers remained strong in the Balkans. In Turkey in the twentieth century, the government of Kemal Atatürk established a secular Islamic state. From the fifteenth to the eighteenth centuries, Islam took over Pakistan and Bangladesh and, passing through Malaysia, made its way to Indonesia, which is presently the most populous Islamic country. Islam actually found its way even to the southern Philippines. During the twentieth century, new Islamic countries were established, not only in Asia but also in Africa, and these have enshrined Shariah as state law. In Europe, the number of Muslims is growing, especially via new immigration and strong demographic growth. Some Muslims claim that they could not conquer Spain by sword, but that now they will be able take it over peacefully. Algerians and Moroccans more typically settle in France, while Germany is home to a large number of Turks.

Muslims are organized on the world stage. They have their own international centers and political power. Their oil fields and wealth, especially those of Arab countries, provide financial subsidies and other forms of assistance. The Al-Ahram University in Egypt is a cultural center that is largely dedicated to their missionary efforts. Pakistan and Somalia supply the university with their "missionaries", while local businessmen and politicians strongly support the spread of Islam throughout the entire world, especially through the construction of mosques in visible places and by establishing religious centers and schools.

The largest concentrations and centers of Islam are certainly in Asia. The Arabic language, in which the sacred Koran is written, as well as Arabic culture, have both deeply influenced Islam. Despite the fact that Islam claims to be a world religion, it is rooted not only in the culture, but also in Arabic traditions, which can be a good or a bad thing. For example, they show great solidarity with the followers of their own religion, but none at all with people of other faiths. Another example is their technical progress, which runs counter to their medieval feudalistic habits. On the one hand, they worship one almighty and merciful God, but on the other hand, they often create obstacles to the religious freedom of other monotheistic religions. Islam has adjusted only slightly to other cultures. Over the centuries, branches developed within Islam, of which we must mention two main groups: the Sunnis and the Shiites. Sunnis, with their traditions and customs, form the majority. Shiites originate with Ali, the first successor of Mohammed, and they submit to the authority of ayatollahs. Presently, most Shiites are concentrated in Iran, Iraq, and Afghanistan.

If we take a closer look at the countries bordering the Mediterranean, and if we consider the state of evangelization, we must leave to one side Israel, Palestine, Lebanon, Turkey, Syria, and Jordan, where Catholics of the Eastern Rites mostly reside, who are under the jurisdiction of the Roman Congregation for the Eastern Churches. These are mostly small groups, divided according to Rite and represented by their patriarchates. Most of them have their original ancient seats in these countries. Difficult societal and living conditions force many Christians to migrate, leaving these lands where Christian communities once used to flourish. We will therefore turn our attention to countries where the Catholic Church has missionary territories that depend on the Congregation for the Evangelization of Peoples. On the Arabian peninsula, these are the United Arab Emirates, Kuwait, and Bahrain. We must also mention the condition of larger groups of our faithful in Saudi Arabia, and smaller communities in Oman, Yemen, and Aden.

A flourishing Christian community existed on the Arabian peninsula in the first centuries after Christ. We possess some data from the fifth century on the evangelization of Yemen. Persecution by Muslims in the early seventh century caused the death of hundreds of martyrs. Experiments in proclaiming the gospel began in the nineteenth century from Aden, which then became the seat of a vicariate apostolic. The task of proclaiming the gospel in this vicariate, which covered the entire peninsula, was given over to Capuchin missionaries. The vicariate has remained in the hands of Capuchins and has its center in Abu Dhabi, United Arab Emirates. It cares for Saudi Arabia, the United Arab Emirates, Oman, Qatar, and all of Yemen. It formerly depended on the apostolic nunciature in Lebanon. Another small vicariate apostolic has jurisdiction over Kuwait and Bahrain. The Holy See recently established a nunciature for this vicariate apostolic, with its seat in Kuwait.

Kingdom of Saudi Arabia

Saudi Arabia is the largest Arabic country in terms of territory and has a population that is growing rapidly thanks to a high birth rate and a high influx of immigrants. The population has already reached 23 million. Of that total number, there are 800,000 Catholics, who are not allowed by the national government to express their faith in any

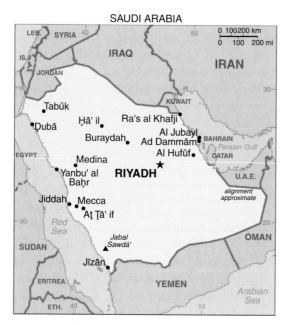

way. Not even a single chapel is permitted to exist, nor are there any priests. The importation of Bibles and other religious articles is strictly prohibited. The reason given is that the entire territory is "holy" by virtue of being the birthplace of Muhammad and as the land where he taught in Mecca and Medina. The state is highly intolerant, and no logical arguments to the contrary are accepted. Any such attempts will conclude with the punishment of the one offering the argument, and this for his so-called "infraction". Appeals for an application of reciprocity, equal to the freedom guaranteed to Muslims by Christians throughout Europe and other parts of the world, elicits no response.

United Arab Emirates

The nearby United Arab Emirates allows Christians to have at least a limited religious freedom, even if it is within the regime of Muslim law or Shariah.

Seven small territories on the Arabian Peninsula, known as "the coast of the pirates", established a common federation of hereditary monarchies. This is headed by a Supreme Council of Seven Emirs, who enjoy absolute power in their territories. They elect among themselves the president of the country. The population is rather sparse, about 3.5 million, but there is great growth, caused especially by an influx of workers from abroad.

In early November 1989, I dedicated five days to a visit to the region, and this at the invitation of the vicar apostolic, Capuchin Bishop Giovanni Gremoli. The fitting occasion for this trip was the dedication of a new church in Abu Dhabi, but I was also delivering a personal letter of John Paul II to the president, Sheik Zayed bin Sultan, who had his office in the same city. From every standpoint, it was a great experience for me. The airport is surrounded by a desert that changes to a rocky waste further inland. The real surprise is the asphalt highway, which is fenced on both sides and lined by street lamps and green bushes. These provide a beautiful contrast to the red sandy dunes. Adjacent to the city, a large factory can be spotted. In reality, it houses machinery for changing salt water into fresh, which can then be used in homes. The city itself has several hundred thousand inhabitants. We could see the villas of the wealthy, twenty-story-high skyscrapers, beautiful beaches, and lovely parks with green trees and flowers. All the plants in the city and along the highway are watered by an interesting sprinkler system, which has its pipes hidden underground and which constantly supplies the vegetation with moisture, drop by drop. The water flows by gravity from large cisterns in the mountains or on

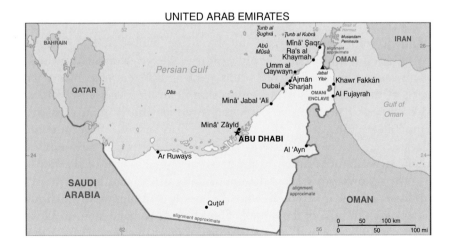

UNITED ARAB EMIRATES

elevated places. We are talking here about huge investments, which are subsidized by oil resources. The people praise the old Sheik Zayed because he built hospitals and provided very inexpensive health care. Of course, we have also to mention the construction of seven hundred nice, modern mosques. During the past twenty years, Abu Dhabi has become a modern city where the palaces of banks and international oil companies have risen, and where, on a lovely seashore along the Persian Gulf, people of different races and colors walk side by side. The streets are filled with comfortable cars and the parks with throngs of children at play.

The Catholic Church especially serves immigrants, those who arrived here as technicians, workers, maids, nurses, and members of similar professions. The emir allowed them to build several churches, but on the condition that these would be sufficiently hidden so as not to draw the attention of the public. I blessed a church that was built in the middle of the yard of the Catholic school complex. It was permitted to have neither a bell tower nor the symbol of the cross on the outside of the building. It had to be hidden behind a steel gate. On the other hand, right behind the walls of the complex, there stood the minarets of the neighboring mosque reaching high into the sky, and from which even the smallest movement on the church property could be observed. The church is modern and air-conditioned. During the dedication, every single place was filled by the faithful. All those who attended the ceremony were very happy and felt moved as they observed the evocative rites, especially as the altar, which is the symbol of the anointed Jesus Christ, was anointed with chrism and as incense was burnt upon it. This produced white aromatic smoke rising toward the sky as the symbol of our sacrifice to God. Also lovely was the procession of the offertory gifts, which were carried by children and adults wearing different costumes from each of the continents. After the solemn dedication and Mass, which two bishops concelebrated with me, everyone lined up to kiss my ring and pectoral cross. This took more than an hour to accomplish because all the people present, mindful of neither the time nor of their own fatigue, wanted to greet me, a representative of the Pope.

The following day I had the opportunity of greeting 1,350 school-children and their teachers, who are mostly Muslims. Five religious sisters are in charge of the school. The Muslims pressure them to allow their children to attend, out of the great respect that they have for the institution. This is an opportunity to work toward a future and quiet preparation for the gospel.

I dedicated an entire day to the visit of the remote parish of Al-Ain, where there is a small church and one priest for more than two thousand faithful. As we departed from Abu Dhabi, both sides of the highway were lined with oleanders, palms, and other shrubbery and, to a certain distance, even with street lamps. The highway cuts through the wasteland to Al-Ain, and its total length is about one hundred miles, fenced-in on both sides. This provides protection against camels, which we saw along the highway, some with their herders, and some without. The collision of a car with a camel, when the animal tries to run across the road, can result in a deadly accident. Most of the time, the camel ends up on the top of the car and, with its weight, crushes the roof down upon the driver. As we proceeded inland, we passed large water tanks nestled on high dunes, and also several small villages with neatly built mosques. After a number of curves, the road started to climb the mountain Jabel Hafit. We got to around 2,600 feet above sea level, where the area consisted of rocky mountain slopes, devoid of any vegetation. On the top was a wire fence, built by the sultan of Oman to mark the boundary of his country. From that point the highway started to descend, and in the distance we saw the oasis of the Sultanate of Oman. The view was not the best, because the hot air rising over the scorched earth created a shimmering sort of effect. Nevertheless, my camera was able to film the flight of the white falcon and other birds. On our return trip, we watched drilling operations—ones seeking not oil but water, which has a higher value in this part of the world.

My special experience consisted of meeting the emir in Abu Dhabi. He received me in his palace. He had just returned from his weekly hunting trip. As he entered the long chamber with his hunting falcon, he gave the trained bird to his servants. He listened attentively to my greeting in English, which one of his interpreters translated into Arabic. My greeting was short and consisted mostly of my commentary on the personal letter of the Holy Father in which the Pope appealed for help in achieving peace in Lebanon. A skeletal-looking Bedouin carefully read the letter from the Pope written in Arabic. After the Bedouin read the letter, the emir began to talk. In his own longer speech, he explained to me his views on Allah's engagement in man's history. With amazement, I listened to this son of the desert, and the faith and depth with which he described the history of salvation as he understood it. Taken simply, his speech could be summarized as follows: God created men not only because of His love, but also because He accompanies them in every age. He sends various messengers to keep mankind on the course of truth, justice, and peace. These messengers, however, have to suffer because of their deeds. And here, he concluded his speech in an unexpected way: that, in our own times, we have just this sort of messenger and prophet for all of mankind in the person of John Paul II. This kind of reasoned explanation from the mouth of a Muslim leader, I had never heard before. At our farewell, I thanked the emir for having granted permission to build several churches, even though this was to be done under certain restrictions. I also promised him that I would inform the Holy Father of his reception and greetings.

The emir of Dubai was sick, and so I was received by one of his sons, who was a member of the government. It was a purely courteous and formal meeting. In Dubai, I was able to admire stores with all kinds of merchandise, and a 1,900-foot-long tunnel passing under the canal and leading to the sea. There were some modern and some older homes. Some of the latter have a tower on top, featuring several chimneylike openings. These serve to catch the wind, which then descends inside the house to cool the living quarters. The proof of the variety of the Dubai marketplace was a decoratively stitched tablecloth from my native country of Slovakia, which was purchased and given to me by Bishop Gremoli. Clearly, one can see that Arabic businessmen do not travel the world for nothing.

Overall, the situation in Arabia is challenging. Like the United Arab Emirates, in nearby Kuwait and Bahrain, the coexistence of the Christian faithful with a Muslim leadership and people, although not easy, is nonetheless possible. But in Saudi Arabia, it is nonexistent and forbidden. They go so far as to have passengers who are passing through Riyadh Airport dispose of any alcoholic beverages and magazines printed in color, even though these people are not even getting off the plane. Is this kind of forced morality sincere? And, from the point of view of international law, is this system of exclusion and suppression of other religions even allowed? When I asked this question of a certain Muslim representative for human rights at the United Nations, he just hesitatingly smiled. But these sorts of things happen in the name of God.

Faithful Catholics are also to be found in the famous port of Aden. There is a church here that the local people have made their own. The situation in this country is difficult as well. Mother Teresa's sisters and the Salesians of Saint John Bosco were allowed to enter Yemen, because of their social and educational work. And in Oman, there is a Catholic priest serving the faithful.

Islamic Republic of Pakistan and People's Republic of Bangladesh

We must now skip over three mostly Islamic countries: only small groups of Christians of the Eastern Rites reside in Iraq and Iran, and in Afghanistan, no groups of Christians are registered at all. It is a different story in Pakistan, where a relatively strong Catholic Church coexists with a strong Islamic presence. Islam has spread even into India, where the number of its followers has reached over 100 million. It is the main religion in Bangladesh, which was united with Pakistan until 1971. A military dictatorship controls Pakistan, and Islamic law, or Shariah, is in force. Almost 60 percent of the population is illiterate.

Pakistan is a large country. Its population is growing fast and has now already reached 150 million, most of whom are Muslim. The number of Catholics stands at over 1.2 million. They are organized into two archdioceses, Karachi and Lahore, and five dioceses. Missionary efforts began in this area in the seventeenth century. The missionaries in the northern region were Jesuits, and those in the south

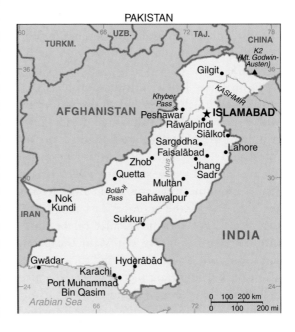

were Augustinians and Carmelites. Cruel persecutions put an end to the missions by the end of the seventeenth century. Only by the end of nineteenth century did the Carmelites attempt once again to proclaim the gospel, with the Jesuits from Bombay joining them. This created good soil for the establishment of the vicariate apostolic in the northern province of Punjab. In 1950, a hierarchy was established with an archdiocese in Karachi. In 1956, the country adopted an Islamic constitution, and the same year, the Bible was published for the first time in the Urdu language. Two years later, the first native bishop, Joseph Cordeiro, was ordained Archbishop of Karachi. In 1973, he became a cardinal. Paul VI visited this country in 1981. At the time I had a flight connection at Karachi airport on my way to Sri Lanka. Right after the Pope's departure, I learned of a small explosion, to which nobody had paid very much attention.

I made a longer pastoral visit to this country in early December of 1994. I started in the city of Karachi, where I stayed in the modestly furnished seminary next to the cathedral. There I admired two rooms that had once been occupied by my good friend Cardinal Cordeiro, who was deceased by the time of my visit. He was a highly intelligent and holy bishop, an excellent co-worker of the universal Church. He was a man well known in the world, but at the same time one who was very humble and poor. This was made evident by the two rooms at the seminary where he lived. The only furnishings were a wooden desk and chair, an old and not very stable cabinet, a metal bed, and an old sink.

From there, I flew into the northern part of the country, which is called the Punjab. It reaches all the way to the Himalaya Mountains of Kashmir, over which Pakistan and India have a long-standing dispute. Although the Himalayas beckoned to me, my obligations brought me into Lahore, the capital city of this region and its surrounding dioceses. There I blessed a new seminary, which was built through the efforts of Italian Dominican Bishop Paolo Andreotti, the zealous missionary of this area. During the outdoor Mass next to the cathedral, I later ordained ten priests. It was a spectacular celebration with the readings in the Urdu language. During the Mass, the parents of these men brought their sons to the altar and offered them to the Lord as priests. The governor of this important region prepared a nice reception for me, which included a luncheon and music by a chamber orchestra. During my visit to the old mosque, the principal imam welcomed me.

I do not know what the agenda of the government was by offering these kinds of gestures, but the fact still remains that in the capital city, Islamabad, I was received by the minister of "justice and law". I was a little surprised by his unusual title, which almost made distinctions between the law and justice, but my main purpose was to express the concern of the Holy See over the consequences of the law against "blasphemy", which was clearly aimed against Christians. For clarification, if any Muslim accused anyone of an offense, not only against Allah, but even against "the Prophet" (Mohammed), the accused person must be put to death. Furthermore, only one Muslim witness was sufficient to prove the accusation. This law became an easy instrument for personal vengeance and for obtaining the property of the accused. Right before my arrival, a certain convicted Christian successfully escaped over the border. This unjust and cruel law was requested mostly by fanatical imams, who can easily convince illiterate members of their congregations to make false accusations. Christians were trying, at the very least, for a fair hearing, and for it to be proven that an "offense against God" had really been committed. They were unsuccessful, however, because angry people were able to kill any judge who had the courage to free a Christian. The minister understood well my complaints, and he was aware of the international scandal that the government had brought upon itself. In reality, he could only promise me that he would clarify some court procedures. It seems that even this small compromise did not help him because later on he was expelled from the government. ·

Islamabad is a diplomatic city, where foreign ambassadors reside, as well as the apostolic nuncio with whom I stayed. Here, I went to visit an expensive beautiful mosque, built in a modern style. Later, during the celebration of Mass, the faithful in attendance were all residents of the capital and most were well educated. I preached about the role of the laity in the world. The local diocese has the double name of Islamabad and Rwalpindi, with the bishop having his see in the latter city. Bishop Anthony Lobo oversees Catholic education throughout all of Pakistan, especially in his own diocese. I blessed property for a new high school and a type of minor seminary. I returned to Rome with the entire collection of wreaths with which I had been honored in this country.

The difficulties of Christians in Pakistan continue to this day, as the bloody attacks from fanatic Muslim groups confirm. Many faithful have lost their lives in those attacks. Despite all these facts, the Catholic

BANGLADESH

Church goes forward, thanks to missionary efforts among the partly nomadic people in the western regions near the border with Afghanistan.

Until 1971, Pakistan and *Bangladesh* were united as one country, despite the fact that their territory was divided by India. It is also the case in Bangladesh that Muslims are in the majority. Among the 141 million people of Bangladesh, only 10 percent are Hindu, and Catholics number only around 291,000. Our Catholics are under the jurisdiction of six bishops, headed by the archbishop of the capital city, Dhaka. Evangelization began in the sixteenth century by Jesuits, Dominicans, and Augustinians. They came to Bangladesh from Goa in India, passing through the Bay of Bengal, but they did not get inland. The vicariate apostolic was founded in 1834 and was named Bengala. In 1850, the mission in the area was conducted by the Fathers of the Holy Cross. By 1950, a hierarchy was established for this territory, with an archdiocesan see in Dhaka. Overall, it is a poor country with rapid demographic growth, frequent floods, and high mortality. Additional missionaries have arrived in recent years, most notably from Italy.

On November 19, 1986, John Paul II made a stop in Bangladesh during his sixteen-day trip to Asia and Oceania, while I was in his company. We had left Rome the previous evening and spent the entire night on the plane that was heading directly to Bangladesh. As we flew over Dhaka, we were able to see the huge delta of the Ganges River, whose mouth flows into the Bay of Bengal and which, during the monsoon season, causes significant flooding. It was already ten o'clock in the morning when, after a short rest, we began a long working schedule that kept us on our feet up until midnight. At five the next morning, they came to load our luggage for the next flight to Singapore. A humorous co-worker of mine made the remark that, with the Holy Father, we have a wonderful division of labor: he worked tirelessly, but it was we who felt tired. This situation was even more pronounced because of jet lag. From this visit, I only remember the crowds of people and the usual meetings with pastoral assistants and laity, those with representatives of other religions and others with the diplomatic corps and military government. Already at that time I spoke with the bishops about the possibility of establishing a new diocese, something that later became a reality. I promised myself a later visit to this country, which is rich in population, floods, and poverty, but my desire during the sixteen years of my prefecture was not fulfilled.

Malaysia

The strip of Islamic countries bordering the Indian Ocean continues with Malaysia, which has about 25 million inhabitants. Of these, 53 percent are Muslims, 24 percent are Buddhists and Hindus, and 796,000 are Catholics. Despite the noticeable presence of different ethnic groups, Islam is trying to develop a strong influence over the government. We are talking here about thirteen federated states, whose leaders, both elected and hereditary, choose among themselves the head of the entire federation for a five-year term. Malaysia is a member of the British

MALAYSIA

Commonwealth, and it has its own parliament and senate. The country consists of two parts, one of which is located on the Malay Peninsula and the other along the north coast of the island of Borneo. The southernmost part of Borneo is included in the territory of Indonesia. Thanks to its natural resources such as oil fields, as well as a fast-growing industry, Malaysia is a relatively wealthy country. The capital city, Kuala Lumpur, surprises every foreigner with its modern architecture, road system, and parks.

Mission work by Portuguese missionaries began on the southern part of the Malay Peninsula in the sixteenth century. This area was traversed by Saint Francis Xavier and other missionaries. A prefecture apostolic was established at Malacca in 1558. An important point in history was reached when French missionaries of the "Missions Etrangères de Paris" built a major seminary in 1808 in Penang (Pulau Pinang). With this, the education of a native presbyterate could begin. When the hierarchy was established in 1955, it was possible to name two native bishops in Malaysia. All of the eight dioceses are now headed by native bishops, including two archbishops in Kuala Lumpur and Kuching.

My first visit to Malaysia was very brief, made during a one-day layover in Singapore, when I was traveling to Papua New Guinea in 1993. The time necessary for the layover afforded an excellent opportunity for visiting the city. Arrangements for a short but excellent visit were kindly provided by Archbishop Gregory Yong Sooi Ngean, who is of Chinese descent. Besides arranging for me to meet a group of faithful in the cathedral, he also prepared a visit to a nearby recreational island, where we were transported by cable car over an active seaport. That green island acts like the lungs of the city. On it were located parks and entertainment centers for young and old. There was a replica of an original house from the Malaysian region and a beach for swimming. Besides all this, visitors could enjoy a panoramic ride on an electric monorail train, which circles the island on tall pillars. The main square of the town is filled with fountains, of which the highlight is an imitation of the Tivoli Fountain in Rome. At certain times of the day, the high waterfalls and streams ebb and flow like charming dancers, creating an endless symphony for eye and ear, and all done to the tune of the famous *Doctor Zhivago* theme song. Magnificent colorful orchids offered further delights to me and for my camera. This city of 4.2 million people definitely needs such a place for rest and relaxation. Our Catholics there number only 166,000. Many are of Chinese origin and display a vigorous faith.

I scheduled a more substantial visit to Malaysia as part of a longer trip to south-central Asia in August of 1995. Right after my arrival from Bangkok, I visited a Catholic school named after Jean-Baptiste de La Salle, the founder of the Brothers of the Christian Schools. Malaysia used to have excellent Catholic schools, but Muslims in power forced these to have Muslim principals. Accompanied by the nuncio in Bangkok, who also has jurisdiction over Malaysia, I visited the local archbishop and took a tour of the modern city. I went to see several Hindu, Islamic, and even Chinese temples. Among the temples of the city, a modern and very beautiful mosque stands out, which cost around a hundred million dollars. Also quite interesting was our visit to a place of Hindu pilgrimage near the city, where a cave containing a temple forms part of a rocky hillside. The long, wide steps leading to the temple were filled with thousands of Hindu pilgrims on foot. On the level ground near the top of the mountain, there were tents belonging to merchants selling food, Indian sweets, flowers, and religious articles. The colorful crowd included dark-skinned girls who had woven flowers into their hair, playful children, and circles of families and friends—all of whom afforded a great opportunity to my camera. At the same time, however, it was a testimony to the revitalization of Hinduism in this area. The Catholic cathedral, where I celebrated Mass that evening, engendered a more European impression.

The next stop on my visit was the town of Semerang in the northern part of the country. The aforementioned major seminary, or "Collège Général", was located here and had just been augmented with some new buildings. The seminary was established by French missionaries for students from Malaysia, and also from Thailand, Cambodia, and Laos. The order left behind a nice foundation for the upkeep of the complex. The seminary has already produced many native priests for the whole region.

My visit to the Diocese of Melaka-Johor was also very interesting, especially from the historical point of view, because it was a port for sailors and an important entry point for missionaries. It is very nicely situated across from Singapore.

The island portion of Malaysia, called Sarawak, has also a Catholic population in the Archdiocese of Kuching and in three other dioceses. The Archbishop of Kuching, as are many Catholics in the area, is of

Chinese ancestry. The influence of Chinese traditions is very much in evidence here in the style of buildings, on the old entrance gate to the city, and in the faces of the people as well. But even here, a grand new mosque was not lacking.

Malaysia gave me the impression of a well-organized Church, but nevertheless one that needs more enthusiasm and *élan* in its life and one that could give better and more visible witness in this challenging region.

Republic of Indonesia and Democratic Republic of East Timor

Indonesia is a nation composed of 17,508 islands, extending 3,100 miles east to west. Eighty-seven percent of Indonesians are Muslims. With a population of 217 million, this makes Indonesia the most populous Islamic state in the world. All Christians taken together represent 9.6 percent of the people, and the number of Catholics is 6,477,000, or over 3 percent of the entire population. The rest of the population is composed of smaller percentages of Hindus, Buddhists, and pagan animists. After long years of Dutch colonial rule, Indonesia declared its independence in 1945 and won it in 1949. The first president, Achmed Sukarno, was relieved of his presidential duties in 1966 during an uprising led by Major General Mohammed Suharto. The latter banned the Communist Revolutionary Party and established a united political power with "Pancasila" as the state philosophy and ideology, which was itself founded on certain fundamental principles. He legalized five religions, including Catholicism. However, he did not allow foreign missionaries to enter the country, unless they were specialists in some field of service. Otherwise, he ruled with authority, until he was forced to resign from office in 1998. In 1975, after the departure of Portuguese colonial authorities from East Timor, the area was occupied by the military of Indonesia. West Timor had become part of Indonesia upon the departure of Dutch colonial authorities in 1949. In a United Nations–sponsored referendum, East Timor chose independence in 1999. This new state has only 824,000 people, almost all of whom are Catholics.

The missionary history of Indonesia is very moving. There are some reports of Catholic missionaries on the island of Sumatra from the seventh century, and on the island of Java from the ninth. More effective missionary efforts began with the Jesuits, Dominicans, and

INDONESIA

Franciscans in the early sixteenth century. Subsequent occupation by the Netherlands brought in Calvinists who were intent on destroying the Catholic missions. The only ones to survive were those on the Island of Flores and others in East Timor, which the occupying power did not reach. Independence actually helped the Catholic Church, because it encouraged the education of native clergy, who could then slowly replace the declining numbers of missionaries from Holland and other countries. Jesuits began to establish smaller Catholic universities, of whom there are currently eleven in existence. In 1961, Rome organized a hierarchy with three Church provinces. There are now thirty-six dioceses. In East Timor, there are two.

I visited this interesting country for the first time with John Paul II in October of 1989, as we returned from the Eucharistic Congress in South Korea. It was not merely a stop, because our visit lasted five days and covered Djakarta, Jogdjakarta, Flores, East Timor, and even Medan in the northern part of Sumatra. I would like to share only a few recollections of this visit as well as to describe very briefly some experiences from my later personal visit on the occasion of the gathering of the bishops' conference of Asia in 1990 in Bandung.

Together with the Holy Father, we arrived in the city of Djakarta on October 9, 1989. Our first appointment was with President Suharto in his presidential palace. The president and the entire government were waiting for us. While John Paul II had a personal talk with the president, we were tended to by the minister for foreign affairs. I had known the minister because for several years I had negotiated with him over the entry of missionaries into the country. He was a well-educated Muslim who, even after his visit to my house in Rome, very politely and with no compromises, continued to deny my request. He supported his decision by arguing that if Catholic missionaries were allowed to enter, fanatical Muslims from other countries would have to be allowed in as well. The local bishops, after unsuccessful negotiations, looked for their own "Indonesian solution", which, while not based on theoretical principles, would nonetheless attempt to bypass certain authorities. In fact, with the help of the ambassador of the Holy See, we were able to obtain visas for several religious sisters and some missionaries but under different titles.

As we continued our trip, the Pilgrim from Rome chose very appropriate topics for his speeches, for example: the faithfulness of citizens to the state and the role of Catholic universities (in Djakarta), the Church as a supporter of culture (in Jogdjakarta), the laity in social collaboration (in Medan), and the participation of laity in the life of the Church (in East Timor). As I was told by the Archbishop of Djakarta, the schedule and themes of this visit were suggested by lay people, who were the main organizers of this visit.

Two parts of this trip were particularly interesting for me. First was the Island of Flores, where my countrymen from Slovakia, the Missionaries of the Divine Word, had served for many years. I knew them personally from their studies in Rome, and through the magazine *Voices from the Missions*. At the time of my visit, I met with Father Vojenčiak, whom, after his retirement, I named to be the director of the Pontifical Missions' Society of Slovakia. Other missionaries whom I met included Fathers Gális, Krčmár, Števko, and Hudec. Fathers Lechovič, Kližan, Černaj, and Brother Šebastián Šoltés used to work there as well. After the memorable celebration of Mass near the airport, we left with the missionaries in their vehicles. By taking a mountain road, we arrived on the top of the hill where two flourishing seminaries stand, the one not far from the other. The first is for diocesan clergy and the second for the Missionaries of the Divine Word. Along the way, we could see entire families gathered around images of the Most Sacred Heart or the Virgin Mary. People live in poverty, but they are rich in their faith, in the number of vocations, and in human values. The results of many years of hard work on the part of German, Dutch, and Slovak missionaries were very much in evidence. Each of the two seminaries had over four hundred students—all candidates for the priesthood. It brought to my mind possibilities for new mission-aries from Slovakia. At that time, since the Iron Curtain still existed in Europe, it was only a dream, but look what happened just a few years later! It was already evening when I had the opportunity to introduce my countrymen from Slovakia to the Holy Father.

The second, much-anticipated part of this trip consisted of a visit to East Timor, where the Indonesian army of occupation sorely oppressed both the local people and the rebels in the hills. We flew from Flores to the capital city, Dili, on a type of army plane called the "Hercules". After we landed, the Holy Father was not allowed to kiss the soil, because the international status of East Timor had not yet been resolved. When we arrived at the cathedral, he asked to have the cross for veneration placed on the ground and he kissed it together with the soil. After that, in a large outdoor space, he cel-ebrated Mass. As Holy Communion was beginning to be distributed, several young men suddenly ran into the center aisle, which was protected by police, and opened their signs calling for a "Free Timor". By the time the Indonesian policemen realized what was going on, the young men were already in the middle of the front rows. Here the experience of our Vatican security services was in evidence: four of our men were able to stop them, and the Mass could continue without any further distractions. The entire incident was viewed in Djakarta, as well as in Lisbon, which was still interested in their old colony. In a 1999 referendum, people clearly expressed their desire for independence, even though, because of the unsettled situation, two hundred thousand people had fled to West Timor and many others had been killed. An unsettled situation persists as well in another region occupied by the Indonesian military, the western part of New Guinea, or Irian Jaya. Also in the Molucca Islands, local Muslims are violently expelling Christians, who in turn blame the army and the government for the situation.

The Catholic Church has a relatively difficult life in this ethni-cally, racially, religiously, and politically complex country, but the Church here continues its mission work through dialogue. Despite the small number of faithful, the Church has a relatively large influ-ence in the area of culture and public life, thanks to its schools and universities. Missionaries need to confront hostile Muslims more often. At the same time, the Church cannot neglect to proclaim the gospel of Christ wherever this is possible. This needs to be done

Indonesia, Diocese of Bandung: Blessing of the Grotto of Our Lady of Lourdes

appropriately through initial evangelization, enculturation, dialogue, and by loyal adherence to the resolutions of the Synod of Bishops for Asia.

2. Region of Hindu and Buddhist Cultures

The cultures of large sections of Asia are influenced by the ancient religion of Hinduism and the related religion of Buddhism. Hinduism is spread throughout India, Nepal, Bhutan, and the shores of the Bay of Bengal. Buddhists form the majority of the population in Sri Lanka, Thailand, Myanmar, Singapore, and the former Indochina (Vietnam, Laos, Cambodia). It can also be found in China, Taiwan, and in Japan in the form of Shinto.

For our purposes, we need to refer to a brief citation on Hinduism from the Vatican II Declaration *Nostra aetate*: "Thus in Hinduism, men contemplate the divine mystery and express it through an inexhaustible abundance of myths and through searching philosophical inquiry. They seek freedom from the anguish of our human condition either through ascetical practices, or profound meditation, or a flight to God with love and trust" (no. 2).

Hindu temples are filled with pictures and statues of gods with animal features—as, for example, the god Ganesh with the head of an elephant—or others with human faces. Hinduism is familiar, however, with a certain explanation of monotheism, according to which there are only different name forms for the same Divine Being. All of creation is in a constant process of conception, development, and destruction, and this is an emanation of the Deity. Men are composed of a spiritual, immortal soul and a body, which is material, temporary, and subject to decay. Every human act brings a recompense in the next life or lives, even in those lives lower than human life. This is a strict law of incarnation and reincarnation. Hinduism has adopted many Christian values but is itself divided into two main branches: one conservative and intolerant, the other more open and accepting. At present in India, political power is held by a nationalistic party that is inspired

India, Agra: The Famous Hindu Temple

by the first religious branch and unjustly creates obstacles for Christians and Muslims. Because of this, the spirit of tolerance and coexistence is disappearing, contrary to the teaching of Hinduism that has always considered all religions as rivers that flow equally into the sea of Absoluteness. In other words, they are thought to bear salvation and freedom equally.

Some Catholic theologians have tried to explain the Christian faith on the basis of Hindu thought, but have rarely done so with any great success. The Holy See, in its Declaration *Dominus Jesus*, points out that only Jesus Christ is the Son of God and the Savior of all people. It is He Who has revealed the truth about God and Who has redeemed us, as we say in the Profession of Faith. Attempts at enculturation, which means the rooting of the faith in some other culture, is very difficult and delicate work. If not successful, the gospel may end up being "corrected" or even changed.

Republic of India

India is the cradle of Hinduism, which developed in the second millennium before Christ. The long history of the country, of

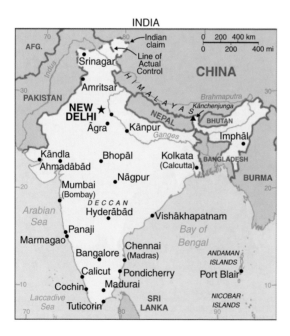

which Indians are very proud, explains why Hinduism is so diverse in its teachings and forms, and why it lacks a central teaching authority to maintain a unity of faith. India covers a vast, triangular-shaped peninsula that commences at the Himalayas and tapers to a southern point in the Indian Ocean. The population is growing fast, having reached more than 1.08 billion, which is over one-sixth of the world's inhabitants. Of the entire number, 81 percent are Hindu, 12 percent are Muslims, 2 percent are Sikhs, and 1 percent are Buddhists. There are over 17.6 million Catholics, which includes a small Malankara Church of Chaldean origin and a larger group, of the Syro-Malabar Church. The total number of dioceses is 156. The social differences in India are great, and in the big cities, poverty makes the situation of the local people even worse. The official languages are Hindi and English, but in different regions other languages such as Tamil, Telugu, Bengali, Marathi, and Malayalam are also used.

I visited India twice with Pope John Paul II. The first time was in 1986, when the people of India, unmindful of religious differences, admiringly and enthusiastically welcomed the Pope as a "White Guru". The trip was rich in events and speeches. In the capital city, Delhi, after the solemn Mass in the cathedral, we attended a cultural event in the stadium where representatives of different religions delivered speeches. The Holy Father gave a very important talk about the relations of the Church with other religions and about dialogue and a proclamation of the gospel that can legitimately bring a person to conversion. We said prayers by the grave of Mahatma Gandhi. In the wall, next to the tombstone, was carved a quotation from this deeply religious warrior against violence. It enumerated the seven "sins of society": politics without rules, wealthy lifestyle without working for it, pleasure without conscience, intelligence without character, trade without moral principles, science without humanity, and success without sacrifice.

At the airport near Ranchi, we later met different tribes among whom the evangelization process continues despite obstacles and persecution from the followers of Hinduism. Also memorable was the visit to the "House of Peaceful Death" in Calcutta where we were received by Mother Teresa. As we were passing by the elderly, sick, or even dying people, for whom she cared with her religious sisters, we could sense her heroic love, fed by Christian faith. Calcutta is a large city and is full of people, but a place of great poverty as well.

From there, we flew to the border state of Assam, and from the plane, we could admire the mountain ranges of the Himalayas covered with snow. There were hundreds of thousands of local people from the mountains who came to attend the Mass with John Paul II, and some of them had traveled for an entire week. In this area, evangelization is successful, thanks to the Salesians, the Divine Word

Missionaries, and the Holy Cross Fathers. From the cold north, we returned to the tropical part of the country where John Paul II celebrated the Eucharist for one and half million people on the seashore at Madras. Only one-fifth of the crowd were Christians. From Madras, we flew south to the warm state of Kerala, where the majority of Indian Christians reside, both of the Eastern and Western Rites. We visited a site where people believe that the body of Saint Thomas the Apostle to be buried. According to local tradition, Saint Thomas brought Christ's teaching all the way to this place. As we returned north, we visited the city of Goa, which used to be the point of entry for missionaries to India in the seventeenth and eighteenth centuries. Toward the end of the visit, we met with large crowds of people from western India in Bombay, currently renamed Mumbai. Our final official stop on this eventful trip was a meeting in a large park with young people of different religions.

At the end of this trip, there was a surprise awaiting us in Italy. The Roman airport was closed due to a heavy snowfall, and we had to land in Naples around midnight. We were cold while a special train was being prepared to take us to Rome. Its heating system did not end up functioning. Along the way, conductors had to warm up frozen track switches. It was a media sensation that ended at the Trastevere Station in Rome, where our special train arrived. Rome was covered with snow, which made its way into my shoes as I walked home with my luggage to the Janiculum. I ended up with a minor cold.

The purpose of the second shorter visit with the Holy Father in fall of 1999 was to publicize the report of the Bishops' Synod for Asia. The government, the official media, and some Hindus were very reserved and cold toward the Pope, even showing open enmity. The reason was the so-called "proselytism" of the Catholic Church, and the attitude that considered each conversion to the Catholic faith (but not in the opposite direction) to be a moral aggression. The Holy Father, during his meeting with the representatives of other religions, clearly explained the Catholic position, and later he received public recognition from all the members present. I am not sure if that speech was broadcast by the local media, but the state television channel broadened their coverage of the Holy Father's visit only after foreign channels began showing more news about the Pope than the local channels. Recent religious and public policies had poisoned the entire societal atmosphere.

Fundamentalist Hindus are currently targeting not so much Muslims as they are the smaller group of Christians.

One could sense the upcoming change during my 1996 pastoral visit to India. This trip just added to my experiences from previous visits. I began in the city of Bombay (Mumbai), which now has 10 million people, of whom 500,000 are Catholics. The local archbishop, Cardinal Ignatius Pimenta, was celebrating the twenty-fifth anniversary of his episcopal ordination and was retiring after many years of ministry in the archdiocese. With my presence, I wanted to express the gratitude of the Holy See for the many years of this ministry. The celebration took place in the spacious yard of the Catholic school. There were many bishops and city representatives in attendance. Even Australian Cardinal Edward Clancy, who was Cardinal Pimenta's classmate from the time of his theological studies in Rome, arrived. I recall my visit to the Church of Our Lady of Perpetual Help, which is located in the poorer section of the city. There were huge numbers of people coming into the church to honor the portrait of the Mother of God

India: Mother Teresa Always Looked for Me in Rome

with flowers. There were so many people that they had to use two long aisles of the huge church, and also two pictures to satisfy all the worshippers, because among them were many Hindus. The downtown was built in the European style during the time of the British colonial government, but cardboard and metal shacks line the main roads and even cluster about the airport. I visited a small city gallery that featured portraits of Mother Teresa. As I stood by a majestic Indian gate that used to welcome sailors from the Indian Ocean, and while I watched peddlers, children playing with their mothers, and tourists, I prayed for the conversion of Asia. I dedicated one day of the visit to a small island, Elephanta, where an old Hindu temple is located. The structure is carved into a rocky hillside and is dedicated to different gods such as Shiva, Vishnu, and Ganesh, which are depicted in tall statues carved out of rock. The island is a recreational, as well as a pilgrimage, destination and is served by regularly scheduled ferryboats.

I flew from Bombay to a completely different area, to the Archdiocese of Ranchi, in the center of a region inhabited by various tribes. In modern times, a Jesuit from Belgium, Father Constant Lievens, began to proclaim the gospel among the members of those tribes. His ministry enjoyed great success. At the entrance of the cathedral, I was welcomed by local musicians and by a group of dancers in colorful attire. The young archbishop, Telesphore Placidus Toppo (now cardinal), prepared a very busy schedule for me, which began by blessing a statue of the Good Shepherd carved in their local style, located in the cathedral's courtyard. The same evening, I celebrated Mass in a nearby schoolyard. Only the altar was lighted, while people sang popular, local religious songs and even conducted a liturgical dance as part of the ceremony. The following morning, we began our round trip of three small new dioceses. As we entered the first one, we were welcomed by a group of Christians who performed ancient traditional ceremonies for us. I stepped out of the car, and they seated me on a throne. A woman waved aromatic incense in front of me, and then, after a short welcome, a young Christian washed my feet and put on my shoes. Meanwhile all traffic stopped and patiently awaited the end of the ceremony. They put a colorful turban on my head, and in this fashion I continued to Torpa, where they again welcomed me, but this time with flower garlands. Christians from near and far gathered on the same spot where Father Lievens had begun his mission. They filled the entire space next to the church and the adjacent, tree-lined road. It made for a beautiful view from the outdoor altar as the large crowd, dressed in various bright colors, sang and looked toward the altar while local music sounded. It reminded me of African Masses, but the people here were more especially attentive. Following the Mass, there was folk dancing and singing.

Similar celebrations continued in the dioceses of Khunti and Shimoga, where they had me step onto a truck and be driven through the town under a round baldachin, accompanied by joyous Christians, until we reached the cathedral. In the Diocese of Gumla, we went by a bumpy road through the rice fields, where poor workers earned their living by the sweat of their brows on farms belonging to Hindu landlords of the higher castes. I made a stop in a village where, in 1994, the Catholic pastor, his chaplain, and a seminarian were murdered. I said prayers at the place of their martyrdom, where their portraits were already depicted. When I addressed the schoolchildren, some Hindu people came to spy and secretly listen to what I was saying. In this whole area, the owners of large farms try to set the people against the missionaries, especially against the Jesuits. They see the social work of missionaries among the poor people from the lower castes as a threat to their own power and social position. They have murdered several missionaries in this northeastern part of India. Many people accuse the government of inaction against those responsible for the persecution. In the evening, as we returned from this strenuous tour, we had a meeting with the priests, religious sisters, and catechists of the archdiocese. Sisters in the nearby monastery prepared a late supper for us. During the meal, I drank from a sealed bottle of mineral water or beer. During the night, I woke up with a violent stomachache, but in the morning I attempted to celebrate the Mass for seminarians I had scheduled. As I got to the Eucharistic Prayer, I fainted for several minutes. I could not continue. Later on, despite an empty stomach and the stressful night, I managed to discuss some questions with the bishops of the local province and to fly back to Delhi in the afternoon. At the nunciature, the medical doctor prescribed some very strong medications because I still had to continue on my long trip to the southern state of Kerala in order to ordain two bishops. India can be dangerous, even for seasoned travelers and despite the fact that preventive care is used. Even bottled water can cause complications.

My trip continued to the state of Kerala, which is relatively Catholic, despite the many Marxist hammer-and-sickles on the walls, left behind by the former government. In Trivandrum, I stayed with the local bishop, but Mar Basilios, the Archbishop of Malankara, whom I knew well from various synods in Rome, arranged a welcoming ceremony for me in his cathedral and new seminary. On November 1, 1996, I ordained the first bishop of the newly established Diocese of Neyyattinkara, Vincent Samuel. The celebration was well attended by bishops, priests, and faithful. I was mesmerized by the beautiful liturgical hymns, litanies, and appropriate liturgical dances, as well as by the colorful crowds of people. The following day I began my trip by car through all of Kerala. Beautiful palm trees and many young people could be seen along the way. I stopped in the dioceses of Allepey and Quilon, were I was again welcomed according to the local practices, by the placing of flower wreaths around my neck and by a solemn procession under a baldachin. Finally I understood why Romans call the Prefect of Evangelization "a red pope". I was red from the sun's rays.

It was already dark when we arrived at Verapoly, where the following day I ordained a new bishop, the former rector of the Urbanium University in Rome, Daniel Acharuparambil. As the high

India, Bangalore: The Opening of the State Catholic Conference

chancellor of this university for the missions, I had worked very closely with the new bishop. This celebration surpassed the others because the two of us were placed on some sort of thrones connected to each together and placed under a baldachin on a decorated truck. We processed in this way to the sound of music, while motorcycles escorted us to the spacious courtyard of the Catholic school, where an altar had been built. Here we heard hymns in the Malayalam language, as well as music and mystical melodies played on stringed instruments and drums. This music drew us into a prayerful state. Also from this visit, I remember the grave of the famous Portuguese traveler Vasco da Gama in the Diocese of Cochin. I was able to take a cruise on the river, which ends at the Indian Ocean near Verapoly. As we traveled down the river, we made several stops at different parishes and communities of the faithful, where we were greeted by the people from under the palm trees on both banks of the river. It was a much-needed rest before my departure for Rome.

A final trip to India brought me to Bangalore, which is located almost in the center of the country. In September 2000, this city hosted a national gathering of the Catholic Church, a very important event lasting five days, which was attended by representatives of the clergy, religious, and laity of 143 dioceses. I opened the gathering with the celebration of a Pontifical Mass and with a homily. Afterward, we gathered in a very spacious hall, where I delivered my speech to the attendees, which included 110 bishops. Considering the overall situation of the Church and society in India, I focused my homily on the person of Jesus Christ, who is the same yesterday, today, and forever (Heb 13:8). He is the hope for a new society. In so doing, I wanted to stress the foundation of our faith, which was threatened. Then in my speech, under the theme "To Be the New Church", I elaborated on this by saying that the Church in India is important, that it should be prayerful and free, and that it should be a missionary Church with a greater involvement of laity.

This was my personal message for the Church in India during the Jubilee Year. That message still remains my wish for the hopeful, but sometimes painful, future of these Christians who constitute the largest Catholic community in Asia outside of the Philippines. As the government erects different obstacles to the entry of missionaries into this country, this Church, which is of the poor but rich in faith and vocations, needs to develop a greater missionary spirit and to be aware of its role within India and even abroad.

Kingdom of Nepal

Nepal is a hereditary monarchy, where Hinduism is the state religion. It is situated north of India and south of China. This country is mostly covered by the Himalayas and by other mountains with deep valleys and has little arable land. The population has reached 25 million. Of these, 8 percent are Buddhists, 4 percent are Muslims, and over 86 percent are Hindus who treasure their own local superstitions and myths. For example, in the capital of Katmandu, a small girl was exhibited in a window, who—until reaching puberty—was supposed to be an incarnated goddess. Of course, if one wanted to see her, one had to pay a fee. Capuchins built a church here in the middle of the eighteenth century, but shortly thereafter abandoned the mission. During all of the next 140 years, the Church had no presence in Nepal.
Finally in 1951, Jesuits opened a school, where children from Hindu families are still educated. This assures that these missionaries will be able to stay legally in the country. Religious sisters have established other schools in Pokhara and Gurka. I

Nepal,
Kathmandu: The
First Catholic Church
Mount Everest in the
Background

visited all three schools during my visit to Nepal in 1995. In 1983, an independent mission was established, and in 1996, the area was declared to be a prefecture apostolic. This is also a certain indication of growth. Currently there are here slightly over 7,000 Catholics.

Another indication of growth was the construction of the first officially sanctioned church in the country, which was finished in 1995. Father Anthony Sharma, a Jesuit of Nepalese origin from the Gurka tribe, who is currently Prefect Apostolic of Katmandu, invited me to dedicate the new church. It was an event appreciated not only by the Catholic faithful, but also by ambassadors from different countries. I arrived safely at Katmandu three days prior to the Feast of the Assumption of the Blessed Virgin, when the celebration was due to take place. I mention my safe arrival because the airport is one of the most dangerous in the world. It is located in a narrow valley, and during cloudy conditions or fog, larger planes can crash into the surrounding mountains, as has been known to occur in the past.

In the capital, I went to see the royal palace as well as temples housing various gods, in front of which people rang bells as a substitute for prayer. Some statues or paintings had a supernatural look. We missed seeing the young, living "goddess" in the window, whom I mentioned above. In the square, a long row of street merchants sell diverse souvenirs to the numerous tourists. Sometimes one can even find beautiful items there, such as carved Tibetan and Chinese statues or short, skillfully decorated knives. I was more interested in the efforts

of missionaries. I spent almost the entire day visiting the Catholic school complex founded by Jesuits from the United States. They were able to get the ear of the king, who henceforth became very fond of them. The school complex is located in the suburbs of the city. On the way there, we admired long tassels of drying hot peppers, hanging outside windows. The people very often use these to season their food. There is also an orphanage in the city, which is operated by Mother Teresa's sisters. Another order of sisters cares for women who have fallen from virtue, whom the sisters are helping on their journey out of a sinful life.

In Nepal, I saw an artistic painting, executed by underground Christians from Tibet, on which the Sacred Heart of Jesus was depicted in the form of Buddha. Each, almost miniature, illustration from the life of Jesus, culminated in the Resurrection and in the symbol of the Most Holy Trinity, enthroned over the Himalaya Mountains. Also, the saints with the Blessed Mother were depicted in the heavens above snow-covered mountains. The persecuted Christians in Tibet, which is currently occupied by China, had used the same technique as the early Christians in the Roman catacombs. They obscured the central person of Jesus, not as a Good Shepherd or in the form of a fish, but by depicting him as Buddha. The painting was brought by our Christian brothers through the mountains to Nepal, and they donated it as a gift to an American Jesuit, who used to care for the drug-addicted and lost youth of Katmandu. When I admired it as an example of faith hearkening to the times of the catacombs, he gave it to me. I now have it hanging in my study.

It rained every day; all the while I looked forward to a possible one-hour tourist flight over the Himalayas. When the sun finally appeared, it was the Feast of the Assumption. Early in the morning, we rushed to the airport, where other tourists were already waiting. I obtained a seat for the flight, and so, for the whole hour, I was able to admire the beautiful view of the peaks, several of which are over 26,000 feet high and are covered with snow. I remembered the story of the mountain-climber Reinhold Messner, who spoke about these mountains with great admiration. This experience served as a fine meditation in preparation to dedicating the church, which took place right after my return from the airport.

The dedication of the first public church in Nepal was, for this small community, a great event. The construction of the church was

Mt. Everest (29,028 feet): A Captivating View from the Air

not yet finished, because the delivery of a steel roof from abroad had been delayed. All the supports for the roof were stored next to the church. To make sure that the inclement weather would not stop the ceremony, they had temporarily covered the building with colorful fabrics and carpets. The great joy of the faithful was demonstrated in their singing and ritual dancing. One could sense their excitement even after the ceremony, as we shared some refreshments under the tents. This reminded me of the atmosphere of the first Christian community, as we know it from the Acts of the Apostles.

The next morning, when we started our day trip by car through the mountains to Pokhara, it was raining. The road toward the highly elevated mountain pass as well as the winding descent to the valley were very arduous for the entire caravan of trucks. The road was covered with mud, which had been carried down the steep mountains by rainwater. It finally stopped raining as we reached the valley, where a mountain creek had formed. Finally, we came to an asphalt road and

Blessing of the Church in Kathmandu

turned into a side valley inhabited by the Gurka tribe, members of whom were once employed by Great Britain as fine soldiers. Those who served in this capacity are still collecting their retirement. As we were approaching, we were met by an Indian priest who works among the tribesmen. This particular village was prepared to receive the gospel by a Pentecostal preacher. We were welcomed with music played on their local musical instruments and by a special dance with masks. After that, the priest took us over to the religious sisters from India, who had opened a school for girls there. These are indications of the budding of the mission.

In the afternoon, we continued our trip toward Pokhara, a tourist center and starting point of many hiking trails leading to the top of the Himalayan peaks. I was able to admire those peaks in the morning, as I was standing on the roof of the Catholic school, which is staffed by sisters from India. The previous evening, a Japanese Jesuit priest and I had concelebrated Mass for the sisters and for a group of tourists from Japan. The tourists were Buddhists or Shinto, but they

The Welcome at Region of Gurka

The Mass with the Sisters of Mother Teresa

Hindu Temple—Stupa

had an interest in Christianity. Mother Teresa had opened a monastery here for contemplative sisters, which we visited as well.

Our return trip to Katmandu on a beautiful sunny day was breathtaking, as we traveled through the Nepalese valleys. Almost halfway through our day trip, we were met by a group of Indian priests and sisters standing by a bridge. They wanted me to bless the cornerstone for their mission church. It was located on a steep hill and to get there by car would have made for a very long trip. The other choice, which we adopted, was to take a steep mountain trail and hike for several hours—something that only trained native people were supposed to be able to do. These trained natives were already well-known mountain porters. They are a short, well-built people. The wilderness furnished us with a picturesque view for the blessing ceremony, after which we enjoyed some refreshments. The following day, I left this difficult but hopeful missionary country. I flew to Bangkok because I had scheduled two more trips, one to Myanmar (Burma) and one to Malaysia.

Our newly established mission in Nepal is only in its early stages, but it has a good start. We have only to hope that the state Hindu religion will not cause persecution of Christians. When our Lord Jesus spoke to his apostles, "Go and teach all the nations!" he also included these 25 million citizens. Christians must work in the mission fields because they are empowered for that. The results are in the hands of the Lord of time and history.

3. Buddhist Territory

Buddhism was originally founded as a sect with the intention of reforming Hinduism. Its founder, Siddhārtha Gautama, lived from 558 to 478 B.C. in northeastern India. After a carefree youth, during which he experienced much human contentment, including a family and a son, he rejected everything and dedicated himself to searching for truth in meditation and the ascetic life. At the age of thirty-five, he reached "enlightenment" and became *Buddha*, which means "the Enlightened One". (When I asked a Buddhist nun in Taiwan, where Buddha is now, she replied, "In you, if you are an enlightened one.") It was under the name of "Buddha" that his fame spread. He began preaching his instructions on how to reach ultimate freedom from pain and suffering (nirvana), and he founded communities of monks. He saw the cause of suffering in a lack of knowledge and in selfish desire, from which it is necessary to free oneself, using eight methods. These include right views, right intent, right effort, and right concentration. The monks have to observe a strict asceticism. Celibacy, poverty, meditation, and begging are their way of life. That is the path to enlightenment.

Therefore Buddhism consists more of instructions in a way of life and a kind of ethical code, rather than a religion; it is a way and desire for absoluteness. Buddhism does not address the question of God, because such things are not accessible to men. Buddha himself is not a god, even though some forms of Buddhism practically consider and honor him as one. When I once somewhat insistently asked a certain educated Buddhist monk in Thailand about their teaching on God, he abruptly changed the topic because they do not like those kinds of questions. Despite that, they believe in an afterlife and a reward for good deeds as well as punishment for bad ones. They believe in a gradual release through different levels of life, or lives, called reincarnation, and this continues until they reach nirvana.

While Christianity was beginning to spread in the Mediterranean world, Buddhism split into two branches, which remain to this day. These are called the lesser and the greater "vehicles", or narrow and wide paths (or instructions) for life. The first branch, Theravada, is stricter and more traditional. It supports communities of monks and is spread throughout Sri Lanka, Thailand, Myanmar, Laos, and Cambodia. The second branch, Mahayana, is more progressive and less strict. It finds its support among the simpler people. Its expressions are to be found in the local cultures of China and Vietnam (Taoism and Confucianism), in Korea and Japan (Shinto), in Mongolia and Tibet (where the Dalai Lama is revered as the Buddha), as well as in Vietnam and Taiwan.

The Second Vatican Council expressed the following thoughts concerning Buddhism: "Buddhism, in its various forms, realizes the radical insufficiency of this changeable world; it teaches a way by which men, in a devout and confident spirit, may be able either to acquire the state of perfect liberation, or attain, by their own efforts or through higher help, supreme illumination" (*Nostra aetate*, no. 2). Without a doubt, this is an honorable human effort for "liberation and illumination",

Sri Lanka:
Next to the Statue of
Buddha in Colombo

which actually is salvation. But it is missing its Savior, "the Way, the Truth and Life", as well as illumination from above, which is God's revelation.

We must note that Buddhism has penetrated the everyday experience of the people and become their approach to life and culture. That is why Christianity, which is considered here as a Western religion, has a difficult time making inroads in these countries. When Christianity tried to adapt to local cultural forms, in several places it encountered nationalistic feelings and the protests of Buddhists who identify their religion with their national identity. As some in India affirm that only Hindus can be 100 percent Indian, some Thai Buddhists are sure that they are the only genuine Thai subjects. Buddhists in Sri Lanka claim for themselves certain privileges as the only loyal citizens.

Following this introduction, it will be sufficient to share only a few experiences from my particular trips to the countries of this region.

Democratic Socialist Republic of Sri Lanka

I have visited the island of Ceylon, or Sri Lanka, several times. We once made a short stop here on the occasion of the Pope's visit to the Philippines, Australia, and Papua New Guinea. It was then that John Paul II beatified the Indian missionary Joseph Vaz, the apostle of Sri Lanka. The beatification celebration took place at the seaside in the capital city of Colombo. An artistically designed altar in the local style, which some would have considered as Buddhist, was designed by a Buddhist architect. It was certainly a positive

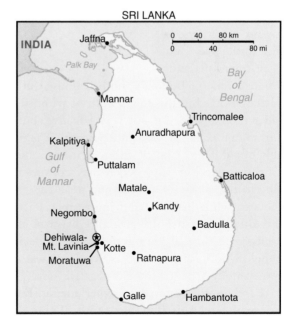

*Kandy (Sri Lanka):
In the Temple of
Buddha's Tooth, with
Bishop Joseph Vianney
Fernando*

step toward dialogue between Catholics and Buddhists. Dialogue is not always easy, as was demonstrated by absence of the Buddhist monks when they did not attend the personal meeting of the Holy Father with representatives of other religions.

I experienced a similar situation during my other personal visit to the holy Buddhist town of Kandy, where a relic of Buddha's tooth is housed in a temple. Two Buddhist patriarchs lived in this town, both of whom I visited. The first was an older monk, who was not very talkative, but nonetheless very pleasant, so our exchange was quite peaceful. The other representative, probably of a different branch, received me in a hostile fashion, asking why Christians steal his souls when they convert Buddhists. He was referring to the action of a sectarian "preacher", who had passed through the area while happily baptizing people. It was difficult to explain to this Buddhist leader that not all Christians have the same principles. Neither do they all show respect for the decisions and consciences of people who hear the Good News. Here was an example of how divisions among Christians yield negative results in the mission fields.

I had another interesting experience in Kandy, in the temple right before the relic of Buddha's tooth. The hereditary guardian of this relic took me to the richly decorated chapel, stopping me directly in front of the honored tooth. He gave me a handful of aromatic lemon tree flowers and asked me to throw them on the relic. At that moment, I was confused, but my guide, the local bishop, immediately, but very politely and strictly said that Catholics do not do this. On our way home, the bishop privately expressed his surprise, because this would have been a religious act. In the past, Christians have sacrificed their lives rather than participate in this, and the guardian knew it.

In the religious history of Ceylon, there have been periods of persecution. Franciscan missionaries used to travel throughout the island in the sixteenth century on their way to China. Saint Francis Xavier stopped here as well and was followed by other Jesuits. Catholics experienced most of their suffering at the hands of European colonists. In the middle of the sixteenth century, groups of martyrs from Mannar spiritually nurtured this soil with their blood. A hundred years later, Calvinists from Holland persecuted Catholics, and then British occupiers began to oppress the Church. Despite these difficulties, a Church hierarchy was established with three dioceses at the end of the nineteenth century. Also, a seminary was founded at Kandy for adjacent India, and many priests and bishops studied there in the nineteenth and twentieth centuries.

Presently well over 1.3 million members of the Catholic Church live in eleven dioceses on this island. The entire population is over 20 million. Seventy percent are Buddhists, who enjoy privileges from the state. Most of these think of themselves as constituting the country's main ethnic group. In addition, the Hindu Tamils reside in the northeast around Jaffna. They form 15 percent of the population and are fighting a war of independence.

Kingdom of Thailand

The culture of Buddhism is alive and well in Thailand. The country has 64 million inhabitants, but only 322,000 Catholics, gathered into ten dioceses. They are spread as a small flock amid the Buddhists who form 93 percent of the population. In addition, 5 percent of the population are Muslims. As one travels through the country, one can get an impression of how Buddhism has become a part of the lives of the people. One can admire beautiful pagodas, not only in Bangkok, but also on both banks of the River Chao Pia, where small pagodas adorn

Thailand:
Bangkok;
Beautiful Pagodas

the fences of houses and function as dwellings for tutelary spirits. Even in small villages one can see monks dressed in their typical orange robes. Every young man must spend one year in the monastery. It is not surprising that citizenship in Thailand is identified with this culture of religion, since young men go to the monastery in the same way they join the military in other countries. Thailand has basically a single ethnic group. Even local Chinese people consider themselves as people of Thailand. One only encounters different tribes in the north and west, such as those overlapping the borders with Myanmar, China, and Laos. Our missionaries work chiefly among these people.

Thailand used to be called "Siam". A point of pride is that its kings never succumbed to foreign powers or to pressure from colonialists. Missionary experiments began in the sixteenth century, but over and over these ended in persecutions. Parisian missionaries settled in the old capital of Ayuthia in the seventeenth century, but once again the missions had to be closed. Finally, at the end of the nineteenth century, King Rama V proclaimed freedom of religion. At that time, many Church communities were established, and these were stronger in comparison to those of the present day. The cause of this decline was World War II, when Catholic missions were destroyed once again. Japanese occupiers put to death the Martyrs of Thailand, who were subsequently beatified on October 22, 1989, by Pope John Paul II. Their entire story was related to me by the Archbishop of Thare and Nonseng, who was but a youngster in 1944 when the martyrs were killed, and who witnessed the executions at the hands of Japanese soldiers. I celebrated Mass at their graves near the Mekong River. Our faithful are very careful and very patriotic, even nowadays. Presently all the bishops are native-born, including Cardinal Michael Kitbunchu, Archbishop of Bangkok.

Pope John Paul II visited Thailand in 1984. Starting in the year 1970, I often

THAILAND

stopped in Bangkok during my trips to Asia because the city is a major crossroads. Most of the time I stayed at the nunciature, but often I visited my Chinese friend Johnny Sue, who ran a store featuring various souvenirs and tourist memorabilia. His was a beautiful Catholic family. "Johnny Gems", as they used to call him, had a very good income, and he built two large, and four smaller, churches. I was introduced to him by the last missionary bishop in Thailand, the Salesian Pietro Carretto, who was a brother of the well-known spiritual writer Carlo Carretto. The Holy Father rewarded Johnny with a knighthood in the Order of Saint Gregory the Great, and I had the honor of bestowing the insignia upon him in the local cathedral. Later he became ill with cancer, but he was still able to visit Lourdes and Rome. There I obtained for him a seat among the sick, and he was able to greet the Holy Father. After that, I visited him in his apartment in Bangkok, and shortly afterward he died, surrounded by his loving family. I still keep in touch with them. This also is a fruit of missionary visits.

Among my various trips, I would like to mention a pastoral visit of the northerly situated Diocese of Chiang Mai. The area is populated by tribal peoples, who are assisted on their spiritual journey by the

Bangkok: With Sister Bošnáková (1910–2003), the Oldest Slovak Missionary Sister

labors of our missionaries. During the solemn Mass in the cathedral, I was greeted by ten delegations, all dressed in different costumes. They keep their traditions, even as they live in an area known as the "Golden Triangle". There, under the strict supervision of reckless nouveaux-riches, illegal drugs are harvested and manufactured. All the while, poor people work in the forests felling trees and, with the help of elephants, drag the wood out to the traveled roads. Despite the danger and the difficulties involved, I was able to visit two villages in the mountains, thanks to an American Redemptorist from Texas who drove me in his jeep. After greeting our new Christians, I celebrated the Mass. I preached in English; the bishop translated into the Thai language; and then this particular priest did the translating into the language of the local tribe. This double translation was time consuming, but the homily got delivered and was graciously received. The women dressed up in their most beautiful costumes, and after the Mass they entertained me with music, singing, and dancing. This entertainment took place in the church building. The church itself is constructed on pillars, but these pillars are not connected by walls, and so the resulting church hall is open to the air. The Eucharist is celebrated in the church above, while the ground floor is more used for socializing. My brave cowboy guide was also caring for a group of immigrants from the Hmong tribe who lived in neighboring China. In the evening, the local bishop escorted me to a folk program, which further enriched my knowledge of these people.

My earlier mentioned visit to the shrine of the Martyrs of Thailand is also very memorable. I was impressed as I stood next to their embalmed remains. They were young people of my generation who gave up their lives for their faith. It is amazing what the grace of God can do, even among these relatively new Christians. The new shrine is spacious and can accommodate very large groups of pilgrims. As I took a walk on the bank of the Mekong River, I looked across the river to the neighboring socialist state of Laos, where the communists obstruct mission work. The Laotian population of 5.7 million is 58 percent Buddhist and 34 percent animist, while our Catholic numbers stand at only about 42,000. Even there, people look forward to better times and to religious freedom when the gospel will be able to be proclaimed. I found out that some of our "underground" Christians sometimes come across the river to obtain their spiritual nourishment. My prayers go with them.

The Welcome at the Shrine of the Blessed Martyrs of Thailand

Several gatherings for Asia have been organized in Thailand, and I attended some of them. For example, representatives of the bishops' conferences have held meetings for evangelization in the town of Hoa Hin, located on the seashore south of Bangkok. Those meetings occurred in 1992, in other words, two years after the publication of the missionary Encyclical *Redemptoris missio* of John Paul II. The delegates consisted mostly of bishops, with a few theological experts. However, India was represented by a certain conceited "theologian" who condemned the encyclical in the name of the "theology of India" and in the name of a group of Indian theologians. I was criticized as well. I listened to him calmly, and afterward I answered him point by point. When I asked him some questions, he did not know how to answer me. Then an archbishop from India stood up and asked him a basic question. In whose name, and about what kind of church was he speaking, since India was represented by the attending bishops? I felt sorry

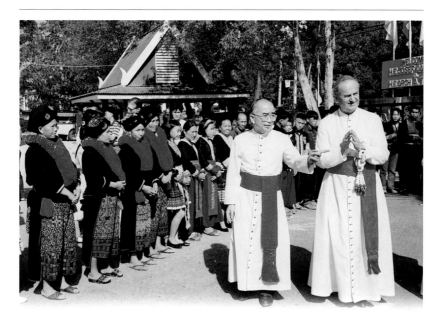

Chiang Mai: Tribes from the North Welcome Us

for our brother theologian who had actually pointed out a matter that troubled certain of his colleagues. Some of them place their own Indian culture above the gospel. They also place the teachings of the Pope, as head of the Church, on a lower level than their own debatable opinions. We must expect a certain cultural pride, which is common in Asia. However, this pride can sometimes manifest itself as haughtiness, which in turn can lead to risky opinions.

Therefore the Federation of Asian Bishops' Conferences (FABC) has an important role in solving pastoral questions, but also in overseeing the purity of the faith. I used to stress this point during my presentations at different general meetings, as I did at the last one in 2000 in Bangkok, which I attended while still Prefect. There is always an important organizational problem at bishops' meetings, namely, the manner of determining the number of theological experts and the role they are to play. The faithful have a right to know who speaks in the bishops' name, since, as Scripture tells us, bishops were commissioned by the Holy Spirit to shepherd the Church.

Among the Mountain Tribes

What Is More Beautiful: She or Her Dress?

Union of Myanmar (Burma)

Myanmar is the new name of this country, and many people are not familiar with it. Since 1989, the military authorities have promoted "Myanmar" as the conventional name for their state. This decision was not approved by any sitting legislature in Burma. The name change was requested by different ethnic groups living in the country, since the name "Burma" is specific to only one ethnic group. The country is located northwest of Thailand on the Bay of Bengal and reaches all the way to the Himalayas. The population stands at close to 50 million, with 87 percent being Buddhist. There are only 623,000 Catholics, residing in twelve dioceses.

Attempts at evangelizing this country have continued repeatedly since the sixteenth century. Only toward the end of the nineteenth century were the missionaries from Milan (Pontifical Institute for Foreign Missions, or PIME) able to conduct deeper evangelization and to do so for a more extended period. British colonial authorities were not very helpful toward the missions, but, in spite of this, Church

Myanmar (Burma): Gate of Welcome

organization survived and continued to spread after 1948, when Burma became independent. However, under the military dictatorship, almost all missionaries were expelled from the country. The only missionary to remain in the country was the zealous Bishop John Baptist Gobbato, who was able to obtain Burmese citizenship. Until he died, he helped the native clergy to build the Church, even during difficult conditions under the socialist-oriented military government.

This regime did not allow the victorious National League for Democracy Party to assume power after the 1990 elections. The leader of the Democracy Party was Ms. Aung San Suu Kyi, who was imprisoned after the elections and later kept as a hostage for almost ten years, this despite being a Nobel Peace Prize recipient. During my visit, I met with this brave lady and was able to spend a few minutes with her. This happened during my complicated trip in 1995, when I visited Nepal, Myanmar, Thailand, and Malaysia.

The local government must have had some kind of interest in my visit, because at the airport in the capital of Rangoon (or Yangon, as the government refers to it), I was met by a small military unit, including the only Catholic general in the government as well as by several bishops. My meeting with the bishops' conference and with seminarians was very cordial. Later I met with three other generals, who were all members of the government. The last one was chief of state, who held the title of "First Secretary" and was the most powerful person in the country. I left for all of them a brief memorandum asking for more freedom for the Church. Basic rights were requested, such as the ability to send theological books and Bibles to seminarians without state censure, of not paying state fees for students in Rome, who were already fully cared for by the Vatican, and other requests, which everywhere else are considered normal rights.

Of great importance was my visit with the minister for religious affairs, to whom I tried to explain the purpose of the missionary activity of the Catholic Church. He received me in the presence of four Buddhist "patriarchs", in other words, representative monks. The answers of the minister were more concerned with the Buddhist monks than with me.

On the last day of my stay in the capital, I celebrated a Pontifical High Mass in a packed cathedral. I was surprised when the entire congregation sang the Latin Gregorian Chant *Missa de Angelis*. The bishops of this country were not able to attend the Second Vatican Council, and the application of liturgical reforms and local hymns was still behind schedule in this city.

During the banquet, which the local bishop organized in my honor, I was seated between two current members of the government. One of them spoke fluent English, and we were able to have an interesting conversation. The opportunity for dialogue began when he mentioned that, as a practicing Buddhist, he would like to resign from his position and, following the example of his wife, spend more time doing good deeds. In this way, he would merit a higher reincarnation and sooner attain the reward of final nirvana. I assured him that we also believe in an afterlife, in reward for good deeds, and even in eternal happiness in paradise. I wanted to find out the idea that the Buddhist had of nirvana, of what it consists, and what causes the happiness of the person who has attained this state. He explained to me the

MYANMAR (BURMA)

Mandalay: Procession through the Streets

purification process of reincarnation, which can happen even through a lower state of being, as, for example, through that of an animal. If the person, after several reincarnations and lives, deserves the final reward, he attains a state where there is no pain, sadness, or suffering. When I asked him in what this state consists, and what nirvana actually is, he replied with the English word "nothingness", or an absence of all evil and unpleasantness. I answered him that our paradise also has an absence of evil and disorder, but most of all it has the presence of Somebody, Who is the fullness of being and happiness and Who is a personal God. Only in that way can I imagine, although to a limited extent, an endless happiness after death, lived out in God's presence, love, and fullness. It will be in my existing persona and not in some other form of life. The final answer to my comments was the declaration by my neighbor that we in the West lack a necessary category in our thought, namely, the importance of understanding the positive value of nirvana as absence or nothingness. I admired him because of his personal search for happiness through good deeds. I felt that he was not too far from the Kingdom, but also I felt sorry that he did not know a personal

God as Father, or Jesus Christ as "the Way, the Truth, and the Life". I thanked God for the gift of faith, which we really do not deserve, and which we value so little.

The next part of my trip took me to the second archdiocese, which has its seat at Mandalay. The welcoming ceremony here was even more solemn. They asked me to stand in a decorated car, and as music played, they took me through the streets of the town to the cathedral. Crowds of people were awaiting our arrival in a spacious square. There I celebrated Mass for those who had gathered. Following the celebration, many Christians wanted to greet me personally. Because of many years of separation from the world, a visitor from Rome was for them an envoy from the Holy Father and a valued guest. My visit strengthened their hope that greater freedom would soon be coming to this country of beautiful pagodas. (Among the huge numbers of pagodas, the golden one at Rangoon and the marble one in Mandalay stand out most in my mind.) While there, I visited the historic fortress on the

Mandalay: Welcome at the Doors of the Cathedral

Buddhist Pagodas Have a Different Style than in Thailand

bank of the river. To smooth relationships with the military governor and his generals, I had to endure a dinner in a Chinese restaurant. I again had recourse to my habit of not asking what was placed in front of me. This time I did not have to suffer any consequences.

The visit in the neighboring Diocese of Taunggyi had a purely pastoral character. The presence of the elderly, but still very strong, Bishop Gobbato was very pleasing. He was a tall man with a white beard. I met also with his spiritual son and successor, whom he mentored from among the native clergy. Even the people from neighboring dioceses arrived here by trucks. Some came all the way from Kengtung, near the Chinese border, led by their short and very zealous bishop, Abraham Than. In the procession to the cathedral, which is dedicated to Saint Joseph, there were not only musicians in their special attire, carrying local musical instruments, but also the faithful from different tribes. After the Mass they presented me with a program of entertainment, during which they demonstrated their most beautiful costumes and talents. For example, Bishop Than brought with him women who wore metal bindings wrapped around their legs and

238

Barefoot among the Pagodas

other bindings that extend their necks. Other performers sang and danced. I went to visit a home for mentally retarded children who were not able to attend the Mass. I was very impressed by young people from the group called the Advocates of the Gospel, who travel to the westernmost villages in the mountains. They remain there for some time and, by word and deed, proclaim Jesus Christ. Also, they educate local catechists who can very easily cross the border into China and spread the faith among members of their tribes. They are Christians who are serious about their faith and their missionary role.

The Church in Myanmar is still living under difficult circumstances, but despite this fact, remains faithful to Christ. It is like a young tree that used to be supported by missionaries, but whose enemies too soon cut off its branches and its outside assistance. At that moment, the tree gathered all its energy and is now growing in both directions, horizontally and vertically. The spirituality of the people is very commendable. They deal with different obstacles and await better times. The universal Church cannot forget about them, even though they still remain cut off from larger activities.

Myanmar: Ladies from the Mountains

Kingdom of Cambodia and Socialist Republic of Vietnam

The territory of Buddhism spreads from Thailand through Cambodia to Vietnam. The last two are well known from recent wars. Both countries were under French colonial rule for almost a hundred years, as part of French Indochina. Cambodia became independent in 1953 and Vietnam in 1954. Recent history has taken the countries in different directions. Both were taken over by communists, but Cambodia was able to free itself from its communist regime. Currently Cambodia has a coalition government, while Vietnam is still under communist rule. The Mekong River waters both countries, too often flooding them.

Cambodia has about 12.8 million people, 90 percent of whom are of the Khmer nationality. There is also a Vietnamese minority

of around 6 per-
cent. The population
is 95 percent Bud-
dhist. There are only
around 23,000 Cath-
olics, but several
male and female reli-
gious work in this
country. Sadly, the
well-known fanatic
General Pol Pot,
who led the "Khmer
Rouge", executed
around 2 million
educated and even
less-educated "class
enemies", among
whom were many
Christians. During a

period of four hundred years, the mission among the Khmer has
experienced successes and reverses. Only now are Christians beginning to gather their senses after a terrible persecution that was supposed to uproot not only the Christian faith, but every other religion
as well. Three territorial units have been reestablished, including the
vicariate apostolic in the capital Phnom-Penh and two prefectures
apostolic. This country too is sprinkled with the blood of martyrs,
which some day will bear fruit for the missions.

Vietnam extends in a long strip from the Chinese border, along the
China Sea, all the way to the Mekong Delta. Its population is around
82 million, of whom 67 percent are Buddhist and around 5.8 million
are Catholics. It has a rather disturbing religious, and secular, history.
The country used to consist of smaller territories, but these were taken
over by France in the second half of the nineteenth century and uni-
fied under the title of Indochina. With the exception of the Japanese
occupation during World War II, the French maintained their colonial
rule until they were finally defeated in 1954. The war for freedom was
led by General Ho Chi Minh. The new state was divided into a northern part under communist rule and a southern part that allied itself
with Western governments. However, the communist military from

VIETNAM

North Vietnam over-ran South Vietnam during a bloody war, and in 1975 they declared all of Viet-nam to be a socialist republic. Even to this day, Vietnam has a communist govern-ment. The capital is Hanoi, while the for-mer capital of South Vietnam, Saigon, was renamed Ho Chi Minh City.

The history of evangelization has been marked by constant alternation between freedom and persecution. At the end of the sixteenth century, Franciscans and Jesuits attempted to proclaim Jesus Christ, but after fifty years of work, perse-cutions began. The Church began to grow once again toward the end of the seventeenth century. At that time, new Dominican mission-aries from the Philip-pines arrived to assist in the process of evangelization. Right after the arrival of the Domini-cans, a new period of persecution began, lasting for around twenty years. In spite of that, by 1759, there were 120,000 Catholics and twenty-five native priests in the northern kingdom of Tonkin. A new period of persecution and a new period of freedom followed, one upon the other. In 1909, Pope Pius X beatified a group of martyrs from Vietnam.

The current communist regime has placed strict limits upon the Church, similar to what people experienced in the former Czechoslovakia. In spite of this, Catholics remain faithful to Christ and to the Church of Rome. The bishops' conference was brought into being in 1951 in Hanoi. In 1960, Rome established ecclesiastical provinces for the Church in Vietnam. When the government expelled the apostolic nuncio, relations between Hanoi and the Vatican became more difficult. Vietnamese communist representatives learned in Czechoslovakia how to oppress the Church. Leaders from both countries who were engaged in this struggle knew and visited each other often, as they later admitted to me. The Vietnamese government still claims the right to approve the nomination of each new bishop, and the Pope cannot name a cardinal without their approval. Seminarians are approved for their studies by communist officials. On one occasion, they permitted a small group of seminarians to study, and then waited six years for the completion of their seminary education, before admitting another small group. Later, after many protests, including some from abroad, they changed their practice and began to admit students every other year.

In the early 1990s, the former Vietnamese minister for religious affairs came to visit me in Rome. During our discussion, which took almost an hour and a half, I asked him—as I did in September 1989, in Prague—to name the international law that gives the right to a government to impose such ridiculous obstacles to the nomination of bishops and the preparation of seminarians. His answer was that they are citizens of Vietnam. I then reminded him that his children are also Vietnamese citizens, but that the state or the Communist Party does not choose their marriage partners. That is a sign, I told him, that there are limits to the competency of political power, and that it is not supreme. There are some areas, in which politicians should not be making decisions. In other words, totalitarianism is nonsense.

During this meeting, my guests three times extended to me their invitation to visit Vietnam. However, when some time later I submitted my application for a visa, they gave me the subtle answer that the Communist Party would be holding its convocation, and that furthermore it would be the rainy season. I then reminded them of their invitation. I also said that I would have nothing to do with their convocation because my visit would be pastoral, and not political. As far as the rain was concerned, I am even used to snow. Their final response was that they were not going to grant me the visa, and that the verbal invitation had only been a formality. I then sent them my own message, wondering which portions of our dialogue had been expressed with sincerity and which had been mere formalities. This is only a small example of how difficult it is to negotiate with this kind of regime. Therefore, the Church in Vietnam remains even deeper in my heart, while my desire to visit these people whom I admire so much even if only once—remains unfulfilled.

After meeting witnesses to these inhuman practices, and hearing the story of one of the Vietnamese bishops who later became a cardinal, I am not at all surprised that then-Bishop François-Xavier Nguyen Van Thuan was not allowed to assume his office. Instead, he was given a jail sentence and imprisoned. Several years later, during the spiritual retreat of the Holy Father and the members of the Roman Curia, we listened to the personal testimony of this faithful man. He shared with us how he lived for many years in a secluded room, with only one window above his head. He was able to celebrate the Eucharist by holding a small piece of bread and a few drops of wine in the palms of his hands. His talk allowed many of us to grasp the perversity of the communist regime. Finally, the government was forced to free him from prison, but, at the same time, they expelled him from the country. In 2001, the Holy Father named him a cardinal in Rome, but he received his real reward in September of 2002, from the Eternal Judge.

Still another example can demonstrate how far the arrogance of the communists reaches. It was the time of the canonization of the Martyrs of Vietnam in Rome. The government of Vietnam with its propaganda forced even the bishops of Vietnam to try to dissuade Rome from holding the scheduled canonization. Without realizing it, the government actually drew the attention of the entire world to these heroes of the faith and to the situation in Vietnam. After they did not get their way with threats, they permitted the celebration of these saints to occur some time later in their homeland.

During my time as Prefect, I got to know several Vietnamese bishops, including Cardinal Joseph-Marie Trinh Van Can and his successor in the Archdiocese of Hanoi, Cardinal Paul Pham Dinh Tung. Some Vietnamese, the "boat people", were able to escape abroad under

Vietnam:
Heroic Cardinal
François-Xavier Nguyen
Van Thuan

very dramatic and dangerous circumstances. These Vietnamese Catholics are great witnesses to the faith in their new home countries around the world. In 2006, the Archbishop of Ho Chi Minh was made a cardinal, and my successor has visited the country. Together let us pray for the freedom of this Church as it undergoes its trials.

4. East Asia

The eastern part of the Asian continent is home to a group of nations, with China surpassing them all in terms of territory and number of inhabitants. In the past, China also used to wield a heavy cultural influence, which included propagating the teachings of Confucius. Confucianism does not constitute a religion, but rather a form of religious and secular culture. In China and in the countries where Confucianism has spread, these teachings help one to understand religion and the manner in which one can live a moral life. As we have clearly seen with Buddhism, which resembles instructions for ascetic human living more than an actual religion, the same is even more true with Confucianism.

Confucius (551–497 B.C.) was at one point in his life a minister of justice and conceived a system of moral and educational instruction that is not in itself anti-religious. He founded his teachings on the religious traditions of the Chinese people. For God, he used the term "heaven", and he called God's commandments, "heavenly patterns". He insisted that education was necessary for all people and not just for the aristocracy. His moral teachings lead to knowledge, which is based on the acceptance of God's decrees. Every person has a conscience and can distinguish between good and bad, all of which makes him different from animals. Familial, societal, and political life should be guided by conscience and should direct everyone toward loving his neighbor. The rules of this moral philosophy are expressed in five points: justice between the subject and his ruler; love between parents and children; honor and respect of differences between man and woman; respect between a ruler and his subjects; fidelity among friends. The foundation of morality is a goodness of heart that imitates heaven (God). As we can see, this teaching could only prepare the way for God's revelation and for Christianity.

In addition, the traditional Chinese religion of Taoism considers Tao (or Dao) as the supreme Divine Being. Over time, this religion became diversified with the adoption of various superstitions. Subsequently, Taoism also adopted the moral teachings of Confucius and also certain aspects of Buddhism. Later, Taoism split into several sects, which then spread throughout China and the surrounding regions. Aside from being affected by this religion, family and societal life are also influenced by sorcerers and by the magic arts. This makes for a mixture of folk spirituality and faith, which the Chinese soul finds very acceptable in its ability to explain the origin of the world from God-Tao. Tao is somehow the soul of the entire universe and functions as a source of unity and harmony. Besides God-Tao, the Chinese are very respectful of their ancestors. Near Hong Kong, I saw a cemetery with interesting monuments and with tokens of respect left behind on the graves.

Visitors to China are left with mixed impressions. It is interesting to observe the remnants in the Chinese soul of a deep spirituality based on Confucianism and Taoism. Revolution has imposed on the people wave after wave of Marxism in its Chinese variety. Chinese people spread throughout the world, however, very easily accept Christianity. For the most part, those who enter the Church become good

Catholics. Who knows if the long-standing rule of atheism, and especially a menacing secularization, will not draw into a spiritual desert a younger generation that is isolated from family tradition? There are signs that the Chinese soul desires, and is thirsting for, eternity and for an absolute God. The missionaries who used to work in China often declared that this deeply spiritual nation would survive even great storms and floods. They could not imagine a total destruction of religion, at least not on a fundamental level. We must also keep in mind the different ways that China has influenced the religions of other peoples surrounding the "heavenly empire".

People's Republic of China

In speaking of China, we should understand the name as applying to its mainland land mass. China is truly a gigantic country. With a territory of nearly 3.7 million square miles, it is only slightly smaller than the United States. After a lowering of the birth rate through the imposition of radical restrictions by the government, the population stands at a current 1.313 billion, or one-fifth of the world's population. Official Chinese statistical data concerning religions does not exist. The Vatican's Annual Statistical Report does not contain data on Chinese membership in the Catholic Church or on the number of dioceses. Jean Charbonnier, an expert on Chinese internal relations, estimates the number of Catholics to be 10 million. According to him, in 1997, they were living in 144 dioceses, headed by seventy-three official, and forty-two underground, bishops. The number of priests was estimated at 1,500, and the number of religious sisters at around 2,000. There were approximately 5,000 churches and chapels.

The history of evangelization in China is long and complicated, and it ought to have its own separate chapter. Mention is to be found of the establishment of an archdiocese in the fifth century. A Syrian monk, Olapen, is known to have arrived later, in 635, at the capital city of the time. Many archeological excavations have provided evidence of the presence of Christians from that era. In the thirteenth century, Franciscan missionaries arrived from Italy. These entered China through Mongolia. At the same time, John of Montecorvino became the first Archbishop of Khambaliq (Peking) and Patriarch of the East. Toward the end of the fourteenth century, there were over 30,000 Catholics in China, but because of difficult conditions, the mission fell into decline. During the entire sixteenth century, missionaries, especially Jesuits, tried to reestablish their posts. Saint Francis Xavier died in 1552, on the island of Sancian, while entering China. Portuguese Augustinians later arrived through Macau, at the same time that a Jesuit missionary, Matteo Ricci was ministering at the imperial court. Experiments at harmonizing Christianity and Chinese culture were multiplying, while differences arose concerning the honors paid to Confucius and to one's ancestors. Jesuits claimed that these were civic honors, and that they should be allowed. Dominicans declared them to be unacceptable religious rituals. This dispute lasted hundreds of years and was brought before the Sorbonne and the papal court. In 1742, after discussing the matter with both sides, Pope Benedict XIV declared the rituals to be definitively condemned. Even so, new dioceses were established, and native-born priests were ordained.

In the middle of the nineteenth century, China was targeted by French expansionism. France had assumed responsibility for the protection of missionaries. In the past, it was a common practice in mission lands for the occupying power to attempt to control mission work as well. This then led to another period of persecution in China. In 1900, when the Catholic population had reached 720,000, and forty missionary territories had been organized in diocesanlike clusters, the Boxer Rebellion broke out. During this uprising, five bishops were murdered, along with thirty priests and 30,000 faithful.

Subsequently, the mission in China greatly expanded. Despite the obstacles of colonialism, the Holy See established an apostolic delegation in Peking in 1922, led by the zealous Archbishop Celso Costantini. The Chinese Church celebrated its first council in 1924, and, a year later, a Catholic university was founded in Fu-Jen. Pope Pius XI ordained the first six native Chinese bishops in Rome in 1926. Also, a native religious order was established, and in 1935, the Congregation for Evangelization allowed people to honor Confucius and their ancestors. In 1943, the Holy See and China established diplomatic relations. The first nuncio was then able, in 1946, to organize a Church hierarchy for the entire country. I recall how joyfully we welcomed the first Chinese cardinal, Thomas Tien Ken-sin, SVD, in Saint Peter's Basilica.

But in 1949, Mao Tse-tung assumed political power. He began to expel foreign missionaries from the country, and later he imprisoned and dismissed the nuncio. The persecution of the native clergy

CHINA

followed. The government tried to establish a "triple autonomy", which forbade anyone to have contact with foreign countries. Pius XII responded with the encyclical *Ad Sinarum gentes* (1954), and a year later he beatified the Martyrs of China. The persecution gradually worsened. In 1957, the government convoked a general meeting of Catholics in Peking, which allegedly "approved" statutes that had been prepared for a "Patriotic Association of Chinese Catholics", created after the example of other communist countries. This was actually an experiment in establishing a schismatic national church, or at least a society that would answer to the communist party. At that time, many bishops protested the decision and "descended into the catacombs" of an "underground Church", one which tried to maintain ties with the Roman Pontiff, the successor of Peter, the Rock upon which the Church of Christ is built. Hundreds of bishops, priests, and religious sisters endured decades in prisons and work camps until the 1980s, when the government somewhat relaxed its policies.

The determination of the regime to control the Catholic Church still remained, however. The government used the same norms for controlling the nomination of new bishops as it used for the "patri-otic" organization, which was itself headed by an illicit bishop. Appar-ently, decisions as to nominations were made by a layperson—a supposed Catholic—but he as well as the new bishops were members of the government and only toys in the hands of the almighty party. The government demonstrated strong opposition against the canonization of the Martyrs of China, whom they wanted to depict falsely with their own incredible propaganda. Attempts by the Holy See to ease the situation from the other side struck up against the real "Wall of China". Rome is striving to keep both the official and secret groups of Catholics together as one Church and, it is to be hoped, will have the opportunity to nominate good bishops. Information has come from several different sources that many "officially" named bishops have reconciled with Rome. The regime, however, has remained unmoved and, in the recent past, has imposed the obligatory registration of churches and chapels. Those that failed to get registered were viciously demolished by the government. Also, the acceptance of candidates into seminaries has not changed. Even so, most seminarians studying in the state seminaries have later become good priests.

The government even tried to organize the ordination of bishops in the Peking Cathedral in January of 1999, by deceiving the candidates into thinking that relations with Rome had been restored, or by simply forcing them to participate. There were supposed to be twelve candidates for ordination, exactly the same as the number of candidates ordained that very day by Pope John Paul II in Saint Peter's Basilica in Rome. The communists were able to force six candidates to attend this ceremony, but the Peking Cathedral was half empty, and the seminarians from the nearby state seminary refused to assist, or even to attend, the illegitimate ordination. This forceful step by the government provoked a protest even from the "official" bishops. One of the bishops ordained during that ceremony was simply not received by the faithful of his diocese. Some of the candidates realized their mistake and sought forgiveness for their weakness. The Church in China is in need of many prayers, especially that it may have sufficient courage to survive a deceitful persecution that continues in so many different ways.

I prayed for a long time that I could visit China as Prefect. Naturally, my expectations were not high. Now, although I am retired from the Congregation, my hope has not vanished, but in fact has become stronger. I have come to love the Chinese through the testimony of missionaries who were expelled from China by the communists and who spoke very highly of the people and their culture. I experienced this as well during my visits to Hong Kong, Taiwan, Singapore, Thailand, Malaysia, and to other Asian countries. I pray that the Catholic faithful will preserve their faith and unity, as they have done during many periods of persecution in the past.

the Arrival in China of John of Montecorvino,

China and Taiwan: The Anniversary Celebration

Mention must be made of two cities, Hong Kong and Macau, both of which came under Chinese control between 1997 and 1999. I spent several days in the latter city in 1988, but I made several stops in Hong Kong, beginning in 1970 on my way to the Philippines. The population of Macau is around 465,000, consisting of 28,000 Catholics. I saw there the façade of the cathedral that had been destroyed by fire. I visited Catholic schools and other institutions, walked by the famous casino, and looked over into Red China, whose border guards constituted obstacles for me and for missionaries who would have wished to enter. At that time, the city was under Portuguese jurisdiction, and even the local Church with its pastoral approach was similar to that of Portugal.

I made a genuine pastoral tour of Hong Kong while visiting Bishop John Baptist Wu Cheng-Chung, who, shortly after my visit, became a cardinal. It is a city whose population stood at 5.5 million at the time of my visit, and which is currently approaching 6.9 million. There are 348,000 Catholics, and after the death of Cardinal Wu they came under the leadership of the dynamic Bishop Joseph Zen Ze-Kiun (who in 2006 was named a cardinal) and his auxiliary bishop, John Tong Hon.

The pastoral difficulties of this large city became even more demanding after Hong Kong passed under Chinese control and was accorded a special status. During my trip, I visited flourishing Catholic schools, a modern hospital, and social institutions that had been built up by a zealous missionary bishop, Lorenzo Bianchi. I also visited the seminary and celebrated Mass in a temporary chapel in the basement of a skyscraper. The chapel was rented on weekends by Catholics and used for other purposes during the week. Churches were lacking because land is extremely expensive. Instead, the faithful gather in rented spaces. The Church depends greatly on the work of the laity. I met with over five hundred of their representatives at the final farewell ceremony. They were worried about the near future. I answered them, in a spirit of Christian hope, that Christ would remain with them even after their absorption into China. I celebrated Mass in English, while my guides concelebrated in the melodic Chinese language. I wanted at least to give my blessing in Chinese, but my guide, an experienced missionary, talked me out of it. He said that my blessing could be changed into a curse if, besides knowing the words, I did not guess the appropriate melodic tone of each of the syllables. The same word can have several meanings according to the melodic tone used. So, the Chinese language is a really musical language. It normally employs five tones, which one needs to know exactly, and is therefore very difficult to master.

Hong Kong is a good city for visitors who are interested in the Chinese mentality, in their culture, religion, and so forth. The local Church has a great role to play here, at the gateway to the rest of China.

Taiwan

When the army of Mao Tse-tung was victorious on the Chinese mainland in 1949, General Chiang Kai-shek moved with his army and many refugees to the island of Taiwan, where he continued to govern. Meanwhile, the government in Peking continued to consider Taiwan as one of their provinces. Many priests, religious sisters, and missionaries moved to Taiwan and there reinforced the home mission that had operated for almost a century. A prefecture apostolic was then erected to cover the entire island. The first Spanish missionaries, who began to preach the gospel in 1626, were removed by Dutch Calvinists to Indonesia. A second evangelization was attempted by Dominicans from the

Philippines in 1859. They began their work in the southern part of the island near Kao-hsiung. Currently, they continue their mission work among the mountain tribes. I visited them in 1994. The Catholic Church has eight dioceses here for 300,000 faithful, who form part of the 22 million inhabitants. Of all the Taiwanese, 40 percent are Buddhists, and a somewhat smaller percentage are Taoists. Gradually, with the passage of time, changes have occurred among the generations, and the number of people born on the Chinese mainland is getting smaller. This is true with respect to lay Catholics and especially priests. This entails a new missionary and pastoral approach.

It was in 1988 that I made my first trip to Formosa, a Portuguese name meaning "beautiful island", which is what Taiwan was once called. My purpose was twofold: to conclude solemnly a symposium on evangelization and to visit all of the eight dioceses. I wished thereby to meet the people responsible for the Church's life: priests, missionaries, religious brothers and sisters, and the laity. I planned to deliver a talk to them, which was to be followed by a discussion and a short prayer service. I began my trip at the southern town of Kao-hsiung and continued along the highway that cuts through the entire island south to north. I dedicated each day to a visit of two dioceses, with the exception of the Diocese of Hua-lien, which is located on the eastern shore and is isolated by mountains. It therefore took me an entire day to visit this latter area, which is mostly inhabited by mountain tribes of Polynesian and Melanesian ethnic origin, who all maintain their beautiful costumes and traditions. Evangelization in this area is still in its first stages.

Following my visits, I met with the members of the bishops' conference in the capital city, Taipei. Later I visited the Catholic University Fu-Jen, which conferred on me an honorary doctorate. After the ceremony, I presented my *lectio coram* to the honored guests who filled the hall to its capacity, speaking on the theme of evangelization and culture.

During my second visit to Taiwan in 1994, when the seven hundredth anniversary of the arrival of the first Archbishop of Peking, John of Montecorvino, was being celebrated, I had an opportunity to send an encouraging message to the Church in mainland China. I stressed for them the importance of remaining united and of not surrendering to the machinations of the regime that was trying to create divisions among them. Later, in the city of Kiayi, I ordained a new bishop for the local Church. A very memorable Mass, which took into account the traditions and costumes of the mountain tribes, was later celebrated in the Diocese of Kao-hsiung, where I had been brought by the local cardinal, Paul Shan Kuo-hsi. Instead of bishops' miters, we wore the native headdresses of chieftains. Before and after the Mass, certain rituals were added, such as the blessing of the fire and a solemn procession through the mountain village. Meanwhile, the faithful from

Haulien (Taiwan): Among the Mountain Tribes

Kaohsiung (Taiwan):
Accommodating Mass
for Hill People

the surrounding areas who were not of Chinese ancestry were waiting for us at the meadow, where we were welcomed by native dancers. Our arrival was solemnly announced by a sentinel, sitting in a tall tree. This is a fine example of enculturation for these people among whom the missionaries work.

We then went with the cardinal to visit a modern monastery of Buddhist nuns. In front of the monastery complex of buildings, where religious meetings are held for large groups, and even for crowds of up to five thousand, there stands a tall statue of Buddha. Our tour guide was a highly educated, but relatively young, nun with a shaven head. She was dressed in orange robes and spoke perfect English. She shared with us their activities and showed us new buildings that had been rendered necessary by the arrival of many candidates, especially from among university students. It was interesting that increased technical development and prosperity have led young people to a contemplative lifestyle. Man really does not live by bread alone. At the end, she tried to explain the basic tenets of Buddhism, which I mentioned earlier.

A visit to the national museum in the capital city, Taipei, broadened my knowledge of the ancient Chinese cultural arts. I refer especially to the making of figurines and various articles out of porcelain, glass, and other materials, as well as accomplishments in mathematics, astronomy, and other fields. Artifacts of historical value were on display, brought there from mainland China before the advent of communism. From out of the large collections, which are safely stored in facilities under the hillsides, valuable pieces connected with the history of China are chosen for exhibition. Nowadays, Taipei is a large, modern city with a spacious central square surrounded by beautiful buildings, as for example, the mausoleum of General Chiang Kai-shek and the national theater built in the Chinese architectural style.

Several years ago, John Paul II suggested to the Church in

Kaohsiung: Hill Lady in Solemn Dress

256

In a Buddhist Monastery near Kaohsiung

Taiwan that it become a bridge to China. To accomplish that, Taiwanese Catholics would have to have a strong missionary spirit. Even
on the island itself, the Church is but a small flock among the Buddhists and Taoists. Besides, the mountain tribes, who learn Chinese
only in schools, need to be evangelized as well. Growing prosperity
does not foster the growth of religious zeal. Despite all this, the
Church in Taiwan is alive and has good bishops and priests. These
are replacing the missionaries, whose numbers have decreased, even
as they faithfully awaited the day of their return to the mainland.
Conditions and statistical data prove that foreign missionaries are still
needed in Taiwan, where they can enjoy an open field for their
missionary labors. Currently, Catholics in Taiwan enjoy an importance that exceeds their numbers. The Catholic University Fu-Jen is
adding to that importance, despite its large, but quite understandable,
number of non-Catholic students. The majority of the faculty, as
well, profess different religions. In the future, it will be a problem
for the university as to how, and in what areas, it will preserve its
Catholic identity. Another significant problem is the decline in population growth, caused by the modern mentality. This entails a decline

in vocations to the priesthood and religious life—a significant challenge for the small Taiwanese flock.

Republic of Outer Mongolia

There are some countries in East Asia where the culture, although grounded in a single religion, possesses its own local color. Still others are marked by a blend of two or more religions within the local cultures. Japan, for instance, is a relatively compact country. Alongside its Buddhist culture, Shintoism is also practiced, which is in fact a typically Japanese version of Buddhism. Then again, in Korea, we find traditional shamanism, Buddhism, and Confucianism, but also Christianity, which, in the North, has been has almost annihilated by the communist regime. The Tibetan variety of Buddhism is practiced by 96 percent of the people of Mongolia. There are, however, a small number of Moslems in Mongolia, as well as an infant Catholic mission, credit for which belongs to the Church in South Korea. Before actually moving along to South Korea, I wish to sketch two other experiences.

I want to mention the beginnings of the Mongolian mission, which for me, is a matter of the heart. Mongolia is a vast country and is almost all desert. About 2.5 million people inhabit this plain of about 600,000 square miles. At the close of World War I, Belgian missionaries of the Immaculate Heart of Mary had already been in the country for more than fifty years. The Church of South Korea has also helped in the evangelization of Mongolia in the past. The ensuing domination of Mongolia by communist Russia ultimately brought an end to their efforts, but this country remained in the memory and archives of the Propagation of the Faith, while hoping for a time of possible evangelization in the future. After the fall of the Soviet Union, the Mongolian minister of foreign affairs requested that the Holy See establish diplomatic relations—a request that was immediately honored. This act allowed for the opening of a mission and for three members of the aforementioned Congregation to undertake their ministry. I consider myself as something of a co-founder of this reestablished mission, to which we initially gave the simplest possible hierarchical form. It was first an "independent mission", but after ten years of successful activity, it was raised by the Congregation for Evangelization to a prefecture apostolic. The following year, in 2003, it received its own bishop. A few years after the reestablishment of the mission, I asked a community of women religious to go there as missionaries. Subsequently, at their general chapter, the sisters voted unanimously to accept the invitation. In addition to these women, Salesians can also be found here. By the tenth anniversary of the modern mission, the missionaries were able to baptize about forty new adult converts at Easter in 2002. Now there are about 200 Catholics. It is in this fashion that Christ's Church is being built up.

Republic of Korea (South Korea)

Since the close of World War II, North Korea has been ruled by a rigid communist regime that has practically destroyed the small company of Catholics that once lived there. As best as can be ascertained, only about 1,000 believers remain. Protestants from the United States of America have maintained certain ties with their co-religionists, however, and the famous evangelical preacher Billy Graham twice received permission in the 1990s to visit this country. Before one of his trips, he came to pay me a visit. A timid sign of openness to the world was apparent after the fall of the Soviet Union. At that time, the regime permitted a delegation from an "independent organization" of Christians to participate in the liturgical celebration of Holy Week in Rome. These persons also came to pay me a visit, but it became clear at once that the government was merely putting on a new "face" toward the West. The delegation was led by a Protestant of some denomination or other, while the only Catholic member was a pious and frightened woman. Accompanying them at every turn was a not-so-secret policeman who constantly and openly jotted down their every word.

A Catholic priest from South Korea had received permission to serve as their interpreter. The leader of the delegation proceeded to describe North Korean religious freedom for me in rosy colors, all made possible by their dictator or "rising sun". I then just urged them all to persevere in their faith and furthermore explained to them that the Church desires nothing more than the liberty to preach the gospel and serve the people. In fact, the regime would later enter into a closer relationship with the Chinese communists and only permit the repeated importation of humanitarian food shipments for its starving inhabitants.

SOUTH KOREA

The situation in South Korea is entirely different. The division of the peninsula into two countries occurred after World War II, but Japan had previously occupied all of Korea in 1910. With the Japanese defeat in 1945, the Soviets seized the northern part and the American army took possession of the south. The 38th parallel became the dividing line. In 1948, both sections declared themselves to be countries, each one with a claim to the entire peninsula. The war that broke out between them in 1950 tended to formalize their existence as two nations, each with a different governing system. A communist dictatorship held sway in the North, while the South was ruled by a military, and eventually a democratic, government.

The beginnings of the Christian faith in Korea have a very interesting history. The first plans were prepared by a certain Chinese Catholic writer at the beginning of the seventeenth century. In 1777, a group of Korean authors undertook the study of Catholic doctrine at a Buddhist convent in Korea. In 1783, Korean layman Yi (Ri) Song Hun received baptism in Peking and took the name of Peter. He brought the Catholic faith back to his native country, where he established the first Christian community. Within a few years, there were already 4,000 Catholics, but these faced persecution, and two early martyrs laid down their lives for Christ. Actual missionaries soon began arriving in the country, and the entire nineteenth century was marked by alternating periods of freedom and persecution, the latter launched on behalf of the ruling state religion, Confucianism. When the Japanese occupied Korea in 1910, in spite of all the obstacles of the previous century, the Church had 73,000 members and fifteen native priests. Evangelization efforts were widely scattered, and subsequent attempts by the Japanese to impose Shintoism failed miserably. The Church increased in numbers, especially after the beatification of seventy-nine Korean martyrs in 1925, the calling of a Korean Synod, and the organization of lay people into the "Catholic Action" movement. Since the Armistice of 1953, the greatest number of conversions has taken place in the South. In contrast, all Christian churches in the North were long ago forbidden any kind of activity, and even the right to exist. Thus have matters progressed until today, when South Korea can count more than 4.5 million Catholics among its 48 million inhabitants, as well as the existence of fifteen dioceses. Their cardinal and my friend, Stephen Kim, went to his deserved rest in 1998. For all Koreans, however, he served as a tireless advocate for human rights and freedom, fending off attacks from the army as well as from dictators.

In October 1989, Cardinal Kim organized the Forty-fourth International Eucharistic Congress, which was held in the South Korean capital of Seoul. He also invited Pope John Paul II to preside at the closing ceremonies. I accompanied the Pope on this trip. Our airplane stopped in Venice and refueled for the trip over the Soviet Union, which was more than thirteen hours. The South Korean capital is a modern metropolis and was then crowded with pilgrims from various parts of the country as well as from neighboring lands, from the rest of Asia, and from the whole world. From North Korea, on the other side of the "Bamboo Curtain" of the 38th parallel, not a soul was permitted to come. In contrast, various bishops and faithful had come from China, Vietnam, and Myanmar in spite of a great many obstacles.

From the airport, we drove directly to the parish church of the Good Shepherd. Perpetual Adoration of the Eucharist is held there, and we were able to join in prayer with those present. After relaxing for a short time at the nunciature, the Holy Father celebrated Mass at the Olympic Stadium, where he administered both baptism and confirmation. On the stage near the altar were twenty empty chairs for youth from North Korea. As the Pope was celebrating Mass, four bishops celebrated another Mass on Mount Tora, at the 38th parallel. In union with the five thousand faithful present, they prayed for peace and for a united Korea. But the strongest impression that remained from the closing of the Eucharistic Congress was the unlikely venue, situated among skyscrapers, and with more than a million faithful in attendance. About 1,500 concelebrants—cardinals, bishops, priests—

were seated on a raised altar platform. They came from all the continents because every country had sent its delegates. The view of this multicolored human multitude was breathtaking. Most prominent were the Korean women in their beautiful native garb. The theme of the Congress was very pertinent: "Christ, our peace". I remember that the Holy Father wanted to insert some Korean words into his homily and asked one of the local priests to teach him the correct pronunciation. For several years, I kept the name of this remarkable priest in my memory as a future candidate for the office of bishop—after a thorough scrutiny. John Paul II has known him very well and willingly appointed him as a bishop.

After a glorious celebration of Mass, the Holy Father addressed a message of peace to the whole world. Amid his remarks, he spoke to the absent faithful in North Korea and China, expressing his admiration and love for them and encouraging them to persevere in the faith.

I nurtured plans for a return trip to Korea and a personal visit to each diocese, but, sad to say, this never materialized. Nevertheless, I heartily admire this Church that was truly established and nurtured by faithful lay people. My heart remains sad over the destruction of the small North Korean flock. I cannot omit noting that native Korean priests and religious sisters are doing missionary service outside their own country and, together with those from the Philippines, are the hope of missionary activity, especially in Asia. I have already met Korean missionaries in Siberia, where many of their compatriots work, as well as other missionaries from Korea who labor in North Africa. Even as civilian laborers, Catholic Koreans in foreign countries give good example and honor the Church founded by their ancestors.

Japan

Japan is an interesting country, even from a religious standpoint. It consists of a large number of islands and possesses an ancient culture and history whose origins the Japanese have embellished with mythological tales. For many centuries, Japan was completely isolated and ruled by Samurai clans. In the twentieth century, the Japanese expanded into neighboring lands such as Korea and earned the reputation of being harsh rulers. After their defeat in World War II, they opened themselves to the world on a large scale. They built up large industries and flooded world markets with their products. Their presence is especially felt in Asia, which is saturated with Japanese automobiles and other manufactured goods. Of the 127 million Japanese, 51 percent practice Shinto and 38 percent are Buddhists. Japanese Catholics number 533,000 (0.4 percent), but when combined with Catholics from abroad who reside in Japan, their numbers exceed 1 million. Christians of all denominations comprise about 1.2 percent of the Japanese population.

History tells us that Saint Francis Xavier and his companions brought Christianity to Japan in the second half of the sixteenth century. Beginning in Nagasaki, the faith spread rapidly. According to the best estimates, the number of faithful eventually approximated that of our own day. Toward the end of the sixteenth century, however, a cruel persecution broke out that claimed many lives, including those of six Franciscans, three Japanese Jesuits, and sixteen Christian laity. They were crucified in Nagasaki in 1597 and canonized in 1862. After a short period of freedom, a worse persecution broke out, during which

Tokyo: In the Girls' School

thousands of martyrs lost their lives. Christianity would remain pro-scribed until the second half of the nineteenth century. This did not prevent Christians around Nagasaki from preserving their faith, how-ever, even though they had to do so without priests. When the French missionary Bernard Petitjean, a priest of the Society of the Foreign Missions, arrived there in 1865, he was asked if he was celibate, if he honored the Blessed Virgin Mary, and if he acknowledged the Pope of Rome as head of the Church. Only after receiving affirmative answers did the people reveal their faith in Christ.

Under the influence of political contacts with European countries, the Japanese Constitution of 1889 accorded religious freedom. Evan-gelization efforts expanded thereafter, but they constantly clashed with the Japanese mentality that had been conditioned by the Shinto reli-gion to regard the emperor as divine and to worship him as a deity. By the time of World War I, Catholic Church organization was solidly established in the country. A seminary was founded in Nagasaki, and in 1927, the first native-born bishop was appointed. A year later, the government approved a Jesuit Catholic university in Tokyo, and in 1937, Tokyo received its first native-born archbishop. The Holy See also published a set of norms governing the participation of Catholics in the civic rituals of Shinto. In 1947, a new constitution recognized the equality and freedom of all religions. Many missionaries arrived at that time to undertake evangelization, but all of the country's bishops are presently of Japanese origin. The sixteen dioceses are divided into three Church provinces, headed by archbishops in Tokyo, Nagasaki, and Osaka. Since 1960, the country has always had its own cardinal. The number of Catholics increases rather slowly, however, and is due more to the arrival of foreign laborers from Korea, Brazil, the Philip-pines, and Peru than to conversions among the Japanese. I was always curious about this phenomenon, and it was the first question I pre-sented to the Japanese bishops when I was named Prefect of the *Pro-paganda Fide*. I suspected that the main reason was a certain moderate reluctance on the part of the Japanese to accept the Christian faith and that this was connected in some fashion with their religion, culture, and mentality.

As statistics show, the Shinto religion is quite strong here, with Buddhism in second place. "The Path of the Gods" (*shin-to*) is the traditional primitive religion of the Japanese. It has its own mythol-ogy and moral values, as well as complicated rituals for worshipping a divinity that lacks a clearly defined face. Divine power is attributed to nature, as well as to the sea and land, to volcanoes, and to growing plants. It subsists in the powerful people of this world, especially the Japanese emperor, but also, after a fashion, in one's own ancestors. The rites for venerating the divinity are carried out in temples constructed in forests or on hills,

JAPAN

or at the very least in parks, as is the case in the great city of Tokyo, where a well-known shrine is located. These sanctuaries function as centers for family and community events, such as births, marriages, and ceremonies of thanksgiving. Shintoism does not pretend to furnish a comprehensive system of belief. It can coexist with other creeds, and especially with Buddhism—so much so that some Japanese consider themselves to be both Shinto and Buddhist.

This was driven home to me by a minor experience I had while visiting the shrine in Tokyo I mentioned above. We entered through a magnificent arch and proceeded up a tree-lined alley to the shrine itself, where we found water for ritual purification. Next to us walked an elegantly attired man, who had hired a pagan priest to celebrate a short ceremony for him. The man spoke to us in English and asked if we were Catholic priests. He informed us that he practiced Shinto, and that it was ultimately immaterial whether we acknowledged Buddha or our Christ. He had come to fulfill a debt of gratitude, because he had undergone a successful operation in America.

One can conclude that Shintoism respects other religions, while remaining connected to family and society, and teaching its own way of life. It emphasizes family, community, and especially external obedience. The laborer who spends all his days in the factory to gain a first-class rating can find a new religion and sense of fulfillment in his work environment and his profit. Shintoism does not concern itself so much with the interior condition of a person, as much as it stresses family and community life. This outlook explains the obedience once given to the emperor and army officers, but also the obedience manifested in work and in many other aspects of Japanese life. It is very difficult for a Japanese person to grasp the notion of sin that can be committed in the heart and in the mind. Catholic morality seems quite foreign to the national mentality, but the Japanese greatly admire it. Because of this difficulty in connecting on the moral plane, and because of the other ceremonies and habits connected to Shintoism, the Japanese find it hard to abandon their way of life with its Shinto traditions. Even after the Japanese opened up to the world after the Second World War, and after they gave up worshipping the emperor as a divine being, Western materialism, technical progress, and a rising standard

Japan: Nagasaki, Martyrs' Monument

of living became so many impediments rather than aids in converting to Christianity. As I said to the Japanese bishops, it is they who are the real experts. It is they who simultaneously understand the Japanese mentality and culture and who know the gospel. Therefore, it is they who are called upon to find suitable ways for inserting the Catholic faith into Japanese society and for enculturating it into the Japanese soul.

These observations and knowledge were gleaned mostly from my pastoral visit in 1994, when I celebrated Holy Mass on the outskirts of Tokyo and confirmed a group of teenage youths. To get out to the site, we traveled one Sunday by auto for almost two hours over modern roads and in peacefully flowing traffic. The small church was crowded with the faithful of various nationalities, who had spent the whole day travelling and waiting just so they could be present at Holy Mass. Among them were Japanese, Koreans, Filipinos, Brazilians, and Peruvians, a true picture of the universal Catholic Church. Many people were preparing joyfully for this meeting for an entire week. It was truly as a parish "community" that they gathered around the Eucharistic table and then at a simple reception after Mass.

I also paid a visit to the modern headquarters of the bishops' conference, where we met with brother bishops, all of whom I recognized. The large seminary building in Tokyo was, sad to say, half-empty for lack of vocations. It was heartwarming to visit a girls' school where Japanese religious sisters exercise their ministry. After that I paid a visit to a seminary of a Neo-Catechumenal Movement in Takamatsu where I blessed the cornerstone for a new building. I also met with seminarians from various countries, mainly from South America, who are preparing for priestly service in Japanese dioceses. In the Diocese of Fukuoka, we had a small session with missionaries who, in spite of their long years of service, could not see any results from their work. I observed their eyes filling with joy when I reminded them that the Lord had sent them to sow the seed and not to harvest the growth. What they sowed with their lives' sweat and blood would yield a harvest that other hands would gather. The Sulpician seminary in Fukuoka made a good impression on me for the expert level of training offered there. The Archdiocese of Nagasaki was headed by Archbishop Francis Xavier Shimamoto, who, as a student, lived in Rome at the College of Saint John Nepomucene. It was there that we first met. The highest concentration of Japanese Catholics lives around Nagasaki, a fact that was made evident at the solemn celebration of Mass at the cathedral. In a nearby marketplace, near the Jesuit residence, stands a monument honoring the Martyrs of Japan. A gracious reception was offered me by the religious sisters who staff a college for girls near Nagasaki. I did not omit visiting the small seminary that the archbishop had founded. A short but warm greeting later awaited me at the residence of retired Cardinal Joseph Satowaki.

The Church in Japan finds itself in a situation that demands heightened attention on the part of bishops, but also intensive prayer on the part of all the faithful of the earth. I carried just such an impression away with me from my first visit there in 1981. But at that time, the recent visit of John Paul II inspired great hopes for deeper consequences in the Japanese soul. I made a stop at the Tokyo airport in December 1992, while returning from Tonga in Oceania. While waiting for the plane that would take me over Siberia, through Moscow, and onto Frankfurt, these old impressions were confirmed. It was just before Christmas, and the whole modern airport was decorated with pictures of Santa Claus and with gold and colored lights.

Slovak Salesian Jozef Figura, Who Served Here for 65 Years

The entire time, American carols like "Jingle Bells" resounded through the terminal. All this was accompanied by advertising. Christianity, with its emphasis on the Incarnation of the Son of God, seemed as little more than a commercial matter in this country. Such "religion" will surely never convert, much less attract, anybody. So how is one to address the Japanese soul? How are the Japanese to convert to the Catholic faith, which has a good reputation among them but seems so difficult for them to embrace? It is said that although some Japanese like the Catholic faith and the Church very much, they put off converting until the end of their lives. I know that the Japanese bishops, priests, and laity face these questions. I hope that these remarks do not seem too cloudy for the Church community living in the midst of this culture.

Oita: Parishioners
of Father Štefan Foltin

Republic of the Philippines

The Philippines consist of over 7,000 islands, both large and small, that lie south of Taiwan and southwest of Japan. They form an appendage of sorts to Asia, and 66 of their nearly 81 million inhabitants are Catholics. Muslims are encountered only on the southern island of Mindanao and account for 4 percent of the overall population. The remainder of the Filipino population is Protestant. The Philippines are rightly called the only Catholic nation in Asia, as well as the place where most Asian Catholics reside. Among its mission territories, certain vicariates apostolic in the mountains and islands can be considered viable. These are to be found chiefly in the central and southern portions of the country. John Paul II more than once reminded the people of the Philippines of their missionary responsibility of caring for other Asian countries. The Filipinos have genuinely embraced this role, not only with regards to the work of priests and religious sisters, but also to the witness given by the ordinary faithful who go there for work. There are eighty-six dioceses in the Philippines. After India, where far fewer Catholics reside, the Philippines contain the largest number of dioceses in Asia. Manila is an important center for international Catholic undertakings, especially as directed toward Asia. The memory of World Youth Day in 1995 remains strong in my mind, when 4 million faithful gathered around John Paul II and constituted what was probably the largest Catholic Church gathering of recent years.

It was from the Philippines that Spanish Augustinians reintroduced the faith to China in the sixteenth century, after the lapse of the Franciscan mission initiated two centuries earlier. Manila became an archdiocese in 1595, and southern Cebu a center for evangelization. Over the next two centuries, the Philippines dispatched missionaries to Japan, Formosa, China, and even Indochina. After the American conquest of 1898, when over five hundred Spanish missionaries returned to their homeland, the local Church continued to grow and was soon endowed with its own national episcopate. After World War II, the country achieved its independence. In 1955, my predecessor as Prefect of the Propagation of the Faith, Cardinal Grégoire-Pierre Agagianian, presided as chairman at a Pan-Asiatic bishops' conference in Manila. Pope Paul VI presided at a similar meeting in Manila in 1970. I was there as well, as a member of the Congregation for the Doctrine of the Faith. Pope John Paul II visited this country twice, in 1981 and 1995. At the time of his 1981 visit, we encountered each other at the airport. After his departure, I was able to visit a few more countries at my leisure. The general assembly of the Federation of Asian Bishops' Conferences (FABC) was held in Manila in 1995. I attended the meeting and delivered a lecture. The Holy Father also spoke before the opening of World Youth Day, which took place in Manila at the same time. The tireless Cardinal Jaime Sin invited me to attend other events, such as, for example, the Conference of the Biblical Apostolate of Penitence. Archbishop José Tomás Sánchez, who was later named cardinal, served for many years as Secretary of the Congregation for Evangelization and was also from the Philippines.

THE PHILIPPINES

The Church in the Philippines has a truly serious mission in Asia. For this reason, it needs inner strength and a deep religious life. Its guarantee of success is first of all the grace of God, and then, in a special way, the faith of ordinary people.

5. Central Asia and Other Territories

After the fall of the Soviet Union, other broad fields of missionary endeavor opened up in what had been forbidden territory under the brutal communist regime. In Central Asia this included five former Soviet republics known as the "Stans", because of the last syllable in each of their names: Kazakhstan, Kyrgyzstan, Tajikistan, Turkmenistan, and Uzbekistan. The last four countries have large Muslim majorities, but we nevertheless organized independent missions (*mission sui juris*) and dispatched at least a small group of missionaries to each of them. Very few Catholics are to be found there and most are former prisoners and deportees to labor camps, as well as their descendants. Mission work is in its infancy and struggles against the greatest of difficulties. Heading missionary activity in each country is a member of a religious order appointed by the Holy See.

Republic of Kazakhstan

Kazakhstan deserves its own mention since it exceeds each of the European nations in the size of its territory. It borders Europe on the west, extends to the frontiers of China, and is home to 15 million people. The number of its inhabitants has decreased by over a million within the last ten years. Just about half of the inhabitants are ethnic Kazakhs, with the other half comprising Russians (less than 30 percent), Ukrainians, Germans, Uzbeks, Tatars, Koreans, and Poles. Many of these are now returning to their countries of their origin. Under communism, Soviet authorities condemned large groups of "untrustworthy" nationalities as well as adherents of certain religions to internal deportation. These included Ukrainians, Germans, Poles, Lithuanians, and various dissidents. Kazakhstan became a country of "gulags" and a place where many faithful priests, bishops, and members of the Russian intelligentsia suffered. Among these was Aleksandr Solzhenitsyn, who situated the plot of his novel *A Day in the Life of Ivan Denisovitch* in this region. This country became the grave of many martyrs and also of war prisoners who succumbed to forced labor, sickness, and freezing weather. It is no wonder that so many of those remaining departed after the collapse of communism. But thanks to the natural riches of crude oil, iron, and other metals, the country is beginning to emerge from its initial postcommunist poverty.

God used the deportations of the Stalinist era for His own purposes. Even after the return of many believers to their countries of origin, about 180,000 Catholics of the Latin and Byzantine Rites remained. In 1991, the Holy See placed Bishop Jan Pawel Lenga in charge of the Catholics of Kazakhstan. Thereafter, many new missionaries also arrived. The situation eventually lent itself to the creation of four administrative units and the appointment of additional bishops and administrators. The freedom of the Catholic Church, as well as that of other religions, is controlled by the state, which fears a rising Islamic fundamentalism. Also of concern are Arabian and Turkish influences among the large Muslim population and that of various sects from America and Europe. Typical mission activity and wrongly understood "proselytism" are forbidden. The government is, however, inclined to favor European culture. Of great support and encouragement for Catholics was the visit of John Paul II in 2001. The Holy Father established a hierarchy for the country in 1999, naming the first archbishop in the capital city of Astana and giving the personal title of archbishop to the great and worthy shepherd Lenga.

The increased freedoms of the postcommunist era open up ever-greater possibilities for historical research and encourage a new interest in Kazakhstan and the surrounding countries. A university professor from Tashkent has claimed that, already in the second century, Roman legionaries introduced Christianity here, after they were taken prisoner in battle against the Persians. Later, Nestorian monks from the Middle East spread Christianity in this area and founded several bishoprics, including one at Maracanda, which is known today as Samarkand. In the thirteenth century, the Venetian brothers Nicolo and Maffeo Polo found 700,000 Chinese families in the south of Kazakhstan who called themselves Christian. At this time, Christians were also to be found in the courts of the Mongolian Khans. Franciscan missionaries traveled through Kazakhstan in the early fourteenth century on their way to China. They established the first bishopric in the south of the country. The Islamization of central Asia put an end to their efforts within a hundred years. During the first half of the eighteenth century, Russian czarist armies intervened in the conflicts between rival Islamic and Buddhist hordes. Russian Orthodoxy arrived in the region some time later, as did the Catholic Church. The Orthodox church is

KAZAKHSTAN

active among the remaining Russian inhabitants, provided these still consider themselves Orthodox. Generally speaking, the Orthodox population gets along well with Catholics. The real challenge is posed by the slow aggressive pressure of Islam, which arrives from the nearby countries of Afghanistan, Pakistan, and Turkey, as well as from Arabic countries.

The journey of Pope John Paul II to Kazakhstan occurred shortly after my retirement as Prefect of the Congregation for the Evangelization of Peoples. I therefore did not accompany him to the country, as had originally been my intent. But in September of 2003, the Holy Father asked me to lead the Vatican delegation to an interreligious dialogue in Astana. Our group consisted of eight members, including Archbishop Renato Raffaele Martino, President of the Pontifical Council for Justice and Peace, who shortly after our trip became a cardinal. Another member of our delegation was Archbishop Pier Luigi Celata, Secretary of the Pontifical Council for Interreligious Dialogue. We first landed at Almaty, the former capital of Kazakhstan, and met with the mayor of this beautiful, very European-looking city. We celebrated the Eucharist in the new cathedral. The current capital of Kazakhstan is Astana, which used to be a small town, but since independence, has grown into a city of 200,000 that is ringed with construction zones. The energetic president of the country, Nursultan A. Nazarbayev, oversees plans for the capital's development. After the meeting of representatives of different world religions in Assisi in 1986, Nazarbayev himself realized the importance of this sort of dialogue, especially in his own country, which is home to about 130 different ethnic groups and some thirty religious groups. It was he who hosted the Astana meeting, which was attended by seventeen different religious delegations, all of which were headed by high-ranking representatives. Islam was represented by many delegates from the World Muslim League, with Shiites and Sunnis coming from Saudi Arabia, Iran, Egypt, Pakistan, and Kazakhstan. Buddhists and Taoists came from China and Mongolia, and Shinto representatives from Japan. A large group of rabbis from Israel, Europe, and America were in attendance, headed by the Chief Rabbi of Jerusalem, David Metzger. Orthodoxy was represented by Metropolitan Mefodij of Kazakhstan and Metropolitan Emmanuel of France, with the latter acting on behalf of the Patriarch of Constantinople. Bishop Nicholas Baines represented the Anglican Church, while Rev. Dr. Ishmael Noko, general secretary of the Lutheran World Federation, represented his own communion. Also in attendance were representatives of the secretary general of the United Nations, the king of Saudi Arabia, the Arab Republic of Egypt, and many others.

The attending delegates agreed on a final declaration, which could be of great importance for the future development of interreligious relations. We can sense this from the important points that I now cite: "Recognizing the right of each human person to be freely convinced, and to choose, express and practice his/her religion, ... we declare: That the promotion of the values of Tolerance, Truth, Justice and Love must be the aim of any religious teaching; That extremism, terrorism and other forms of violence in the name of religion have nothing to do with genuine understanding of religion." It was shame that other, sensationalistic, headlines overshadowed the publicity that this important document deserved.

In addition to the official meetings, I had interesting discussions with President Nazarbayev, Metropolitan Mefodij, and with Rabbi Metzger. At the local university, I delivered a speech to the students, of whom most were Muslims. My topic was "The Need for Jesus Christ for the Modern Era". It was there that I also introduced the first volume of *The Catholic Encyclopedia* translated into the Russian language.

Siberia

I undertook a very interesting visit to Siberia, located to the northeast of the five aforementioned countries and hence part of the continent of Asia. I had been invited to consecrate a new church in Chita in the Diocese of Irkutsk. I did not wish to cancel what I had promised the year before, and so in June 2002, I flew first of all to Irkutsk near Lake Baikal. I had always been fascinated by the Siberian taiga and by the deepest lake in the world. Of additional interest were the new cathedral and a visit to the city where the governor and local officials have their headquarters. In the center of town stands an old dilapidated church that caught my attention with its European style of construction. It was a Catholic church that the Soviets had transformed into a concert hall. Even now, only a small lower area is allowed to be used as a chapel. When larger numbers of believers are present, they can cover the stage and celebrate Holy Mass on a portable table. This has compelled Catholics to build a new cathedral that now inspires envy.

At the river that flows through town, I saw a group of boys roaming about. I was informed that they are "bastard" children who were cast out of their homes after their mothers acquired new partners. There are substantial numbers of these illegitimate children. Many local people are addicted to drugs, while the lives of still others are being destroyed by alcoholism. To those in hospitals, we must add the growing numbers suffering from AIDS. In spite of these genuine needs, our mission work among such people elicits envy. This in turns leads to the feeding of false information to the authorities, who then erect barriers to all "mission" activities. The Russian Orthodox hierarchy claims the exclusive right to conduct mission work in the "canonical territory" of Russia, which is said to include the five aforementioned countries. I consecrated the church in Chita for local Catholics who had finished by leaving the old church building to Orthodox believers and building this new one for themselves.

After the blessing and ceremonies, we went to the nearby lakes and passed through some villages that are inhabited by the aboriginal "Buriats". Driving through the birch forest, we spotted a group of trees on which ribbons and other ornaments were hanging. This indicated that people stopped there to conduct short ceremonies and take refreshments. This is also where they honor the gods and their ancestors, according to the long-standing shamanistic customs of the local Mongolian clans. Of course, no one has yet announced Christianity to these people. They are neither Russian nor Orthodox, but nevertheless live in "canonical territory". Then there are those modern atheists who were born without faith or lost it because of the atheistic regime.

Ecumenical dialogue is confronted by many such problems of a missionary nature, namely, how one is to carry out the decisive command of Jesus Christ, to "Go therefore and make disciples of all nations" (Mt 28:19).

The peoples of Asia need Jesus Christ and his Gospel. Asia is thirsting for the living water that Jesus alone can give (cf. Jn 4:10–15). The disciples of Christ in Asia must therefore be unstinting in their efforts to fulfil the mission they have received from the Lord, Who has promised to be with them to the end of the age (cf. Mt 28:20). Trusting in the Lord, Who will not fail those whom He has called, the Church in Asia joyfully makes her pilgrim way into the Third Millennium. Her only joy is that which comes from sharing with the multitude of Asia's peoples the immense gift that she herself has received—the love of Jesus the Saviour. Her one ambition is to continue His mission of service and love, so that all Asians "may have life and have it abundantly" (Jn 10:10).

Part Three

The Americas

On October 17, 1992, I stepped onto the small island of San Salvador (or Guanahari) in the Bahamas. It was a hot day, and I blessed the Jubilee cross on the shore of a turquoise-colored ocean. At that moment, I probably experienced the same feelings as did Christopher Columbus when he anchored his ships at this very island five hundred years earlier. After a long adventure at sea, while looking for a western route to India, he had discovered a new world. It was October 12, 1492, and his discovery somehow expanded the boundaries of the earth. During their first moments on this new and still mysterious soil, the brave sailors raised the cross and named the island "San Salvador"—the Island of the Holy Savior. There I stood, half a millennium later, as a special envoy of the Roman Pontiff, head of the Church. At that moment, I reflected on the deeper meaning of the event, which connected the history of two continents and which opened a new field for the evangelization of the nations. The discovery of America, which was later named for another explorer, Amerigo Vespucci, must have been as symbolically important for our forebears as the lunar landing was for our own. In the history of salvation, it was an event of far-reaching importance, which was acknowledged by the cross that was raised at the ocean's edge.

The gradual exploration of the Americas makes for interesting reading—almost as good as a novel. Even more interesting is the history of evangelization, which has already furnished the subject matter for a good many books. In fact, the story of this mission work has not yet been concluded, as there are still many locations where people do not yet know Jesus Christ the Son of God or His message of salvation.

Guanahari—San Salvador, Where Christopher Columbus Landed

In his Apostolic Exhortation of 1999, *Ecclesia in America*, Pope John Paul II invited his readers to consider the Americas as constituting a single entity, encompassing the materially prosperous north as well as the less prosperous central and southern regions. All should form a single community within the bonds of Christian fraternity, just as all have a common stake in advancing the progress of the gospel. Traditional historical usage, however, divides the Americas into four parts: North, Central, and South America, as well as the Antilles, or islands of the Caribbean. Their land mass extends from the Arctic to the Antarctic Circle, while their combined area is only slightly less than that of Asia, or four times that of Europe. Their combined population of nearly 900 million is greater than that of either Europe or Africa. French is spoken in eastern Canada. English is the predominant language everywhere else north of the Rio Grande River, although because of immigration, Spanish is making inroads in this area. Latin America commences south of the U.S.-Mexican border. With but few exceptions (Belize, Guyana, Surinam, French Guiana), the people in this zone speak either Spanish or Portuguese. In the Antilles, Spanish, French, English, and Dutch are spoken.

The original inhabitants of the northern arctic area were the Eskimos—presently called the Inuit. The rest of America was inhabited by different native tribes whose struggles against European immigrants and invaders are well known. Some of these peoples developed great cultures, as for example the Aztecs of Mexico, the Mayas in Central America, and the Incas in Peru. In Latin America, Europeans brought with them their different cultures, which gradually mingled with those of the natives. These peoples and their cultures gave rise in many places to a new population of mixed ancestry. We must also make reference to the black population, whose ancestors were brought by force from Africa. In the United States, they are known as "African Americans", although large numbers also reside in the Caribbean and on the South American mainland. In recent decades, especially in North America, the number of immigrants from Asia has dramatically increased, with people coming especially from the Philippines, Vietnam, and India, as well as from Oceania. In this way, a new colorful society is coming into being, especially in North America.

The multiethnic origins of the population are also visible, at least partially, in the religions that they practice. Americans are mostly Christian, despite many divergences of belief. The number of Catholics in the Americas in 2003 stood at 552 million, which is close to half the entire membership of the Catholic Church. In Latin America, Catholics constitute 86 percent of the population, while they represent 44 percent of Catholics worldwide. Nevertheless, in all parts of the Americas, not only a new, but also a first, evangelization is necessary.

In northern Canada and in Alaska, we are talking mostly about Inuit-Eskimos and Native Americans, who live in eight missionary dioceses. In the United States of America, most Native Americans are baptized. Nevertheless, there remains a need to proclaim the gospel to immigrants from Asia and Oceania who are not yet Christians. In Mexico, in Central and South America, as well as in the Antilles, there are still large groups of native peoples or people of African descent who are in need of an initial—or at the very least a more intense—evangelization. These inhabit about seventy-four dioceses, located in the Andes Mountains, the Amazon basin, and the smaller islands of the Antilles. Missionary work in all these territories is directed by the Congregation for the Evangelization of Peoples. After this explanation, it will be easier to understand why the Prefect of the missionary Congregation had to travel into these regions.

The Church in America celebrated a special assembly of the Synod of Bishops from November 16 to December 12, 1997. The title of the meeting, which also pointed to a future plan of action, was "Encounter with the Living Jesus Christ: The Way to Conversion, Communion, and Solidarity in America". The resolutions of the synod were later compiled by Pope John Paul II in his Post-synodal Apostolic Exhortation *Ecclesia in America* (*The Church in America*), published on January 22, 1999, one year before the Great Jubilee Year 2000. In this document, the Holy Father John Paul II and the bishops of America strongly pointed to the need for a new evangelization, "new in ardor, methods, and expression". The Pope also stressed the need for a missionary ministry on the American continents, as well as in other parts of the world. Together with the Synod Fathers, he emphasized the need for collaboration in ecclesial matters between North and South America, even in places where cultural differences are involved. Their common faith and an increased level of exchanges demand more effective collaboration. It is also important that the ecclesial communities of North and South share their experiences: the North, which excels in organizational spirit and a more rational approach, and the South, which is marked by material poverty but also by its ardor and a more heartfelt approach to the faith. During the synod, it was demonstrated how faith can foster unity among nations and across vast distances. The synod also underlined the already existing points of connection that work on behalf of the common welfare. Cooperation of this sort in mission work can be very effective. I therefore suggested that the well-known Latin American Missionary Congresses (COMLA), which I shall treat later, might also include North America and consequently change its name to American Mission Congresses (CAM).

1. North America

Missionary efforts in North America began within a few decades of the discovery of the New World. The missionaries had no choice of transportation if they wanted to travel to the new continent but needed to use the ships of the Spanish, French, and British colonizers. Starting in 1565 in Florida, Spanish Jesuits and Franciscans took turns introducing the native inhabitants to the faith. Franciscans were present in New Mexico by 1580, and they entered California in 1769. French Jesuits and members of other communities traveled up the Saint Lawrence River, reaching the area of the Great Lakes by the 1630s. They then expanded to the south, setting up mission stations in the vast drainage basin of the Mississippi. A martyr's death endured by many of these early missionaries prepared the spiritual soil for the spread of the Catholic faith among the native people. Already, by the end of the seventeenth century, there bloomed forth from among the Indians "the Lily of the Mohawks", Blessed Kateri Tekakwitha. When England conquered Canada and the eastern Mississippi Valley in 1763, the Golden Era of the missions ended. The Treaty of Paris of that year ended the influence of the French in North America. Since it was no longer possible to reinforce mission personnel from France, work among the native peoples largely came to an end. In all the colonies that would become the United States, the few Catholics present lived under some sort of penal legislation until the federal Constitution was passed in 1787. While most states did away with their anti-Catholic legislation at that time, some did not do so until well into the nineteenth century. A brief experiment in religious toleration had been tried in Maryland in 1634, but this came to an end in 1692.

The United States declared its independence in 1776 and acquired its first bishop in 1790. In the latter year, there were but 35,000 Catholics of European origin in the country, as well as some Catholic slaves in Maryland. These tiny numbers grew to 12 million by 1900, thanks to successive waves of emigration from Europe. Mission work was aided, in both a material and spiritual sense, by the Society for the Propagation of the Faith, founded at Lyon, France, in 1822. Two other great mission societies, based in Vienna and Munich, also rendered invaluable assistance in keeping the immigrants Catholic and in reaching out to Native and African Americans. Because of this aid, and because of increasing numbers of Catholics, the Church in the United States and in Canada eventually attained a high level of organization. In both countries, the Catholic Church exists alongside strong Protestant bodies and other Christian groups and societies. In addition, religious variety is increasing through emigration from other continents.

There remain seven dioceses in northern Canada, and another in Alaska, that are under the jurisdiction of the Congregation for the Evangelization of Peoples. This territory extends over 2.7 million square miles and is mostly characterized by snow, tundra, and lakes, as well as by forests and prairies. A large majority of the people living in this area are Inuits (Eskimos) and native Indians, who presently are called the "First Nations". The Oblates of Mary Immaculate have been ministering to them for a very long time. The number of these religious men, however, is in constant decline. The Jesuits labor in the Diocese of Fairbanks, Alaska. The cooperation of other missionaries and the temporary loan of diocesan priests are quite necessary. In the meantime, an effort continues at solidifying the condition of at least some dioceses so as to allow them to be placed under the jurisdiction of the Congregation for Bishops. This happened in the case of the Diocese of Prince George, British Columbia, during my term as Prefect.

This mission territory is quite vast but sparsely populated. To visit it in its entirety would consume much time. I therefore decided to assemble all the Canadian bishops from these mission territories in one place and at the same time during my ten-day visit, which occurred in June 1996. I gained additional experiences and insights through excursions by land and air, all of which are valid for the various parts of northern Canada.

I started my trip from Winnipeg, because it was possible to fly directly from there to the northernmost regular airport at Rankin Inlet, located on the northern shore of the Hudson Bay near the Arctic Circle. The bishop of the Diocese of Churchill-Hudson Bay, the missionary Reynald Rouleau, OMI, organizes an annual meeting of Inuit delegates from all the Church communities scattered over this wide diocese. Its territory covers 888,000 square miles, but it contains only 27,000 inhabitants, of whom just about 7,800 are Catholic. This conference presented a timely opportunity for me to bring some encouraging words and a blessing from the Holy Father John Paul II to the delegates. Early in the morning of the day of my projected trip from Winnipeg to Rankin Inlet, I learned at the airport that the airline had reassigned our plane to transport other passengers to Ottawa. These had earlier been obliged to make an emergency landing in Winnipeg during a severe storm, after extremely large hailstones had broken the glass in the plane's cockpit. We were eventually able to depart, but only in the afternoon. We flew over the Hudson Bay for a very long time and watched the ice floes below us that even a July sun could not manage to melt. Polar bears were resting on some of them.

At Rankin Inlet, we were greeted by our eager audience, most of whom were of the Inuit people. Many of them had to return home that evening on small planes or by other modes of transportation. It was almost seven o'clock when we were finally able to gather in the church. The whole town has only 3,000 inhabitants, but its location makes it an important stop for the people of the region and for NATO, which maintains a rather large military base there. The delegates were most gratified that people in Rome and in other parts of the world had remembered them. After reciting prayers in common, and singing some songs, and after what, for me, were interesting conversations with the local people, we all departed together to take supper. Right at the door of the dining hall I was offered a half-inch cube, which looked like a thick piece of skin, but which in fact was whale blubber. For the local people, it served as an hors d'oeuvre and was savored immensely by everyone. And so I tried to chew my cube of blubber. The people assured me that it was a piece of whale skin, which consists of four layers. It was difficult to chew, and it reminded me of rubber, so I discreetly got rid of it. During the meal, I greeted quite a few participants from the meeting, including a young, American Oblate priest of Polish descent. He worked at the northernmost mission station in the world and had to leave that same evening.

After farewells, I took a walk through the parish, as the sun sank slowly beyond the horizon. I went down to the small harbor, where the local fishermen set out to work the broad bay. At around ten-thirty, the sun finally set. I had been merrily filming the scenery up until then. The night proved to be too bright and too short, because at four in the morning it was once more broad daylight. The thought then crossed my mind that a missionary must be physically prepared to adjust himself to all sorts of situations. In addition, he must not be discouraged by the small number of people to whom he must minister, because in God's eyes every soul has eternal value. The Inuits are a gracious people with Mongoloid features. They have broad faces and rounded physiques, the result of their diet and the way their bodies adapted to the climate to protect them from the cold.

The following morning we took a flight to Ariata, a small parish located on the tundra and in a region of many lakes. At the small airport, we were greeted by a group of schoolchildren accompanied

Northern Canada: *Official Welcome*

by their eager teacher, singing songs and holding a welcome sign. There were also two Canadian police officers clad in red uniforms and hard, round hats. The village is situated near a lake, has a well-managed hospital, and also possesses quite a number of churches to accommodate the various sects, which are numerous there. After Mass, I blessed many children, even non-Catholics, by touching their heads. We then had some time left for a leisurely trip to the vast area of tundra between the lakes. Finally, it was time for dinner. The trees are not able to grow in this area. The grass was of a greenish-brown color and sprinkled with many colorful flowers that live but a short time. Nature utilizes the short summer to speed up their growth. For us, the wind was moderately cold, but the local children and youth were bathing in the cool water of the lake. Not far away, on another lake, there rested a hydroplane, most likely owned by a hunter who had flown in for the abundant hunting and fishing that the area afforded. The Catholic women of the parish cooked some meat and sausages for the entire assembly and then sang their religious songs for us.

Before midnight, we took a flight toward the actual seat of the Diocese of Churchill in Manitoba. From the small plane, looking down on the ice floes, we tried to spot the polar bears that sometimes approach the town. The following day, we flew to the industrial center of Thompson, which lies amid forests and lakes. I celebrated an evening Mass there and met with a large group of parishioners. The town is famous for its precious metal mines. In honor of our visit, we were taken to the deepest shaft and shown the modern process of excavation, which has very much lessened and eased human labor. The workers come from different countries and continents and are gradually forming a new community. I was accompanied here by Archbishop Peter Alfred Sutton of Keewatin–Le Pas, whose diocese is located in this region where industry has penetrated and where many new Canadians live alongside the native Indians on their reservations.

In spite of a storm, we were able to take a small plane from Thompson to the tiny mission station at South Indian Lake, which is completely isolated from the world. An Italian oblate, Father Bignami, provides the ministry here. It is an independent Indian parish and is accessible even in winter by cars driven over the frozen lake. Parish membership is small, and the people are mostly fishermen. We spent a few hours with them. During our return car trip, we passed the mining and industrial town of Flin Flon, Manitoba, known for its famous hockey team and for its inhabitants of mixed European and native ancestry. The sight of two churches constructed in an Eastern style attested to the presence of Ukrainian immigrants as well.

A good road took us south through a beautiful forest, where we stopped at an Indian reservation to greet a group of waiting faithful in a small interfaith church. They were indeed Indians, but one would not have known this from their garb and jewelry. Reservation life is neither psychologically nor physically healthy. The government pays them not to work, and this deprives their life of a purpose. Inactivity promotes alcoholism, reckless gambling, drug use, and other vices. The young are incapable of setting goals for themselves. Material security disconnected from labor creates emptiness in the soul, and this in turn often leads to suicide. Even missionary work among them is difficult under such circumstances. This clearly illustrates the importance of human work, of a job, and even of struggle, in the human condition. Many of them flee from this artificial welfare into the towns, even if they must sacrifice their material advantages. In the towns, however, they must accustom themselves to living in a commercial environment, and the adjustment is not easy.

Welcome at the Indian Festival

When we came to town of The Pas, which is the archdiocesan seat, I had an opportunity to take a closer look at the life of Canadian Indians and their problems. A young, elegantly dressed Indian lawyer and parliamentarian came to see me. He wore some of the insignia and decorations of his tribe, which consisted of jewelry and a necklace. He stressed the reality of the "First Nations" and protested against the arrival of colonists who placed them onto reservations or into disadvantageous living environments. A festival was then in progress in the town, and quite a few tribes had gathered to celebrate. I chose to visit them clad in my festive cassock. They had erected an enormous tent on a broad plain, where they conducted their dances and rituals. The chiefs displayed their colorful traditional garb and headdresses, as did the older tribe members, while the younger people danced with vigor. They greeted me as a great chief and put a warm blanket on me. Then they continued with their performances, which lasted several days.

After these events, my pastoral visit was still not at an end. A good airline connection enabled me to travel to the great city of Edmonton, Alberta, located in the southwestern part of Canada. From there, we drove over a highway directly to Lake Saint Anne. Several bishops from missionary dioceses met me there. The lake has become a pilgrimage destination for the Indians, who gather there around the Feast of Saint Anne (July 26). They are joined by members of various tribes, including some from the United States. About 20,000 usually gather for this occasion. Their cars, campers, and tents fill a broad meadow, where an outdoor shrine is located, complete with a covered altar and presidential chair. The pilgrims can follow the celebration of the Mass from the adjoining meadow. The small, older church of Saint Anne accommodates more modest-sized groups throughout the year.

An Indian tent was pitched near the outdoor shrine and served as a sacristy for the celebrants. Here I put on an Indian chasuble and then processed to the outdoor altar in the company of several bishops and priests. We did so to the sound of drums and Indian melodies. Near the altar, some Slovaks from Edmonton had placed a Slovak flag and a welcome sign. Also close by the altar stood a large enthroned portrait of the founder of the Oblates of Mary Immaculate, the canonized Bishop Charles-Joseph-Eugène de Mazenod, who was the great father of the missionaries of this region. The penitential rite was performed in the Indian style and included incensing with smoke, which symbolized purification from evil spirits. The sound of their drums and other musical instruments accompanied the celebration.

After the Mass, the entire crowd relocated to the lake shore, where the rite of blessing of water took place. I stood on a small platform with Archbishop Sutton just a few yards from the shore, but the people stepped into the water until it reached up to their knees. After the blessing, the whole crowd moved further into the lake until the water reached their waists. The bishops and priests also followed the crowd into the water, while still wearing their liturgical robes. I remained on the platform, because I had not brought spare clothes to change into afterward. After that, the people returned to their tents and shelters, where they prepared lunch for themselves. I rode afterward in a small car throughout the encampment, to the sound of music and singing, and was cordially greeted by everyone.

My journey concluded with a meeting of the Canadian bishops of the missionary area, who had all came to Edmonton. We shared our experiences and impressions. I informed them of my own experiences on this visit. I emphasized two important needs, without which this difficult missionary ministry could not develop: the formation of laity for active witness, and the education of native candidates for the

Northern Canada: Lake Saint Anne, *"Pilgrimage into the Lake"*

priesthood. The vocational crisis afflicting other dioceses of Canada should not be used as an excuse for not allowing some diocesan priests to minister for several years in the northern area. A temporary sacrifice such as this would give a new impetus to elevating priestly spirits and to fostering priestly vocations.

2. Latin America

The central and southern portions of America are also known as Latin America, because, with few exceptions, the various languages utilized in the region are all traceable to Latin. These are chiefly the modern Romance languages of Spanish and Portuguese, to which can be added the French spoken in French Guiana and on several islands of the Caribbean. In the Antilles, we can also encounter people speaking English or Dutch—a living reminder of their own colonial history. The unity or similarity of language facilitates cooperation in Latin America, which in Church matters is supervised by the

Consejo Episcopal Latinoamericano (CELAM) or Latin American Episcopal Council.

According to official statistics, as of 2004, this territory counted 551 million inhabitants, which included 468 million Catholics, or 85 percent of the entire population. These indeed constitute a strong majority of Catholics, who currently represent 43 percent of Catholic numbers worldwide. Once again, compared to the data from North America, there is a noticeable difference. The 80 million Catholics in the United States of America and Canada represent only 24.5 percent of 327 million inhabitants of the two countries. These numbers demonstrate Latin America's importance for the Catholic Church, but also that the two regions are the product of very different mission histories.

Without delving too deeply into the history of the evangelization of Latin America, we must recall that it commenced immediately after the discovery of the "New World", which itself constituted a critical moment in the history of mankind and also of the Church. Twenty-five years after the landing of Columbus, the Protestant Reformation broke onto the European scene. Along with the English Reformation, this caused a rupture of ecclesial unity and subsequently influenced the development of evangelization in North America. To the south, missionaries arrived on the same ships that transported colonists and *conquistadores*. They encountered pre-Columbian cultures, but also polytheism and exceptional practices such as human sacrifice and slavery. Approximately five thousand missionaries came to Latin America in the sixteenth century, chiefly from the Franciscan, Dominican, Jesuit, and Augustinian orders. These missionaries lived in radical poverty and helped the local Indians—the *indios*—to adapt economically and socially, as well as agriculturally, with newly introduced plants and animals. By the middle of the sixteenth century, they had authored 109 volumes treating of local cultures and languages. During this same century, missionaries founded 149 hospitals and six universities. The number of the latter eventually grew to twenty-five. Juan de Zumárraga, the first bishop of Mexico City, who took office in 1530, established the first printing press in the New World. The procedure for episcopal nomination nonetheless depended on ancient customs of royal patronage, under which the secular power exercised immense privileges.

The coexistence of conquistadors and missionaries was at times difficult. The sword versus the Cross; the quest for gold versus the quest for souls—all were fraught with contradictions. Missionary methods that sought to improve the lot of the people often confronted the exploitative methods of the conquistadors. The Jesuit Reductions in Paraguay are a fine example thereof and were depicted in the famous film *The Mission*. Pope Paul III (*Sublimis Deus*, 1537) affirmed the human rights of Indians. Several bishops did the same, including Bartolomé de Las Casas (1474–1566) and Saint Toribio de Mogrovejo (1538–1606). In Europe, the theologians of Salamanca defended the rights of Indians. The Church would elevate Saint Rose of Lima to the honors of the altar and do the same with Martin de Porres, who had been born to a Spanish father and a mother of African descent. The Church canonized bishops and missionaries and approved of the veneration of Our Lady of Guadalupe, who appeared in 1531 to the now-canonized Indian, Saint Juan Diego.

Evangelization was made even more difficult by a long-lasting traffic in African slaves. These unfortunates were acquired in Africa by cruel white traders and exported to the New World for hard labor on plantations and other forms of work. Intermarriage between persons of European and African descent would eventually produce a mulatto caste, just as the mixing of European and Indian blood resulted in a class of people called mestizos.

Thanks to a tireless evangelical outreach, many people became Christians. Starting in the eighteenth century, however, the governing classes began seeking their inspiration in Enlightenment philosophy and in anticlerical movements, especially Freemasonry. The "Black Legend", which arose in Elizabethan England and Netherlands, as a means of justifying English cultural and religious hegemony at the expense of Spain, has been embroidered upon in recent decades by liberal, Protestant, and Marxist historians. The "Black Legend" originally cast Spain in the role of a brutal colonizer, and the Catholic Church as a purveyor of evangelical darkness. In later years, the Church has been accused of assisting in exterminating native civilizations and in destroying their cultural and historical artifacts. The Catholic Church has also been decried for encouraging economic and cultural backwardness. According to certain writers, Protestant nations are poised to bring the light of capitalism to the countries of Latin America. Still others claim that the Catholic Church never proclaimed the gospel in depth, but instead contented itself with merely conferring the sacraments. This is exactly the sort of propaganda that is being propounded by representatives of North American sects, who arrive

South America: *Devotion to the Holy Cross*

in the region with significant financial resources and are attempting to bring about a second *conquista*.

The Catholic Church experienced a decline in newly independent Latin America during the nineteenth century, since the Spanish Crown was no longer able to subsidize the works of religion. The Congregation for the Propagation of the Faith, as the Congregation for Evangelization was once known, began encouraging missionaries from different parts of the world to engage in more effective ministry, especially among the native peoples inhabiting the most difficult regions, e.g., the Amazon jungles and the high plateaus of the Andes. Popular devotions were encouraged, such as devotion to the Holy Cross and to Our Lady. Over the last two centuries, the Holy See and the local bishops have intensively fostered an organized mission program and the education of local priests. Clerical numbers, however, still remain insufficient. The hierarchy established the previously mentioned Latin American Episcopal Council, which held its first assembly in 1955 in Rio de Janeiro, Brazil. Pope Paul VI attended the second assembly of the Latin American episcopate in 1968 in Medellín, Colombia. Pope John Paul II delivered his great, memorable speech at the plenary assembly of Puebla, Mexico, in 1979. He spoke of the need for a "new evangelization"—a topic whose importance he once more underscored at the 1993 conference at Santo Domingo, in the Dominican Republic. I attended the last two of these assemblies. I was for many years a member of the Holy See's Committee for Latin America, which carefully monitors and assists evangelization efforts in this region. We must also note that religious priests and brothers have established their own organization, the Latin American Confederation of Religious (CLAR).

I cannot conclude this short sketch of the history of evangelization in the southern part of the Americas without mentioning the superb field work carried out by the Latin American Missionary Congress, or COMLA. I served as papal delegate at COMLA III, held in Bogota in 1987, and at the subsequent fourth and fifth congresses held at Lima, Peru (1991), and Belo Horizonte, Brazil (1995), respectively. I also represented the Holy See at the 1999 assembly in Paraná, Argentina. In the spirit of the Special Assembly of the Synod of Bishops for America, which took place in Rome in 1997, a new title of the missionary congresses was used to include North America: the American Missionary Congress (CAM). The 1999 gathering used a transitional title, COMLA VI–CAM I. The most recent gathering was simply called Second American Missionary Congress (CAM II), and it was held in Guatemala City in 2003.

I have made several trips to Latin America. Apart from attending official meetings and congresses in cities that are large and atypical for missionary countries, I tried to visit territories with a clear missionary character and where living conditions were difficult. I have still not visited Chile and some of the smaller countries of Central America and the Antilles. I am aware of conditions in those countries only from meetings with local bishops and from official correspondence. Latin America deserves our attention, however, so I therefore offer the following account of my personal experiences as well as my comments.

United Mexican States

Mexico is one of the largest of Latin American countries, with a territory of almost 760,000 square miles and a population of over

Mexico:
Our Lady of
Guadalupe

106 million. Ninety-five million of these people are registered members of the Catholic Church and are organized into eighty-nine dioceses. Relatively speaking, we can call it a Catholic country. The only diocese under the jurisdiction of the Congregation for Evangelization is that of Tarahumara, located in the northern Sierra Madre. It will nonetheless be graduating soon to the status of a full-fledged diocese, such as all the others of Mexico enjoy.

I took my first trip to Mexico in February 1979, when, as Vice Secretary of the Congregation for Bishops, I attended the Conference of Bishops of Latin America in Puebla. It was to be opened by the recently elected Pope John Paul II. I arrived in Mexico a few days before the beginning of the conference with the intention of visiting some important sites in this historically rich country. I flew via New York City to the Mexican capital, which is located in a broad valley more than 6,500 feet above sea level. After the exhausting trip, I went straight to bed. During the night, I was suddenly awakened by the sound of my door being opened. I turned on the light and saw the hanging light fixture swinging and my bed moving as well. I quickly ran into the hallway, but everything was dark and no one was getting up. I therefore returned to bed, only to learn the next morning from the other guests that this sort of small earthquake occurred almost every night. Mexico City now has a population of 9 million and is located in a crater-shaped valley that once harbored a small lake. The city also sits adjacent to volcanic hills, for example Popocatepetl, which rises 17,953 feet above sea level. The city reminded me of a lively anthill, replete with loud traffic noises, as we made our way northward along the main highway to the Basilica of Our Lady of Guadalupe. It took me several hours to reach the basilica, but spiritual rewards awaited me. I was able to observe in all tranquility the devoted pilgrims as they approached the new basilica on their knees, advancing through a spacious plaza. Next to the new basilica stands the older, original one, which was built on the spot where Our Lady appeared to the Indian Juan Diego in 1531. John Paul II declared the visionary to be a saint in 2002, at this very site of pilgrimage. The image of Our Lady of Guadalupe, the patroness of Mexico and Latin America, is universally recognized throughout the region.

A large square called El Zócalo is located in the center of Mexico City and represents three cultures. Until 1521, an Aztec temple stood there. Currently, a large and beautifully decorated cathedral stands on one side of the square, while on another stands the spacious National Palace. The latter is built on the ruins of the palace of King Montezuma, who was killed in 1520 after the arrival of the Spanish conquistador Hernán Cortés. The best-preserved historical structures, however, are located approximately thirty miles northeast of the city. I refer to Teotihuacán, the "City of Gods", with its admirable temples and pyramids. These are located along a central thoroughfare, the Avenue of the Dead, with the Pyramid of the Sun to the east and the Pyramid of the Moon at the avenue's northeast extremity. Truly, I was short of breath after managing to climb both of them. These pyramids testify to the high level of culture among the Toltec people, who preceded the Aztecs by hundreds of years as the dominant force in the region. My visit to one of the best museums in the world, the Museo Nacional de Antropologia, broadened my knowledge of the secular and religious history of Mexico. The facts I learned at the museum were of use to me during the rest of my travels, as I walked in the paths of ancient Indian cultures.

MEXICO

I dedicated a few days preceding the arrival of the Holy Father to a visit to southeastern Mexico. A number of pre-Columbian historical structures of great importance are located in that region. I visited some rather well-preserved Mayan buildings at Palenque and some of their temples and pyramids at Chichen Itza, as well as sites associated with the Toltecs mentioned in the guidebooks. I will not even attempt to express my feelings when gazing upon those gigantic and precisely aligned buildings, which dated back to the first millennium, to a time when the various tribes were competing with each other in their cultural activities. Even the capital of Yucatán state, the beautiful Mérida, is located on the ruins of a Maya settlement. Overnight accommodation was provided for us at the tourist center of Cancún. The following day, we continued south along the Caribbean coast, where I was to stay with a missionary priest on the island of Cozumel. The priest ministered to people on the island but also on the mainland. He also visited the descendants of Maya Indians in the forest. The Mayan women, old and young alike, usually wear white dresses with richly decorated blouses. They are shorter and heavier in stature and very kind in character. Gazelles and jaguars, which were considered sacred by the Maya, still inhabit the forests. My host owned a small gazelle and a young jaguar that the local people had brought him. When they were young, the two animals would play together, but later the jaguar turned into a danger for its companion as well as for men, and the priest had to donate it to some sort of zoo. I was able to swim and snorkel above the coral reefs near Cozumel Island. There were colorful fish to admire there, as well as other animals living in the warm waters of the Caribbean.

After my return flight to the capital city, I attended the welcoming ceremony for the Holy Father John Paul II upon his arrival at the airport. The streets through which he later had to pass were transformed into rivers of people. Even the long road to Puebla was lined with people, whom the Holy Father joyfully greeted. The assembled bishops of Latin America, as well as a huge crowd of people, were waiting at Puebla, or, to use the official name, Puebla de los Angeles. I managed to situate myself in a narrow passageway through which the Roman Pilgrim would walk. As he passed by, I shouted loudly in Slovak, "*Vitajte Svätý Otče!*" (Welcome, Holy Father!). He spun around sharply, looked at me with surprise, and blessed me with a smile. Among the hundreds of thousands present, I was probably the only Slovak.

John Paul II opened the conference with a speech, which was eagerly anticipated because of then-current tensions with advocates of liberation theology. Many will recall that his talk was divided into three parts: Truth about Jesus Christ, Truth about the Church, and Truth about Man. It was a clear lesson on the part of the Successor of Peter, who had come to strengthen the faith of his brothers. The lesson was so clear that missionary Cardinal José Clemente Maurer of Sucre, Bolivia, observed in German at the end of the speech, "Die Konferenz ist schon gemacht!" (The conference is already completed!) The answers to the disputed points, which were supposed to have formed part of the conference agenda, had just been delivered.

I recall several interesting incidents from this trip aside from the conference itself. At the beginning of the Puebla meeting, the chefs gave us all the same food, which, out of consideration for the guests from Europe and North America, lacked local spices and "pimiento", a sharp, local hot pepper. But the fare was not appetizing enough for the bishops of Latin America. Finally, the decision was made to divide us into groups. Separate food was then cooked for us, the people of "the weaker stomach". Among my memories, I can also recall a kind family with a young daughter, who offered me their hospitality. During one of my visits to the Church of Saint Dominic (if memory serves), I met Roger Schutz, the well-known founder of the Taizé Movement, who, although a Protestant, was praying on his knees in front of the Marian altar. He asked me about the situation in my homeland, and together we offered a prayer for Slovakia.

Almost two years later, I had the opportunity to visit another part of Mexico. This was on the occasion of the General World Synod on the Christian Family held at the famous tourist destination of Acapulco, where I was invited to speak on the subject of the family. I found myself looking out over the city, which is very heavily promoted, especially in the United States and Canada. The town is located in a mountainous area and surrounds a lovely bay. It boasts of many swimming pools and new hotels. Doctors John and Evelyn Billings, the married couple known for their method of determining a woman's fertile and infertile days, were staying at a hotel to which guests were shuttled back and forth in pink jeeps. One morning, they found some young coral snakes in their bathroom. I do not know if the snakes are as poisonous when young as they later become. They are native to the area and live on rocks exposed to the sun. I also went to watch young boys jump from a pretty good height into a narrow spot among the rocks just as a wave was hitting the shore. As the wave receded into the sea, the rocky bottom was revealed. If the boy did not anticipate the wave correctly, he would be killed. These brave fellows received applause, as well as some money from the bystanders.

I also visited Oaxaca, which is located in the center of the country. It is famous for its beautiful sixteenth-century church. Nearby is Monte Alban, the ancient city of the Zapotecs, with its royal graves and temple ruins. Also nearby is Mitla, the center of Mixtec culture, which is worthy of its own visit. In Villahermosa, I was able to admire a twenty-ton statue of a human head, whose features reminded me more of African art than American. This artifact actually sparked a debate on the ancient connections between Africa and America. I still have problems understanding how the cultures of ancient Mexico, which were so advanced in the fields of art, architecture, and astrology, could preserve certain practices that were more indicative of savagery than humanity. I am thinking here of human sacrifice and the conviction that the bravery of a defeated enemy would be transferred to the winner when his heart was removed and eaten. There were other moral discrepancies that belied the advanced state of their culture. In this regard, Christianity surely allowed them to make a great stride forward.

Christian Mexico has also undergone some difficult times. The country gained its independence in 1821, but soon thereafter the national government turned very unfriendly toward the Catholic Church. Portions of the 1917 constitution were actually designed to oppress the

Church. Active persecution broke out in 1926, and many Christians died a martyr's death. Father Miguel Pro, for example, was executed while exclaiming, "Long live Christ the King!" Even after the visit of the Holy Father in 1979, some stubborn Freemasons in parliament threatened the president for not punishing priests who appeared in public in cassocks, which were prohibited. Only recently has political power been acquired by a different party. The people, however, have always remained faithful to Christ and the Church and are deeply devoted to Our Lady of Guadalupe. Currently, Mexico has many priestly and religious vocations, as well as a strong missionary movement with many representatives abroad. When John Paul II sent me in October 2004 as his legate to the Forty-Eighth International Eucharistic Congress in Guadalajara, I could confirm the missionary spirit of the Mexican Church, especially during my visit to the city's major seminary. They showed me there the artifacts and relics of their thirteen seminarian-martyrs, who had been beatified only three years earlier by John Paul II. During the concluding ceremony of the Eucharistic Congress, which took place in a large stadium, the enthusiasm of the faithful in attendance, in response to the missionary appeal in my homily, revealed their fervor and fidelity to the gospel.

Central America

I have not had the opportunity to visit the countries of Central America, but I did have a working relationship with a number of them. Among these I will mention Guatemala, a very much poverty-stricken neighbor of Mexico, which is ruled by a military government. Its population exceeds 12 million, of whom 80 percent are Catholics. One of its dioceses, El Petén, with an Indian population, is still under the jurisdiction of the Congregation for Evangelization. Also under the jurisdiction of this Congregation is the small country of Belize, located on the shore of the Caribbean. It has more than 283,000 inhabitants, most of whom are black or intermarried with native Mayan Indians. Of the population, 215,000 are Catholic. The country gained its independence from Great Britain in 1981, and English is the official language. Several dioceses in Central America still have missionary status, including Bluefields in Nicaragua, San Pedro Sula and Trujillo in Honduras, and Colón and Darién in Panama. With effective evangelization, all these dioceses might leave their mission status behind in the near future.

Antilles Islands

There are many islands in the Caribbean, and with few exceptions, these are under the jurisdiction of the Congregation for the Evangelization of Peoples. Because of their warm climate, fertile soil, and excellent location, they became an early prey of European sailors and colonists. Even today, some of them are under British, French, and Dutch jurisdiction. The majority of the islands are independent, however. The total number of Catholics exceeds 1 million, but these are spread throughout small dioceses, whose borders are the same as the islands where they are situated.

In the past, slaves were brought from Africa to labor on most of these islands. These in turn mingled with the native population and later with the descendants of white colonists. In the nineteenth century, the British also imported indentured workers from India, with the result that the current population of the islands shows a colorful mixture of races. Evangelization in this region was very much hampered by powerful landowners. The process of evangelization was able to develop more freely after the abolition of slavery. In more recent times, native-born men have been ordained and are assisted by missionaries from abroad, who are chiefly members of religious orders.

I admit that for a long time I considered this area more a tourist destination than as a field for evangelization. Some of my later visits, however, showed me the necessity for great missionary effort and for strong faith in this region. One of those opportunities for learning about the needs of the area was the five-hundredth anniversary of evangelization in connection with the discovery of America. I have already mentioned my visit to San Salvador, where the Spanish caravels dropped anchor in 1492. There was also at the same time a centennial celebration of Catholic mission work in the Bahamas, where I represented the Holy Father as his personal legate.

I made this official visit to the Bahamas in October of 1992, flying by private airplane from the meeting of the Bishops' Conference of the Dominican Republic. We flew fairly low, so I was able to admire the magical sea with its different hues, especially around the islands. In Nassau, I was welcomed by the local bishop, who was a native of nearby Jamaica, and by the governor, who represents the British queen. I celebrated the solemn Eucharist in a small, open-air stadium. In attendance were the representatives of the local government and of different

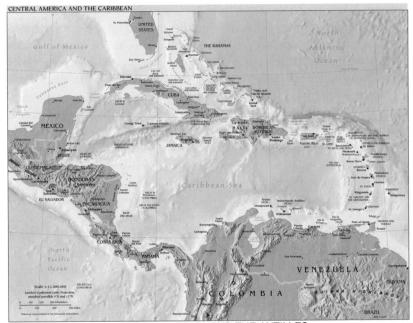

CENTRAL AMERICA AND THE ANTILLES

religious denominations, including an Orthodox priest. In the spirit of ecumenical cooperation, the chorus was provided by a Methodist church. There are over 49,000 Catholics in the area, which makes for one-seventh of the overall population. The old cathedral of Nassau sits on a nice, elevated spot and is interesting for its relatively long and narrow form. Therefore, the altar, with its large overhanging crucifix, is centrally located in the only nave of the building. During my other visit, Bishop Lawrence Burke, who is currently Archbishop of Kingston, Jamaica, took me to the island of Great Abaco on their small diocesan airplane, which was operated by his female secretary. On this island, a certain zealous priest had built a beautiful church and was also extending pastoral care to workers from Haiti. The Haitian people were working on a fruit plantation whose owner, himself the descendant of slaves, allowed them to worship during the only break of their workday. The late Štefan Roman, a Canadian of Slovak ancestry, used to have his summer residence near Nassau. He once took me there on his own airplane and spent a couple of days with me. He sent me deep-sea fishing with his sons. After we crossed the coral reef and got out on the ocean, we cast our fishing lines. Eventually, we caught something big: a five-and-a-half-foot-long shark, which yanked the steel fishing line back and forth enough to break it and then disappeared into the depths with the hook. I was luckier, when I caught smaller fish: a barracuda with a long mouth full of sharp teeth. Despite the fact that it was only slightly more than three feet long, this beast with the double saw blades was frightening. We gave it to the workers in the port, who savor barracuda. So we salvaged our fishermen's pride by catching a tasty fish that was large enough for all the company.

I traveled to the region of the Bahamas on another occasion, toward the end of December 1998. A small airplane took me to the tiny but beautiful islands of Turks and Caicos, located an hour's flight from Nassau. The islands had turned into a popular tourist destination and were in need of a level of pastoral care that the Bishop of Nassau could not provide. Archbishop Theodore McCarrick of Newark, New Jersey, was willing to assume responsibility of these islands and send over needed clergy as well as build another church. He and I joined the Bishop of Nassau on Grand Turk Island, where I installed the Archbishop of Newark as local superior in the presence of the British governor and the faithful. Once more I was able to admire the beauty of the sea, whose colors shifted from light green to darker green and blue the farther one moved from shore.

After we returned to the Bahamas, I celebrated Christmas Midnight Mass for the tourists. Later I had a Mass in French with hymns in Creole for poor Haitian workers, who are served in this area by their own priest. I also visited "Paradise Island" near Nassau, where Americans have built huge, expensive hotels, complete with luxurious rooms and all manner of entertainment for young and old, for people with high and even lower budgets. At one of the hotels, I encountered a walk-through aquarium, where the visitor is completely surrounded by glass walls. Behind these, different kinds of fish swim among "ruins" depicting the legendary and fanciful Atlantis. A large aquarium full of sharks is located at another establishment. There is even a casino, where I wanted to film the tension that sometimes spread across the faces of the players as they watched the roulette wheels spin. The employees did not permit me to do so, however, suspecting perhaps that it would not make very good advertising for roulette gambling, which devours people's money as well as their composure.

While making allowance for certain geographic differences, the islands of the Antilles have their own special character. The local people are in need of a "new evangelization" to deepen a faith and devotion that is often mixed with non-Catholic elements. The Church in Latin America as well as in other countries should take some responsibility for building up ecclesial life in this region. They could do this by helping the people lay more solid foundations, especially for family life, for the fostering of vocations, and for the quality of religious life in general.

Republic of Colombia

Colombia shares much of the northern coastline of South America with Venezuela, both of which are large countries. Venezuela extends from the Caribbean coast through the deep forests of the Orinoco River basin, to the borders of Amazonia. In the west, the country reaches to the Andes. The population of Venezuela has attained 26 million, 87 percent of whom are Catholic. Despite the high number of Catholics, there are still four vicariates apostolic of missionary character, located along the country's borders. I did not have an opportunity to visit them. Essentially we are speaking of mission territories inhabited by Indians that are similar to those that I visited on the other side of the border in Brazil or Colombia.

Colombia is a large country with great geographical diversity. To the north, it borders on the Caribbean and to the west on the Pacific Ocean. The Andes divide the country into western and eastern rain forests, with the latter descending through savannas and forests into the flat lands of the Amazon basin. The faith was brought here by Spanish Franciscans, and it spread very quickly. Different

groups of missionaries built schools and "reductions" for the native Indians. After Colombia declared its independence in 1819, this period of growth gave way to a period of difficulties, and even of persecution, on the part of the state. The Holy See established several vicariates apostolic in the tropical zones of the west and southeast, where living conditions are difficult. There was a need to deepen the faith among the native Indians, among people of African descent, and among various other ethnic groups as well. Currently, Colombia has 45.4 million inhabitants. The Catholic population stands at 39.5 million, who live in seventy-five dioceses and vicariates apostolic. During my time as Prefect, I tried to elevate the status of some missionary territories to that of regular dioceses, and so lower the number of vicariates dependent upon the Congregation for Evangelization. The example and help of well-established dioceses, especially those in the central Antioquia region, could speed up this process.

The main obstacles, however, are political and social. The country has been immersed for several decades in a state of civil war. The central government, which is democratic and headed by a president, must confront two, large organized military groups, both of Marxist inspiration. These groups exploit the poverty of farmers, who began the profitable cultivation of the coca plant. The Colombian army experienced difficulty in moving about in the forested areas, and so the richer landowners established their own paramilitary groups. This makes it even more difficult to reach an agreement between the rebels and the government. Several missionaries, and even bishops, have been murdered by the rebels, or by the organized Mafia-like producers and smugglers of illegal drugs. The rebels cover their financial needs through theft or by kidnapping, especially of tourists and visitors. Besides causing all these problems, they behave on their widely occupied territory as the only dispensers of law. Despite all this, life in the country moves along, in both the secular and religious spheres.

Bogotá, a city of 7 million inhabitants, is the capital of Colombia and seat of the General Secretariat of the Latin American Episcopal Council (CELAM), which is a motivating force in pastoral life. The Catholic University of Colombia is located there, as are other Church institutions. The International Eucharistic Congress of 1968 took place in the city, and Paul VI presided at its conclusion. John Paul II visited Bogotá and several other places in Colombia in 1986. A year later, Bogotá hosted the third missionary congress of Latin America

(COMLA III), which I attended as papal legate. The latter was only one of several visits that I have made to Colombia, however.

While at this congress I began to implement my plan for making this Catholic continent into a source not only for their own ministerial needs, but also for overseas missionaries. In this way, the commitment of the bishops gathered at the Puebla conference could be fulfilled, namely, their decision "dar desde la pobreza" or to give from their own poverty. This also means to share the faith they have preserved so well. On my way to Bogotá, I developed a complete case of laryngitis, so I introduced myself to the packed hall as "the voice of the voiceless", i.e., the poor and oppressed faithful of Christ. My speech was read with South American fire ("fuego latinoamericano") by one of the bishops. The results were immediate: two diocesan priests signed up for the missions as *fidei donum* (gift of faith), and many more became enthused about the overseas missions.

Following the congress, I left chilly Bogotá and went to visit a missionary vicariate located in a hot inland portion of the Amazon basin. Following the visit, I began my journey by helicopter to a forested region on the Pacific side of the country. As we thankfully cleared the ridges of the Cordilleras, we began a long search for an opening in the low, thick clouds. We knew it was risky, but we wanted to get to our final destination, the vicariate in Quibdo. Missionary priests and religious sisters from Spain were at work there among small groups of Indians who are spread throughout the forest. After the usual meetings with mission workers and faithful, we left the area and before evening flew to Istmina. This time the flight was safer. In Istmina, I received a rather modest-sized key to the city, which was made of gold. The local Indians still sluice gold from the mountain streams. Istmina was a vicariate, but ready to become a diocese, thanks to their zealous bishop. He had made sure that the territory was well organized as a Church community and had solid missions and ministries. He even saw to it that they would share their own missionaries with others. After my return to Medellín, I stopped in the missionary seminary, in the flourishing region of Antioquia. Passing through the city of Cali, which used to be known for drug trafficking, I visited the port town of Buenaventura, located on the Pacific coast. The city is the center of a vicariate, where most of the inhabitants are of African descent or of mixed ancestry. It is a very unhealthy tropical town, built partially on pilings at the shoreline, so that the high tide washes against some of the homes, bringing with it mud and dirt. A small cathedral and a simple church, which was still under construction and built of wooden beams, were the signs of religious life of these deprived people to whom our missionaries minister.

I also visited Colombia on other occasions. I flew there last in October of 1998. The purpose of the visit was to ordain a young missionary bishop for a vicariate in rebel-held territory. To perform the ordination at the actual seat of the vicariate would have been too dangerous, and so it took place instead in the Bogotá cathedral. The ceremony was attended by many bishops, who had come to the city for a regular meeting of their episcopal conference. The Bishops' Conference of Columbia has seventy members, and they invited me to address them at their meeting. After my speech, which I read in Spanish, I had to answer some questions. As in the past, on similar occasions, it was not difficult for me to answer in basic Spanish. Now, however, in some tight situations I had to use a few Italian expressions. So I ended up using the "itagnolo" (italiano-espagnol) language—as I jokingly called it. My presentation was immediately followed by the solemn ordination. I was then able to impose hands on the candidate and welcome him into the ranks of bishops with a brotherly kiss of peace. All the while, the choir and people sang lovely South American melodies.

With the government's permission, I was able to travel to our vicariate at Mitú, located in the easternmost area of the country, in the midst of Amazon forests, near the Brazilian border. This large territory, which is accessible only by boat and over footpaths, has a population of only 28,000 people. Of these, 25,000 are Catholic. The town of Mitú is built adjacent to a large river in the midst of thick forests. It has its own airport, which is protected by military guards. It was there that I arrived by plane. The aircraft, which had the words "Policia nacional" written on its side, was also used to transport civilians. As we arrived to the airport, it was clear why the facility is guarded. Right behind the fence, the bishop pointed out two buildings to me, both of which had been destroyed by bombs and fire. One of them was a recently constructed Catholic school for girls, and the other was an office building for local government. Not too far away sat the new bishop's house. It was not yet finished, but someone had already destroyed parts of it with a homemade bomb.

When we arrived at the cathedral, we saw windows that had been destroyed by gunfire. The people were very kind and grateful that someone in Rome had shown an interest in them. They were, how-ever, very careful and afraid of spies. With the exception of some teach-ers, governmental officers, and soldiers, all were poor farmers, fishermen, or craftsmen. One could sense their fear and insecurity. When I asked about the cause of all this, I was informed that the surrounding forests were inhabited by communist rebels. They had attacked the town and were destroying the symbols and property of those whom they con-sidered enemies, namely, the state and the Church. Just before my arrival, the soldiers caught one of the rebels in a nearby forest. My visit, however, went peacefully and brought a little bit of relief and encouragement to the people and to their tested missionary person-nel. I could see that the bishop was tired but ready to continue his ministry under these difficult circumstances. He was losing his sight in one eye and was close to seventy years old.

When I asked what the people did for a living, I was told that some were cultivating the coca plant on tiny clearings in the forest as their sole source of income. One of the missionaries shared with me a conversation that he had had with one of those farmers. The mission-ary was trying to discourage him and explained that the farmer might be causing the death of drug addicts in New York. The farmer told him that drug users somewhere or other in New York are free and do not have to use it. But he, who is growing it, has no choice if he does not want to see his children die from hunger.

The government is trying to solve the problem by destroying the coca fields and subsidizing the farmers for planting other, more useful, crops. The government is also fighting the very profitable drug trade. Drug traffickers have their own small airplanes, employ Mafia tactics, and are in league with the rebels. When we were returning from Mitú, we made a stop at San José de Guaviare, where forest and savanna meet. The place has a military base, but the sight of many small pri-vate aircraft at the airport was enough to raise questions in one's mind. This vicariate was detached from that of Mitú because the number of its diocesan priests, schools, and faithful, as well as the vitality of Church life, indicated that it was ready to become a regular diocese. My visit only confirmed this decision, but did not show me any clear answers for the social and civil conflicts afflicting the region.

I must mention that during my previous visits I also acquainted myself with various other parts of Colombia. I met with some impor-tant cardinals, bishops, and priests, as well as with excellent lay workers. These are the guarantee that the Church will not only flourish in this relatively prosperous, yet war-torn country, but also that a more abundant mission harvest will be forthcoming.

Republic of Peru

Two countries share a border with Colombia: Ecuador on the Pacific coast and Peru, further inland in Amazonia.

Everyone has read about the classic country of the Incas, which even today attracts many visitors and historians because of its mystifying history. If anyone wants to become more familiar with Incan culture, he absolutely must visit Peru. The modern-day country is a large one, which the Andes Mountains divide into three parts: a western coastal zone, a highly elevated mountain plain or "sierra" in the middle, and an Amazonian forest zone or "selva" to the east. Differences in elevation are great. From Lima, located on the coast, one can fly in an hour's time to Cuzco (11,810 feet above sea level) and then descend to the Amazonian plain at Iquitos (elevation: 413 feet). The Andean Cordillera divides itself into three chains, which attain rather high elevations, e.g., the Nevado Huascaran at 22,204 feet. Peru has about 27.6 million inhabitants, 24.3 million of whom form part of the Catholic Church and live in forty-five dioceses or vicariates apostolic. One can say that opportunities for missionary work here are few. But difficult living conditions on the mountain plains and in the forests complicate missionary activities. There are not enough native priests, who are the supporting pillars of the Church as an institution. In addition, foreign aid is necessary for alleviating poverty. Therefore, relatively speaking, the Congregation for Evangelization has many vicariates apostolic in the country.

Despite a promising start, evangelization in Peru has not been easy. In the first half of the sixteenth century, the Holy See was able to establish dioceses in Lima and Cuzco. In the seventeenth century, another encouraging step for the Church was the canonization of Saint Rose of Lima. Peru was a Spanish colony until 1821, when, with the help of Simon Bolívar and José de San Martín, it declared its independence. A number of anti-Catholic governments followed in succession. Evangelization of the mountain dwellers and the people of Amazonia, however, would eventually provide the opportunity for establishing new centers of evangelization. At various times in the twentieth century, the country has had military governments. About the time that civilians resumed power in 1980, the Maoist Sendero Luminoso, or "Shining Path", guerrillas were founded. These were eventually beaten by the government. In 1990, Alberto Fujimori, who was of Japanese descent, became president. Ten years after assuming power, he was forced to leave office. In his place, an Indian by the name of Alejandro Toledo was elected. Through trying times, the Church has continued its efforts and has gradually gained the trust of the people. Peruvians have a very deep sense of devotion, especially to the Holy Cross and to the Blessed Virgin Mary.

My first extended journey to Peru took place in 1983, when I was invited to give a lecture at a symposium in Arequipa. The topic of my lecture was reconciliation and penance as well as the recently concluded Sixth World Synod of Bishops. The area around the city looked like a moonscape, with volcanic peaks exceeding 16,400 feet in height. In the center of the city is the well-preserved monastery of Saint Catherine, which has a very interesting history. I had two more presentations to make in the city of Lima. From the capital, I then traveled about two hundred miles south on the beautiful Pan-American Highway. On a rocky plain, near the town of Nazca, images and symbols are traced in the ground and date from prehistoric times. We were able to observe them from a small airplane. Their origin and meaning have still not been explained. On our way back to Lima, we stopped at the shore near Paracas, where we visited a museum dedicated to the ancient local culture. For example, preserved skulls were on display, all covered with gold and with

evidence of drilled holes. A visit to another museum in Lima, with its gold artifacts from ancient times, expanded my knowledge of the highly evolved culture and religion of that era. Cuzco is situated at 3,600 feet above sea level. The city and its environs are invaluable not only for the awareness they can impart of Inca history, but also for their rich Christian art from colonial times and for the original style of painting that flourished there called *cuzqueño*. After a day trip by a train that climbs through the picturesque mountainous countryside, I visited Machu-Pichu, the famous Inca settlement. The following day, I traveled to the small town of Pisac, passing through a poor countryside with its narrow strips of farmland and occasional herds of llamas. I enjoyed visiting the market and watching the religious customs and rituals of present-day Indians. The change in elevation is noticeable immediately upon one's arrival at the airport. The local people suggest at least a half-hour's rest after arrival and the consumption of some calming *maté* tea.

The trip over the mountains to the Amazon plain was very interesting. The town of Iquitos lies in the center of this mission territory bordering on Brazil. It is part of a vast zone of forests and tributaries of the Amazon River and is sometimes called the "lungs of our planet" for the great amount of oxygen that it produces. Amid tropical heat, we traveled upstream in a motorboat. We came ashore and visited a small village of the forest-dwelling Yagua tribe. They welcomed us in their light clothing and showed us their thatch-covered homes and storage places. They performed dances for us and also demonstrated the art of blowing poison darts through a hollow reed. They live by hunting and fishing. Most of the Indians are civilized, and many are moving into larger villages and towns. The missions in this area are difficult, but successful.

Another very interesting trip consisted of my visit to Peru, in early February of 1991, as the papal legate to the Latin American Missionary Congress, COMLA IV, in Lima. The congress was well organized. In attendance were not only the delegates and bishops from Peru, but also others from different countries, including Cardinal Jaime Sin from Manila in the Philippines and Archbishop Laurent Monsengwo from Kisangani in Zaire, to mention but the better known ones. It seemed advisable to divide the participants into smaller groups, according to their area of interest. These included children, youth, missionaries and delegates, and the ill and elderly, all of whom had their own agenda. The general session took place in a spacious schoolyard.

After the solemn welcome, I delivered my opening lecture. This was right after the publication of the new encyclical letter on the permanent missionary role of the Church, *Redemptoris missio*. (I had introduced the encyclical during a media conference only ten days prior to my arrival in Peru.) During the entire hour of my talk in Lima, I explained and built upon the main points of this "Magna Carta" for missions of our time. The whole assembly received this with great attention; even the hot sun (it was summer in Peru at the time) did not tire them. The newness of the document gradually piqued their interest. I stressed the parts that were very appropriate for the situation in Peru and Latin America, which could broaden the peoples' vision and engender in them an enthusiasm for the missions. John Paul II published this encyclical as a "cry" to the conscience of all the faithful. He wrote that Catholics should realize that

> the mission of Christ the Redeemer, which is entrusted to the Church, is still very far from completion. As the second millennium after Christ's coming draws to an end, an overall view of mankind shows that this mission is still only beginning and that we must commit ourselves wholeheartedly to its service.... Above all, there is a new awareness that missionary activity is a matter for all Christians, for all dioceses and parishes, Church institutions and associations. (nos. 1–2)
>
> The Pope sensed that the moment has come to commit all of the Church's energies to a new evangelization and to the mission *ad gentes*. No believer in Christ, no institution of the Church can avoid the supreme duty of proclaiming Christ to all peoples. (no. 3)

This clear challenge of the Pope, the foremost missionary of the Church, fostered an enthusiasm that made itself heard several times during my speech. In this country of poverty and Marxist military groups, but also of liberation theology, it was important to stress that we must first address physical hunger, but that we must also feed the hunger for God and Jesus Christ, and the yearning for divine justice and love. For those who wanted to limit their missionary activity to their own country or only to Latin America, I reminded them of the commitments their bishops had made at the Puebla Conference, "dar desde la pobreza" (share from one's own poverty), and also to share especially from one's own wealth of faith. In conclusion, I called upon the entire Church of Latin America to "step beyond the borders" and to open themselves up to other continents, such as Africa and Asia: "Latin America, send missionaries from out of your own faith!" At this point, the enthusiasm of those gathered exploded as a glowing flame.

It was not merely a temporary flame, as with burning dry grass that flares up and dies back quickly. At the concluding Eucharist, which was celebrated in a spacious stadium, I was able to entrust missionary crosses to a number of priests, religious sisters, and lay volunteers, who registered for missionary service not only in Latin America, but also in Africa, Asia, and Oceania.

I was able to take advantage of this trip to travel to a valley located some fifty miles from Lima. There, among the bare mountains, stands the church where Saint Rose of Lima received the sacrament of confirmation. The road was in a very bad state of repair and led through an uninhabited countryside toward mountains bereft of any vegetation. Only in the valley, which became ever more narrow, did we see the bronze, tanned "Indios". They struggle against the difficult conditions of nature, as they seek grazing land for their little goats. Weather conditions contribute their own difficulties on the high plains. Poverty engenders social problems, as was evidenced by the shanties constructed by families seeking work in the capital city. On this particular trip, I was escorted by the police, because the host government is responsible for the safety of the papal legate, who is entitled to diplomatic protection. At that time in Peru, the Sendero Luminoso still posed a genuine danger.

Geographical conditions, as well as the climate and economy of this diverse country, make the normal evangelization process more challenging. Peru is a typical country in need of reevangelization. There are only small groups of Indians in the Amazon basin who need initial evangelization. Even today, many foreign missionaries are at work in Peru. Besides the members of religious missionary communities, there are also diocesan priests from Europe who come here for a period of several years. The number of local vocations is growing slowly, and these people are assuming leadership positions in the Church. However, the number of territories still under missionary jurisdiction indicates that this process is advancing at a really slow pace.

Republic of Ecuador

After a week-long stay in Peru in February 1991, I flew north to neighboring Ecuador. The airport of the capital city Quito is one of the most dangerous in the world. As we were approaching the airport, I got some idea as to why it is so risky to land there. Our big "jumbo jet", known for its two stories in height and its ability to carry over four hundred passengers, approached a mountain, directly behind which sat the airport. In turn, its runway resembled one of the streets of Quito, because of the family dwellings that lined it on both sides. The capital itself is located in the center of a high plateau, with even higher mountains as a backdrop. The Andes Cordillera runs through the country from north to south. It includes a number of peaks of volcanic origin, of which Chimborazo is the tallest, at 20,560 feet. As I stepped from the plane, I could feel the high elevation and thin air, and so my luggage felt doubly heavy. Thankfully, my friends from the nunciature met me at the airport. The nunciature became my base of operations for the trips I took through the country.

Ecuador is a tropical country located on the equator, a fact which gives the country its name. There are significant variations in elevation, especially if one travels westward toward the Pacific Ocean or in the direction of the eastern Ecuadorian forests in Amazonia. My agenda called for visits to missionary territories in both areas. Apart from these, I needed to fly to the Galapagos Islands out in the Pacific. Despite the fact that this is not a large country, my schedule was not an easy one. I was obliged to use some sort of

jeep in passing over mountains with different elevations and for covering longer distances. The population of Ecuador stands at 13 million, 92 percent of whom are Catholics. The native Indians and those of mixed racial ancestry form the majority of the population, while 15 percent are white and 5 percent are of African descent. There is a need here to deepen the faith and to reevangelize the faithful. It is also necessary to encourage vocations to the priesthood and religious life from among the native population. Ethnic diversity, as well as geographical factors, explain why there are still areas under the jurisdiction of the Congregation for Evangelization.

Missionary activity started in the sixteenth century. The first diocese was established at Quito in 1545. In 1599, Jesuits began to evangelize the upper reaches of the Amazon River, while in the central part of the country, near the capital city, they established their schools and colleges and educated many Christians of the upper social classes. After Ecuador became independent in 1822, the Church had to go through difficult times. In the middle of the nineteenth century, governments dominated by Freemasons expelled the Jesuits from several countries of Latin America. Even at the start of the twentieth century, the Church experienced persecution. Meanwhile, missionary activity among the Indians continued. Before World War I, the Holy See reached a *modus vivendi* with the government, which resulted in a lessening of restrictions against the Church. After World War I, a Catholic university was founded, and in 1953, the Archbishop of Quito became the country's first cardinal.

Currently bishops head twenty-four dioceses or administrative divisions. One-third of these are still in the process of evolving into dioceses, which means that they are under the jurisdiction of the Congregation for the Evangelization of Peoples. I lacked the time to visit vicariates that are not easily accessible, and so therefore I limited myself to one area in Amazonia, to another on the Pacific coast, and to a third one located in the Galapagos Islands. From the missionary point of view, these territories differed among themselves as to population, level of evangelization, and the methods used. They gave me an overview of the entire region for which I had responsibility.

First I decided to go by car to the coastal Vicariate Apostolic of Esmeraldas, which was then administered by an excellent missionary bishop, Enrico Bartolucci. From highly elevated Quito, we descended on a winding main road through humid valleys with forest vegetation all the way to sea level. Not too far from the capital we could see the tops of volcanic, snow-covered peaks, but then came a rapid descent along roads that hugged the curved sides of hills. Sometimes, a waterfall appeared on one side of the road, while a mountain creek ran along the other. The weather also changed from a damp chill to a coastal heat—everything that might be experienced in the tropics. The Pacific Ocean here did not look very appealing, but appeared very rough and dirty. We had extra time to visit some centers that were staffed by missionaries or by religious sisters. In the evening, I celebrated Mass for the faithful from the cathedral area, who were mostly of African descent or of mixed racial ancestry. Many of them worked at the seaport and surrounding areas, but others did not have jobs and lived only from day to day. The tropical climate can have an affect on human nature, rendering some people satisfied with a few fish and fruit and removing any enthusiasm for work. This makes for great problems in families and within marriages, where the danger of alcoholism and other pathologies lurks. The devotional life of the faithful is typically South American, with some African characteristics.

The following morning we arrived at a military airport, from which we had been promised transportation to Quito. However, there was no airplane, and no pilots were to be found. After several attempts to find out what was going on, we learned that our flight had been canceled. Suddenly it dawned on us, that it was the time of Carnival and someone had simply forgotten his promise. There was no other solution but to climb back into the car and get on the road, but this time ascending into the mountains. We arrived in Quito sometime before midnight, and, after a light supper, I had to go to bed because we had to start very early the next morning.

The next day we began our five-hour trip at five o'clock in the morning. Our destination was the Vicariate Apostolic of Napo, located in Amazonia. We traveled in two vans, one driven by the tireless vicar apostolic, Bishop Julio Parise Loro. Despite his seventy years, he bravely navigated the dangerous narrow curves on the road through the Andes Cordillera. Before six o'clock, we were at a mountain pass at a high elevation surrounded by thick fog. Suddenly we stopped in front of a pile of dirt, which bulldozers had piled up during road construction. We were disoriented and did not know if we should go around the pile and follow the tracks of heavy machinery and trucks. The thick white fog and the darkness kept us from finding our way. It was only a few minutes before six, which usually means sunrise in Ecuador. We waited a few moments. Then, sure enough, the morning sun revealed a sharp curve around a rock that had limited our view. We then sped up so as to be on time for the beginning of ten o'clock Mass in Napo. I had gotten used to the fast driving of Africans, but these local drivers on narrow, winding roads and hidden curves were unsurpassable. Only once did we almost have an accident, when a large bus came barreling toward us from behind a curve. Whoever has traveled through high mountains can imagine a narrow ribbon of road with steep rocks on one side and a sheer drop on the other. It was more comforting when we got to lower elevations and to the Amazon plain with its deep forests.

We eventually started spotting people, and near Napo, we saw others hurriedly converging on the cathedral. While the vicariate had 55,000 faithful at the time of my visit, the number of Catholics has now reached 87,000. These are mostly Indians who farm small forest clearings or make their living by hunting. They are isolated from the world, which in this case means from Quito, and the work of missionaries also includes the cultural uplifting of the faithful. The Missionaries of Saint Joseph have even opened a broadcasting station here. We missed meeting with the youth, because in February all students have a summer vacation. The vicariate is centered on the small town of Tena, which was honored to be visited by a cardinal all the way from Rome. Local representatives expressed how much they value the work and zealous activities of the missionaries, which constituted the only form of cultural enrichment in this region. Five years later, I was glad to ordain a new and younger apostolic vicar for them in Rome. At this time, it is still an Italian missionary who serves in this capacity. The number of native-born priests is growing slowly, however. They are the hope for the future.

As we took our leave of these kind people, it was already late in the afternoon. We wanted to take advantage of whatever daylight remained before sunset, which always arrives here at six o'clock in the evening. To our misfortune, while rounding a sharp curve, one of the tires of the first vehicle, in which I was riding, threw a sharp stone backward, breaking the windshield of the new van right behind us. We did not notice the accident, and as we began the ascent, dusk fell. It even started to rain, and we had to slow down and wait for the second vehicle to catch up. The van with the broken windshield had

had to slow down because of the rain, which was sharply penetrating the interior. Then there was the cold wind, the effect of which was increased as the van moved along. We were at least together at that point, and so we were able to continue our trip through the mountains. It became dark, and a thick fog caused the drivers to be more preoccupied with the shoulders of the road than with looking straight ahead where the fog seemed to solidify into a white wall. On top of everything else, we were slowed down by some trucks that were not easy to pass. I sat next to the driver and admired his skills, as he confronted a new danger with each bend in the road. When we arrived at Quito, it was already the middle of the night. The elevation of the city and the stress of the day's activities caused me nightmares, as I found myself swimming through narrow gaps among rocks. Luckily, there remained just one plane ride to the Galapagos Islands.

The flight to the Galapagos included a stop of several hours in Guayaquil, a city of 2 million people. I took advantage of the layover to rest. The Galapagos are a good distance from the mainland and consist of several islands. The airport as well as the ecclesiastical offices are located on the Island of San Cristóbal. While the population has now risen to 18,000, it stood at only 9,000 at the time of my visit. One-third of these lived on San Cristóbal, because of its government offices and military base. Also favoring settlement on the island were its small village, its church, and the prefect apostolic, who at that time was a Franciscan bishop from Ecuador. He was then in charge of 8,000 faithful, who have now grown to 14,000. Generally, a prefect apostolic is not a bishop. There are, however, many factors that warrant the presence of a bishop in the Galapagos: the distance separating the residents from the mainland; the pastoral needs of both permanent and temporary residents; and the ministry to international tourists, who come here for a few days on cruise ships, especially from the United States, Japan, and even faraway Europe.

My visit was directed especially to the prefecture apostolic, but I also availed myself of the opportunity to examine the local fauna. It is well known that many rare species of animals and birds live here, which tourists have been admiring for decades. Accompanied by the prefect apostolic and the youthful secretary from the nunciature in Quito, I traveled to the small island of Española. It is uninhabited by man, but a paradise for animals and their admirers. We went there on a small military ship, which the navy had put at the disposal of military families and other government workers. The ocean excursion was quite entertaining, because we were escorted by a school of dolphins that leapt in and out of the water. They swam past us and dove underwater, only to surprise us by appearing once more next to the ship. Then they resumed swimming and leaping until they disappeared in the distance. I do not know who was more entertained, the people on the ship or the dolphins in the water. When our ship dropped anchor close to the island, we were transported in smaller boats into shallow water. From there, we had to walk barefoot to the island, where still more entertainment awaited us.

A small bay was occupied by a large group of seals of various sizes, small as well as large. Some of them were swimming in shallow water, while others were sunning themselves on the rocks or on the sandy beach. They were not afraid of us, and the children who had traveled with us began to pet them and play with them. Later, colorful iguanas appeared, and we occasionally spotted large lizards, almost three feet in length. Each animal was jealously protecting its living area and would attack any intruder. Different kinds of birds were nesting right at the shoreline. While walking through the center of the island, we saw increasing numbers of birds. There were white pelicans, albatrosses, sea ducks, and birds resembling geese—only smaller and with blue feet. Some of them had just hatched, while others were covered with fine fuzz. Their mothers were flying along the shore looking for fish or else simply fighting with each other. Then we came to a rocky inlet, where powerful waves had worn holes through the rocks. As the waves hit the rocks, water gushed, geyserlike, through the holes and sprayed the seals. Among these animals, one stood out who gave us the impression of dominating all the others, almost like an ogre. The seals were fighting among each other, sometimes even to a bloody end, but none dared challenge the ogre. Colorful iguanas could be seen in the sun, and red lobsters in the water. Even though we were so close to the ocean, it was very hot. I did not mind the heat, because each square foot of the island offered exquisite opportunities for the eye and the camera. Picturesque scenes were so abundant there that it is difficult to describe them in words. I must point out that there were no snakes on the island.

As we returned to the port, my guide, the secretary from the nunciature, was red as a lobster. In the yard of the prefect's residence, we were entertained once more by feeding a huge tortoise with bananas.

Old "José", as they called him, had attained a truly venerable age. After an evening meeting with the faithful at the Eucharistic table, we visited a local radio station. It was run by a young volunteer, who taught, catechized, and entertained all the people of the Galapagos with music. Our exciting day was followed by a good night's sleep.

The next morning we returned to Quito. The capital is a typical colonial city and is spread over several hills, which are then interconnected with ascending and descending streets. The main square next to the cathedral serves as a large marketplace. One can see, side by side, Indian men, merchants loudly hawking their wares, and women with small hats on their heads sitting in front of their houses, while their dark-eyed children hold onto their skirts. There are always many people inside the cathedral. Some come to pray, while others are tourists who have come to admire the rich decoration. Jesuit churches with baroque façades possess high altars reaching from floor to ceiling. The one in Quito is exquisitely carved and richly decorated with gold. Even the ceiling sparkles with gold—justifiably so because we are in Inca country. It was because of their gold treasures that Spanish sailors named the region simply "El Dorado", or the gilded country. A unique style of colonial architecture developed here, as well as a colonial style of painting and carving. The city has its wealthy neighborhoods, while the poor inhabit surrounding villages. These social differences lead to frequent turmoil and changes in government. My visit to the city also included a stop at a public square where a stone memorial and a line in the pavement remind visitors that they are crossing the actual equator. During my visit, I met with all the missionary bishops at the nunciature and later with all the bishops of the country. I saw the retired, elderly cardinal, Pablo Muňoz Vega, at his residence near Quito. I knew this cardinal from Rome, when he had served as rector of the Gregorian University.

I was fortunate to be able to visit Slovak Salesian Ján Šutka. He had labored for a very long time among the Shuar Indians, and I had read interesting articles about him and his mission. In our conversation, we touched upon the "why" and the "how" of appropriate mission work. Some South American theologians were asserting at the time that the main goal of mission work is to free Indians and blacks from their economic and social poverty, heal their bodily ills, and otherwise enhance their humanity. Only after achieving all this was it time to proclaim the gospel. Some of these thinkers expressed themselves with a single phrase: First make them "humans", and afterward Christians. Others claimed that it made no sense to disturb their consciences with our moral prescriptions, while they were happy with their lifestyle. The Holy See and the local bishops challenged these mistaken and seductive opinions and methods, and with time, the matter of "liberation theology" was clarified and settled.

Among South American countries, Ecuador had one of the highest percentages of Catholics to the general population, and one of the smallest indigenous populations in need of initial evangelization. Most, however, need a "new evangelization" to deepen their knowledge of the faith, to enhance their devotion, to encourage vocations, and to mobilize everyone for the missionary needs of Latin America and of other continents.

Federative Republic of Brazil

Brazil is the largest Latin American country, in terms of territory as well as population. Its territory of nearly 3.3 million square miles is home to 181 million people. Of these, 153 million are Catholics, living in 268 dioceses and ecclesiastical territories. The basic religious problem is visible as we look at their statistical data: there are 9,359 parishes and 6,991 missions without a priest. At the same time, Protestant sects, especially from North America, make a tremendous effort to attract Catholics to their own faiths, especially those who are not well catechized or who have little contact with a priest. With these few remarks on the status of the Church in Brazil, we can understand why Brazil is even today of missionary interest, in spite of its being under the jurisdiction of the Roman Congregation for Bishops and not the Congregation for Evangelization.

As history tells us, Brazil was colonized by the Portuguese. The Church in Brazil was also run under a system of royal patronage, where the Crown gave material assistance to the Church and drew ecclesiastical boundaries in return for being able to name bishops who then were confirmed by the Pope. The whole system resembled the one in use in the Spanish Empire and in Austria-Hungary. Missionaries from Portugal and various other lands were forced to accept a situation where secular interests limited the freedom of the Church and her missionary activity. The history of the Jesuit missions is only partially described in the well-known movie *The Mission*. We can therefore understand better why a certain aversion arose toward the Church in the Spanish and Portuguese colonies, as well as toward certain religious orders who tried to protect the Church's freedom of action. This aversion arose in spite of an apparently successful missionary effort. In the end, the Church had to suffer for the transgressions of the colonial powers. European governments, in which Freemasons had gained influence, forced the Pope to suppress the Jesuits. Wars of independence in Latin America also produced effects on the Church. The evangelization effort suffered, on top of the fact that previous efforts had not always penetrated to the depth of people's souls. These factors enter into play in Brazilian history. Apart from these complications, Brazil's proximity to Africa led to the importation of slaves by unscrupulous traders. This explains why today 6 percent of the population are black and 38 percent are mulatto (which includes intermarriage between blacks and Indians). Of the remainder, 55 percent are white and are the descendants of Portuguese, Spanish, German, Ukrainian, Italian, Polish, and other immigrants. In the forests along the Amazon River and Mato Grosso live smaller groups of native Indians. In the city of São Paulo, I was delighted to observe young people of different races and colors as they walked together and amused themselves, without any sign of discrimination.

I traveled to Brazil for the first time in 1979, on the same airplane that brought Pope John Paul II for an extensive pastoral visit. The leadership of the Latin American Episcopal Council, CELAM, had invited me to their twenty-fifth anniversary celebration. The festivities themselves constituted a stop on the papal visit, even though I was not officially accompanying

the Holy Father at the time. I separated myself from the papal entourage when we reached the Brazilian capital in order to pursue my own itinerary. It took me through all of Brazil, at some points intersecting with papal events, but without the limitations that would have been imposed by a series of mass gatherings. This allowed for a very interesting visit to the principal regions of the country.

I traveled from Rio de Janeiro to São Paulo and from there to Foz do Iguaçu, located on the border with Argentina and Paraguay, where I admired the great waterfalls. On my return, I ran into the Holy Father in Curitiba and made a stop at a Marian shrine in Aparecida. Then I continued on to Salvador de Bahia for a Eucharistic Congress in Fortaleza, where the Holy Father was present. While the Pope continued on his trip to Manaus in the Amazon region, I visited the large city of Belém, located next to the mouth of the Para River, not far from the Atlantic Ocean. Here I found myself in partial mission territory. The local population is composed of native Indians or people of mixed ancestry, who are baptized but not sufficiently catechized.

From Belém, I continued to Manaus, flying over massive forests and broad stretches of the Amazon River and its tributaries. The city of Manaus was just then emptying itself of throngs of pilgrims after the departure of John Paul II. I was therefore able to move more freely in the surrounding areas. Manaus is located near the confluence of the Rio Negro, whose black water flows down from Venezuela, and the Amazon River with its yellowish brown waters and clay from the mountains of Peru. After the juncture of the two rivers, the waterway retains the name of Amazon. On Sunday, I accompanied a missionary into the forest, about sixty miles to the north, where a mission church was located. Before Mass. I baptized seven children, while the missionary priest witnessed the weddings of several couples. Then on a small boat we continued inland, trying to navigate around fallen trees in the river. We carefully studied the thickly wooded riverbanks, as a caution against an attack by a jaguar or some other creature. The following day I went on a fast motorboat to another mission station, where construction on a small wooden church had just finished. Walking along the street, we came upon the skin of an anaconda hanging up to dry. The local people had killed and removed the skin so as to be able to sell it. The huge snake had been coming into the village to snatch chickens and piglets. These farm animals are allowed to strut about and live freely under the floors of houses, which are elevated more than a foot off the ground.

From Manaus, I flew to the nearby river island of Parintins, where an Italian bishop, Arcangelo Cerqua, began the evangelization process by first building a brick factory. He was then able to erect a cathedral and other buildings. The landing strip was situated in the midst of a housing area, where people were walking and goats were grazing. Whenever a plane was about to land, a man with a horn warned everyone to leave the airfield. It happened to be the Feast Day of Our Lady of Mount Carmel, and many Indians from along the tributaries had gathered for the celebration. The local bishop had too many candidates for confirmation, so I eased the burden by confirming some of the faithful. The celebration lasted several days. When I inquired about how so many people were getting fed, my attention was directed toward the river, from which an Indian was just returning. In one hand, he held a good-size fish, and in the other, a spear tied to a rope. He had killed the fish with the spear and brought it to the riverbank to feed the whole family.

There are some tribes in broad Amazonia who still need initial evangelization. I witnessed a different missionary situation near Bahia, where many Afro-Brazilians live, and even in the city Manaus itself. Theirs is a very shallow Christianity, mixed with old pagan customs such as venerating a statue of an angel with a feminine appearance, dressed in a swimsuit, which is supposed to symbolize some sort of water goddess. Also, along the mountain road above Rio de Janeiro, I saw altars for sacrificing black roosters, according to the rites of Macumba. A new evangelization is really necessary in this area.

I was able to update my impressions and examinations in July 1995, when John Paul II sent me as his legate, to the fifth Latin American Missionary Congress, COMLA V. The gathering took place in Belo Horizonte and lasted the entire week. Hundreds of delegates and guests gathered in a large, enclosed stadium and participated in a rather busy program. Interesting small-group discussions on various mission-related topics were also held at the local Catholic university. I dropped in on some of them and participated in the exchanges. Some of the theologians stressed the need for mission work solely among the native Indians—who in Brazil account for only 180,000 people. Some broadened their view by including people of African descent. But the delegates from missionary movements emphasized the foreign missions, especially those overseas. They considered proclamation of the gospel as the primary role of the missionary, who is not to limit his activities to social work. It was there that I discovered that some of the less-educated attendees had better views on the missions than did some professors. The final resolutions of the congress were well balanced. My visits to the parishes in this city of 2 million, as well as the presence of the local faithful during the solemn moments of the congress, were most edifying. Many families provided hospitality to less fortunate delegates. At the opening Mass, which was concelebrated by hundreds of bishops and priests, the spacious stadium literally shook with the combined voices of the delegates and local people, all raised in song. I celebrated the solemn closing ceremony of the congress in a spacious hillside square. A broad avenue descended toward the city center. The crowds exceeded all expectations, numbering in the hundreds of thousands. The view from the altar toward the city below and toward a beautiful distant horizon encouraged me to point out during the homily that the city of Belo Horizonte is really worthy of its name of "beautiful horizon". By meeting at Belo Horizonte, this congress was also opening up beautiful horizons for mission work in Brazil and in Latin America. Also, according to the Lord's command, they should go out into the whole world and proclaim the gospel "to the end of the earth" (Acts 1:8).

After this successful congress, I went to the capital city, Brasília, where the Papal Mission Works (or Society) has its office. I had to tend to some business there and also visit the nunciature and the office of the bishops' conference. The capital is located at the geographical center of this huge country. On paper, the plans for the capital city remind one of an airplane drawing. They were commissioned by Juscelino Kubitschek, a Brazilian president who was born in what is now the Czech Republic. The presidential palace is located in the "cockpit". Nearby are the parliamentary buildings and other legislative offices, while the cabinet ministries are located on the "wings". Place was allotted on the main street for a modern, but not very large, cathedral. Foreign embassies occupy their own quarter, while yet other districts are designated for commercial activities and housing. Satellite suburbs have sprung up in a sometimes chaotic fashion around the periphery of the city and are inhabited by new immigrants with their own pastoral problems.

I was more intrigued by the vast territory of Mato Grosso, where the endless plain gives way in places to swamps and forests. The capital of the state of Mato Grosso is Cuiabá, with over 400,000 inhabitants. Campo Grande, with 700,000 inhabitants, is the capital of the state of Mato Gross do Sul, or Southern Mato Grosso. Salesian missionaries have been ministering in the northern part for many years. The local archbishop organized a one-day visit for me by military helicopter. We headed to the heart of the forests and plains, where villages belonging to the Shavante tribe are located. The pilots of this huge helicopter knew the correct path of approach, and our missionary guide knew the area of the forest where this village was hidden. After a long flight, we discovered that our knowledge was insufficient. We had to land twice next to solitary farms to get information about the precise location of the Indian village. Even after doing so, our knowledge was still deficient. We had to fly into a small airport, refuel the plane for the return trip, and obtain directions to the village that, finally, were accurate.

When we finally landed in a clearing next to the village, we were solemnly welcomed. The Indians had decorated their bodies with red paint. They stood in a row, with their wives and children hiding in the shadow of nearby trees because of the extremely hot noonday sun.

Brazil: With the Shavantes Indians in Mato Grosso

The chief decorated me with a headdress of blue parrot feathers, while the rest of those present sang typical Indian songs and danced according to their own rhythms. Suddenly two moving piles of grass came closer to me, and under the moving bundles, two small boys were hiding. After this welcome ceremony, we had a Mass in the mission chapel, followed by a meeting in the yard of the mission station. I was greeted there by old Chief Benjamin, who a few years earlier had met the Holy Father. When I introduced myself as the papal legate and greeted him in name of John Paul II, he felt much honored and ritually tied my wrists as a sign of our friendship.

After the speeches, the dances, and the singing, we had a short lunch and then visited the entire village. There were about twenty large houses there, built of wooden posts with thatched roofs that were attached to a central pillar. In the central place of the house was a fireplace, and in each corner married sons and daughters lived with their small children. There were no windows in the houses. The only light came in through the entrance, if the door was open. Next to one of the houses I spotted a large satellite dish, which was a sign of progress. It was actually the home of the local teacher. A missionary had placed a water turbine into a nearby creek, and it produced electricity.

So the Indian village is slowly adjusting to technical progress. After roads and other links are constructed, we can also expect a change in their lifestyle. Indians are not friendly to the sort of progress that destroys their lifestyle. I have in mind the difficulties that were caused by the construction of the Pan-American Highway and other roads in South America, which cut through the forests. Also notorious are the disturbances caused by destruction of the woodlands, the clearing of land, and gold fever. (On our return flight by helicopter, we observed rivers with rapids, which at one time were sources of gold.)

From Mato Grosso, I had a good flight connection to São Paulo. In São Paulo, I was able to visit with Cardinal Paulo Evaristo Arns, whom I had known for a long time from our meetings in Rome. After this visit, I got on a flight bound for Rome.

This visit to Brazil confirmed my impression of a country with great social differences and economical possibilities, but also as a country of many jobless and landless people ("sin terra" people). The Church is poor and close to the poor. The bishops' conference is one of the largest in the world. There are not enough priests. The devotional life of the people is extensive, but is sometimes mixed with almost magical expressions. The faith has a weak catechetical foundation, and so the people fall victim of all kinds of native-born and foreign preachers. There is ample room for a new evangelization. Despite that, Brazil initiated the preparation of missionaries from their own poverty. It is my impression that the missionary congress of Belo Horizonte broadened missionary awareness.

Argentine Republic

The "southern cone" of South America is covered by several countries that do not contain numerous missionary territories. Of these, Argentina is the only country I was able to visit; thus I will make only a brief mention of the others before discussing my visit there. Bolivia and Paraguay are landlocked states with some regions under the jurisdiction of the Congregation for the Evangelization of Peoples. I saw Paraguay from a distance as I stood on the Brazilian border, at the famous waterfalls of Foz do Iguaçu. A visit to Bolivia has remained part of my plans and dreams. The small country of Uruguay, located northeast of Argentina, is considered to be a Christian country, but a new and deeper evangelization is necessary there. The continent narrows toward the south, with the Andes Cordillera dividing it into two states. Chile, to the west, possesses two missionary regions, the Diocese of Villarica and the Vicariate Apostolic of Aysen, which are on their way toward full-fledged diocesan status. Argentina, in the east, possesses all the resources to increase the number of its missionaries abroad. I personally visited Argentina only in 1999, as the papal legate to the missionary congress COMLA VI—CAM I in Paraná.

Argentina is a vast country that reaches all the way to cold Patagonia, a land evangelized by the Salesians of Saint John Bosco. The 38.8 million inhabitants of Argentina are mostly white and immigrants or the descendants of immigrants. Nearly 91 percent are Catholics, organized into seventy-one dioceses. The Church is relatively well structured, self-sufficient in vocations, and able to sustain itself economically. As of late, wild experiments in neo-capitalism have brought economic crises down upon the country.

The zealous Archbishop of Paraná, Monsignor Estanislao Karlic, took upon himself the role of organizing a missionary congress for 1999, which in the spirit of the 1997 Synod of Bishops on America, would also include the northern portion of the Americas. Participation from

Argentina: Missionary Congress COMLA VI–CAM I in Paraná

the north did not in fact live up to expectations, and so it became our fond hope that North America would be better represented at the 2003 congress in Guatemala. When the organizational talent of North America unites with South American enthusiasm, it could generate a strong impetus for missionary work all over the hemisphere. We cannot omit mentioning the growing number of Hispanics in the United States. Therefore, the idea of a united missionary congress has a future, and I have supported it from its inception.

I began my visit to Argentina on September 27, 1999, at the University of Buenos Aires, where I received an honorary doctorate. On this occasion, I dedicated my lecture to the enculturation of the gospel, pointing out some problems in this area and their effect on the missions. I was pleased to know that some of my countrymen living in Argentina were present at this lecture. The following day, I opened the Paraná congress by celebrating a solemn Mass. Hundreds of bishops were present from Argentina, from the rest of the Americas, and from other continents. Delegates from various countries were in attendance, as were diocesan faithful. In the homily, which I gave in Spanish, but with a few insertions in English, I repeated the theme of the Congress: *"América, con Cristo, sal de tu tierra!"* ("America, in the company of Christ, leave your homeland!"). I touched on a number of issues in my opening speech, which I delivered from a central podium in an enclosed stadium. The delegates and attendees became enthusiastic about the education of missionaries, especially those for the overseas missions. I adjusted my lecture to their lively style of dialoguing between speaker and audience. Many young people were in attendance, to whom I addressed practical questions. At some points, I asked them to sing and then led them to deeper reflection and to resolutions for missionary collaboration. They were expecting a serious official Roman cardinal, but soon discovered that I was able to converse well with them and find a way into their hearts. Before long, they titled me an "excelente comunicador" (excellent communicator). That opened the way for my lectures to special groups of laity, youth, and bishops.

During the cooler evenings, I was pleased to have a warm South American poncho over my shoulders, which somebody gave to me. Evenings were our time for entertainment, and this consisted of folk dancing and singing from various regions. During the six-day congress, filled as it was with many speeches, meetings, and experiences, I was privileged to receive another honorary doctorate, this time from the Catholic University Buenos Aires. For that occasion, I had prepared a theological lecture about the deeper meaning of the missionary vocation for different groups of people, including bishops, priests, and faithful. (Every year, my speeches and homilies are bound into a single volume, and in 1999, these amounted to over four hundred pages, thanks in part to all the material required at the congress in Argentina.) I delivered my concluding homily in a spacious open stadium, where tens of thousands were in attendance. Following a festive celebration of the Eucharist, which reminded me of some African celebrations, I personally greeted each national delegation, who were dressed in their colorful costumes. I presented mission crosses to the priests, religious sisters, and lay volunteers.

The missionary congress of Paraná was the fourth one I attended, not only as Prefect of the missionary Congregation, but also as papal legate. From Bogotá through Lima and Belo Horizonte, and all the way to Paraná, it made for an ascending line in building missionary awareness in Latin America as well as in the North. I am sure that with time, efforts in the Americas will produce a plentiful harvest for the Church and for the missions. As John Paul II declares in his encyclical *Redemptoris missio* (no. 2), mission "renews the Church, revitalizes faith and Christian identity, and offers fresh enthusiasm and new incentive. Faith becomes stronger when it is shared."

Part Four

Oceania

Someone once called Oceania a floating continent. It is more like a submerged continent. Whether one flies from the American mainland in the east or from Asia in the west, the great mass of water and the enormous distances leave a lasting impression. The first explorer of these regions, Ferdinand Magellan, named these waters the Pacific Ocean. From an airplane on a clear day, one can see only water, out of which a small island might occasionally appear. Of the 3.2 million square miles of land making up Oceania, nine-tenths is taken up by Australia. Next comes New Zealand and Papua New Guinea, and finally several small island countries. Slightly more that 32 million people live in this area. Of these, more than 20 million reside in Australia, while Papua New Guinea has about 5.5 million, and New Zealand 4 million

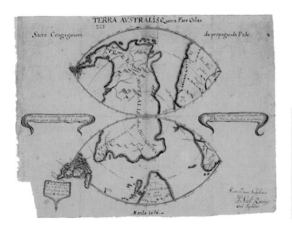

The Oldest Map of Australia

inhabitants. The remaining 3 million are scattered among the smaller islands, some of which are trust territories and colonies. Still others are independent countries, whose status is made necessary by the great distances that separate them from their neighbors and by differences in culture and language. By their number, names, and data, they are a dread for students of geography.

From the religious standpoint, 8.5 million claim to be Roman Catholics and live in seventy-eight dioceses. Given the small population of faithful, this number of dioceses may appear high, but one must make allowance for the isolation of Church communities and the distances between the islands. Catholic missionaries came to Oceania chiefly in the nineteenth century and arrived only after representatives of other denominations, which today are more strongly represented.

Systematic Catholic evangelization actually began in the middle of the seventeenth century, but did not encounter much success. In the archipelago of Guam, the Jesuits had to abandon their efforts due to opposition from the natives. For their part, Franciscans had to withdraw from the Caroline Islands. It was not until the nineteenth century, and after the Congregation for the Propagation of the Faith (now called the Congregation for the Evangelization of Peoples) had entrusted certain parts of Oceania to several new religious orders, that the efforts and sacrifices of missionaries began to bear fruit. Their sacrifices even included the shedding of blood by martyrs. The presence of colonizers from Europe and America only complicated the situation. Active competition among the different Christian churches also rendered difficult the work of many male and female religious. In addition to this, the multitude of languages spoken in the region impeded the timely preaching of the gospel on the part of missionaries. In Papua New Guinea alone, there are more than seven hundred languages. Here the cooperation of native catechists proved to be very effective. They subsequently became leaders of Church communities in the villages and often even missionaries among neighboring tribes and islands. I visited an institution in Papua New Guinea where these simple individuals were being formed, and at a Mass in Mount Hagen I was able to admire the sincerity of their devotion. Other missionaries ministered through good schools. Even today, along with certain women's religious congregations, the Marists are known in all of Oceania as the best educators.

Thus over two hundred years, the Church in Oceania has penetrated the local culture and in some regions has become firmly rooted.

The faces of the people have also changed with the advent of new immigrants from Europe and Asia. Nowadays, very few of the people of Oceania are not Christian. The ecumenical atmosphere is also changing. The formation of a native priesthood, however, is not keeping up with the decline in missionary numbers. Therefore, the transfer of Church leadership into native hands goes slowly. With a few exceptions, such as Australia and New Zealand, the deepening and strengthening of the faith require the presence of missionaries. One can say that the Church in Oceania is in a state of maturation and transition, with a disquieting side as well as a bright side.

The Holy See directs missionary activity in this region. The Roman Congregation of which I served as Prefect has concerned itself with the evangelization of Oceania for a very long time. All of Oceania lies under its jurisdiction, with the exception of Australia, which has an established hierarchical organization. After World War II, the naming of Australian bishops ceased to be the duty of the Congregation for Propagation of the Faith and was assumed by the Congregation for Bishops. Pope Paul VI visited distant Samoa in 1970, and Pope John Paul II did the same to the Solomon Islands and Papua New Guinea in 1984. In 1986, John Paul II paid a lengthy visit to the faith communities of Fiji, New Zealand, and Australia. He returned to Australia and Papua New Guinea in 1995, at which time I accompanied him. We might also include another of my trips under the missionary heading, namely, that of 1973, when as a representative of the Congregation for the Doctrine of the Faith, I attended the gathering of the bishops of Oceania in Sydney, Australia. Apart from those journeys when I accompanied the Holy Father, I also made some individual visits and gathered experiences that I would now like to share.

We should mention the special Bishops' Synod for Oceania, which was held from November 22 to December 12, 1998, in Rome, in which I participated. This was the last continental synod among those that preceded the Jubilee Year 2000, and John Paul II summarized its results in his Post-synodal Exhortation *Ecclesia in Oceania* (*The Church in Oceania*). Because of his health, he could not personally promulgate the exhortation in such distant places. He did so in the Vatican, however, in the presence of the Roman Curia and invited guests, through a simultaneous Internet connection that was the first of its kind in Church history. This synod embedded itself into the memory of those present and also those who witnessed it on television. Of special note was the

Mass in Saint Peter's Basilica, which was celebrated to the accompaniment of native melodies and dances that are typical to Samoa and other parts of Oceania. The principal theme of the exhortation reflected the program of the synod: "Jesus Christ and the people of Oceania: Follow his way, proclaim his truth, live his life." The exhortation, of course, encompasses a set of pastoral conclusions.

Despite the tremendous distances, Oceania can be divided into three cultures and racial regions. This incidentally excludes Australia and New Zealand, where the Aboriginal and Maori peoples were overwhelmed by immigrants from the British Isles and the influence of their culture and mentality. The three regions of Oceania are Polynesia, which includes Samoa, Fiji, Tonga, and other smaller islands; Melanesia, which takes in the extensive territory of Papua New Guinea, as well as the Solomon Islands and New Caledonia; and finally Micronesia with its many small islands, such as the Carolines, the Marshalls, and others.

Traveling throughout Oceania requires time and money. Time considerations alone would prohibit a visit by ship, while air transportation is complicated and expensive. For these reasons, the meetings of

Tonga: One of the Many Choirs

the Episcopal Conference of the Pacific (CEPAC) are infrequent. For us Europeans, it was amusing when a certain bishop described his diocese as being as vast as Italy. Another bishop observed that one of his parishes is as wide as the distance between Moscow and Lisbon. Still another one wrote about the amount of time necessary to visit the small groups of Christians in the scattered atolls of an archipelago, where a transport ship sails but once every few months and stops only for a few hours at this or that island. A bishop dependent on such transportation would therefore require years to visit communities of faithful. We cannot begin to imagine the sorts of pastoral problems such situations impose on bishops and priests, and on the faithful. But the Son of God came into the world and gave His life for the salvation of these people. It is this truth that preserves the missionary spirit, even under such difficult conditions.

My journeys to Oceania offer but a small glimpse at this gigantic and diverse part of the world.

Kingdom of Tonga

In December of 1992, in the company of one of my staff members who knew Oceania very well, we began our journey to Tonga, located northeast of New Zealand. The flight to Australia lasted about twenty-four hours, after which we continued to Auckland, New Zealand, where we stopped for one day and met with local bishops. As is usually the case, the stopover afforded a fine opportunity for fraternal discussions about their joys and concerns. We

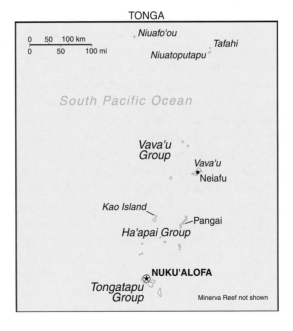

also celebrated an evening Mass together in the cathedral. Auckland is located on the North Island of New Zealand. Only about 10 percent of its 1.5 million inhabitants are Catholic. Because of the location of the city, as well as its industries and trading activity, Auckland surpasses the capital city Wellington, which is only two-thirds as large. The bishops spoke to me of the new wave of de-Christianization in public and private life, which was arriving from Great Britain and from the United States. In addition, they shared with me the desire of the native Maori to have their own diocese, administered by their own bishop. This request was impossible to fulfill because the native population is scattered over the whole country and also because of the difficulty involved in naming an ethnic bishop for a single group of faithful. The problem was eventually solved by naming an auxiliary bishop of Maori descent for one of the dioceses, who could also occasionally minister at Maori religious rituals.

The following day, in the company of several bishops, we flew for hours over the ocean to the archipelago of Tonga. This kingdom consists of 169 small islands, gathered around a central island, where most of the 95,000 inhabitants reside. The king lives there, as does a Catholic bishop who presides over 16,000 of our faithful. Protestants number more than 40 percent, because their missionaries came here much earlier. Tonga has been a monarchy for many centuries. It became a British protectorate in foreign affairs in 1896 and only recovered its full independence in 1976. While popular customs remained intact, the British left their mark on public life, and English was adopted as an official language. The climate of Tonga is tropical, hot, and humid.

I traveled to Tonga at the invitation of the local bishop, Patelisio Punou-Ki-Hihifo Finau. As the Holy Father's special delegate, I was to rededicate the cathedral that had been damaged by one of the region's frequent typhoons and then subsequently rebuilt. Representatives of the government and of the local Church met me at the airport, after which I was escorted to a large meadow for the traditional welcoming ceremony. Tents had been set up on one side of the field for the principal guest, the local bishop, and several local chieftains. A crowd of people had gathered on the other side, all attired in colorful native costumes and richly decorated with tropical flowers. Their spokesmen sat in front of them. The majority of the Tongans, the women as well as the men, are tall, strong, and well built. They enjoy putting on these traditional ceremonies and delivering the welcomes that follow.

The whole celebration lasts about two hours and is named *kava* for the drink that is prepared behind the scenes during the singing, dancing, and oratory. Water is added to the pounded roots of a certain species of tree and the resulting mixture is put into a bag. Strong hands then wring out the juice into a carved hardwood bowl. While the drink is prepared, the spokesmen and guests exchange gifts and greetings about 150 feet away. When the drink is ready, the elders of the group have to taste it and praise it. Only after doing so can they present a coconut shell cup to the guest. The drink has a mildly bitter taste and easily induces a sense of euphoria. To be sure that I would not be too affected by it, I did not finish the entire cup, but handed the rest of it to my neighbor. That was a mistake, for which they reprimanded me after the ceremony. The songs were really beautiful and typical of the Pacific region, the choirs were enormous, and the dances consisted of slow bodily motions with hand and finger gestures that we could only partly understand. Among the gifts that were exchanged were large mats woven from tropical plants and fibers and fattened pigs, which were taken away after the ceremony for use in a communal meal. Afterward, I was tired and went off to the bishop's residence to relax and refresh myself. I was not able to sleep that night, because someone had died in a neighboring home, and the survivors were singing mournful melodies. It was not until morning that I was able to sleep a little and prepare myself for the dedication of the cathedral.

The dedication turned into a great celebration for all the inhabitants and was attended even by the Methodists and by the king and queen. Bishops from other parts of the Pacific, and still elsewhere, waited with me in front of the cathedral for the arrival of the royal couple. When the large Cadillac stopped in front of the cathedral entrance, the door of the vehicle opened wide. Then the king, who is known for his weight (about 300 pounds after undergoing a special diet), extended his right leg. His foot sported a very manly looking sandal. He then drew himself up majestically to the full extent of his gigantic height. I noticed that after he stepped out, the car rose considerably. Incidentally, I learned from the newspapers that the king rode a bicycle escorted by four strong bodyguards, and that this had helped him lose about ninety pounds. The king was a lawyer with a doctorate from Cambridge University and was therefore a well-educated, as well as a kind, gentleman. The sandals and short socks, as well as the traditional skirt and jacket or shirt constitute men's formal attire for ceremonial occasions here. The queen looked matronly in colorful clothes, as did the rest of the ladies. In spite of the fact that she was Protestant, in a spirit of ecumenism, she did one of the liturgical readings at the Mass. Ecumenism is well developed in this region.

We started the ceremony by welcoming the king in front of the cathedral. Against the seaside background and the coastal palm trees, he appeared as a giant. He wore no royal insignia, and his behavior was unexceptional but dignified. He thanked us for the welcome and then walked toward the closed doors, which he solemnly opened. Together with the bishops in attendance, we began the procession to the altar while the Methodist choir sang. The king sat in a large chair of appropriate size to the right side of the altar, but a little behind the celebrants, while the queen sat at his side. In the center of the spacious cathedral stood a round altar made from rare tropical wood, which I blessed. The interior of the renovated church had a look of great dignity about it, despite the reinforced walls and heavy roof that will protect it against future typhoons. The heat was bearable, and the rite shorter than in Africa during similar celebrations.

After the ceremonies in church, everyone gathered outdoors in a broad meadow. Long tents with transparent partitions had been erected there, and in the center of each were wide benches covered with fruits and other food. The king, his royal escort, and distinguished guests had a tent of their own. All the people, regardless of their faith, were welcome to attend the meal, which was sponsored by the king. They could take some food and then go sit in a tent or under the trees. The local bishop and I got a place in the king's tent. I even received the exceptional honor of sitting close to the king on a linen folding chair. All the others present, including the bishop and the queen herself, sat on the ground with crossed legs and ate from plates that they held on their knees. When I examined the food on the tables in front of us, especially the roasted pigs in this tropical hot weather, I noted the large flies that were drawn to the dripping fat, and which tireless ladies kept chasing away; I did not have much of an appetite, but I was saved by the queen, who strictly supervised her husband's diet. All I had to do was smilingly ask her to serve me the same food that she prepared for His Highness, but only in smaller amounts. I conversed with the king during the meal, so as not solely to eat and get indigestion. He told me that he was familiar with my country because he had once ordered trumpets and other musical instruments from there for his local band.

After a few hours, when the heat had subsided, the entire group moved to a nearby outdoor area, where groups of singers and dancers from Tonga and other countries performed. It was a colorful display, not only for the eye but also for my video camera. After awhile, the king arrived informally with his guards. Typical Polynesian melodies could be heard throughout the site, and this was without the use of microphones. A single person was in charge of the whole performance, which reminded me of wedding celebrations in my homeland, where all is choreographed and directed by "the best man". The best local female dancer performed a slow piece while the chorus accompanied her with their singing. Her shoulders were bare and anointed with oil. Various people came to her as she danced and pasted money onto her shoulders. It reminded me again of how we used to reward the violinist by placing a 100-Crown banknote on his forehead, if he had done a good job with a requested number. As the performances continued, other groups of people were in charge of selling hand-woven carpets and doormats as well as other homemade objects. The proceeds of the sale benefited the cathedral rebuilding project. My own task was to bestow awards or blessings from the Holy Father on the praiseworthy catechists.

The familiar local songs and dances continued into the night. I had to leave for the airport, however, because of a flight that would be taking me to Fiji. From there, I would continue in larger aircraft via Japan, Russia, and Germany before getting back to Rome. After all these ceremonies I was obviously exhausted, but I still had a long and adventuresome trip ahead of me. In Fiji, a jumbo jet awaited us, which had to take off immediately because of an approaching typhoon. It was already midnight when we finally departed. I buckled myself into my seat, and, as soon as we were permitted, I lowered the seat into a comfortable position. I covered my eyes and then fell into a deep sleep. The flight to Tokyo was supposed to last eight hours. The seats on the plane were very comfortable, and one could lower them further than on any other plane. After two hours I awakened. My traveling companion was completely pale and was surprised that I had been able to fall asleep. He asked me if I had not felt the typhoon shaking our plane, which was trying to outrun the storm under full power. He expected disaster at any moment, but my sleepy smile calmed him down. We eventually broke away from the destructive winds, and I was able to resume my peaceful sleep in the assurance that exhaustion would overcome the fears of my companion and would allow him to fall asleep as well.

In Tokyo, we landed at the new international airport and waited for a Lufthansa that would take us over Siberia to Moscow, and ultimately to Frankfurt. As I mentioned earlier, it was shortly before Christmas, and the modern air terminal was filled with sounds of American Christmas carols. The walls were covered with commercialized decorations taken from Western cultures. Among these, Santa Claus reigned as the representative of Western Christmas, replacing the image and name of Jesus on this Church holy day. This is how Christmas is portrayed in the Buddhist and Shinto religious heartland! Who cares about the real Christmas? The chief concern is the sale of merchandise! My heart was really saddened as I pondered the commercial aspect of Christmas, and not even the familiar Christmas melodies could cheer me up.

The flight over Siberia lasted more than ten hours. I found our stop in Moscow very interesting. This was the first time I had ever stepped onto Russian soil, which I had never been able to do before for obvious reasons. I was amused by the Russian shopkeepers in the air terminal, who artfully tried to augment their income in the duty-free shops by always claiming to lack sufficient change. They tried to explain this in Russian to every foreigner, who in the end would just leave them the entire sum in foreign currency. For these shopkeepers, even fifty cents meant a great deal, especially if the opportunity repeatedly presented itself.

When, after this seemingly unending journey, I finally reached Rome, I delighted myself with thoughts of medieval missionaries, who would spend months on ships before reaching their destinations. Restful sleep puts an end to exhaustion, but beautiful experiences enrich a person forever.

Papua New Guinea

Papua New Guinea constitutes an extraordinary phenomenon for Oceania, from the standpoint of geography, the racial composition of its inhabitants, and the length of time that it was isolated from the rest of the world. The country consists of the eastern half of the island of New Guinea, as well as three moderately sized islands and numerous smaller islands. Taken together, their territory is slightly larger than that of California. The significant population growth of the past ten years is quite apparent. Since the official census of 1990, the number of inhabitants has risen from 3.7 million to the current 5.5 million. Most of the population is Papua New Guinean, with the exception of 15 percent who are Melanesian.

The country's double name is rooted in its history and geography. The islands of New Britain and New Ireland were named by early explorers, but, along with their neighbors in the Bismarck Archipelago, were absorbed into German New Guinea in the late nineteenth century. The island of New Guinea was henceforth occupied by three colonial powers. The Dutch controlled the western half, the Germans the northeast, and the British the southeast. In 1906, British New Guinea passed to Australian administration and became the territory of Papua. After the German defeat in World War I, Australia exercised a League of Nations mandate over what had been German New Guinea. During World War II, the Japanese occupied the northern part of the island, but at war's end the eastern portion was returned to Australian administration, and the west was claimed by Indonesia, which had just declared its independence from the Netherlands. The western portion was then renamed Irian Jaya. In 1975, Papua New Guinea became an independent member of the British Commonwealth. The head of state is therefore the Queen of England, who is represented by a governor general. A nine-year secessionist revolt on the island of Bougainville ended in 1997, after claiming some 20,000 lives. It appears that the agreement still endures, and that the population was satisfied with autonomy. The revolt was organized in the center of the island, which contains valuable copper mines. The local bishop also lives there and was forced to remain isolated for many years from the rest of his flock because of war conditions.

In general, we can say that Papua New Guinea, with its complicated past, has undergone a significant transformation in the last hundred years. Primitive conditions have given way to a modern state, in spite of the mountainous terrain that creates obstacles to standardization and to easy communication among regions. It was not very long ago that an Australian physician came upon some native people in one of the valleys who had never before encountered the civilization of the outside world.

Rapid change can also be ascribed to matters of religion. Spanish missionaries came to the area in 1855 and celebrated the first Mass on Yule Island next to a beautiful bay where they had just landed.

Evangelization work was later undertaken in the English and German zones by members of religious orders such as the Marist Fathers and Italian priests from the Pontifical Institute for Foreign Missions. The latter were recompensed for their work with the martyr's death of one of their brothers. Later, Divine Word Missionaries arrived in the German colony. British Methodists and German Lutherans began their own missionary work earlier than the Catholics, with the result that today they claim over 60 percent of the inhabitants. The Catholics have 31 percent, while the rest are still animist, or pagan. After some initial sacrifices, our missions have met with great success. Today, the Catholic Church is divided territorially into nineteen dioceses, which are mostly administered by missionary bishops. The education of native priests lags somewhat; the first two native men were only ordained in 1953. The first regional seminary was established in 1968 in Boman, near the capital city of Port Moresby.

Pope John Paul II visited this country for the first time in 1984 as head of the Catholic Church, but had previously visited it as a bishop. I saw a photo displayed in a bishop's residence, showing him in his cassock, in spite of the islands' tropical climate. The first papal visit was limited to the capital city, Port Moresby. A papal visit of the city of Rabaul, on New Britain Island, was out of the question because of the acute danger posed by a nearby erupting volcano. The beatification ceremony of a young catechist-martyr, Peter To Rot, was planned for Rabaul in 1995, but the volcano had grown even more menacing, and the Holy Father had to beatify Peter To Rot in Port Moresby instead. I accompanied

PAPUA NEW GUINEA

NORTH PACIFIC OCEAN

INDONESIA

Wewak

Bismarck Sea

Rabaul

New Ireland

Mount Wilhelm

Madang

New Britain

Kieta

Mount Hagen

Goroka

Lae

Bougainville

New Guinea

Gulf of Papua

PORT MORESBY

Solomon Sea

SOLOMON ISLANDS

Daru

Torres Strait

Coral Sea

AUSTRALIA

Equator

SOUTH PACIFIC OCEAN

the Pope on that journey, which took us to Australia and then to Papua New Guinea and included a stop in Sri Lanka, where the beatification of a great Indian missionary priest to the island, Joseph Vaz, took place.

I became fascinated by Papua New Guinea when I was young. I read about the ministry of the Divine Word Missionaries, and I remember an article about the flying American missionary, Leo C. Arkfeld, who would land his small one-engine airplane in mountain and forest clearings to spread the Good News of Jesus Christ. I was also drawn to this poor country and its Church community, which was already experiencing rapid growth, and whose development showed such promise. During my time as Prefect, the local Church had its share of internal problems that needed to be resolved. I therefore planned a long pastoral visit, to last from October 28 to November 14, 1993. I flew to Papua New Guinea through Singapore, where I stopped for the one-day visit described earlier in the section on Malaysia. I flew on an airplane belonging to Air Niugini, which employs the indigenous spelling of "New Guinea" in its name. On my return trip, I made a stop in Hong Kong. It suffices to take a look at a map to understand the distances involved and the need to wait for connecting flights. Such one-day stopovers can then be seen in context.

The night flight from Singapore to the capital of Papua New Guinea did not give much time to rest. After we landed and unpacked at the nunciature, it was time to leave for the cathedral, where local bishops and a group of the faithful awaited us. The men with their typical curly hair and large cheekbones, as well as the local women with small children, filled the church and wholeheartedly sang hymns in English. The entire service had an Anglo-Saxon character. There were only a few native elements incorporated into the liturgy. The prevalent British culture was evident elsewhere in the capital as well as in the Church's celebrations. Besides English, the people here speak pidgin-English or "vantok" (from "one talk"). This is in addition to about seven hundred tribal languages.

Port Moresby is not a very large city. With its population of close to 200,000, it is located on a beautiful bay, but surrounded by an arid region. It almost never rains on the narrow strip of land where the city is situated, but about seven miles away one can find mountains and green forests. With a few exceptions, the homes in Port Moresby are built low to the ground, and the vegetation is very

Papua New Guinea: *Welcoming in the North*

limited. The nunciature was built on top of a hill above the bay, in a beautiful, picturesque location, but the wind blows constantly through its windows and doors. The advantage of this location is that it is surrounded by a number of other diplomatic residences and in a secure neighborhood, away from the crime that affects other parts of the city. Youth in the area are numerous, while job opportunities are few. The Salesians have charge of a technical school for youth, which I visited, and where I met with the students. I visited the construction site for a large church, which was close to completion and under the administration of the Salesians. Right behind the school and maintenance buildings rises a tall, parched knoll, on which the young men had erected a sign bearing the name of the Salesian founder,

Don Bosco. That afternoon we drove to a nearby forest to see a beautiful waterfall.

The next day we flew northeastward, to New Britain Island, where we visited Kimbe. There we saw giant, centuries-old trees that were being taken from the forests by Japanese and Malaysian companies and exported without any concern for eventual replacement. Decorations lined the road from the Kimbe airport to the city. Groups of people sang alongside the road and gleefully threw large bouquets of tropical flowers at our car until the windshield was covered. When we arrived in front of the governor's residence, I had to step into a portable chair. Strong men lifted me up and carried me along to the sounds of happy, rhythmic singing. Conforming to their ceremonial custom, I stood up while trying to maintain balance. I was glad when they put me down and took me through the door of the governor-general's office. He discreetly informed me that the western part of New Britain needed its own diocese. Next to me sat the Archbishop of Rabaul, Karl Hesse, MSC, who could testify that this matter was already under consideration, but needed further research and preparation. The evening Mass showed that the faithful in this area are much more lively in comparison with those of Port Moresby. We spent the night at a large mission station. The next morning, we vested and readied for a prayer service, which took place in a larger church at a picturesque site near the shore. Before we began the procession toward the church, the local people tied a red band around the forehead of the Archbishop Hesse and of the apostolic nuncio, as well as my own. This red scarf is worn only by chieftains. This entire island is still mostly administered by German missionaries under the leadership of Archbishop Hesse. These missionaries have built up beautiful communities here and have organized Church life.

Our next flight took us to Rabaul, the principal city on New Britain, which lies beneath two volcanoes. The population of the city is catching up quickly to that of the capital, Port Moresby. Nevertheless, because of Rabaul's location next to two perpetually threatening volcanic peaks, the city's expansion is limited. The airport where we landed in 1993 was located rather close to one of the volcanoes. It was among the first areas destroyed in 1994, in an eruption that buried half the city. The local people call the main volcano the "mother" and the other one the "daughter". They are interconnected and equally dangerous. The town is situated on a beautiful bay, which is actually a

Kimbe:
Greeting to the Faithful

gigantic caldera con-
nected to the sea. A
disastrous eruption oc-
curred in 1937, dur-
ing which the city
was almost destroyed.
Many faithful were
trapped and entombed
while partaking in a
procession near the
eruption. The whole
area around the bay
is like a single live
volcano, which can
erupt at any moment
and obliterate the city
and the surrounding
country.

Germans built a large missionary station on an elevated spot above
the bay a few miles from Rabaul, and they called it Vunapope, or "the
Pope's town". By using this name, they clearly wished to distinguish
themselves from Protestant and Anglican missionaries. In spite of this,
however, relations among them are good and make for an example of
ecumenism. The mission station now serves as an archdiocesan administration center. On several occasions, it was suggested to the Holy
Father by the distinguished Archbishop Hesse and by me that he should
visit his town, but the power of natural subterranean forces prevented
this on two separate occasions. After the last eruption in 1954, Vunapope sustained minimal damage from the volcano. Its small airport was
spared, which then permitted disaster relief to be organized for the
devastated region. Over time, several structures have been added to

the mission station, such as a school, a church, and a hospital, as well as housing for the employees and their families. German organizational efficiency, as well as material support, proved once more to be excellent in this part of the world.

Before the 1954 eruption of the volcano, Rabaul was a beautifully maintained city. Our cathedral was located downtown and already was in need of expansion. I met there in 1993 with the priests and the faithful when we celebrated the Eucharist. I went to Vunapope, where a pleasant surprise awaited me. A sizeable group of native children stood under a large mango tree with its fragrant fruit. All of a sudden, they began to sing in Slovak the hymn "Hej Slováci" (Hey, Slovaks) and to wave Slovak flags. After the singing, one of the native boys stepped out and greeted me in Slovak, from a message he had written on a piece of paper. I tried to find an explanation for this remarkable surprise. As it turned out, there, hidden behind a tree, stood an American religious sister of Slovak descent, who labored here as a schoolteacher. After a luncheon with local representatives and missionaries, the community gathered on a broad grassy field in front of the mission station for their ceremonial celebration. Groups had arrived from different villages, each attired in their particular costumes, in order to display their singing and dancing skills. My video camera was in constant use and caught scenes that even television stations do not have. The scenes were spontaneous and not at all planned or staged by the camera people. My collection of valuable (at least to me) videotapes was enriched with this new, precious addition. The speeches in my honor were short, but the dances and songs were long and lasted until sunset, when all departed in big trucks or walked home. Imagine what these people would have shown to the "White Pope", after so beautifully honoring his representative, whom the older people of Rome call jokingly "the Red Pope".

I completed my visit by touring the surrounding country and by celebrating two solemn Masses. From the elevated area around Vunapope, I was able to view the entire bay, and the peninsula that had once been devastated by the volcano. A Japanese ship was anchored not far offshore, and gigantic logs were being loaded onto it. Even now, it is possible to see World War II–era cannon in the hills, where they were left by the departing Japanese. The coastline is dotted with seaside caves where Japanese soldiers hid their smaller ships and tanks, as they prepared an attack on Australia. The bombing of Hiroshima put an end to these plans.

Blessed Peter To Rot

During the occupation, the Japanese prohibited all missionary activity. For the most part, priests were imprisoned, while the faithful were rallied by lay catechists, who secretly led devotions and instructed the people. The enthusiastic Peter To Rot was just such a catechist. Neither threats nor concern for his young family could dissuade him from carrying out his ministry. The Japanese finally took him into a hilltop cavern and injected him with deadly poison. I met an old friend of his who kindly shared with me his recollections of the man. Two years after my visit, the Holy Father beatified Peter To Rot in Port Moresby. A large assembly of his countrymen participated in that celebration, attired in their various costumes. Also present was Peter To Rot's daughter.

By the grace of God, I was able to pray on the spot of his martyrdom, in the aforementioned cavern, in front of which now stands a monument. I also went to visit his grave and blessed the cornerstone for the church. Construction had already begun, and it was awaiting the beatification in order to be named for Peter To Rot. The church was already partly roofed, but the walls were not yet filled in. Mass was supposed to be celebrated outdoors near the church, but a strong tropical rain moved in and forced us (although not all of us) to run under the roof. We had to wait for the noise of the torrential rain to stop and for the drenched crowd to stop chattering. In spite of it all, we were eventually able to complete the celebration of the Mass. After visiting the local seminary, where I celebrated Mass for the young students and delivered a suitable homily, I received permission from the central government to visit the northern part of the island of Bougainville, which was then a war zone.

My journey began in a small, rented airplane, piloted by an Australian. I was accompanied by Archbishop Hesse, who was also the apostolic administrator of the part of Bougainville that was not occupied by rebels. Native-born Bishop Gregory Singkai administered the area that was in revolt. The archbishop also had to tend to his large Archdiocese

of Rabaul and was seldom able to assemble the missionaries, sisters, and catechists of Bougainville, who ministered to the scattered faithful during this period of unrest. With my visit in this area, I wished to encourage everyone to persevere and to resolve certain problems of a practical nature. Our workers gathered in Buka, near a strategically important

The New Church of Blessed Peter To Rot, Which I Blessed

strait guarded by the government military. Its small airport was then used primarily for military purposes. Upon leaving Rabaul, we flew over the aforementioned active volcanoes. I must admit that flying low over a volcano is not the most comforting experience. We quickly flew out over the sea and shortly thereafter found ourselves once more above forested land, a position we maintained until reaching our final destination. Upon arrival, we were greeted by the enthusiastic faithful with a portable chair, on which I had to sit while they carried me—not into the church, but toward the army commander. A high-ranking officer of some sort then privately explained to me the government's view of the rebels and the status of the military operations. He also instructed us as to how to conduct ourselves in case of an unexpected attack from the nearby forest or from the sea. Only then were we able to prepare for Mass.

Meanwhile, melodies filled the air, produced by skilled musicians with small and large bamboo whistles. Along with the missionaries, we began the procession toward the church. The temperature was over 100 degrees Fahrenheit and was only aggravated by the high humidity. It was even worse in the overcrowded church, where perspiration soaked our shirts and other apparel as well. The hymns were beautiful, with familiar English ones mingling with others of local composition. We were able to tolerate the heat, and my audience could have endured an even longer homily than the one I gave, in which I affirmed their faith and hope. They could scarcely believe that someone had come to visit them all the way from Rome and had brought greetings and blessings from the Holy Father. For me also, there were moving moments that were well worth the effort that it had taken to get myself to the island.

After the Mass, I had a very useful discussion with some pastoral workers, who shared experiences from their ministry among the people. Their stories bore witness to much courage, heroism, and acceptance of daily crosses. After taking some light refreshments, we departed, because time was passing. It was furthermore not advisable to linger since this would mean risking some sort of a surprise attack on the airport or our airplane. A cardinal from Rome would have made a good catch for insurgents and their propaganda.

The day after this adventurous visit, we flew south to New Guinea proper, and to the town of Madang, which is the seat of an archbishop. The archbishop was one of the few native bishops and was already in poor health. The day's schedule consisted of a short ceremony at the cathedral and two other excursions. At the minor seminary, we were greeted by the sight of students assembling to the sounds of pounding on a hollow carved tree trunk. Very quickly, not only the "young" seminarians gathered, but also grown men with thick beards and curly hair. They were still in minor seminary because they did not yet possess a basic education, in spite of the fact that some of them were over twenty-five years of age. They sported the hairstyle typical of a mature man, which is in fact worn by all students. I had a lively and interesting discussion with them. It took the form of questions and answers, rather than a formal speech. The second visit took me to a spiritual center run by the Divine Word Missionaries, and located on a beautiful bay. There we were able to relax before the evening flight to Wewak.

A large group of the faithful in their native costumes awaited us alongside the poorly illuminated runway at Wewak. At the welcome, they gave me a garland of tropical flowers, as well as a pectoral cross, made from the teeth of the local wild boar. At the mission station, there was already a lively bustle, because delegates from all the local "parishes" were assembling to commemorate the fiftieth anniversary of the priestly ordination of their beloved Archbishop Leo Arkfeld. After retiring in 1987, he had chosen to remain among them. Six years later, he was still there, in spite of his eighty years and diminishing strength, and the fact that the diocese was being administered by his successor.

A tall, slender American of German descent, Arkfeld had spent his entire missionary life here, evangelizing the northern coast of New Guinea, as far as the mountain plain and doing so with his single-engine plane. As I already mentioned, I had read about him in my student days, but now in the early morning light, I could actually see his airplane hangar near the mission station. From here, this courageous missionary would push his Piper into the street that also served as his runway. He would start his trusty engine and then set out over the palm trees on excursions into the hinterlands that could last one or more days. I was told that while he was in the air, he would set the autopilot in the appropriate direction and then serenely pray his breviary. He would glance at the ground from time to time and search out a field or grassy spot on which to land. Then he would descend to the ground and come out to educate both young and old in the faith

Papua New Guinea*: Buta: Procession on the Portable Chair*

of Jesus Christ. His adventures with sorcerers, tribal leaders, and children; the youth that he sent to the seminary; as well as the times he confronted storms in his airplane would all make for interesting reading. Of course, he never had time to write those stories. Only when he became very old was his pilot's license revoked, and this put an end to his dangerous flying.

The Holy Father, Paul VI, elevated him to an archbishop, and John Paul II knew him personally. Current statistics for the Diocese of Wewak testify to his fruitful ministry. Out of a total population of 293,000, there are 193,000 Catholics, to whom we must add those living in newly erected dioceses. With our own eyes, we could see proof of his fruitful ministry, as many groups of local people gathered to celebrate the anniversary of their father in the faith, filling the town for an entire week. I adjusted my itinerary so as to be able to concelebrate his Jubilee Mass, in the company of many other bishops and priests from all over the country and from abroad. Our elder brother kept up with the pace of the entire ceremony, but he had to excuse himself from the banquet out of a need to rest.

I cannot allow myself to summarize my stay in Wewak with such a short reference. The sacred ceremony marking the jubilee began with

Wewak: Congratulations Given to Archbishop Leo Clement Andrew Arkfeld

a ceremonial procession from the missionary center to the nearby cathedral. The procession consisted of boys and girls in colorful native costumes that were decorated with the beautifully colored feathers of the "bird of paradise" and other ornaments. This transpired to the sound of drums and the enthusiastic singing of all those present—to the point that even the walls of the cathedral shook. During the Mass, two processions caught my attention. During the first, the precious "message from the Great King" was brought forward wrapped in an embroidered scarf. It was unwrapped and exposed with great ceremony before the altar, then handed over to the main celebrant so he could share it and read it to the people. The article was none other than the Holy Bible. The second procession brought up the offertory gifts, from which, for practical reasons, the sheep, hens, and pigs had been excluded. The homily was translated into "Melanesian Pidgin", which was understood by almost all those present. The whole Mass was celebrated in the same language, which consists of a mixture of English and native words and expressions. For instance, possessive pronouns are always replaced with the word "belong". Consequently, the word "belong" is constantly repeated. After a little while, one gets used to it, and with the help of English, one can guess the meaning of a sentence. After the Mass and after a number of commemorative photographs were taken, we sat down to dinner.

Afterward we took a short rest and then went out to a broad meadow where the faithful were being entertained. They came from the various regions, from the seaside and from the hills and forests. Right in front of the mission station, I saw two people carrying a long snake. It was a rare, green python, whose skin was very much coveted by tourists. The government had had to forbid the exportation of the skin of this rare animal as a means of preventing its complete extermination. Similar steps were taken with respect to the colorful "bird of paradise". The old Archbishop Arkfeld passed in a jeep as we were going down the street. He had already taken his rest and was on his way to the airport. It was evident that he had not yet had his driver's license revoked. The celebratory mood of the people continued to occupy me for several hours. It would have been difficult, under other circumstances, to gather so many costumes from so many areas into one place. The people danced and sang, not to boast, but to demonstrate their joy. The celebration was supposed to continue for a whole week, but I had just a few hours to use my faithful video camera. The picture of these diverse types of people, as well as their dress, costumes, and songs, was so varied and rich that I will not even attempt to describe them in words. A large group of people came to escort us all the way to our airplane. We took off, leaving the seaside country, and continued our flight toward the center of a mountainous plateau, where Mount Hagen, the seat of an archdiocese, is located.

This smaller town is the administrative center for an extensive hilly plain in the midst of the mountains that cover the entire island from east to west. The flora here is green and rich because it is sustained by the tropical heat and by sufficient rainfall. The Divine Word Missionaries were quite successful in spreading the word of God here, as evidenced by the fact that during their seventy-year ministry, they gained for Christ more than one-third of the inhabitants. My visit fell on a Sunday, and this made it easier for the faithful from town and country to attend the solemn Mass that was celebrated on a green public square. The altar was placed on the bed of a truck, which was strategically parked at the edge of the square. The canopy and background were

Mount Hagen: Dressed-up Youth

covered with a plastic material so that the celebrants had some shade over their heads. The tropical climate, combined with the merciless sun of the mountains, only made the heat seem worse. The people tried to protect themselves against the sun with scarves or with woolen hats. Despite all this, the crowd sang reverently, and a charismatic group enlivened the liturgy. I was fascinated, not only by the long, red shirts of the diocesan catechists, but also by their great reverence. They render such enormous assistance to the missionaries in the diffuse villages. It was here that I worked up the courage to celebrate and sing an entire Mass in "Melanesian Pidgin". At the distribution of Holy Communion, I was burned unmercifully by the sun. When the procession of celebrants was leaving the square, a member of the faithful who was either grateful or who wanted to play a joke, inserted a colorful bird-of-paradise feather into my miter. I think that in Saint Peter's Basilica in Rome, this would either scandalize or cause people to laugh. Amid this radiant group, however, it was accepted as an act of gratitude.

In Mount Hagen, I visited a girls' school and teachers' institute and prayed at the graves of the first missionaries, one of whom was also the first bishop of the diocese. Elsewhere I saw a burnt village. This was a sign that tensions still exist among the tribes and villages, and that differences sometimes culminate in this way. It might be over the theft of a cow or a sheep, or a dispute over a beautiful girl, or other such things. These passions and traditional disputes frequently occur even among the Christians. Bloody battles used to erupt on a daily basis, but today the gospel is slowly penetrating into the morals of society.

I also visited a group of thirteen seminarians who were spending an entire year preparing for the diaconate and for lifelong celibacy. This culture is marked by great promiscuity, and a man who does not leave any offspring is considered a weakling. Even living out the holy state of matrimony is relatively difficult. In my dialogue with the candidates for the diaconate, I stressed that they would never be happy if they did not consistently live out celibacy—or matrimony if they ultimately chose to marry. They would furthermore not be happy if they did not make a firm choice according to God's call. I pointed out to them the importance of a clear decision before God and before their own consciences, without which they would never find inner peace and contentedness. The next day some missionaries asked me what I had said to the seminarians, since two of them had immediately left the seminary. My response was "Better now, than later!" I found out that in this country, as well as in some others, celibacy is not discussed clearly enough with seminarians. We must never think that in some cultures it is impossible to live a celibate life faithfully. This is difficult to accomplish everywhere in the world, but it is not impossible if one lives a prayerful life and maintains a necessary vigilance. Happy priests are then able to witness to a healthy tradition of celibacy among their people. We also had an open discussion on this and other topics in the large seminary complex in Fatima, where the students of philosophy undergo two years of formation prior to entering the regional theological seminary in Port Moresby.

I was touched by my visit to the first church in this region, with its painted depictions of the Most Holy Trinity and various holy missionaries on the front wall, above the altar. Among these was Saint Thérèse of the Child Jesus, the contemplative Carmelite from Lisieux, France. In spite of the fact that she never left her convent, she became the patroness of the missions because of her spiritual works on their behalf. I cannot forget the warm reception I was given at an important primary and middle school. These are conducted in a beautiful natural setting by the Marist Fathers, who are renowned for their education of youth. Amid tall trees, we were welcomed by a number of students, both boys and girls, dressed in native costumes. Thus does the Church help to promote the education of the people. This is fortunate since the state has only recently begun to concern itself with education on a large scale.

From Mount Hagen, we journeyed all day by car with a police escort, which guaranteed my security as the Pope's delegate. A beautiful asphalt road led through the hills and smaller valleys from Kundiawa to Goroka, which is another diocesan seat. We went through a mountain pass at an elevation of about 8,200 feet. In Goroka, we surveyed the work being done in the diocese and visited the well-known Melanesia Institute, which studies the local culture. After meeting with missionary workers, we returned to Port Moresby by airplane—an absolute necessity, given the distances and travel conditions involved. The following day, I would set out on the final leg of this rich and fascinating trip.

The last part of the journey yielded its own varied experiences, but was a bit unusual compared to the earlier days of the trip. We flew by rented helicopter, which took us out from the capital city, over the sparsely populated lowlands along the southern coast of the island, and then on to Yule Island. We landed in a schoolyard, where we were greeted by the students and the local bishop. From there, we traveled a short distance out onto a small peninsula that borders a beautiful bay. It was there that Spanish missionaries once landed and celebrated the first Eucharistic sacrifice on the island. Native men in traditional attire, holding spears in their hands, greeted me with warrior shouts, according to their ancient custom. I had already witnessed this shouting tradition in the Pacific while visiting the Maoris of New Zealand. It was intended as a warning, so that the guest would put aside any warlike thoughts. It was also meant to test the peacefulness of his spirit. I was not familiar with the next part of their custom and instinctively jumped aside when they imbedded their sharp spears in the ground exactly three inches in front of my feet. The spears were really sharp and could probably have passed right through the bones of my feet! Those present could only smile at the fear of the cardinal. The greeting ceremony then took a friendly turn as we proceeded toward a memorable site featuring an altar that overlooked a light blue bay. I was greeted there by students and faithful in traditional costumes, which hereabouts cause no scandal to anyone. Even so, the style of their clothing is slowly changing.

Following the Mass, we returned by helicopter from Yule Island to Bereina on the mainland, where another bishop has his seat. The terrain of this diocese is very difficult, because it extends all the way into the high mountains. The former bishop utilized a small plane for his missionary visits. One day, however, it crashed while landing at an elevated spot on a mountainside. Although the bishop survived, he lacked the money to purchase a replacement. The Church provides various public services in Bereina. In this place, which gave me the impression of a large chaotic village, the Church runs schools and operates clinics. It also transports the seriously ill by plane to Port Moresby. Once more, the faithful streamed in from remote missionary stations. The celebration, which took place in the cathedral and overflowed into the adjacent streets, was a joyful one. I blessed some new buildings belonging to the diocese, and that afternoon we took off so as to be able to land our helicopter at Port Moresby while it was still daylight.

I paused in the capital to visit the regional seminary, which until recently was the only institution in the entire country that educated priests. That was before Archbishop Hesse built his own seminary in the north. I once again had a very interesting conversation with the students about priestly happiness and celibacy, and I blessed a large auditorium that had been financed by an elderly Austrian priest, who was also present at the ceremony.

Afterward, the nuncio arranged a farewell reception, which gathered all the diplomats and some representatives of the government. (I had met the governor previously.) Cultural opportunities are not numerous in the area, and so diplomats very gladly attend this sort of gathering. After kind greetings were exchanged and refreshments were served, the attendees clustered into small groups. I visited them one after the other. I approached the British and American ambassadors, who were enjoying an exchange with a representative of the international organization for Asia and the Pacific territories, who was of Asian origin. They asked about my experiences on Bougainville, after which we chatted about the need for religious freedom and dialogue to foster public peace. Our Asian companion asserted that international law should

Bereina: Native Welcome

ban every kind of "proselytism", in other words, activity that seeks to convert someone to another religion. I explained to him that I was against the use of physical or psychological force, but that I could not allow for a general prohibition against a person changing religious views. This would constitute a restraint on personal freedom. I gave him an example: if the two of us were to debate and have different opinions, might I change my opinion and accept his own, if he succeeded in convincing me? "Of course!" he agreed. I followed this up by asking, why such a change should be forbidden with respect to religious opinion, where human freedom is the most sensitive? Then I explained to him that in proclaiming the gospel, the Church only proposes Christ's teaching, but imposes nothing. Our companion insisted, however, that conversion had to be prohibited for the sake of "public order". The two ambassadors just smiled at his reasoning. I then remarked that my own experiences had taught me about dictatorships that hide behind the cloak of "public order". That is when I understood how battles are fought against Catholic missions at the highest international forums. Also, by invoking this sort of reasoning, conversions to Christianity are forbidden in many parts of India. Such is never the case with conversions to Hinduism. This debate constituted my last useful experience in Papua New Guinea. The next day we flew to Hong Kong and, after a two-day layover, continued onward to Rome.

The Church in Papua New Guinea is developing nicely. During the past hundred years, the country has leapt forward centuries in its material and technological development and has entered into modern times. Meanwhile, its people preserve many beautiful traditions. Only in the remote forests and barely accessible mountains is the progress slower. Missionaries play an important role in human advancement. They still face enormous tasks, especially in penetrating the souls and the morality of the inhabitants such that lives may be transformed without destroying the positive elements of the local culture. The great and fundamental task is the educating of good diocesan and religious priests. The field is also open for spiritual cooperation with prayers and sacrifices. This much being said, there is still a need for foreign missionaries.

Republic of the Fiji Islands

The year 1994 marked the 150th anniversary of the beginnings of evangelization in the region of Fiji in southwestern Oceania. The cathedral of the Fiji capital, Suva, was renovated for the occasion, and the archbishop, Petero Mataca, requested that the Holy Father send a papal legate for the blessing ceremony that would reopen it. So it was in that capacity that I began my long journey, flying northwest from Milan over the Arctic Circle and Canada to Los Angeles. My faithful co-worker, Joseph McCabe, and I then rested after an eleven-hour flight. The next day we flew eight hours to Honolulu and continued for several hours more to the international airport at Nandi, on Viti Levu, the principal island of Fiji. During the flight, we crossed the international date line and skipped a day. We arrived in Fiji on August 13, 1994, two days before the Feast of the Assumption, when the jubilee celebration in Suva would culminate.

The beginnings of missionary work in this region were difficult and required many sacrifices. In 1841, Peter Chanel died as a martyr on the neighboring Futuna Island, and in other places the Catholic missionaries were persecuted not only by the native rulers but also by the colonial authorities and members of other religions. In spite of all these difficulties, and because of the work of the Marist missionaries

Fiji: The Ritual of Kava

in the Fiji Islands, Rome established a prefecture apostolic there in 1863 and raised it to a vicariate apostolic in 1887. Evangelization progressed at such a rate that in 1966 the vicariate became an archdiocese, with its seat in Suva, the capital.

Fiji is actually composed of 332 greater and smaller islands. It has 982,000 inhabitants, 51 percent of whom are Melanesians. Of the remainder, 43 percent are of Indian origin, and less than 2 percent are Europeans. All Christians taken together comprise 53 percent of the population. Catholics number 92,000, or not quite 10 percent of the population. Of the remainder of the inhabitants, about 40 percent are Hindu and somewhat more than 7 percent are Muslim. The climate is tropical and humid. The forests yield lumber for export, and the ground is fertile, especially for the raising of sugar cane. Since 1987, Fiji has been a republic.

The government felt honored by the visit of a papal legate and appointed a Catholic member of the cabinet to oversee the official escort. The government sent a special helicopter from the capital

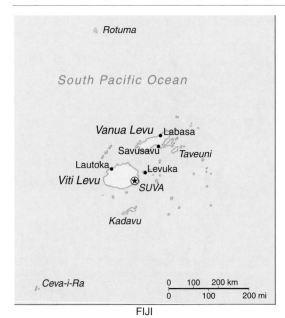

FIJI

city, Suva, to the international airport in Nandi for our transportation back to the capital. The small helicopter had to fly quite high to cross over the mountains. These maneuvers were not safe because of extremely strong winds. The pilot, however, was skillful and took his craft through various mountain passes. We breathed a new sigh of relief every time we left a hill and its treetops behind us. We encountered some rain, but after flying for over an hour, a bay appeared in front of us, and with it Suva, which is home to 77,000 people.

The local archbishop was waiting for us, along with other bishops from far and near. Also present were a representative of the government, local members of my delegation, and the secretary of the nunciature in Wellington, New Zealand. After a short greeting, we were taken to a residence for state guests and were extremely well cared for. The home is located on a hill with a beautiful view of the bay and the city. Before lunch, the president of the republic welcomed us in an official audience.

The *kava* welcoming ceremony was performed according to Melanesian or Maori custom. I was already familiar with it from a previous visit to Fiji while accompanying the Holy Father in 1986. I also encountered it on my journey to Tonga, which is about a two-hour flight southeast of here. This particular ceremony featured interludes of folk entertainment, with traditional dancers in their warrior attire, ritual incensations, and the placing of wreaths about our necks. These were made by local women of Indian origin, who were dressed for the occasion in elegant saris. I am not going to describe the entire ceremony, which lasted about two hours. This time, I drank the bitter *kava* to the bottom of the coconut shell cup, not repeating my mistake at Tonga. As a result, I received a triple ceremonial applause. I also had a speech for the people who had gathered on a broad meadow for the official welcome. The ceremony had so many different features to it that it helped me overcome my sleepiness and exhaustion. We had, after all, spent twenty-four hours aloft. According to the clock, we had arrived only shortly after we had started, and this was after flying halfway around the globe passing through the date line; therefore, we had the same date twice. By now, we were experiencing a good case of the infamous "jet lag".

Fortunately, the next day we had a easier schedule. We concelebrated Mass with the bishops and priests at the regional seminary, which I remembered from my previous visit with the Holy Father eight years earlier. I preached a homily appropriate to the occasion and later delivered a speech to the professors and other educators. Afterward, we left on a tour of the city.

Suva (Fiji): Welcoming Dance and Song

On the Feast of the Assumption, the newly renovated cathedral was filled with the faithful, some of whom had even come from nearby islands. The altar was entirely new, and the ceremony whereby it was anointed with chrism and incensed with fragrant white smoke was itself mystically evocative. The homily offered me the opportunity to describe the history of evangelization and the heroic faith of the first missionaries. I encouraged the faithful to be grateful for all this, imitating the Blessed Mother's recognition that "the Almighty had done great things for me", since the Lord had done great things for them as well. I also encouraged them to grow in faith. The joyous atmosphere inside the cathedral overflowed into the square outside, where friends and relatives from different islands met and socialized.

Right after the celebration, I had a very difficult working day. First I met with the priests and religious of the archdiocese, in the presence of Archbishop Petero Mataca (pronounced "Matasa"). I depicted the jubilee celebration as an appeal from God for an intense new evangelization. I then responded to their questions. After that, came an even more important meeting with the members of the Episcopal Conference of the Pacific, or CEPAC. Most of the bishops had come to attend the ceremony at the cathedral and, of course, to meet the Prefect of the Congregation for the Evangelization of Peoples. In my opening address, I analyzed certain issues and problems, such as the preparations for the upcoming Jubilee Year 2000; the situation of the Church in Oceania; and the future missionary role of this Church, not only with respect to its maintenance, but also to a dynamic new evangelization. A lively debate followed, because circumstances differed from one region to another. Later, I realized that this meeting had been a good preparation for the special Synod of Bishops for Oceania, which preceded the Great Jubilee of the Universal Church. In the afternoon, fifteen seminarians showed that they had not forgotten their roots or their traditional dances, the latter of which made for a truly athletic performance. That evening, the aforementioned Catholic member of the government held a reception at his home, where I was able to greet the prominent members of local society.

Early the next day, we started northward along the seashore, with our ultimate destination being the international airport. The trip to the airport took several hours. The picturesque seacoast featured calm bays ringed with high mountains and forests. On the way, we stopped at a modern church and school, where we greeted all the young

A New Hindu Temple

students. We also came upon a typical Hindu temple. The descendents of Indian immigrants own many stores thereabouts and preserve their ancestral religion. We stayed overnight at an international beachfront hotel, and in the morning, we took a stimulating boat ride to the nearby islands. Aboard ship, we met some tourists, whom we joined for the excursion that followed. On a small, beautiful island, we ate our lunch in the shade of a tree, while the ship's crew performed some native songs for us. The color of the ocean shifted from dark to light blue, and light green and to foamy white, according to the depth of the water. The water itself was very warm, and the coral sand absolutely white. All this time, we were escorted by our kind host, the cabinet minister.

We could not linger because a large crowd of the faithful were expecting us in a local church for the celebration of Mass at five o'clock in the afternoon. They had also prepared a great entertainment for us afterward. The Mass started as scheduled, but toward the end one of our escorts arrived to inform us that we had to say our good-byes quickly. The plane that would take us to Los Angeles via Honolulu was awaiting our arrival at the airport in order to depart. Our escorts, however, could not bear to see us leave without offering us the traditional farewell. Our government host reserved a separate room for us at the airport where we partook in the *kava* ritual. Of course, the drink could not be made from fresh tree roots, but rather from a sack of roots that had already been prepared. The airplane was waiting for us at the gate. We did not want to appear anxious to leave, so we patiently drank the traditional beverage and offered our heartfelt thanks to the entire escort. They were greatly pleased with the papal medals and other small mementos that I distributed.

Early the next morning, when we departed from Honolulu after a short layover, I wanted to pray my breviary. That is when I realized that we had gone "backward" a day on the calendar, and that I would once again have to pray the same prayers. I recalled how the old moral theologian Noldin had studied the question of crossing the international date line, and the impact that this would have on the recitation of the breviary and the celebration of Mass. For us, the whole issue had always seemed humorous and improbable, but behold, here I was living out the experience! So, on my way to Fiji, I skipped a day, and on my return trip I relived the exact same day of the week.

On the return journey, we had a free day in order to gather our strength for the flight to Europe. We took advantage of it and went sightseeing in Los Angeles. We visited Beverly Hills and Hollywood, and especially the Disney central production studios, where we were shown how the popular movie *The Lion King* was made.

The experiences I gleaned from my several trips to Oceania proved very beneficial for the special Synod of Bishops for this region of the world, which took place in 1998 in Rome. The resolutions of the synod were articulated in the Post-Synodal Apostolic Exhortation *Ecclesia in Oceania* (*The Church in Oceania*), which was published on November 22, 2001, on the third anniversary of the opening of the synod. All the region's bishops were present at the synod because, in comparison with those of other continents, their number is small. With great openness, they analyzed the state of the Church in the Pacific and analyzed the principal problems facing the individual regions. They spoke of their difficulty in assuring the regular celebration of the Eucharist and the sacrament of reconciliation because of the shortage of priests and the great distances between the small groups of faithful. They also shared their thoughts on such questions as the formation of local clergy and religious sisters, marriage and family life, Catholic education, and so on. Those questions are the challenge, the task, and the hope for this area of the world.

The Church in Oceania is indeed clearly in the process of moving from complete reliance on missionaries to a situation of greater independence. It needs to intensify its efforts, especially as concerns the improvement of priestly training for native candidates and the preparation of couples for marriage. Also, it must further develop its missionary outreach in the spirit of the new evangelization.

The synod drew its principal inspiration from those gospel events that evoke the sea and shore, such as Matthew's account of the calling of Peter and Andrew: "As he [Jesus] walked by the Sea of Galilee, he saw two brothers, Simon who is called Peter and Andrew his brother, casting a net into the sea; for they were fishermen. And he said to them, 'Follow me, and I will make you fishers of men.' Immediately they left their nets and followed him" (Mt 4:18–20). At the end of his Post-Synodal Exhortation, John Paul II turned in prayer to the Blessed Mother as "the Star of the Sea". Let us adopt his prayer of petition for the Church in Oceania: "O *Stella Maris*, light of every ocean and mistress of the deep, guide the peoples of Oceania across all dark and stormy seas, that they may reach the haven of peace and light prepared in him who calmed the sea. Keep all your children safe from harm for the waves are high and we are far from home."

Part Five

Europe

Europe: a missionary region? Some find this a bewildering statement, but at least they do emphasize the question mark at the end of the sentence. I remember, that toward the end of the Second World War, two French priests, Henri Godin and Yvan Daniel, published a book with the title *La France, pays de mission?* (France, a mission country?). They demonstrated therein the extent of dechristianization in France and also provoked a great debate on the validity of the proposed question. Today we can, with good reason, apply the same question to Europe: Is the situation of our old continent now one of a mission territory? The decline of Western civilization, which frequently is identified with Christianity; the decline of faith; the crises of married life and family; complete moral laxity, which presents itself as the attainment of freedom; the loss of fundamental natural values; the steadily increasing influence of non-Christian religions; the shortage of priestly and religious vocations in the Church—these and other problems incline one to respond positively to the above question: yes, at least in some countries, Europe has become mission territory. With certainty, it can be said that all of Europe needs a new intensified evangelization, as well as a complete renewal of private and community life with a restored Christian spirit and understanding.

The bishops of Europe gathered in a special synod for the continent toward the end of 1999, shortly before the advent of the third millennium. They understood the gravity of the issue and the importance of the discussion. The central theme of the synod was "Jesus Christ: Alive in His Church, Source of Hope for Europe". The shepherds of Europe confronted with intensity the "question of faith", as well as the need for a new evangelization of the old continent.

The Holy Spirit is in charge of spreading the message of Christ, sometimes even working through the historical events. In this way, the Christian faith was brought to almost all of Europe over a period of a thousand years. But it was on this continent that human weakness produced two broad and profound cleavages within Christianity. East and West separated at the beginning of the second millennium, and then the Protestant Reformation occurred five centuries later. Despite these divisions, Europe remained a Christian continent. However, the invasion of Muslim Turks into the Balkans in the late Middle Ages led to the abandonment of the Christian faith on the part of some already Christianized nations. This explains why there are mission territories in Europe that for many centuries have been under the jurisdiction of the Congregation for Evangelization. Its Prefect is involved in the life of every missionary Church, but his activity is greater is some regions than in others. After the fall of communism, this involvement became much stronger in the mission territories of previously communist countries.

Despite an influx of immigrants from Asia and Africa who practice different religions, Europe remains a Christian continent. Its Catholic numbers are surpassed by those of America, however. The old continent covers not quite 4 million square miles, which is less than a quarter of Asia or America, and only one-third of Africa. Leaving aside Oceania, Europe's population of nearly 705 million, places this continent behind all the continents. The number of the Catholics in Europe stands at almost 280 million, while the Americas counts 552 million; Africa 149 million; and Asia 113.5 million Catholics. We also need to remember that Europe is home to other Christian denominations. Besides the Catholics in Europe, the second most numerous religious group are the Muslims, with their high percentage of the population in the Balkans, where they have lived since the time of the Turkish occupation.

The Prefect of the Congregation for the Evangelization of Peoples is directly involved in dioceses located in Albania, in Bosnia and Herzegovina, in the current Yugoslavia, and in the diocese of Skopje in Macedonia. Gibraltar has also been supervised by the Congregation for a very long time. During my term in office I visited Albania several times. I also accompanied John Paul II to Sarajevo, the capital of

Bosnia and Herzegovina, and on one occasion I went to Gibraltar. So as to conform to the title of this book, I will pay close attention only to these regions.

Republic of Albania

As everyone knows, this country of tall mountains borders the Adriatic Sea. Its present population stands at over 4.1 million. Christianity arrived here after the apostolic period from Greece, Dalmatia, and Macedonia. Dioceses were established by the fourth century. In 1912, after four centuries of Turkish occupation, Albania became independent. It remained free until 1939, when Fascist Italy took it over. Albania reacquired its independence only in 1944, but under a strong communist regime that, with time, completely isolated the country from the rest of the world. Communism was finally toppled by a people's revolution in 1990. Under the communist dictator, Enver Hoxha, the Catholic Church was cruelly persecuted. From the time he assumed power at the end of World War II, he closed over two thousand churches and other places of worship. Some of these were demolished, while others were turned into gymnasiums or halls for sports and social gatherings. Priests were unable to perform religious activities. In 1967, Hoxha proudly declared Albania to be the first completely atheistic state. It was once a chiefly Muslim country with a Catholic minority and small groups of Greek Orthodox in the south. From the onset of communist rule, all religions had to cut their ties with their centers abroad. Practically all the priests who survived the initial persecutions were confined in prisons or work camps. Religious orders were abolished, and all religious rituals, including the celebration of the sacraments, were prohibited and punishable even by the death penalty for those officiating. The people were not even allowed to have religious necklaces or to wear such things as small crosses. Many priests and laity suffered martyrdom. Other survivors shared with me almost unbelievable stories of the cruelty that they had experienced at the hands of the regime. In spite of it all, the Catholic Church endured this test of faith and right after the fall of communism came alive. Currently 506,000 Catholics live in Albania, within six dioceses. Five of the six are under the jurisdiction of the missionary Congregation.

During the time of oppression, the Congregation for the Evangelization of Peoples could not have direct contact with this country. Reports were very few, and most of the time very sad. News was also sparse concerning Albanian Bishop Nikolle Troshani. But in 1989, Mother Teresa of Calcutta stopped to see me and shared some good news. Everything was in a ferment all over the communist bloc at that time, and even isolated Albania began to be influenced by the events. The brave Albanian ambassador to Italy was able to obtain the permission of his government for a world-famous Albanian woman to visit the land of her ancestors. Mother Teresa was indeed an ethnic Albanian, although she had been born outside Albania, in the territory of nearby Macedonia. She told the ambassador that she would visit the country only if clad in her religious habit and carrying her cross and rosary. And, in the end, that is the way she went to Albania. During her visit, she proposed to start a ministry to the sick, especially to children. The communist government was under pressure from the rest of the world, but Mother Teresa clearly declared that she could open no home without the Eucharist and consequently a priest was essential. She even looked for space in a former chapel that had been converted to other uses. She wanted to ask for the chapel building to return it to its original purpose. The authorities told her to talk to the wife of the late dictator Hoxha, who was then studying the matter. The latter told Mother Teresa that she could have the building only if she would offer more money than any other foreign investor. The tiny religious sister smiled at the severe woman, answering, "And you do not understand that I am giving you an opportunity to do something good?" When the tiny, stoop-shouldered Mother Teresa shared this story with me after returning to Rome, I asked her where she had gotten such a great idea. She answered only with a smile, pointing toward heaven and saying, "From the Spirit".

It was my Congregation that had responsibility for overseeing the translation of the Roman Missal and other liturgical books into modern Albanian. During this process, certain priests living in neighboring Kosovo proved to be very helpful. Contact with these priests was less complicated than with persons in Albania, prior to the fall of communism in that country.

After the revolt against communism, we increased our assistance to the different religious orders and to local European churches. Native priests were able to take up pastoral work once more, the faithful became more courageous, and atheistically educated youth became interested in religion. The organizational structure of the Church

ALBANIA

also became more visible, but bishops were lacking. In February 1993, I spent several days in Albania. One of my priorities was to prepare the trip of the Holy Father, who had scheduled his visit to Shkodër to coincide with the ordination of new bishops at the end of April. The Archdiocese of Shkodër is located in the north, near the border with the former Yugoslavia, and our faithful constitute a majority in the area. The only international airport is located in the center of the country, however, in the capital city of Tirana. I was welcomed at the airport by my good friend and the apostolic nuncio, Archbishop Ivan Dias, who was a native of India. At the time of my visit, the nuncio lived in a wooden house.

After a visit with the president of the country and with the prime minister, I continued on my journey by car to Shkodër. The main road was paved but very rough and winding. As soon as I got out of Tirana, I saw a poor country that seemed to be covered with military bunkers and resembled a field of mushrooms. The bunkers were everywhere: among the houses, in yards, near the roads, in the middle of farm fields. They were made of heavy concrete and steel and created an eerie impression. Apparently, each of them had cost the same amount as an ordinary apartment building. There were 620,000 of them spread over the entire country, witnessing to the senseless phobias of the dictator. With the same money, he could have built new apartments for every family in Albania. Hoxha lived in absolute terror that the capitalist West, especially Italy, would attack him. He had also built a huge subterranean bunker for members of the government and their families. How many other unnecessary expenses and sacrifices were made, of which we are still only dimly aware? In the meantime, the people not only lived without freedom, but also in poverty.

On the way to Shkodër we passed through villages and small towns. They pointed out a suburb, where a certain priest had been shot, simply for having been caught baptizing a child. Further north, we came to a marshy area that Hoxha had had drained. He had included many priests in the work details for these unhealthy and compulsory labors. As I was told by witnesses, many of those who worked in the marshes became infected with malaria, losing first their health and, several years later, their lives. Shortly before getting to Shkodër, I was shown the ruins of an old shrine dedicated to Our Lady of Good Counsel that the regime had decided to demolish completely. During my third visit to Albania in 1998, I had the pleasure of rededicating this pilgrim shrine, which was rebuilt in the original style and is now frequented by many faithful. The dedication ceremony was attended by large numbers of Catholics.

The principal destination of my first visit, however, was the cathedral in Shkodër, which the Congregation for Evangelization had helped renovate and repair with many financial sacrifices. It is a spacious church, bordering on the main square. Under Hoxha, the church had been transformed into a sports arena. A playing field was laid out in the central nave, and along both sides, concrete and steel walls were erected, complete with bleachers. The altar and sanctuary of the church were removed. The worst part, even from an architectural point of view, was the wall that covered up the façade of the church. Thus, all traces of the church's identity were be obliterated. I saw a similar wall on a different street, which covered the entrance to yet another church and looked really horrible. I rededicated the cathedral and its new altar in the presence of a great crowd of people. The entire rite was very moving and lasted several hours. It, therefore, could not be incorporated into the ordination of the four new bishops by Pope John Paul II, which was scheduled to take place two months later. In Shkodër, I also visited the future archiepiscopal residence and offices, which the state had just restored to the Church. The first group of seminarians were wedged into one part of the building, where they had to sleep in bunk beds. I encouraged them by saying that even in Bratislava in Slovakia seminarians had to make do with modest accommodations. I assured them that we were trying to solve the matter by building a seminary. In fact, we were offered a tract of land adjacent to a dry riverbed, but one that could be flooded in time of heavy rain. We were able, some time later, to obtain the former seminary and to erect a new modern facility. I drew great profit and encouragement from a short visit and conversation with some heroic elderly priests. I was overwhelmed by a visit with the aged former vicar general of Shkodër, Mikel Koliqi, who lived with his relatives in great poverty. He had suffered a great deal, but his eyes radiated a peaceful and kind disposition. Two months later I was able to introduce him to the Holy Father and later to greet him after he had been made a cardinal in his nineties. This was how the Holy Father honored this faithful confessor of the faith.

After returning to Tirana on a sunny but cool day, I went to the small village of Biac, about twenty-five miles from the city. Our Catholic faithful used to have a small, ancient church on the hillside next to the village, but Hoxha commanded its demolition and the reuse of the stones in the construction of sheep pens. After the fall of communism, the Catholics asked to have their church rebuilt in the original style. So they tore down the sheep pens and used the very same stones in reconstructing the church. They were assisted financially by Catholics from Italy. At the time of my visit, the church was not yet finished. I therefore celebrated an outdoor Mass that was attended by a good number of faithful from the area, all dressed in their traditional costumes. The people were summoned to Mass with an old bell, which was temporarily hanging on a tripod prior to its final installation in a small tower. The bell itself had an interesting history, because when the military and police arrived to demolish the church, the faithful hid the bell by burying it in the ground. They only dug it up after the communists fell from power. This bell served for many years as a symbol of hope that things would change, and that the Church, as well as faith in Jesus Christ, would return. The same Christ came to them on that cool and sunny day in the Eucharist, which I celebrated on the hillside in front of the church.

The capital city, Tirana, has a population of less than 400,000. Along with the historic ancient seat of Durrës, the city forms part of the Archdiocese of Durrës-Tirana. Approximately 1.2 million people live in the archdiocese, but of these, only 105,000 are Catholics. In Tirana, I saw the remains of a wall that had been erected in front of the façade of the Church of the Sacred Heart, which is administered by the Jesuit Fathers. Catholics become less numerous the more one travels south, but even there we can find many religious in ministry, as well as some foreign diocesan priests, all of whom are animated by a genuine missionary spirit.

I informed these servants of the gospel that I wished to meet with them in the industrial city of Elbasan, which has not a single Catholic church. This necessitated a trip through the mountains, where a substantial snowfall and the skidding of a heavy truck on one of the curves had caused the temporary closing of the road. With significant delay, we were able to get through the snow, which had not fallen at all at the lower elevations beyond the mountains. We gathered at a hotel and opened this gathering of co-workers with the celebration of Mass. A few of them who ministered in the mountains were not able to attend the meeting. I communicated the greetings of the Holy Father to those present, as well as some warm words of appreciation and encouragement for their hard work. After lunch, we discussed the problems that they share, but which they nevertheless experience from different sources. I then continued my travels across flat land to the seaport town of Durrës, where I stopped to see the damaged old cathedral, completely surrounded as it was by newly erected structures. I also saw some newer buildings and schools then returned to Tirana late in the evening.

I returned to Albania two months later in the company of John Paul II for his one-day visit. On this occasion, he ordained four bishops for the resurrected Albanian Church. The ceremony took place in the renovated cathedral of Shkodër. Among the newly ordained was Archbishop Franco Illia of Shkodër, who had once shown me the places where he was forced to work in labor camps. The second candidate was Zef Simoni, his auxiliary bishop. The third was Rrok Mirtita, an Albanian priest who was born in Montenegro, who had served in New York, and who was now becoming Archbishop of Durrës-Tirana. Lastly, there was the Franciscan Robert Ashta, who became Bishop of Pult. The southern part of the country remained under the jurisdiction of the apostolic nuncio until a suitable candidate for bishop was found.

My third opportunity to visit Albania occurred in 1998, after I was invited by the Archbishop of Shkodër to dedicate the rocky hillside shrine of Our Lady, Mother of Good Counsel. Monsignor Simeone Duca, who is of Albanian origin but lives in Rome, had generously funded the rebuilding of the church on its old ruins and according to its original plan. This Marian shrine is located just outside the city of Shkodër and has occupied a significant place in Albanian history. The painting of Our Lady of Good Counsel it once harbored attracted many people. A large crowd attended the dedication ceremony and completely filled the neighborhood adjacent to the church. There were even some Muslims among them. Among other things, I shared the following thoughts in my homily:

> The demolition of this ancient monument from your history was supposed to signify the complete destruction and dissolution of faith and religion. And along with these, the memory of Our Lady of Shkodër was supposed to evaporate as well. Her memory was to be uprooted from the minds of your sons and daughters and from that of the whole nation. However, as soon as you regained your freedom, you persevered in your decision to rebuild this Marian shrine on its original location, to serve as a sign of the renewal of your life and as of the return of Our Lady, Mother of Good Counsel to your homes and hearts. . . . Today her home rises from the ruins as a symbol of your resurrection and as a sign of her presence and constant protection, not only for Shkodër, but for all Albania.

Another sign of the resurrection of this nation is the new seminary, which is filled with students. Our Congregation substantially assisted in building it.

The situation looked a good deal worse on the other side of Lake Shkodër, west of the city. On the northern side of the lake is Montenegro, and further Kosovo, which are under the jurisdiction of the Congregation for Evangelization. In Kosovo live 65,000 Catholics, who used to be ministered to by the auxiliary bishop from the Macedonian Diocese of Skopje, who resided, however, in the capital of Kosovo, Pristina. The bad news about the war and the complaints of suffering people were reaching us in Rome. Only in 2000 did we manage to establish an apostolic administration there, headed by the Bishop Marko Sopi.

The number of Catholics in Montenegro stands at only 15,000. They are pastored by the Archbishop of Bar, the Salesian Zef Gashi, whom I ordained bishop in Rome. An even smaller number of Catholics resides in the Diocese of Skopje in Macedonia, which for many years was headed by Bishop Joakim Herbut. For different reasons, especially lack of time, I was not able to travel to these dioceses. This was in spite of the great inclination I felt to visit Skopje and the nearby monastery of Ochrid, which is connected to the lives of Saint Gorazd and other disciples of Saint Methodius.

Bosnia and Herzegovina

After the dissolution of Yugoslavia, some dioceses under the jurisdiction of the Congregation for the Evangelization of Peoples found themselves in new countries. Since the end of the civil war, Bosnia-Herzegovina is home to three distinct groups: Croatians, Serbians, and Muslims. While the first two are ethnic, the third is quite obviously religious in nature. The territory is mountainous and slopes downward in the north toward the valley of the River Sava. Because of the war, and because of ethnic cleansing and emigration, the population has fallen below 4 million. The presidency is occupied for an eight-month rotating term by a Serbian, a Muslim, and finally a Croatian. The capital of the country, Sarajevo, is well known for the assassination of the Austrian-Hungarian Archduke Francis Ferdinand, which took place there in 1914 and led to the outbreak of World War I. The city has approximately 350,000 inhabitants.

The Catholic Church suffered greatly during the civil war of the 1990s as well as from the war's aftermath. Many faithful of Croatian ethnicity fled to neighboring Croatia, and many others died in battle and through ethnic cleansing. According to available statistics, the religious disposition is as follows: 40 percent Muslim, 28 percent Orthodox, 13 percent Catholic, and 4 percent Protestant. Three dioceses are home to 467,000 Catholics. These are the Archdiocese of Vrhbosna-Sarajevo, with its young cardinal, Vinko Puljič; the Diocese of Banja Luka under the leadership of Bishop Franjo Komarica; and the Diocese of Mostar-Duvno, which is led by Bishop Ratko Perič and contains the well-known pilgrimage site of Medjugorje. The number of Franciscans is quite large, and they were very helpful in preserving the faith during the five centuries of Turkish occupation. To this day, Franciscans serve in parishes, but there are also increasing numbers of diocesan clergy who are educated primarily to serve parish communities. Franciscans do not like to leave the parishes, in spite of the express orders of the Holy See. This sometimes produces tensions within the Church. The people have a strong faith and a deep devotion. There is still a high level of mistrust among the ethnic groups, which is proving difficult to overcome.

0 20 40 km
0 20 40 mi
17 CROATIA 18 *Danube*
Sava
Prijedor Bosanski Brod
• •
45 45
Republika Srpska Brčko
•Bihać •
Banja
Luka
Tuzla•
Zenica SERBIA
•
44 44
CROATIA SARAJEVO Republika
★ Srpska
Federation of Bosnia
and Herzegovina Goražde•
Mostar
•
Maglić
43 43
MONTENEGRO
Adriatic Sea CROATIA
ALB.
16 17 18 19

BOSNIA AND HERZEGOVINA

During the time of conflict, the Holy See made some very well-known pleas on behalf of dialogue and reconciliation. Pope John Paul II accepted an invitation for a two-day visit to Sarajevo in April 1997. I accompanied him on this visit. We were welcomed at the airport by the three men who make up the presidency. Our cars were parked a short distance away, where we observed buildings that were lacking windows and doors, as well as an area devastated by wartime explosions. On the main street, the picture got even worse. We saw a number of multistory houses that had been destroyed by artillery fire. Cardinal Puljič pointed out the mountains to us, which he had to cross if he wanted to leave the region of conflict. Right after arriving at the cathedral, the Roman Pilgrim delivered an interesting speech, in which he encouraged the faithful to rebuild their homeland in unity and harmony with other citizens and to work for unity within the Church community. He also praised the Franciscans for preserving the faith, of which the present sons of Saint Francis are the modern-day heirs. But he also challenged them to be obedient to their bishops and to become part of a united apostolate under the leadership of the bishops. The Franciscans took this as a fatherly reminder.

After that, we proceeded to a large and spacious cemetery, with many new Catholic and Orthodox crosses, as well as Muslim symbols on the graves from the recent war. The large crowd who met us had endured a great deal. Even though it was already the middle of April, an extremely cold wind was blowing down from the mountain passes to our right. Thankfully, I had worn my topcoat under my alb, but the wind found its way through my vestments and layers of clothing. Not quite as fortunate were the cardinals and bishops from other parts of Europe, who were not prepared for such cold weather conditions. The young men and women in traditional costumes suffered even more from the cold. Several times during the Mass, wild snow showers descended from the mountains and occasionally removed our miters. The one who was most exposed to the wind was the Holy Father, since the altar and pulpit were in nature's direct line of fire. We noticed the master of ceremonies' repeated attempts at covering the Holy Father's trembling hands with his chasuble. All of us joined the Pope in uniting our own physical sacrifice to that of Christ, offering it for peace and reconciliation in this country that for years had been tested by a tragic war and by persistent hatred. When we returned to the tent to change out of our vestments, one of my colleagues quipped that it would be good now to have some local *slivovitz* (plum brandy) to warm up our cold bodies. Such humor bore witness to the brotherly attitude that reigned there among us and continued later at the luncheon served in the renovated and fully functional seminary.

I had an opportunity to speak in person with two bishops, who shared with me their worries and problems. I also met with various other persons of note. Of special importance was the visit of John Paul II to the office of the triple presidency, as well as his meeting with representatives of Orthodox, Muslim, and Jewish communities. As he had done in other parts of the world, the Pope strengthened the people in their faith. He also invited all factions to overcome their centuries-old mistrust, to look for spiritual reconciliation, and to foster reconciliation within society.

The Church in this Balkan region grows stronger as it confronts challenges and difficulties. The local Church carefully seeks out occasions for dialogue with non-Christians. Sometimes improved understanding is more possible with non-Christians than with our other Christian brothers. If not on the level of theology, this can occur on the level of community. As the Church in this country grows and stands increasingly on its own, it can be considered stable enough so as no longer to need missionary leadership from Rome. And in fact, since January 2006, the dioceses in the Balkan region and Gibraltar have changed the official status from "missionary" to "established" churches.

Gibraltar

Sometimes the spiritual care of the faithful and the missionary call of the Church require that unusual solutions be found for exceptional circumstances. Included here would be a diocese of 2.5 square miles under missionary jurisdiction where local Catholics number 21,000 out of 27,000 inhabitants. Some larger city parishes would have bigger populations than the Diocese of Gibraltar. We must, however, consider the geographical location, and especially the historical circumstances, responsible for establishing this diocese.

As everyone knows, Gibraltar is essentially a gigantic rock, strategically situated north of the Strait of Gibraltar, which separates Europe from Africa and stands between the Mediterranean Sea and the Atlantic Ocean. This tiny territory is connected to Spain by a narrow strip of land. In Roman times, Gibraltar's pointed rock was considered one of the pillars of Hercules, and the edge of the known world. The Muslim conquest of Spain commenced in the year 711 at Gibraltar. The Christian *Reconquista* reached Gibraltar in 1309, under Ferdinand IV of Castile and León. Until the Muslims retook Gibraltar in 1333, a small mosque at the southernmost tip of the Rock was used as a Christian church. The Moors were finally expelled from Gibraltar in 1462, after which the little mosque was converted into a shrine honoring the Blessed Mother as Patroness of All Europe. This decision has special significance in our own day, as the countries of Europe continue on the path of unification. During the intervening centuries, sailors passing through the Strait of Gibraltar have been able to gaze at the statue of Our Lady, asking for protection and safe travel as they have journeyed southward to Africa and Asia or westward to the Americas. When this fortress was taken by Great Britain in 1704, Catholic worship and all ties with Rome were abolished. Only a hundred years later was the Congregation for the Propagation of Faith able to send a priest to minister to immigrants who came from Italy. To avoid various ecclesial and political difficulties, the Congregation established a vicariate apostolic in 1816 that was answerable directly to Rome. In 1910, the vicariate was elevated to a diocese. Since 1704, Gibraltar has been under British jurisdiction, with its own chief minister and governor, who represents the Queen of England.

In the past, the city was a transit point for soldiers, sailors, traders, and refugees, to mention but a few. Even today, it remains essentially a fortress, with miles of road below the rock, military storehouses, and even, according to some sources, hiding places for submarines. The inhabitants reside mostly on the northern side of the hill and on the plain. They are mostly of Maltese, Italian, and English descent, although many from Spain commute daily to their jobs.

Bernard Devlin, the local bishop between 1985 and 1998, who was Irish by birth, invited me several times to visit this interesting missionary diocese. For political and other reasons, it cannot join the Conference of Bishops of Spain, nor accept a bishop of Spanish nationality. Also, the territory is quite far from England and has few Catholic British faithful. In the late 1990s, the old bishop wanted to resign, and it was necessary to begin to look for a replacement who would be worthy of the position and be knowledgeable in dealing with the political situation. Also under discussion was the question of the territory's continuance under the missionary Congregation.

I therefore decided to visit Gibraltar in May of 1997, passing through the nearby Spanish port of Malaga. The timing of my visit allowed me the opportunity to enthrone the statue of the Blessed Mother and to rededicate Europe to her. We arrived in a midsize plane at the airport, which is located on the narrow strip of land that connects Gibraltar to Spain. The runway juts westward into the Bay of Gibraltar. The airport sits in the middle of an uninhabited area. When a plane is landing, the authorities simply block the main road to Spain, which crosses the runway. Landings can therefore be both entertaining and picturesque.

Mass was celebrated in an open area, right at the foot of the Rock. The upper portions are of military interest and off-limits to the general public. It was a beautiful, sunny day, and to the south, we could see the not very distant shoreline of Africa, where the Spanish enclave of Ceuta lies on the Moroccan coast. Not quite twenty miles to the west, the Strait of Gibraltar gives way to the Atlantic Ocean, while to the north and northeast we could see the Iberian Peninsula and, behind it, all of Europe. Many of the faithful and invited guests, along with representatives of the government and diplomatic corps, were gathered under a huge tent. In the homily, I pointed out the historic background and symbolic significance of the enthronement of the statue of Mary and the rededication of Europe to her care. The fact that some children were making their First Holy Communion fit the celebration well, since children are a sign of hope for Europe. A glance at nearby

---

Africa and out toward the broad ocean once again reminded us of the missionary role of the European continent.

I also visited the British governor and toured the city and Rock of Gibraltar. We went by automobile then walked toward the top of the hill until we got to the ramps where the military zone began. Along the way, we were surrounded by blossoming trees and bushes, and by monkeys who gather here by the hundreds. In the evening, I met with the lay faithful and delivered a lecture. After that I attended a ceremonial reception given in my honor. In the meantime, I conversed with both priests and laity, who informed me of current conditions and the need for a diocese.

A visit to this little peninsula at the extremity of the European continent could encourage many to reflect on the future of the faith and of missionary activity in Europe. The continent definitely needs a new evangelization to keep it from getting lost in the crisis of Western civilization. As the European bishops appropriately described matters during their first Special Assembly of the Synod of Bishops for Europe in 1991, "A mentality and type of behavior is spreading culturally in which only one's own personal satisfaction and economic interests find validity. These mistakenly make the freedom of an individual absolute and reject the possibility of encountering the truth and the values that go beyond a personal or communal vision." The bishops continued even more clearly in stating, "Even though imposed Marxism has fallen, an effective atheism and materialism remain widely spread through all of Europe. Without being imposed by anyone or clearly labeled, they lead to such a way of thinking and such a way of life as if God does not exist." At the second Special Assembly of the Synod of Bishops for Europe in 1999, the bishops emphasized the need to proclaim "the gospel of hope" by word and example (*martyria*), by celebrating it at worship (*liturgia*), and by spreading it through service to one's neighbor (*diaconia*).

However, Europe cannot isolate itself from missionary endeavor. As John Paul II states in his Encyclical Letter *Redemptoris missio*, "It is in commitment to the Church's universal mission that the new evangelization of Christian peoples will find inspiration and support" (*RM*, no. 2). It is with these thoughts in mind that I labored, visited, and even tried to stir up various European churches. The lectures I delivered in Italy, France, Spain, Poland, Slovakia, and other places bear witness to these efforts, as do in a special way, the annual addresses I gave to the 115 assembled leaders of the Pontifical Mission Societies from all over the world.

The field of missionary cooperation in the universal Church and my own humble contribution to it would make for yet another story, and one that would exceed the scope of the present recollections and experiences.

Conclusion

As I was handing over the office of the Prefect of the Congregation for the Evangelization of Peoples to younger hands in April 2001, the International Missionary Press Agency "Fides" asked me for an interview. Later the interview was published in several languages. My sincere answers are expressions of personal feelings as well as some important characteristics of the Catholic missions throughout the world. My answers express views after many years of ministry in that capacity and after countless experiences in the field of missionary evangelization. I think that they may serve as a conclusion to this book. Therefore, I would like to use parts of the interview in that meaning.

Your Eminence, what are your feelings as you leave "Propaganda Fide"?

After sixteen years of service at the missionary Congregation, I leave carrying mission in my heart. In these years, I have learned a great deal: *Propaganda Fide* is a sort of observatory on missionary activity among the peoples of the world. It has in its care peoples of Asia, Africa, Oceania, and also those still to be evangelized in the forests of Latin America, in the frozen lands of North America, and here in Europe, in the Balkan mountains. To this variety of peoples, civilizations, cultures, and religions, God in his love sent His Son: the historical and mysterious event of the Incarnation commemorated during the Great Jubilee. All my years here have been part of the Incarnation event, a great gift from God. I have received much more than I was able to give. I have shared the "passion" of mission, with its joys and with pains.

What signs justify your judgment?

I have lived the adventure of the Spirit at work among the peoples. I have seen the Church take root and grow in travail of poverty and hunger, amidst persecution and oppression, the heroism of missionaries and new Christians, amidst human weakness and the slow opening of fossilized cultures. I made more than fifty journeys to peoples in Africa and elsewhere. From them, I learned to "celebrate God" in spirit and in dance. With my hands, I helped the planting and growing of new churches: the mystical Christ born among the nations, His body moving in new communities and ecclesiastical circumscriptions. I felt something like the fatherly joy Saint Paul mentions in his letters. Almost every time I went to the Pope in audience, I carried a request for recognition of a new diocese or apostolic prefecture, feeling as I did so like a godfather for a "newborn" church. The number of these churches has grown: from 877 in 1985 to no less than 1,059 in 2001. Thirty-seven percent of the Catholic Church has almost doubled in recent years, not to mention the growth in vocations. To be brief, the Lord achieved my episcopal motto: *Ut Ecclesia aedificetur* (That the Church may be built up).

How does **Propaganda Fide** *work?*

In my years as Prefect, I have always sought above all to improve the quality of formation at all levels: special courses for bishops and for formation staff, pastoral and apostolic visits, missionary congresses, preparation of bishops' appointments (today for the greater part, local men), missionary animation at all Church levels. The increase in vocations demands also an increase in funds to build new seminaries, form the future leaders of the young churches, to build new "houses of God" (467 churches in one year!)—which become places and means of evangelization and other activities, pastoral, social, educational humanitarian. At present, we assist 29,000 major seminarians and 52,000 minor seminarians. In a word, a fascinating task, which starts anew every morning.

Your Eminence, when you came to **Propaganda** *in the 1980s, Marxist-style liberation theology was very much in fashion and so was the temptation to limit the Christian message to social commitment . . .*

Faced with the threat of mission being reduced to social commitment (Marxist) or sociological dialogue in which the person of Jesus Christ disappeared completely ("missionaries without Christ"), we worked to give once again central place to proclaiming Christ, who by His death and Resurrection frees us from slavery and is the answer to all genuine religious longing for the one true God. This is one of the challenges put forward by John Paul II for the third millennium: to rediscover Jesus Christ and focus on dialogue as a "dialogue of salvation"; this work continues.

We are also faced with globalization of the economy, ever speedier communication between the continents. How are the missions affected by this problem?

To globalization of markets, the fact that the world has become smaller, we answer with "globalization" of mission. I have made every effort to encourage the young churches to contribute personnel and means to the universal mission. Mission is no longer from the West to other countries; it travels in all directions. Africa too is beginning to send missionaries to Africa and abroad. One of the most significant proposals have been the COMLA, the Latin American Missionary Congresses, which in 1999 embraced also North America and became the American Missionary Congresses (CAM). In this way, we supported the sending of missionaries to Africa, Asia, and Oceania from countries such as Peru, Colombia, and Mexico: poor countries, with problems, but able to give of their poverty, revealing a mature missionary spirit. The Church in America is called to make a great contribution in human and economic resources for mission in the future. One of the fruits of globalization is the Internet, immediately put to use by Fides, the international news agency that depends on the Pontifical Mission Societies. Fides was among the first of the Vatican offices to use the Web to connect Rome and the world. Today Fides' website is visited by more than 100,000 browsers, including people in Vietnam and China.

In the 1990s, the "Asian tigers" emerged with their impact on world economy and politics. How did it affect the missions in those countries?

Asia, seen by everyone as the world's most attractive market, is for us the continent where mission is most urgent, where the Church is still a small minority. In his Encyclical *Redemptoris missio*, Pope John Paul II said that mission is still only beginning and that Asia is the challenge for evangelization in the third millennium. He said it again in Manila in 1995 and at Delhi in 1999.

And China, this illustrious and populous land, with a Church under cruel control?

For China, Asia's great tiger, we ask always and only full religious freedom and respect, freedom for the Catholic Church to appoint bishops and respect for her identity and unity. We rely on the help of China's martyrs, to whom all her Catholics, official and unofficial, are deeply devoted.

Africa has been abandoned with its poor economy, interethnic wars, and widespread poverty. What kind of role can the missions and the Church play there?

In Africa, we accompanied the emerging of a fully African hierarchy. I myself ordained two of the continent's great bishops. The first is martyr and Archbishop of Bukavu (formerly Zaire), Christophe Munzihirwa, killed in 1996; the other, Bishop Augustin Misago, who stood trial for genocide and was acquitted, completely cleared of the charge. Africa is searching for a path that will guarantee it equal dignity with other peoples while preserving the best in its cultures (the family, religious sentiment, etc.). These bishops are leaders for the African people, in their ability to dialogue with the rest of the world while maintaining their dignity of their culture. With the Great Jubilee, the African hierarchy became the most authoritative and precise voice in proclaiming Christ and denouncing violation of human rights. A great communion has grown among the African churches, lived as "family of God".

What to say about the Islamization of Africa and its conflicts?

In many African countries, for centuries a tolerant Islam has existed, and this facilitates peaceful coexistence. Fundamentalism is a limited slice of religions often exploited for political ends. At the world level, *Propaganda* works hard to defend the rights of Christians, as well as religious freedom for all believers, calling for reciprocity. We stood to defend Catholics in East Timor, and we worked to restore peace in

Indonesia among Christians and Muslims, Madurese and Dayak, and for peace and reconciliation in the Great Lakes region of Africa.

What prospects do you see for the third millennium?

Very positive. There is a new fervor around the person of Jesus Christ not as a sacred hero of the past, but as a living person. I will never forget the impressive gathering of 2 million young people in Rome for the Youth Jubilee, many of whom came from our young churches. The Pope asked them, "What have you come for, who are you looking for?" Rome and the universal Church must rediscover the living person of Jesus Christ and a clear Christian identity. In his Letter *Novo Millennio Ineunte*, the Holy Father stressed that the third millennium will be marked by dialogue and proclamation: "Inter-religious dialogue cannot replace proclamation, it must be directed towards proclamation" (no. 56). Mission is today younger than ever. The Good News never leads to religious conflict; indeed, it brings religions together against all that conspires against the absolute dignity of human life and religious freedom. In his *Redemptoris missio*, Pope John Paul II said, "Mission renews the Church, revitalizes faith and Christian identity and offers fresh enthusiasm and new incentive" (no. 2). Mission is a medicine also for the West, overfed and dispirited but in its depth still hungry for God and thirsty for Christ.

The Great Jubilee 2000: Missionary Impetus into the Third Millennium

Acknowledgments

The illustrations used in this book are under the copyrights of His Eminence, Jozef Cardinal Tomko, with the exception of the following: page 214: parish of Katmandu, Nepal; and page 389: Pontifical Mission Societies of Canada.

The maps used in this book are copied from *The World Factbook*, which is in the public domain.